**Iain S. Maclean** is Associate Professor of Western
Religious Thought at James Madison University,
Harrisonburg, Virginia, USA.

# RECONCILIATION, NATIONS AND CHURCHES
## IN LATIN AMERICA

*In memory of my parents*

*William Mathie Maclean*
*Elizabeth Symes*

# Reconciliation, Nations and Churches in Latin America

*Edited by*
IAIN S. MACLEAN
*James Madison University, Harrisonburg, USA*

ASHGATE

© Iain S. Maclean 2006

Iain S. Maclean has asserted his moral right under the Copyright, Designs and Patents Act, 1988, to be identified as the editor of this work.

Published by
Ashgate Publishing Limited
Gower House
Croft Road
Aldershot
Hampshire GU11 3HR
England

Ashgate Publishing Company
Suite 420
101 Cherry Street
Burlington, VT 05401-4405
USA

Ashgate website: http://www.ashgate.com

**British Library Cataloguing in Publication Data**
Maclean, Iain S., 1956–
    Reconciliation, Nations and Churches in Latin America.
    1. Christianity and politics – Latin America. 2. Truth commissions – Latin America –
    3. Reconciliation – Religious aspects – Christianity. 4. Reconciliation – Political aspects
    – Latin America. 5. Latin AMerica – Politics and government – 1980– . I. Title.
    323.4'9'098

**Library of Congress Cataloging-in-Publication Data**
Maclean, Iain S., 1956–
    Reconciliation, Nations and Churches in Latin America / Iain S. Maclean.
        p.    cm.
    Includes bibliographical references and index.
    1. Reconciliation – Religious aspects – Christianity. 2. Christianity and politics – Latin
    America. 3. Church and state – Latin America. 4. Reconciliation – Political apects –
    Latin America. 5. Christianity and culture – Latin America. I. Title.
    BT738.27.M33   2006
    261.7'098–dc22                                                        2005016697

ISBN 0 7546 5030 8

Printed and bound in Great Britain by MPG Books Ltd, Bodmin, Cornwall.

# Contents

**PART III: NATIONS AND CHURCHES IN THE FUTURE**

# List of Contributors

**Mario I. Aguilar**

Mario I. Aguilar is Dean of the Faculty of Divinity at the University of St. Andrews, Scotland. He is the author of *The Rwanda Genocide and the Call to Deepen Christianity in Africa* (Amecea Gaba Publications, 1998) and *Current Issues on Theology and Religion in Latin America and Africa* (Edwin Mellen Press, 2002) and is Chair of the Ritual Studies Group of the American Academy of Religion and a Senior Lecturer in Divinity at St. Mary's College, University of St. Andrews, Scotland. He and is currently preparing a three volume work on 'A Social History of the Catholic Church in Chile.'

**Michael Battle**

A priest in the Episcopal Church, Michael Battle has taught spirituality and moral theology since 1995. Formerly, Assistant Professor of Spirituality and Black Church Studies at Duke University, he is not Associate Dean of Academic Affairs at Virginia Theological Seminary. A participant and worship committee member of the Seventh Assembly of the World Council of Churches, he has served on its central committees in Geneva and Johannesburg. A research fellow in residence with Archbishop Desmond Tutu, Dr. Battle was ordained by the Archbishop in Cape Town, South Africa. He is the author of *Reconciliation: The Ubuntu Theology of Desmond Tutu* (Pilgrim Press, 1997) and *Blessed are the Peacemakers: A Christian Spirituality of Nonviolence* (Mercer University Press, 2004).

**José Comblin**

Professor of the Faculty of Theology, Louvain University, Comblin is a Belgian priest who has worked since the Sixties in Latin America, primarily in Mexico and Brazil. He teaches at the diocesan seminary at Recife, Brazil and is the author of over forty books, *including The Church and the National Security State* (Orbis, 1979) *The Meaning of Mission,* (Orbis, 1977), *Cry of the Oppressed, Cry of Jesus* (Orbis, 1988), *The Holy Spirit and Liberation* (Orbis, 1994), *Retrieving the Human: A Christian Anthropology* (Orbis, 1990), and *Reconciliación y Liberación* (Ediciones Chile y América, 1987).

**Brett Greider**

Brett Greider previously Assistant Professor of Religious Studies at the University of Wisconsin in Eau Claire, is now teaching in the Social sciences Department of the University of California at Santa Cruz. He is a scholar of Latin American religious movements, indigenous cultures, Maya revitalization, cross-hybridization of cultural traditions, and Buddhism. Numerous journeys in Central America and Mexico influenced his Maya research, including a 'Maya Worlds' Summer Institute of the National Endowment for the Humanities and the Community Colleges Association. Dr. Greider's publications include 'Academic Buddhology and the Cyber-Sangha: Researching and Teaching Buddhism through Multimedia and Internet Sources' in *Teaching Buddhism in the West: From the Wheel to the Web* (Curzon Press, 2002) and the 'Instructors Manual' to *Experiencing the World's Religions* (McGraw Hill, 2001). He has a Ph.D. from the Graduate Theological Union in Berkeley, an M.A. from Western Washington University, and an M.A. from Fuller Theological Seminary.

### Margaret E. Guider, O.S.F.

Margaret Guider, O.S.F. is Associate Professor of Religion and Theology at Weston Jesuit School of Theology in Cambridge, Massachusetts. Her work focuses on contemporary spiritual renewal movements; women and religion; theological education; Franciscan spirituality; and the question of childrens' rights. She spent many years working with the Franciscans in Brazil, and is the author of the award-winning *Rahab's Daughters: Prostitution and the Church of Liberation in Brazil* (Augsburg Fortress Press, 1995), and *What Child is This? Children in Christian History and Theology* (Augsburg Fortress Press, 2005). She is the past President of the American Society of Missiology.

### Iain S. Maclean

Iain S. Maclean is Associate Professor of Western Religious Thought at James Madison University. His interests might be summed up broadly as encompassing the field of religion and politics. Dr. Maclean has authored *Opting For Democracy: Liberation Theologians and the Struggle for Democracy in Brazil* (Lang, 1999), and co-edited with J. Schultz, *The Encyclopedia of Religion in American Politics (Oryx, 1998)* and with Gabriel Palmer-Fernandez *The Encyclopedia of Religion and War,* (Routledge, 2004). He researches the religious and theological dimensions of contemporary political phenomenon of national reconciliation commissions. He was ordained by the Presbyterian Church of Southern Africa.

### Nelson Maldonado –Torres

Nelson Maldonado-Torres is Assistant Professor of Comparative Ethnic Studies in the Department of Ethnic Studies at the University of California, Berkeley and Ford Foundation Postdoctoral Fellow in the Center for Global Studies and the Humanities at Duke University. He specializes in critical theory, postcolonial studies, and modern religious thought. He is interested in theories of decolonization as they emerge in different contexts and from different points of view in the Americas. He is the current co-chair of the 'Religion in Latin America and Caribbean Group' of the American Academy of Religion. He has published several articles and is working on two book-length projects: *Against War: Views from the Underside of Modernity*, and *Fanonian Meditations*.

**Margaret R. Pfeil**

Margaret Pfeil is Assistant Professor of Moral Theology/ Christian Ethics, University of Notre Dame. After receiving a B. A. in Government and International Relations from the University of Notre Dame in 1987, she worked with the Holy Cross Fathers as a lay associate in Chile (1987-89) and then worked in Hispanic ministry in a Catholic parish in Akron, Ohio (1990-92). She received an M.T.S. from Weston Jesuit School of Theology in 1994 and a Ph.D. from the University of Notre Dame in 2000. Her book, *Naming Social Sin. Developments in Magisterial Teaching*, will be available from the University of Notre Dame Press in 2005.

**David Tombs**

David Tombs is a political theologian working in Belfast as Lecturer in Reconciliation Studies for the Irish School of Ecumenics, Trinity College Dublin. He formerly worked at the University of Surrey Roehampton in London and studied at the Universities of Oxford, Birmingham and London and at Union Theological Seminary, New York. His publications on Latin America include *Truth and Memory: The Church and Human Rights in El Salvador and Guatemala* (edited with Michael Hayes, published by Gracewing 2001) and *Latin American Liberation Theology* (by Brill, 2003).

**Charles Villa-Vicencio**

Executive Director, Institute for Justice and Reconciliation, Cape Town, South Africa, formerly Professor of Religion and Society, University of Cape Town and Minister of the Methodist Church of Southern Africa. He was the Director of the South African Truth and Reconciliation Commission Research Division. He holds the degrees of B.A., Rhodes University; M.A., Yale University and Ph.D., Drew University. He is the author, amongst others, of *Between Christ and Caesar* (Eerdmans, 1986), *Trapped in Apartheid* (Orbis, 1988), *Theology and Violence: The South African Debate* (Eerdmans, 1988), *Apartheid is a Heresy* (With J. De Gruchy) (Eerdmans, 1983), *Resistance and Hope: South African Essays in Honour of Beyers Naude* (Eerdmans, 1985) and (With H. Verwoerd) *A Theology of Reconstruction* (Cambridge, 1992), and *Looking Back, Reaching Forward: Reflections on the Truth and Reconciliation Commission of South Africa* (Macmillan, 2000).

# Introduction

In late 2003 the Peruvian Truth and Reconciliation Commission presented its report to the nation which then began considering ways of moving forward in the process of national reconciliation. This was now beginning to be understood as a much longer and more difficult task than perhaps first envisioned almost twenty years earlier when Chile and Argentina initiated such commissions. Some years before the Peruvian commission, the South African Truth and Reconciliation Commission had, during the late 1990s, televised its hearings to the nation, and thereby captured national and international attention. Interest in such commissions has continued to grow, as has the amount of literature devoted to the phenomenon. Why then add to the number of books and articles on the subject? Because this volume seeks to address an area often assumed and rather less written about, namely that of the role of religion, theology, and churches (and religious movements) as social and political actors. Thus while the South African commission, chaired by an archbishop and co-chaired by a Methodist clergyman, did in fact highlight the role of theology and religion, few works, especially in the English-speaking world, have focused on the role of the Churches in such truth and reconciliation commissions in Latin America.

This then is the primary reason for contributing this volume to the literature on national truth and reconciliation commissions. The literature on such commissions (and note that not all were explicitly 'reconciliation' commissions) has primarily been focused through the disciplines of political science and law since these have in fact been the primary sources from which the various national commission resources have been drawn. As more has been written and as the victims have found their voices (perpetrators typically do not often speak unless they have to do so), sociologists and psychologists have added to the literature.

Precisely because national reconciliation is a national objective, other elements than the role of the Church or the religious come to the fore. The role of amnesty and impunity decrees, the place of the truth about the past, justice for both perpetrators and victims, and restitution or reparations, are all elements in such envisaged reconciliation, all contributing, as John de Gruchy so pithily puts it, to 'restoring justice'. This step of course depends upon the truth being told and known. Perhaps because perpetrators and victims are of the same nation (though often not of the same race, ethnicity, language group, political persuasion, or religion) and have to live together in some manner, truth-telling has led to remarkable instances of public apology, pardon, and forgiveness. The complex relations between these components provides the second reason for this volume, in providing specific case studies of how in particular cases not only were some or all of these elements related, but also how the Churches or religious institutions interacted or shaped the processes of national reconciliation.

Churches, often as the only surviving institutions of civil society, served as mediating structures between the ruling regime and opposition parties. In almost all cases they provided neutral territory for opposing sides to meet and in both Latin American (with varying degrees of success) and the South African cases, they often functioned as the upholders of moral values, specifically of international human rights' norms. The South African case is mentioned (and used for comparative purposes in some of the chapters in this volume) as it serves as the primary example of a nation that was deeply and directly influenced by the Latin American experience of such truth and reconciliation commissions. In its turn, the South African case was to provide an example for the Peruvian commission which only published its report in 2003. The study of Latin American truth and reconciliation commissions provides the third reason for offering this volume: for the history of such commissions reveals their dependence upon earlier and other peace or reconciliation processes and such comparative study enriches the understanding of such processes and of the roles of Churches and religious organizations intricately involved.

Thus while this collection of essays is primarily focused on the Latin American case, at least two of the authors relate their chapter's contributions directly to that of the South African Truth and Reconciliation Commission. It should also be clear that the issues raised by attempted post-conflict resolutions are complex and require attention to specific cases and indeed from differing perspectives. Consequently the essays in this collection are focused on specific national examples of truth or truth and reconciliation commissions, whether official (Argentina, Chile, El Salvador, Guatemala, Peru, and South Africa), or not (Brazil). Further they approach their subjects with differing methodologies and challenges for institutional religion. For example, Mario Aguilar provides a detailed analysis of one aspect of the Chilean process and views its failure to obtain the truth about the past as indicating the overall failure of the Chilean reconciliation process; while David Tombs offers a powerful comparative analysis of two commissions (El Salvadorean and the Guatemalan) and their differing treatments of sexual violence, and brings the results to bear upon traditional cultural and theological avoidance of such taboo subjects.

This volume is divided into three parts, gathering together essays that focus on specific nations and aspects of religion or theological materials. The first part comprises contributions that offer specific examples of Latin American national commissions and explores, in differing ways, the role of Churches or religious organizations in the truth and reconciliation processes. The second part comprises two chapters that focus specifically on Christian understandings of reconciliation in the ecclesiastical, social, and political spheres. The third and final part encompasses those chapters that draw on lessons from the past to indicate future directions for both religious institutions and nations on the path of reconciliation.

Chapter one, by the editor, has two major goals. The first is to argue that national processes of reconciliation are practical political compromises. Thereby the parties engaged in peace negotiations hope to achieve what was envisaged as parties in conflict negotiated peace. The second goal is to offer in the process a brief overview of the major Latin American Truth Commissions or Truth and Reconciliation

Commissions (note that not all were both truth and reconciliation commissions) and the South African Truth and Reconciliation Commission, primarily in order to provide a historical framework for the other essays in this volume. The following chapters provide detailed case-studies of specific national commissions and examine the role of the churches or religious institutions in such processes, and note either theological and ethical bases of such involvement or the implications of such involvement for Churches and for theology. Thus Mario Aguilar offers an analysis of an aspect of the negotiated settlement in Chile and underscores its weaknesses. David Tombs takes a different tack, highlighting, due to cultural and theological reasons, the inability of both the El Salvadorean and the Guatemalan truth commissions and Churches to deal directly with unspeakable (and deadly) sexual torture in Central America. He poses the question of what heinous crimes and the inability of victims to forgive means for the Church and its sacramental practices. Brett Greider offers another perspective on reconciliation, from the perspective of resurgent indigenous Mayan movements in similar regions examined by Tombs. How does a non-Christian religion address the situation/s and understand reconciliation? Margaret Guider offers an essay that explores the question of 'what difference does a truth and reconciliation commission make?' This involves examining the case of Brazil, which never had an official commission, but did produce an unofficial report, *Brazil: Never Again,* which became the paradigm-and lent the name-to numerous other official national reports.

The second part provides directly religious, theological, and ethical resources on the phenomenon of national reconciliation. A major reason for producing this volume has been to address the relative absence of specifically religious analyses of this contemporary phenomenon which, in a modern and increasingly secular (so it seemed) world, was utilizing specifically Christian terminology such as 'reconciliation', 'apology', 'forgiveness', and 'restitution' to name the most prominent. The chapter on 'The Theme of Reconciliation in Theology in Latin America' by José Comblin, available in English for the first time here, provides a major overview of how this term has been understood in theology in Latin America during the twentieth century. It is a privilege to have Padre Comblin's permission to include this important essay in this volume. His concluding analysis of social sin provides an appropriate preparation Margaret Pfeil's analysis of this concept in Church Social Teaching, the thought of the late Pope John Paul II, and liberation theologies, utilizing the Peruvian Truth and Reconciliation Commission as a case study.

The third part directs the reader to the possible futures that such commissions have for nations and religious institutions. They have influenced each other nationally and across national borders, most publicly in the case of the South African Truth and Reconciliation Commission's experience with the earlier Latin American Commissions. Charles Villa-Vicencio, the Research Director of the South African commission, reflects on his experiences and argues that, in divided nations, such reconciliation commissions' work is not limited to a year or two of investigation, but instead should be an ongoing process at as many social levels as possible. Michael Battle, an Episcopal priest (ordained by Archbishop Desmond Tutu) provides an interesting comparison of the Chilean and South African Commissions, arguing that both have lessons for the other. The Chilean experience of failed amnesty decrees highlights the weaknesses in approaches that fail to deliver justice, while the South African case illustrates the importance of trusted leadership in bridging vast political and social gaps. Critical to Archbishop Desmond Tutu's success in chairing the South African Truth and Reconciliation Commission was his theology and philosophy of *ubuntu* which enabled him – and others – to see the common humanity of both black and white peoples. Finally, Nelson Maldonado-Torres, current co-chair of the Religion in Latin America and Caribbean Group of the American Academy of Religion (out of one of their conferences this volume originally developed) reflects on the whole volume, and provides a much needed commentary on the necessity for reconciliation to move well beyond the present truths, to the historical truths of 'coloniality' and the history of imperial powers that have created unbalanced and thus unjust societies with racist and class distinctions that hinder true selfhood and thus lasting reconciliation amongst individuals and peoples.

Clearly there is overlap between all three parts and some chapters perhaps could have been situated elsewhere. Thus there are connections between the situations described by David Tombs, Mario Aguilar, and Brett Greider and the theological analysis of such situations in Margaret Pfeil's chapter. Tombs, Guider, and Battle are, in differing ways, comparative studies. Both Guider and Battle emphasize the role of prominent individuals in forming history, while Greider, Pfeil, and Maclean indicate the importance of national and international linkages in influencing national events. Guider, Pfeil, Battle, and Greider also reveal the importance of communal solidarity in effecting change, and the role – in Greider and Battle-of indigenous values in enabling change. If reconciliation is the organizing theme, then not only do the case studies 'problematize' individual cases of national reconciliation, but they also raise further questions as to the nature of humanity, of society, of sin, of the role of the Churches in the political, and the courage of individuals willing to remember, to tell the truth, to forgive, and to apologize.

So much remains to be done and while the focus in this volume has been upon some major examples of truth and reconciliation commissions, this is not to forget the numerous other processes that have begun in Uruguay, Paraguay, and Bolivia, central Africa, and Eastern and Southern Europe. Thus this volume is best understood as both a road map to the subject and as a prompt to further research and study in the areas of one's own concerns. To this end a cumulative bibliography has been included at the end of this volume, divided into three sections: primary documents, ecclesiastical documents, and then secondary literature. It is hoped that this will be a helpful tool in further exploring the roles of the Christian Church and other religions in the processes of ascertaining the truth and fostering national reconciliation. Since the work on Mayan religion is relatively unknown, a separate bibliography has been retained at the end of that chapter.

Finally thanks are due to the contributors, all of whom have experience in the nations and situations of conflict and reconciliation they describe, who have sought to present in print critical aspects of the reconciliation and truth-telling processes in order that this work might benefit readers seeking better understandings of the role of religion in the contemporary world. The editor also wishes to thank Mrs Linda Wandless and Mrs Karen Harris who both patiently edited and corrected the numerous versions of this volume!

# PART I
# Nations and Reconciliation

Chapter 1

# Truth and Reconciliation: Hope for the Nations or Only as Much as is Possible?

Iain S. Maclean

## Introduction

The publication of the Final Report of the South African Truth and Reconciliation Commission (TRC) in 1998, and the dramatic televised hearings that preceded it, sharply focused that nation's and the world's attention on such commissions. A recent phenomenon in national politics, such a truth and reconciliation project seemed to be offering a more peaceful and constructive route for nations seeking to emerge from periods of great internal strife, indeed of civil war. As the political scientist Samuel Huntington expressed it, such transitions were in fact part of a historic 'third wave of democratization', bearing with them hopes for a better future. The South African TRC caught the world's attention not only because it was conducted in public and nationally televised, but also because it seemed to have found a means to overcome the conflicting demands of victims and perpetrators, between those of justice, (and truth and reparations) and amnesty, that had hindered and often marred the hopes of earlier Latin American commissions seeking national reconciliation.

The attention focused upon the South African TRC had been roused by an earlier report, that of the 1993 United Nations Commission on the Truth for El Salvador, and prior to the El Salvador report there had been a rather long series of earlier attempts in other nations. In fact there have been over twenty earlier commissions, primarily in Central and South America, and then scattered examples in other conflict-ridden nations in former Communist Eastern Europe and in Africa. In these situations truth or truth and reconciliation commissions were often established by successor governments to assist the transition to democracy. These are official fact-finding bodies set up to formally investigate the past violations of international human rights' standards. They were charged to uncover the truth about the past, ioften granted amnesty to perpetrators, and apportioned reparations to victims or their survivors. The work of such commissions, it is hoped, will result in a more unified, or reconciled, nation.

In practice, such commissions produce diverse results, depending upon the scope of the specific mandates, period, scope of operation, ability to satisfy all the participants, and finally, their ability to project their recommendations into future national structures and policies. Put simply, did such commissions produce the truth and did this in turn produce justice, reparations, amnesty and national reconciliation for all or most of the nation? In order to ascertain the truth, such commissions have found that either impunity or amnesty has to be offered to members of the previous government, and victims, in exchange for dropping their demands for full justice, have to be offered reparations. Thus the early commissions tended to grant amnesty to perpetrators and some compensation to victims. However, as the Argentine and Chilean cases soon demonstrated, this approach favoured the perpetrators, who escaped justice, and left the nations with no guarantees that the full truth had been told. This resulted in popular distrust of the successor government, and in some cases, with the subsequent revelation of previously concealed human rights' violations, amnesty, and/or impunity decisions were soon reversed, all leading to great political unrest. In such cases, then, reconciliation had not been achieved.

Such experiences are reflected in part in the history of the publication of such reports. Thus they can range from formal published studies issued with government approval, such as the Report of the Chilean Truth Commission, the Argentine Report on the Disappeared, and the Guatemalan one on the recovery of historical memory,[1]

---

1   Commission reports are listed below for Argentina: Comisión Nacional sobre la Desaparición de Personas (CONADEP), *Argentina Nunca Más* (Buenos Aires: Editorial Universitaria, 1984) and in English, Commisión Nacional sobre la Desaparición de Personas. (CONADEP) *Nunca Más: The Report of the Argentine National Commission on the Disappeared* (New York: Farrar, Straus, 1986); Brazil (non-official): *Brasil: Nunca Mais*.(Arquidiocese de Petropolis: Vozes, 1985) and in English, *Torture in Brazil. A Report by the Archdioceses of São Paulo*. Translated by Jaime Wright and edited by Joan Dassin, (New York: Vintage Books, 1986); Chile: Comisión Nacional de Verdad y Reconciliación, *Comisión Nacional de Verdad y Reconciliación: Informe Final* (Santiago: La Nación, 1990) in English, *Report of the Chilean National Commission on Truth and Reconciliation*, trans. Phillip Berryman (Notre Dame, Ind: Notre Dame Press, 1993); El Salvador: La Comisión de la Verdad para El Salvador: *Informe de la Comisión de la Verdad para El Salvador: De la Locura a la Esperanza: La Guerra de 12 años en El Salvador* (New York: United Nations, 1992); United Nations, United Nations Commission on the Truth for El Salvador, *From Madness to Hope: The 12-Year War in El Salvador: Report of the Commission on the Truth for El Salvador* (New York: UN Security Council, 1993); Guatemala: Comisión para el Esclarecimiento Histórico (CEH), *Guatemala: Memoria Del Silencio, Informe de la Comisión para el Esclarecimiento Histórico*, 12 vols (Guatemala: Comisión para el Esclarecimiento Histórico, 1999), and the Roman Catholic Church independent report by REMHI, *Recuperación de la Memoria Histórica* (REMHI and Menschenrechtsburo des Erzbistums Guatemala ODHAG, 1998); REMHI and Menschenrechtsbüro des Erzbistums Guatemala ODHAG (eds) *Guatemala: Never Again!*, The Official Report of the Human Rights Office, Archdiocese of Guatemala. Trans. G. Tovar Siebentritt (Maryknoll, NY: Orbis Books) London: Catholic Institute for International Relations and Latin America Bureau, 1999; Paraguay: CIPAE. *Nunca Más: La Dictadura de Stroessner y los Derechos Humanos* (Asunción: Comité de Iglesias para Ayudas de Emergencia, 1990); Peru: Comisión de la Verdad y Reconciliación, *Comisión de la Verdad y Reconciliación, Informe Final*, 9 vols (Lima: Comisión de la Verdad y Reconciliación, 2003); South Africa: Truth and Reconciliation Commission, *Truth and Reconciliation Commission of South Africa: Final Report*. 5 vols (Cape Town: Juta and Co.,

to the more informal reports from Brazil (no formal commission). Some countries have not been able – for reasons ranging from lack of documentation, to active prevention of access to certain sectors (e.g. military granted immunity) – to obtain a full picture of the past, or only a slice thereof as in the cases of Haiti and Uganda. Other reports have been suppressed or have never been published, as occurred with those of Bolivia, Zimbabwe, and the Philippines.

The Latin American and the South African commissions emerged during a process of democratization following earlier periods of national authoritarian military dictatorship and apartheid respectively. An essential part of these democratization processes (somewhat delayed in the Argentine, Brazilian, and Chilean cases) was the establishment of national commissions (not official in Brazil) to investigate the past, so that its truths might illumine the present and guide the national future. In other words, the hope was – and is – that the truth about the country's past would somehow contribute to present nation-building and democratization, and so, it was hoped, end the ongoing 'spiral of violence'. And foster national reconciliation. Did national truth and reconciliation commissions actually achieve these ends?

José Zalaquett, a Chilean lawyer and participant in the Chilean Commission (and consultant to the South African TRC) famously remarked that in reality such commissions can only strive for 'as much justice as possible'.[2] Taking a cue from this observation, and extending its range, a study of the most prominent such commissions reveals that the process of developing Truth, or Truth and Reconciliation Commissions in fact represents a balance between the claims of the perpetrators and those of the victims, for as much justice, amnesty, and truth as possible. The extent to which this balancing act succeeds in satisfying all parties, represents the extent of possible reconciliation. This position will be presented in three parts. The first part offers a brief chronological overview of selected Latin American commissions and, for further comparative purposes, the South African TRC. The often under-noted role of the Churches, both Roman Catholic and Protestant (and other religions) in these processes is outlined. The second part presents an evaluation of the result of the demands for truth, justice, amnesty, and reparations in the process of national reconciliation. The third part examines the specifically religious, ethical, and theological evaluations that have arisen from these commissions.

1998); Uruguay: Servicio Paz y Justicia de Uruguay, *Uruguay Nunca Mas*: *informe sobre la violacion a los derechos humanos* (1972–1986) (Montevideo: Servicio Paz y Justicia Uruguay, 1985); in English, *Uruguay: Nunca Mas: Human Rights Violations, 1972–1985*. Trans. Elizabeth Hampsten (Philadelphia: Temple University Press, 1992).

2    José Zalaquett, 'Balancing the Ethical Imperatives and Political Constraints: the Dilemma of New Democracies Confronting Past Human Rights Abuses', *Hastings Law Journal*, 43/6 (1992), 1426–1432.

## Overview of Truth and Reconciliation Commissions

Priscilla Hayner, one of the early scholars to examine comparatively this phenomenon, has briefly defined truth commissions as 'official bodies set up to investigate a past period of human rights' abuses or violations of international law', while a truth and reconciliation commission seeks both the truth and some form of unification within a nation deeply divided by political violence ranging right up to open civil war.[3]

Due to the national situation of conflict, usual means of dealing with human rghts' abuses are often not available or cannot be utilized for fear of continuing conflict. Thus, in the transition from authoritarian or military control to democratic government, both sides made compromises. So the outgoing government agreed to step down if guaranteed amnesty or impunity for any crimes committed. The incoming democratic government, not powerful enough to ensure justice through the courts, and feared a military reaction if too stringent demands were made, agreed. Such a political compromise, based on the pragmatic power situation, offered enough to each side to pave the way towards national reconciliation. After all, to pursue charges through the criminal justice system assumed that there was such a national justice system functioning after years of dictatorial rule, that there were a sufficient number of untainted judges, funds to provide for lengthy trials, and that there was enough available evidence. The experience of such a process in Germany post-World War Two revealed the difficulties of pursuing such a course rigorously.[4] Nevertheless, such commissions have served important roles in helping divided nations deal with a past history of human rights' crimes as well as providing a voice for the victims. The victims witness to the truth which serves to preserve the memory of the past, to assist in re-writing national history, and to provide a framework for a better society through which the nation might be reconciled.

The earliest such commission, that set up by the then ruling president of Uganda, Idi Amin Dada, in 1974, did not live up to these expectations, largely because its results were not published and its recommendations were not implemented. However, this rather unimpressive performance was to improve as successive commissions took place in Africa (Chad, again in Uganda, and then in South Africa), in Latin America (starting with Bolivia in 1982 and most recently with Peru in 2003), and in Europe (Germany in 1992 to investigate the abuses in the former East German Democratic Republic and in the former Yugoslavia). Not all states have resorted to such commissions, particularly when genocides have occurred. Thus the successor states to the former Yugoslavia have resorted to a justice option and so to an International Criminal Tribunal at The Hague, as has Rwanda. While the case of Brazil does not fit those briefly outlined below in this chapter, in that there

---

3    Priscilla B. Hayner, 'Fifteen Truth Commissions – 1974 to 1994: A Comparative Study', *Human Rights Quarterly* 16 (1994), 597–655, 598. Further details and updates are contained in this author's book, *Unspeakable Truths: Facing the Challenge of Truth Commissions* (New York: Routledge, 2001).

4    See the discussion of this issue in Donald W. Shriver, Jr., *An Ethic for Enemies: Forgiveness in Politics* (New York: Oxford University Press, 1995), 73–118.

has been no official 'Truth Commission', the results of non-governmental agencies' activities, specifically those of the Roman Catholic Church, in collecting, preserving and publishing records of human rights' violations, do offer an alternative by which the efficacy of such national commissions in other Latin American nations, can be compared and evaluated.[5]

## Argentina (1976–1983)

Argentina and its truth commission has drawn the attention of legal and political scholars ever since its inception in 1983 after the military's handing over of power partly as a result of its dismal military failures against the United Kingdom in the Falkland's (Malvinas) crisis. The successor government under President Raúl Alfonsín, elected in October and taking office in December 1983, seeking swift democratization, looked to the example of Bolivia in setting up a truth commission to investigate abuses committed during military rule from 1976 to 1983.

President Alfonsín set up a ten-member commission, with further members nominated from both chambers of the Congress, and headed by the well-known author Ernesto Sábato, after whom the commission report is commonly known as the Sábato Report. Its formal name is 'Comisión Nacional para la Desaparición de Personas' ('National Commission on the Disappeared' abbreviated as CONADEP).[6] As the name of the commission makes clear, its task was to examine the many cases of disappearances of those taken into custody during military rule. The final report, issued in 1984, documented about 9,000 cases of disappeared persons, and set in motion the trial of some high-ranking military officers. The report vindicated the suspicions of the 'Mothers of the Plazo del Mayo' who since 1977 had been holding weekly protests outside government offices demanding to know the truth about the fate of their children and grandchildren.

Though the military government left in disgrace and without time to negotiate a transfer of power, it did issue a justification for its actions, released in 1983 as the 'Final Document on the Struggle against Subversion and Terrorism' (28 April 1983).[7] This report sought to justify the military's actions and called for a new sense of national unity as all citizens sought 'reconciliation' with a 'Christian spirit'. This document denied the existence of clandestine detention centers and the practice of secret executions.[8] However, what was most striking about this document was

---

5 See the chapter by Sr. M. Guider in this volume for a Brazilian case study.

6 The report was published, borrowing a title from the Brazilian non-governmental report on human rights' abuses there, as *Nunca Más: The Report of the Argentine National Commission on the Disappeared*. Trans. Writers and Scholars International, Ltd. (New York: Farrar, Strauss Giroux, 1986).

7 The Argentine Military Junta's "Final Document": A Call for Condemnation.' *An Americas Watch Report* (1983).

8 Congreso Argentino de la Cooperación, 'Documento Final' (Buenos Aires: Consejo Intercooperativo Argentino, 1983).

its open admission that the 'disappeared', if not still underground or in exile, were probably all dead. . Then, on the 23 September 1983 just weeks before the first civilian democratic elections, the military government passed a self amnesty law, providing a general amnesty for all criminal acts committed between May, 1973 and June, 1982.[9]

However, just days after taking office, President Alfonsín annulled this military amnesty and ordered the heads of the past three military governments arrested. Thus the trials of these officers proceeded as the national Truth Commission was doing its work. After the military refused to try these officers, they were transferred to the Federal Court of Appeals in Buenos Aires in 1984 and on 30 December 1986 the Supreme Court ratified the judgments handed down. These included life imprisonment for General Jorge Videla and Admiral Emilio Massera, and prison terms for other military and police officers.[10]

While the spectacle of citizens judging former military leaders gripped Latin American, and indeed international attention, President Alfonsín was facing increasing pressure from the military to desist from such trials. So, in 1986, in attempts to placate the military and obviously to avoid another military coup, the Argentine Congress passed the 'Law of Final Termination' which set a statue of limitations on initiating any further trials. Then in April 1987 the first of a number of military uprisings occurred, and under pressure the Congress passed the 'Law of Due Obedience' by which lower ranking officers were exonerated of any culpability in crimes, on the grounds that they had only been following orders. This de facto amnesty decree was followed, by Alfonsín's successor (since July 1989), President Carlos Menem, who in October of the same year, issued a general pardon to 277 military officers and civilians who had been condemned in the courts for human rights' violations or for mutiny. This was followed in December 1990 by a general pardon that included the former high-ranking military officers imprisoned since 1986.

Such actions did not meet with popular approval and indeed the 'Mothers of the Plazo del Mayo' had continued their weekly vigils as many remained missing. Their persistence was rewarded almost two decades later with the shocking confessions in 1994 of Captain Adolfo Scilingo on national public media that drugged detainees were thrown from naval aircraft into the South Atlantic.[11] This was followed by General Martin Balza's confession in 1996 that death squads had in fact been operating under military control. The nation was outraged and this led as recently as September 2003, to the Argentine Congress declaring all amnesty laws null and void. Amnesty, often a useful process, had here served only to hide the truth and

---

9   Larry Rohter, 'Argentina: Military Amnesties Repealed', *New York Times* (22 August 2003), Section a, Column 4, 6.

10  Details of individual sentences can be found in Jeffrey Klaiber, *The Church, Dictatorships and Democracy in Latin America* (Maryknoll: Orbis Books, 1998), 88.

11  Marcela Valente, '"Repentant" Captain Adolfo E. Scilingo Arrested,' *Press Service* 7 October 1997.

protect the guilty. Further, such revelations only served to destabilize the present government, as citizens distrusted the military and police.

A popular – though mistaken – perception of the Argentine Roman Catholic Church is that it did little or nothing to resist the human rights' violations of the military dictatorship, especially during the so-called 'dirty war' perpetrated during the years 1976–1983. This perception was encouraged by a series of revelations that military chaplains had been present and associated with the military units connected with now infamous detention centers. The Church it was charged, was so concerned with maintaining its status, as well as supporting the regime's public opposition to Communism, that it failed to speak out against its abuses of power. These and similar charges were powerfully brought to the public and indeed world attention, through Emilio Mignone's *Witness to the Truth: The Complicity of Church and Dictatorship in Argentina, 1976–1983.*[12] The Church had to respond to these accusations almost at the same time as Argentina moved to civilian democratic government, and had a new president, the Radical Party's Raúl Alfonsín, whose domestic political agenda regarding legalizing abortion, divorce and separating Church and State, was opposed by conservative clergy. This opposition, combined with economic distress, led to Alfonsin's replacement in 1989 by the Perónist, Carlos Menem

When in early 1980 the political parties had created the *Concordia Multipartida* in order to negotiate with the military, the Church negotiated between the military government and the civilian politicians. The Church then issued an important Pastoral Letter in 1981, entitled *Iglesia y Comunidad Nacional,* which called for open public debate on the nation's political future, a return to a social ethic based on the common good, and advocated democracy as the only means to achieve these and preserve the rights and duties of the human person. Then as the democratic transition was underway, the National Episcopal Conference of Argentina (CEA) issued a number of declarations and pastoral letters calling for order and for reconciliation. Thus in their pastoral *Camino de la reconciliación*, the bishops drew on John Paul II's proclamation of a Holy Year to call for national unity and reconciliation. This message of reconciliation was repeated often, and in fact three bishops met regularly with the military government during the year of 1983.[13] Shortly after this the CEA issued a further document, *La Iglesia y los derechos humanos* (The Church and Human Rights) which listed earlier declarations on human rights and also listed official meetings held between the bishops and the military.[14]

The military governments' passing of an amnesty law in 1983 had in fact been preceded by favourable comments by the Catholic episcopacy. In fact, Monsignor

---

12 Emilio Fermin Mignone, *Witness to the Truth: The Complicity of Church and Dictatorship in Argentina, 1976–1983*. Trans. Phillip Berryman (Maryknoll, NY: Orbis Books, 1988). Mignone was founder of The Center for Legal and Social Studies (CELS) and writes out of a personal attempt to discover the fate of his 'disappeared' daughter, and relates many attempts to gain help from the Church hierarchy.

13 Quoted in *Clarín* (17 March 1983).

14 Conferencia Episcopal Argentina, *La Iglesia y los derechos humanos* (Buenos Aires: CEA, 1984).

Antonio Quarracino, on his return from the recently concluded Latin American Episcopal Conference (CELAM), where he had been elected the president, had even proposed a law to forget the past as a prelude to the amnesty declaration.[15] Indeed the bishop went on to state that such laws would assist national reconciliation by removing sources of hate, revenge and further injustice. It should be noted that while this statement reflects their conservative support of the military government other bishops' critical statements reflect the division within the national episcopacy on these issues. Thus the close ideological agreement between the military's position and some of the high-ranking clergy was well illustrated in the statements made by the Papal Nuncio Pio Laghi –subsequently appointed Papal Nuncio to the United States until 1991 – that the Church supported the military in its goals and actions.[16] In contrast, Bishop de Nevares declared that a supposed 'law to forget' does injustice to the 'disappeared' and citizens should rather look for truth and justice from the law.[17] The most blunt statement came from Monsignor Miguel Hesayne who, in appealing to the principles of truth and justice, declared that 'Human rights conform to the nucleus of evangelical values, therefore the Process of National Reorganization is anti-Christian because it has violated them...'[18]

The conciliatory attitude adopted in the episcopal document outraged public opinion.[19] Thus, as Michael Burdick summarized this period, he noted that as the public's outrage grew, their interpretation of the bishop's mediating efforts grew increasingly negative.[20] In addition, by 1987 Rubem Dri's study *Teologia y Dominación* undertook a detailed examination of the Argentine episcopacy and a comparison of its stances with those of the military government. He discerned three strands of opinion within the episcopacy. The largest strand had been most supportive of military rule, while the smallest one had been critical of the military's policies and actions.[21] For the church and its bishops had been involved with the military government prior to seeking to work out a transition of power. The military government policy, centered around the twin programs of economic restructuring and state terror, included the suspension of the Constitution, dissolving the National Congress, the banning of political parties and of trade unions, as well as censorship

15 Quoted in *Convicción* (3 April 1983), 2 and in Michael A. Burdick, *For God and the Fatherland: Religion and Politics in Argentina* (New York: The State University of New York Press, 1995), 249.

16 Michael A. Burdick, *For God and the Fatherland*, 233.

17 Dom de Navares, quoted in *Clarín* (19 April 1983).

18 Msgr. Miguel Hesayne, quoted in *Clarín* (6 February 1983).

19 See the editorial by José Luis Ignacio in *Clarín* (10 May 1983), 19.

20 Michael A. Burdick, *For God and the Fatherland*, 232.

21 Rubem Dri, *Teologia y Dominación* (Buenos Aires: Roblanco,1987), and for further detail see his *Processo a la Iglesia argentina: las relaciones de la jerarquia eclesiástica y los gobiernos de Alfonsín y Menem* (Buenos aires: Editorial Biblos, 1997).

of the press. These measures, as well as the broader social and political conceptions that propelled them, were supported by a National Security Doctrine.[22]

According to Burdick's thoughtful analysis of the Argentine Church, three themes[23] illustrate Church–state relations during the dictatorship and the transition to democracy. First, the Catholic bishop's support for the military government, even support of the Falklands invasion, and limited criticism of human rights' violations. The second theme was the Church's handling of human rights' violations after the transfer to full civilian rule in 1983. The bishops responded to public criticism by publishing the record of their criticism of the military government's abuses. The third theme that ran through church and state relations was that of the implications of democratization for traditional Roman Catholic social teaching and for the church's position in society.

Perhaps the Church's position is best described by the summary offered in the conclusion of the 1984 Report of the Argentine National Commission on the Disappeared (*Comisión nacional sobre la Desaparación de Personas*), which recognized the Church's positive contributions and role in the democratic transition, but did record individual cases of clergy or of chaplains present at clandestine torture centers.[24]

## Chile (1973–1990)

Six weeks after taking office as President of Chile on 11 March 1990 the Christian Democrat Patricio Aylwin established a *Comisión Nacional para la Verdad y Reconciliatión* (National Commission for the Truth and Reconciliation, also called 'The Rettig Commission') headed by former Senator Raúl Rettig, to examine deaths and disappearances during the past seventeen years of military rule under General Augusto Pinochet. Working for nine months, this commission recognized 2,920 cases of human rights' violations, and by February 1990 had produced a massive 1,800 page report.[25] In offering this report to the Chilean people, President Aylwin offered formal apologies to victims and survivors and called upon the military to acknowledge its role in the past acts of violence. While political assassinations and right-wing violence dampened public debate over this report, it set a high standard

---

22 The classic theological analysis of this doctrine is provided by José Comblin's *The Church and the National Security State* (Maryknoll, NY: Orbis Books, 1979). For specific examination of Argentina see David Pion-Berlin, 'The National Security Doctrine, Military Threat Perception and the "Dirty War" in Argentina,' *Comparative Political Studies*, 21/3 (Oct. 1988), 382–407.

23 Michael A. Burdick, *For God and Fatherland*, 220.

24 See *Nunca Mas* (New York: Farrar, Strauss Giroux, 1986), 248.

25 Comisión Nacional de Verdad y Reconciliación, *Informe de la Comisión Nacional de Verdad y Reconciliación, Informe Rettig. Texto Oficial Completo*, 3 vols (Santiago, Chile: La Nación, 1991). In English, *Report of the Chilean National Commission on Truth and Reconciliation*, trans. Phillip Berryman, 2 vols (Notre Dame, IN: Notre Dame University Press, 1993).

for documenting cases and for its recommendations. Not only did it call for continued investigation of unresolved cases, archival preservation of the commission's records and accompanying evidence, the initiation of national dialogue, forums and national educational programes, but also for the establishment of a 'National Corporation for Reparations and Reconciliation'. Such a corporation was in fact established by the Chilean parliament, and reparations, including medical, educational, and pension benefits paid out to survivors of those executed or still classed as 'disappeared'.[26]

Again, as in the case of Argentina, President Aylwin and the Truth and Reconciliation Commission had to negotiate the amnesty decreed by General Pinochet as far back as 1978 which granted immunity to all military personnel for human rights' violations committed since the 1973 coup. Further, the new government was well aware that the military kept a close watch on activities, in this case, in the person of General Pinochet, Commander in Chief of the military till 1998 and after that date, a senator for life. The Truth and Reconciliation Commission in part, by focusing on obtaining exact records of past human rights' violations, was seeking to obtain the truth and thus to circumvent the earlier amnesty law. The national debate over this report was stifled by General Pinochet's public disagreement and by numerous assassinations.. However, when he stepped down as Commander in Chief in 1998 and was arrested in London on charges pressed by Spain, the issue of human rights' violations resurfaced in Chilean society. Was the Truth and Reconciliation Commission's mandate excessively limited when it disallowed cases of torture, only dealing with fatal or unresolved cases of disappearance? Further, questions were raised about the failure to achieve justice when the military had refused to cooperate, the complete truth was not known, and amnesty laws shielded the guilty.

While the result of the Argentine commission, was to 'forget the past,' Chilean human rights' lawyer Cerio Helvia Larenas has stated that the proper 'trick is how not to close the book'.[27] So Chilean lawyers representing the families of alleged victims were permitted to approach the military and verify claims – but no names of military personnel could be revealed. Despite this secrecy the Chilean government did agree on an extensive reparations settlement for the families of victims. Yet, the inability to ascertain the complete truth of the extent of the atrocities committed has continued to undermine successive governments and as recently as late 2004 former President Pinochet had his presidential immunity removed by the Chilean government, opening the way for investigation, trials and possible future prosecution.

The Chilean Church was far more involved and active in social issues than probably any other national church in Latin America. That however did not prevent criticism being raised against the hierarchy. Like the Argentine, the Chilean Church played a role in mediating the transition to civilian power, though unlike the Argentine Church, it had a long record of sharp protest against the military dictatorship's human rights'

---

26 Details of the reparations proposed (and ultimately acted upon) are contained in the *Report of the Chilean National Commission on Truth and Reconciliation*, volume two, part four, 837–878.

27 Quoted by Priscilla Hayner in 'Fifteen Truth Commissions', 609.

record. In fact the two successive cardinal archbishops of Santiago stand out, though in differing ways, in their public political commitment. Archbishop Cardinal Raúl Silva Henríquez (Santiago, from 1961–1983) became a national symbol of protest against General Pinochet's military government, while his successor, Archbishop (and later Cardinal) Juan Francisco Fresno Larrain (Santiago, from 1983–1990) became an agent of national reconciliation amongst the national opposition parties. While scholars have discerned changing stages in the relationships between General Pinochet's military junta and the Church, the focus here will be on the Church's role during the transition to civilian and democratic rule.[28]

Like other church hierarchies, the Chilean bishops (less than a third supported the coup openly) were cautious in their support and criticism until at least 1976. This did not prevent Cardinal Silva, as early as one month after the military coup of 1973, from visiting detained suspects and forming the Committee for Peace. This committee was led by Christián Precht and was to evolve into the Vicariate of Solidarity, the victims' rights and support association.[29] Then shortly afterwards, having taken stock of the national situation, the Episcopal Conference itself on the 24 April 1974 issued the statement 'Reconciliation in Chile.'[30]

However by December 1975, Cardinal Silva, acceding to General Pinochet's criticisms, dissolved the Peace Committee. Slightly earlier, in September, the episcopal letter 'Gospel and Peace' signaled the Church's recognition that the Pinochet government was indeed there to stay, and was indeed treading a dangerous authoritarian path. Then in January 1976 Cardinal Silva Henríquez announced the formation of the Vicariate of Solidarity to protect human rights. This organization lasted until 1992. It was under the personal patronage of the Cardinal. Under the dynamic leadership of Precht, the vicariate not only tracked and recorded every case of detention, arrest or disappearance, but provided legal advice, took every case to court, and founded both the Chilean Commission on Human Rights and the Group of Twenty-Four, co-chaired by Patricio Aylwin, which was to study and draft a new national constitution.

The bishops' fears were realized by the abolition of all political parties in 1977 and the promulgation of a new constitution that guaranteed Pinochet involvement in the nation's political life, by allowing him to be appointed a senator for life. Consequently, in their statement 'The Rebirth of Chile' of 17 December 1982 the bishops directly called for the return of democracy. They proceeded to criticize the 1980 constitution, the government's economic record, and the lack of respect

---

28 See, for instance, the analysis offered by Michael Fleet and Brian H. Smith, *The Catholic Church and Democracy in Chile and Peru* (Notre Dame: University of Notre Dame Press, 1997), chapters 2 and 5.

29 Further information on the Vicariate of Solidarity is provided in Jeffrey Klaiber, *The Church, Dictatorships and Democracy in Latin America*, 54–65.

30 Conferencia Episcopal de Chile, 'Reconciliacion en Chile' (Santiago: CEC, 24 April 1974). See Eduardo Araya, *Relaciones Iglesia-Estado en Chile 1973–1981* (Santiago: Instituto Chileno de Estudios Humanísticos, 1982), 98.

for human dignity and Christian moral values.[31] Successive letters laid down the conditions for ensuring national peace and called upon the government to enter into dialogue with civilian political parties.[32]

Then in June 1983 Cardinal Archbishop Silva announced his retirement, and was succeeded by Juan Francisco Fresno, Archbishop of La Serena. After a difficult first year, with Church and state relations at an all-time low, Cardinal Fresno invited representatives of all political parties to a meeting in his residence on 22 July 1985. At this meeting, critical for creating a combined political opposition to Pinochet, eleven political parties nominated three members to produce the 'National Accord for the Transition to Democracy'.[33]

This was the accord that produced the candidate, Patricio Aylwin in the 1989 election who was to defeat General Pinochet and take office in March 1990. A further important point is to note the effect not only of Church Social Teaching mediated through national hierarchies, but also the impact of direct papal teaching and visitations. As early as 1987 (1–6 April) the visit of Pope John Paul II, according to Precht, not only helped mobilize the populace but also encouraged them to create national reconciliation.[34]

Then, as if to underscore the weaknesses of the Chilean reconciliation process, on 16 October 1998, former President Pinochet was arrested in London while undergoing some needed medical procedures. Spain had laid charges in connection with Spanish citizens who had 'disappeared' under General Pinochet's rule. These and other charges were later dropped on medical grounds, though the Chilean Supreme Court has since allowed charges to proceed against the former ruler.

**El Salvador (1980–1992)**

A civil war raged in El Salvador for close on twelve years between the government and the armed Leftist opposition, the Farabundo Martí National Liberation Front (abbreviated as FMLN), resulting in over 75,000 deaths. The El Salvadorean conflict had been particularly savage, encompassing the whole gamut of human rights' violations from totture, killings, massacres of entire rural settlements, and including the assassination of an archbishop in 1980 and subsequently the execution of six Jesuits priests and their housekeepers in the capital in 1989; an act that spurred international intervention in the conflict. As part of the peace agreements reached between these parties in 1991, was the establishment of a United Nations' Commission on the

---

31 Episcopal Conferrence of Chile, *El renacer de Chile y otros documentos* (Santiago: Centro Nacional de Comunicación Social del Episcopado de Chile, 1984), 35.

32 Episcopal Conferrence of Chile, *El renacer de Chile y otros documentos* (Santiago: Centro Nacional de Comunicación Social del Episcopado de Chile, 1984), 36–43.

33 For a brief overview of the National Accord, see Jeoffrey Klaiber, *The Church, Dictatorships and Democracy in Latin America*, 60–65.

34 C. Precht, quoted in Jeffrey Klaiber, S.J. *The Church, Dictatorships and Democracy in Latin America* (Maryknoll, NY: Orbis Books, 1998), 62.

Truth for El Salvador. The commission was given a mandate lasting eight months, to investigate human rights' abuses over the previous twelve-year period. While this commission was modeled on earlier ones conducted in Argentina and Chile, such were the tensions and suspicions within the country, that this commission had to be staffed and run by the United Nations. The commissioners, were appointed by the United Nations and included Belisario Betancur, past-President of Colombia, Reinaldo Figueredo Planchart, ex-Minister of Foreign Relations for Venezuela, and Thomas Buergenthal, Professor of Law at George Washington University and past President of the Inter-American Court.

As early as 1993 the commission published its report entitled *From Madness to Hope: The 12-Year War in El Salvador: Report of The Commission on the Truth for El Salvador.*[35] It included names of perpetrators both from the military and the armed opposition, leading to its prompt and public denunciation by the El Salvadorean military. Critics of the report questioned its silence on the role of death squads and the part played by the United States in supporting the government forces. Significantly, the President of El Salvador, Alfredo Christiani, informed the media that the report had 'failed to meet the Salvadorean people's yearning for national reconciliation', which he then defined as 'to forgive and forget this painful past'.[36] Any further attempts at finding the truth and establishing justice was effectively cut short five days after publication of the report, when the El Salvadorean Legislature passed a General Amnesty Law.[37]

While the Commission on the Truth for El Salvador dealt with a specific period of the immediate national past, the conditions that led to that civil conflict of course existed long before. These conditions had moved the Church from a traditional acceptance of social inequalities to one of sharp criticism of the treatment of the poor. Archbishop Oscar Romero (San Salvador, 1977–1980) assassinated during a church service, symbolized for many Salvadoreans, as well as others in Latin America, a church that sided with the poor and oppressed. His predecessor, Luis Chávez y González (1938–1977) had not only endorsed the reforms of the Second Vatican Council and its regional endorsements made by the Episcopal Conference of Latin American (CELAM) at Medellín, but supported both Catholic Action and Christian Trade Unionism. Archbishop Romero was a conservative, driven to opposition by attacks on clergy, in particular the savage murder of Fr. Rutilio Grande S.J. in 1977. After the reformist coup in 1979, he offered conditional support. Nevertheless, up to the time of his death, Romero was involved in mediation attempts between the government and armed opposition.

---

35  *From Madness to Hope: The 12-Year War in El Salvador: Report of The Commission on the Truth for El Salvador*, UN Security Council, UN Document 2/25500 at 18 (1993).

36  Martha Doggett, *Death Foretold: The Jesuit Murders in El Salvador* (Washington, DC: Georgetown University Press, 1993), 266.

37  For further analysis of the El Salvador Truth Commission, see Margaret L. Popkin, *Peace Without Justice: Obstacles to Building the Rule of Law in El Salvador* (University Park: Pennsylvania University Press, 2000).

After his assassination on 24 March 1980 there was a dramatic increase in death squad activity-four priests murdered and by year end, four American women (three nuns and one lay woman) kidnapped, raped, and murdered. The reaction was soon to follow and by January 1981 the first dramatic offensives by the FMLN were underway.

In 1983, on the eve of the papal visit to the country, Bishop Arturo Rivera y Damas was named Archbishop. The new archbishop was a conservative, yet supported mediation between the warring sides. To this end he founded 'Legal Defense', an organization which investigated human rights' violations and kept complete records of all known cases. The complex and delicate process of mediation was well handled by the Archbishop, who was a friend of President Duarte and also knew that the progressive wing of the Church supported the FMLN. This radical Marxist group knew that the Archbishop supported the memory and work of his murdered predecessor, Oscar Romero, over against the views of many conservative bishops.

President José Napoleón Duarte (1984–1989) came to support dialogue between the government and the rebels, and the Archbishop and the National Episcopal Conference acted as facilitators, messengers, as well as working to provide neutral meeting places for peace talks. The last mentioned began rather sporadically in 1984, restarted in 1985 at the urging of the rebels, but ceased when the rebels objected to statements in the August 1985 Episcopal Conference document entitled 'Reconciliation and Peace'. Their primary objections were that the document did not mention United States involvement in the national struggle and that the bishops' statements placed rebel and army atrocities on the same moral level. Despite this setback, the Archbishop continued efforts at mediation, including negotiating the return of the kidnapped President's daughter Inés Guadelupe, in 1985 (in which he was assisted by Fr Ignacio Ellacuría, rector of Central American University), and facilitating further negotiations in Mexico City with rebel leaders in 1988 This was in the spirit of an earlier agreement reached by the Central American presidents meeting on 7 August 1987, in Guatemala City (the 'Equispulas II Agreements') that urged each government in conflict to establish dialogue, declare cease-fires, and establish a national commission of reconciliation.

Then, in 1988, the Archbishop proposed a 'national debate for peace', held on 3–4 September, which was a great success. This debate included four non-Catholic churches and about sixty other organizations. Political parties held their own National Forum and even Alfredo Cristiani, candidate of the rightist ARENA party agreed with most of the proposals. The results of such mediation efforts became clear in May 1989, when President Duarte turned power over to the Arena Party and Alfredo Cristiani,.who on assuming power on the first of June, announced a new dialogue with the opposition.

Numerous meetings were held between the government and the FMLN in Mexico and then in Costa Rica. Bishops, including the president of the Episcopal Conference, were present at both these meetings,. Also for the first time, at a successor meeting in Costa Rica, the Organization of American States and the United Nations sent representatives. The subsequent 1990 meeting in Geneva had as principal mediator the United Nations and this meeting led to a series of dialogues culminating in the Mexico Agreements of April 1991. The next month the United Nations Security Council created The Mission of the Observers of the UN to El Salvador (CONUSAL) which had the task of overseeing the transition to peace. These peace efforts were aided within the country by the National Commission for the Consolidation of Peace (COPAZ). This latter commission had representatives from the government, the FMLN, all political parties as well as the Archbishop and the Lutheran bishop, Medarno Gómez. This commission provided the 16 January 1992 Chapultepec Peace Accord, which ended twelve years of civil war. The conditions stipulated the demobilization of rebel forces, the abolition of rural police and the national guard and reforms of the army, as well as the establishment of a national Commission on the Truth for El Salvador.

Two critical events, one internal, the other external precipitated the conclusion of this peace accord. First, internally, the 1989 murder of six Jesuits and their cook and her daughter on the campus of the Central American University shocked the nation and the world. The victims included the Rector and the vice-rector, the well-known theologian and peace negotiator Ignacio Ellacuria. The military blamed the FMLN, but on 13 January 1990 President Cristiani admitted that the army was responsible and nine soldiers were brought to trial. Second, externally, the cessation of the Cold War in 1989, and the dramatic cut in United States' military support, combined with increasing international pressure on the government, dramatically focused combatants' desires for a negotiated peace.

When the El Salvadorean Truth Commission published its Report on the 15 March 1993, it named those thought responsible for human rights' abuses, including those responsible for the murders of Romero and the six Jesuits and their cook and her daughter. Further, the Report found that 85 percent of the violence was perpetrated by agents of State, while only five per cent was committed by the FMLN. Unfortunately, and certainly in defiance of national and international expectations, the ARENA-dominated National Assembly passed an amnesty law almost immediately after the Report's publication.

## Guatemala (1954–1996)

The report of the Guatemalan Historical Clarification Commission (CEH), issued in February 1999, marked the end of one of Latin America's longest and bloodiest civil wars, This conflict between the government and the leftist *Unidad Revolucionaria Nacional Guatemalteca* (Guatemalan National Revolutionary Unity or URNG) lasted for over thirty years and left over 200,000 dead or disappeared.[38] The government counter-insurgency tactics peaked in the decade of the 1980s, and

---

38 Guatemala: Comisión para el Esclarecimiento Histórico (CEH), *Guatemala: Memoria Del Silencio, Informe de la Comisión para el Esclarecimiento Histórico*, 12 vols (Guatemala: Comisión para el Esclarecimiento Histórico, 1999) and the Roman Catholic Church independent

involved large-scale clearances and massacres in rural regions, largely of Native American Indian settlements. Only United Nations' participation was finally able to end conflict and broker a peace. The peace agreement sought to deal with the issue of past human rights' violations in the process of negotiation, and much impetus was given to this issue by the publication of the El Salvador Truth Commission during the negotiations. The agreement to establish a 'Historical Clarification Commission' was signed in Oslo, Norway, in June 1994, though the actual peace accords between the government and the URNG were only finally signed in 1997 and the commission's work initiated. The commission and its work was surrounded by controversy, particularly from victims and survivor groups, since the terms of the commission's mandate included not attributing any individual responsibility for human rights' violations, nor enabling any judicial procedure, and being given a six-month period of operation. However, the commission, chaired by a non-Guatemalan United Nations appointee, Christian Tomuschat and two Guatemalan commissioners, Otilia Lux de Cotí and Edgar Alfredo Balsells Tojo, assisted by additional field staff of almost two hundred non-nationals for security and impartiality reasons, gained the trust of both the government and opposition, and eventually had eighteen months to complete its investigations.

The report documented 23,000 deaths, 6,000 cases of disappeared persons and a staggering 626 massacres, primarily directed against the indigenous Mayan peoples. Over 90 percent of the atrocities were attributed to the military or state-supported paramilitaries, while only 3 percent were traced to guerilla activity. In accordance with its mandate to analyze causes of the violence, the report attributed such activities largely to racism, structural injustice, the national security doctrine followed by the military, support by the United States and the anti-Communist Cold War strategy, and the non-democratic nature of much of the national institutions. The report concluded with proposed recommendations, some of which were adopted reluctantly and tardily by the next President, Alfonso Portillo.

The commission established up to fourteen field offices, visited many isolated villages, and even managed to obtain declassified United States documents regarding the Guatemalan military, which in turn declared that it had no records of the period under investigation. The commission received much help from the Roman Catholic Church, which turned over its 'Recovery of Historical Memory Project' (REMHI) archives from its own Human Rights Office, the results of a project begun years before the official commission had been established.[39] In addition, the results were also turned over from the non-governmental *Centro Internacional para Investigaciones*

---

report by REMHI, *Recuperación de la Memoria Histórica* (REMHI and Menschenrechtsburo des Erzbistums Guatemala ODHAG, 1998).

39  The Roman Catholic Archdiocesan Office of Human Rights had launched this unofficial CEMHI years before to document violations of human rights. It published on 24 April 1998 an unofficial report entitled *Guatemala: Nunca Mas. Informe projecto interdiócesano de recuperación de la memoria histórica* (Guatemala City, 1998). The English, abridged edition is entitled *Guatemala: Never Again!* (Maryknoll: Orbis Books, 1999).

*en Derechos Humanos* (International Center for Human Rights Investigation, or CIIDH). Together, these two sources provided much of the evidence used by the commission.

The question of how human rights' violations were to be handled was being discussed in Guatemala when the El Salvadoran report was released in 1993. This report served as the central reference point for the Guatemalan situation and the military insisted that the El Salvadoran precedent of naming the military perpetrators would not be tolerated. In fact as early as 1996 the National Assembly passed a 'National Reconciliation Law ' which made amnesty possible for both soldiers and guerrillas, but excluded those involved in the crimes of disappearances, torture and genocide.

Guatemala differed in significant aspects from other Latin American nations. It was the least developed, with roughly 85 percent of its population comprising a rural peasant class. In addition, and exacerbating division, roughly half if not more of the population was Native American Indian, primarily of Mayan ancestry and speaking 22 differing languages. Further, according to research by David Stoll, the percentage of Protestants in Guatemala had increased during the decade of the Eighties, from just one point eight to almost 20 percent and some estimates place the percentage even higher.[40] Two of the recent Presidents of the country have been Protestant, Efraín Ríos Mont (1982–1983) who came to power through a military coup and Jorge Serrano Elías (1990–1993) who was democratically elected. Partly as a result then of perceived Protestant growth, the divisions between the conservative and progressive tendencies within the Roman Catholic Church were exacerbated.

The Archbishop, Mario Cardinal Casariego y Acevedo, C.S.R. was conservative and hindered any progressive deviation from traditional approaches. However, Cardinal Casariego died in June 1983 and was succeeded by Próspero Penados del Barrio, who brought new vision to the Guatemalan National Bishops' Conference and encouraged the issuance of episcopal letters critical of the government.[41] It was this Archbishop who involved the Church in the National Reconciliation Committee formed in 1989, and led by Bishop Rodolfo Quezada of Zacapa, who in addition encouraged broad participation in the National Dialogue, a body comprised of fifteen commissions seeking ways to end national strife. He also, in 1990, formed the Social Service Office of the Archdiocese, and appointed the previously exiled bishop, Gerardi Conedra to direct the office. In 1998 Bishop Gerardi was murdered days after submitting the Church report mentioned above – one that differed from the

---

40 David Stoll, *Is Latin America Turning Protestant? The Politics of Evangelical Growth* (Berkeley: University of California Press, 1990), 9 and chapter 7. See also the estimates in Tim Steigenga, 'Guatemala', in Paul Sigmund's *Religious Freedom and Evangelization in Latin America. The Challenge of Religious Pluralism* (Maryknoll, NY: Orbis Books, 1999), 150–174.

41 For instance see the letters 'Para Construir la Paz' (1984), Conferencia Episcopal de Guatemala, *Al servicio de la vida, la justiticia y la paz: Documentos de la Conferencia Episcopal de Guatemala, 1956–1997* (Guatemala de la Asunción : La Conferencia, 1997) and *El Clamor por la Tierra: carta pastoral colectiva del episcopado Guatemalteco* (Guatemala de la Asunción: Impr. Gutenburg, 1988).

official commissions by naming those responsible for murder and genocidal activities and rejecting the military and government consensus on a general amnesty.

Nonetheless, much cooperative work was completed by both Roman Catholics and Protestants in determining the extent and duration of human rights' abuses, both through the National Reconciliation Committee and the National Dialogue.[42] Despite the reactionary reputation of President Rios Montt's rule, not all Protestants were conservative politically and political support by Protestants tended to be regional. Added to this complexity is that of the relations between these differing Christian traditions and the religious traditions of the indigenous Native Americans (Mayan). Religious pluralism in Guatemala remains and presents challenges to all religious communities.[43]

### South Africa (1960–1994)

On 29 October 1998 the Final Report of the South African Truth and Reconciliation Commission (TRC) was due to be submitted to the State President, Nelson Mandela. The presentation of this report was the last of the TRC's four mandated objectives. The others were first, to establish as complete a picture as possible of gross human rights' violations between the years 1960 and 1993; second, to grant amnesty in exchange for complete and truthful disclosure of such violations during this period; third, to ascertain victims' fates, enable victims (or their survivors) to tell their stories, and finally; to arrange reparations. The ruling party, the African National Congress (ANC) in the person of the country's Vice-President Thabo Mbeki, objected to the report apparently equating human rights' abuses by the ANC with the National Party's (NP) crimes and sought legal action to stop the report.[44] The erstwhile National Party Prime Minister F. W. De Klerk threatened legal action to prevent its publication on the grounds it misrepresented and slandered him.[45] The TRC chairperson, Anglican Archbishop Desmond Tutu defended the report and singled out the ANC for sharp criticism in attempting to halt the report. President Nelson Mandela overruled his own political party and the report was issued on schedule. What did the Report in fact report and what were the criteria by which it claimed to be about truth and reconciliation?

---

42  On the extent of ecumenical cooperation, see Karla Ann Koll, 'Struggling for Solidarity. Changing Mission relations between the Presbyterian Church (USA) and Church Organizations in Latin America during the 1980s' (Ph.D. Dissertation, Princeton Theological Seminary, 2003), chapter 3.

43  See, for example, Veronica Melander, *The Hour of God: People in Guatemala Confronting Political Evangelicalism and Counterinsurgency, 1976–1990* (Uppsala: Uppsala University, 1999). On Mayan identity and religion, see Brett Greider's chapter in this volume.

44  K. Owen, 'Can South Africans Really Face the Past? The Truth Hurts', *The New Republic* (23 November 1998), 21.

45  F. W. De Klerk, 'South Africa Panel Didn't Serve Truth', *New York Times* (28 November 1998), A14.

The TRC Report was mandated by the South African Interim Constitution, and represented a political compromise between some who wished justice for human rights' violators, and violators who sought amnesty. The compromise was to offer conditional amnesty in exchange for the truth. It should be noted that the South African TRC was deeply influenced in its planning stages by participants of earlier Argentine and Chilean commissions.[46]

While on one level a political compromise, the idea of such a commission can be traced back beyond the release of Nelson Mandela and the unbanning of proscribed political organizations in 1991, to numerous and repeated suggestions made by then Bishop Desmond Tutu in 1985, the 1989 South African Council of Churches' document, *Confessing Guilt in South Africa: The Responsibility of Churches and Individual Christians,* the 1990 Rustenburg Conference, the General Secretary of the World Council of Churches, Dr E. Castro in 1991, and the 1992 Western Cape Council of Churches' 'Statement on Amnesty', reiterated by Gerald West and James Cochrane in 1992.[47] Thus the role of Protestant Churches in the South African political process becomes evident. The country is predominantly Christian, with small minorities of Jews, Muslims, and Hindus, and adherents of African Traditional Religions. Thus the Roman Catholic Church, while it played a critical part in protesting apartheid, did not have the central role it played in Latin America.[48]

Further, political discourse in South Africa was often conducted in theological terms, with the predominantly Afrikaner National Party defending apartheid because it was justified on a theological interpretation of racial differences being maintained as a part of God's order for creation.[49] Thus critique of the political was often couched

---

46 Iain S. Maclean 'Truth and Reconciliation: Irreconcilable Differences?' *Religion & Theology* 6/3 (1999), 272.

47 Desmond Tutu, 'The Process of Reconciliation and the Demands of Obedience', *Transformation* (1985), 3–8; South African Council of Churches, *Confessing Guilt in South Africa: The Responsibility of Churches and Individual Christians* (Johannesburg: SACC, 1989); L. Alberts and F. Chikane (eds), *The Road to Rustenburg: The Church Looking Forward to a New South Africa* (Cape Town: Struik, 1991); World Council of Churches, *From Cottesloe to Cape Town. Challenges for the Church in a Post-Apartheid South Africa. The WCC Visit to South Africa, October, 1991* (Geneva: PCR Information, No. 30. 1991), 69; Western Cape Council of Churches, 'Statement on Amnesty', *Journal of Theology for Southern Africa.* 81 (December 1992), 94; and Gerald West, 'Don't Stand on my Story: The Truth and Reconciliation Commission, Intellectuals, Genre and Identity', *Journal of Theology for Southern Africa* 98 (July, 1997), 3–12.

48 On the Roman Catholic Church in South Africa see Garth Abraham, *The Catholic Church and Apartheid. The Response of the Catholic Church in South Africa to the First Decade of National Party Rule 1948–1957* (Johannesburg: Ravan Press, 1989) and Joy Brain and Philippe Denis (eds), *The Catholic Church in Contemporary Southern Africa* (Pietermaritzburg: Cluster Publications, 1999).

49 See the Classic statement in Algemene Sinode van die Nederduitse Gereformeerde Kerk, *Volk, Ras en Nasie en Volkeverhoudinge in die Lig van die Skrif* (Kaapstad, Pretoria: NG Kerk Uitgewers, 1975) translated into English as *Human Relations and the South African Scene in the Light of Scripture* (Cape Town: Dutch Reformed Church Publishers, 1976) and the critique

in theological terms, for apartheid also divided the Church along racial lines instead of fostering unity.

In addition, powerful political impetus was given to the concept of a reconciliation commission through the protracted negotiations between the ANC and the then ruling NP, both of whom desired amnesty conditions in any future settlement. Professor Kader Asmal suggested the idea of a 'truth commission' in his installation lecture as Professor of Human Rights' Law at the University of Western Cape on 25 May 1992.[50] This suggestion was picked up by the ANC which had just concluded its own internal investigation of human rights' abuses in ANC guerilla camps. Thus from the outset there existed a convergence of political and ecclesiastical interest in setting up a commission to examine the recent South African past and to consider the issue of amnesty and its role in future national reconciliation. Consequently, the TRC clearly understood itself as a 'bridge', using the words of the Interim Constitution, between a divided past 'of untold suffering and injustice' and a future 'founded on the recognition of human rights, democracy, peaceful co-existence, and development opportunities for all'.[51]

Precisely because the political and racial divisions were thought irreconcilable, the TRC has gained much attention. It drew the attention of social commentators, politicians and social scientists because it so consciously sought to be inclusive, to hear from both perpetrators and victims, from the extreme left and the extreme right, and because it sought to avoid the errors of earlier attempts at national reconciliation attempted in Latin America. It thus sought to avoid the 'cheap grace' approach taken in many nations where the departing military or succeeding civilian governments had granted blanket amnesty to those who had violated human rights' norms.+ The Latin American cases revealed that such approaches, by too swiftly granting amnesty, also led to national amnesia about the past, denial (that is, 'no truth') and no justice or reparations for the victims (not possible as the truth was not known). The perpetrators, it seemed, never did anything, the victims remained victims and deep suspicion of the government developed with profound implications for national unity.[52] What then has happened to justice for the victims? Further, if the perpetrators are not brought to justice how will the truth of what occurred under military dictatorship be known? Certainly the self-serving justification of such perpetrators, claiming that one must forgive in order to foster national reconciliation must be recognized for what it is, a simple attempt to avoid the

---

offered by Douglas Bax, *A Different Gospel: A Critique of the Theology Behind Apartheid* (Johannesburg: Presbyterian Church of Southern Africa, 1979).

50  TRC, *Report* Vol. I/4, Section 6.

51  TRC, *Report*, Vol. 1/5, Section 1.

52  See Patricia Hayner, *Unspeakable Truths*; Robert I. Rotberg and Dennis Thompson (eds), *Truth V. Justice: The Morality of Truth Commissions* (Princeton: Princeton University Press, 2000) for a discussion of the Latin American cases and further on South Africa, see J. Aldunate, 'The Christian Ministry of Reconciliation' in Gregory Baum and H. Wells (eds), *The Reconciliation of Peoples: Challenge to the Churches* (Maryknoll, NY: Orbis Books, 1997); and Alex Boraine, J. Levy, R. Scheffer (eds), *Dealing with the Past: Truth and Reconciliation in South Africa* (Cape Town: IDASA, 1994).

consequences of their actions, one which subsequent experience revealed, produced neither truth nor national reconciliation. When terms such as truth, justice, reparations (restitution), confession, and reconciliation are used it becomes evident that the political realm is dependent upon some accepted norm or system of value. Language typically associated with religion is now being applied to the political sphere.[53] Differences then emerged over the appropriate theological and ethical principles that should predominate in the TRC, as did controversy over what was regarded as an overly Christian cast to the commission, given the presence of an archbishop as the chairperson, and numerous Christian clergy and theologians among the seventeen commissioners.[54] Nonetheless, despite these criticisms, and sharp reaction to the TRC's reparations policy, the South African TRC is regarded as one of the more successful commissions to date.

## Peru (1980–2000)

The latest of the national commissions, the Peruvian Comisión de la Verdad y Reconciliación (Truth and Reconciliation Commission, abbreviated as CVR), after completing its two-year investigation into the conditions and victims of the country's undeclared 'civil war' stretching over twenty years from 1980 to 2000, presented its report to President Alejandro Toledo on 28 August 2003.[55] The Peruvian case is significantly different in that the atrocities occurred not under military rule but rather under two democratically-elected governments and the authoritarian rule of the erstwhile President Alberto Fujimoro. In 2001 President Fujimoro fled into self-imposed exile and his successor, interim President Valentin Paniagua, appointed a Truth and Reconciliation Commission to investigate and to uncover the truth about the twenty-year period from 1980 to 2000. This was a period of the country's history that was marked by increasing guerilla violence which in turn led to government reprisals and fueled the classic 'spiral of violence', coined by Brazil's Dom Helder Camara, in which government retaliation spawned further violence. This commission differed significantly from earlier Latin American ones, both in its methods and in its proposals. The CVR was comprised of twelve members and one observer and was directed by Salomon Lerner Febres, and was given a two- year mandate to uncover the truth. The commission examined the situations that gave rise to such violations, sought to allocate responsibility, to propose reparations, and to recommend reforms. The CVR began its work in July 2001.

The Shining Path guerilla movement, led by Abimael Guzmán, deeply influenced by Mao Tse Tung, initiated a terror campaign against the state that eventually left 25,000 dead and billions of dollars in destruction. Unlike other terrorist movements in Latin America, the Shining Path movement did not just attack government officials

---

53 Tinyiko Sam Maluleke, 'Truth, National Unity and Reconciliation in South Africa. Aspects of the Emerging Theological Agenda', *Missionalia 25/1* (April 1997), 59–86.

54 See Iain S. Maclean 'Truth and Reconciliation: Irreconcilable Differences?' *Religion & Theology* 6/3 (1999), 288.

55 Comisión de la Verdad y Reconciliación, *Comisión de la Verdad y Reconciliación, Informe Final*, 9 vol (Lima: Comisión de la Verdad y Reconciliación, 2003).

or the rich, but systematically targeted all popular leaders, the rich and the poor, urban and peasant populations. Unlike other leftist movements in Latin America, the Shining Path had no links to any leftist clergy, either Roman Catholic or Protestant, because it was violently anti-religious, to the extent of holding public trials of religious leaders then openly executing at least five priests, two religious women and many lay catechists. There was a much smaller, more traditional leftist guerilla movement, the Tupac Amaru Revolutionary Movement (MRTA), which targeted landowners and the military but did not promote systematic killing and destruction of the civilian infra-structure on the scale that the Shining Path initiated.

The Peruvian CVR produced dramatic results in its search for the truth. The number of victims had to be revised dramatically to over 69,000 killed and 6,000 'disappeared'. Over 40 percent of the victims were from the poor South Western department of Ayachucho, and primarily from ethnic groups and social classes that have been marginalized in Peruvian society. Thus three quarters of the victims were in fact Quechua-speaking and from rural areas. The report attributes over half (54 percent) of the casualties to the activities of the 'Shining Path' movement, 30 percent to the Peruvian military and police forces, and the rest to the actions of the rural or peasant self-defense militias.[56]

The Peruvian CVR process represents a significant advance in such processes, as building on the widely recognized South African TRC, the Peruvian one included public hearings. This was a first for Latin America and it included not only the public, but also a special unit that worked on bringing specific crimes to the justice system. Thus justice, often overlooked in the rush of nations seeking to avoid a 'Nuremberg approach' or occluding the truth through amnesties, has returned to prominence here. Again, perhaps building on critiques of the South African TRC, the Peruvian CVR has recognized that it is only the start of a much larger and long-term national reconciliation process, one that includes reparations, education, and renewed structural, social, and legal safeguards. In fact, the Peruvian CVR understood its work as a long-term process involving not simply its immediate results, but long-term action in three spheres, namely those of the political, the social and its connection to political institutions, and individual and inter-personal relations.

The Peruvian Roman Catholic Church had a much more traditional hierarchy than, say, Chile, or even Argentina. Comment on the state of the nation was left to individual bishops and in terms of social amelioration, this was up to individual priests or religious workers in specific locations. As a consequence, the laity were divided along the political and theological spectrum with no overall leadership emerging from the bishops or from the Peruvian Episcopal Conference which tended to focus on the implications for Church teaching of government proposals to separate Church and state or to reform the educational system.

While some of the bishops were actively involved in ameliorating social conditions, and organizing the poor of their parishes into self-help movements, others were more interested in defending a traditional relationship between Church

---

56  Comisión de la Verdad y Reconciliación, *Informe Final*, VIII, 315.

and society. An indicator of how divided the Peruvian Church's responses were to oppression and human rights' abuses, the conclusion of the CVR comments on the Church's mixed record and candidly expresses the need for other social actors outside of the Church to contribute to the reconciliation process. It is perhaps indicative of the situation that the Archbishop, Cardinal Juan Luis Cipriani, a member of the conservative society Opus Dei, in a public Mass attended by the country's President, condemned the CVR Report and its recommendations in particular.

Ironically this is the official ecclesiastical response in a nation that provided Latin America – and the world – with the articulator of liberation theology, Gustavo Gutiérrez. Drawing on traditional catholic Augustinian themes, as interpreted by the Second Vatican Council and subsequent regional bishop's conferences, Gutiérrez formulated a new way of doing theology by rejecting a dualistic interpretation of history and advocating a three-step methodological theological hermeneutic. This involved first involvement and analysis of the actual historical context of specific peoples, reflecting theologically on the results thus obtained and, finally, engaging in action to change the inequities discerned in the situation. This was directly expressed in his 1971 work *A Theology of Liberation*, where the use of the term 'liberation', rather than salvation, expresses his rejection of spiritualizations of the human condition that ignore harsh this-worldly realities.[57] Liberation became a technical term for freedom from social and economic oppression, freedom from traditional fatalism and discounting of the underprivileged, and freedom from individual and social or structural sin.

This theology directed a sharp critique against traditional assumptions common on the Latin American rim of a fast-decaying Christendom: assumptions that authority was ordained by God and thus unchanging, that one's class was determined, and that poverty was in fact a Christian virtue. Rather, in an Augustinian manner, sin was expanded to include structures and institutions of society, and human agency encouraged as the agents of altering the unjust and thus sinful structures that kept the people poor. While Gutiérrez had written his theology in part as a response to Marxist ideas, rapidly gaining currency and influence in the late 1960s, more conservative clerics and certainly political leaders, saw such a theology as representing a threat to the established order. In later years, many liberation theologians –and of course other critics- doubted talk of 'reconciliation' as they understood such as underplaying the realities of structural oppression.

**Evaluation**

Is reconciliation then possible in countries that have experienced civil division, indeed war, marked by atrocities and human rights' violations by every side? To answer briefly, yes, but with qualifications, for, as the Chilean José Zalaquett summed up the

57 Gustavo Gutiérrez's title in Spanish, *Theologia de la Liberación* (published 1971) and translated into English and edited by Sr. Caridad Inda and John Eagleson. *Theology of Liberation. History, Politics and Salvation* (Maryknoll, NY: Orbis Books, 1973).

process, only 'as much as is possible' is accomplished in each case. So, what actually occurred and what has been learned from the now rather extensive experience and documentation of such truth (and reconciliation) commissions, reaching back over a quarter of a century? How did the Churches and religious organizations contribute (or not) to the process?

I will now briefly address each of the critical elements identified through the summaries presented above of selected commissions, namely amnesty provisions, the necessity of truth, justice, and, finally, reparations. Then I will briefly note the role of the Roman Catholic churches primarily in Latin America, and of the Protestant churches in South Africa. It is striking in this post-Cold War world, that here terms are used in political contexts that are in fact profoundly theological. Thus, the political application of an old theological term, reconciliation, emerged or was first used in this way in Latin American nations. Significantly, and more about this will be stated below, it seems the use of the term 'reconciliation' was used in contexts where similar religious language was being utilized. Thus for instance, not only the term reconciliation, but also apology, forgiveness, pardon, truth, reparations, and unity came into common political usage.

## Impunity/Amnesty (as reconciliation)

As many Latin American nations democratized, beginning in 1974 with Brazil, transitional or successor governments established fact-finding commissions and in most cases passed amnesty laws. Such was the case in Chile (Commission 1990, amnesty1978), Brazil (no official commission, but amnesty 1977), Argentina (Commission 1982, amnesty 1983, 1989), Guatemala (Commission 1999, limited amnesty 1996), El Salvador (Commission 1991, amnesty 1992) and Peru (Commission, 2003 amnesty decrees, 1995, 1996). No doubt these commissions bore the hope that internal conflict would cease and that one 'must forgive and forget' in order to reconstruct, unify, and reconcile, the nation. However for many nations this was not to be. The Chilean and Argentine cases were to result, not in national unity and reconciliation, but rather in suspicion, doubt, and questions about the legitimacy of the successor government, police, and armed forces. Then, in situations where the military operated from a position of relative strength, such as in Guatemala and El Salvador, rapid amnesties were decreed almost immediately after the publication of the national commissions' reports. The rapid granting of amnesty meant that the truth was hindered and without truth, justice was denied the victims and their families. The fact that the truth cannot be ascertained meant that the 'official version' was all that remained and the victims suffered yet again in that their stories were discounted. The nation also suffered in that without truth, it remains trapped in a less than accurate history, and uncertain paths to the future.

The cases noted above led to the recognition that amnesty was but a blanket impunity for terrible crimes. The protest against it by survivors and their families was a cry for justice, for the recognition of wrongs, for the holding accountable the perpetrators, for the events of past history to be recognized and to be told to the present. It is perhaps too obvious, but we must recall that the word 'amnesty' itself is derived from 'amnesia' – the loss of memory – the loss thus of history and so also of truth. Thus, as Harper has pithily phrased it, impunity or amnesty is the 'enemy of democracy'. If amnesty serving to grant impunity is the norm, then how will differing groups of people, especially victims and perpetrators, ever be reconciled and live together?[58]

These amnesties brought the recognition that without at least some of the truth, justice, let alone reparations, and so national reconciliation over the long haul, is not possible. What was now apparent was that such 'reconciliation,' without considering justice, or truth, was but – to rephrase Dietrich Bonhoeffer – 'cheap reconciliation'. The recent revelations of the truth in the Argentine case (see the earlier case study in this chapter) were so shocking and their implications for the legitimacy of the current government and police and military so damaging, that as recently as September 2003 the Argentine government decided to revoke all earlier amnesty decrees.[59]

So amnesty laws were no longer sufficient. Without truth, then, there was no record of what happened in the past, no justice in the present, and no basis for any reparations and national reconciliation in the future. It had become clear that actual practical outcomes have meant a move from 'amnesty' proclamations to truth commissions, and from these most markedly in the South African case, to a truth and reconciliation commission that included amnesty provisions only on the condition of telling the truth. As South Africa's Archbishop Desmond Tutu succinctly expressed the point:

> You see there are some people who have tried to be very facile and say that let bygones be bygones: they want us to have a national amnesia. And you have to keep saying to those people that to pretend that nothing happened, to not acknowledge that something horrible did happen to them, is to victimize the victims yet again. But even more important, experience worldwide shows that if you do not deal with a dark past such as ours, effectively look the beast in the eye, that beast is not going to lie down quietly; it is going as sure as anything, to come back and haunt you horrendously. [60]

## Truth (as Reconciliation)

The abuses surrounding the amnesty process in Latin America, and the failure of national commissions to ensure justice, led to a focus on truth as a critical factor in national reconciliation. However truth, as Pilate once observed, is not easy of

---

58  Charles Harper (ed.), *Impunity: an Ethical Perspective. Six Latin American Case Studies* (Geneva: World Council of Churches, 1996), ix.

59  These repeals effectively annulled the 'Due Obedience' law of 1987 and the 'Full Stop' law of 1986 which granted amnesty. See report noted in footnote 12.

60  Desmond Tutu, 'Healing a Nation', *Index on Censorship: Wounded Nations Broken Lives – Truth Commissions and War Tribunals* 25/5, 172 (September/October 1996), 38–42.

definition. According to numerous scholars of truth commissions such as Raoul Souza and Fanie du Toit, truth is to be understood as a multi-faceted element of a national commission. Rather than being something abstract, static and other-worldly, it should be understood as a reality exposed in time, historical and progressive, revealed by what is done.[61]

In other words, truth is understood pragmatically, in terms of what is accomplished by specific national commissions. In summary form then, such an emphasis on truth enables certain other features to occur more easily. First though, such an emphasis on truth should have critical individual and social consequences in that it frees individuals from pathological ideological perversions of both past and present lies and reveals the depths of both individual and social corruption. This freeing from the negative, from untruth, should enable the truth to transform the present realities into a hopeful future. As such it places these present 'realities' into crisis by placing them in judgment and thereby pointing to alternatives.

From the perspective of victims, knowing the truth about the past, or having it re-affirmed, enables the victims or their survivors to have their history acknowledged and finally affirmed as also a more accurate account of part of the national past. National commissions precisely provide the social and psychological 'space' for this to happen, for both perpetrators and victims, as the South African TRC's public hearings dramatically illustrated. In this way then another 'version' of the past is made public so that it can engage in conversation, struggle, and debate in order to arrive at a broader national consensus about the nation's past. Learning from the past enables the truth about the past to be more fully known and so furthers possible justice in the present and reconciliation for the future.[62]

The public acknowledgement of injustice and the uncovering of the truth facilitates both individual and collective grieving, remembering, and resolutions to avoid future recurrences of such atrocities. Such victim-centered definitions of "truth" do posse troubling questions for a legal system that seeks truth, not only from victims, but evidence to implicate the perpetrators. This has led to a widespread debate which can

---

61  Raoul Souza, 'The Church: A Witness to the Truth on the Way to Freedom', in Charles Harper (ed.) *Impunity*, 60–72. Stephanus Francois Du Toit, 'Ideas of Truth and Revelation in the Light of the Challenge of Postmodernism' (Ph.D. Dissertation, Cambridge University, 1995); TRC, *Report, SA Truth and Reconciliation Commission*, 5 vols (London: Macmillan, 1998), vol. I, 110–122. An evaluation of the role of truth in the TRC process is offered in James L. Gibson, *Overcoming Apartheid: Can Truth Reconcile a Divided Nation?* (Cape Town: Institute for Justice and Reconciliation, 2002).

62  Kader Asmal, L. Asmal, and L. Roberts (eds), *Reconciliation through Truth: A Reckoning of Apartheid's Criminal Governance* (Cape Town: David Philip, 1996); Alex Boraine, Janet Levy, and S. Scheffer (eds). *Dealing with the Past: Truth and Reconciliation in South Africa* (Cape Town: Institute for Democracy in South Africa (Cape Town: IDASA, 1994); José Zalaquett, *The Ethics of Responsibility: Human Rights, Truth and Reconciliation in Chile* (Washington: Washington Office on Latin America, 1991).

only be noted at this point.[63] Finally, and most critically for reconciliation, if there is truth then a provisional basis is laid for establishing who are eligible for reparations; ndeed, how reparations or restructuring of national society are required in order to ensure justice for all citizens.[64]

## Justice (as Reconciliation)

Because of the perceived weaknesses of the Argentine, Chilean, El Salvadorean, and Guatemalan national commissions, focusing on the too-rapid issuing of amnesty decrees, the decade of the 1990s witnessed a shift away from such approaches. Instead there was a renewed emphasis on justice, as can be observed in the reversals of amnesty in the Argentine and Chilean cases, and the decision for international justice tribunals in the aftermaths of the Bosnian and Rwandan genocides. So a primary issue in the early 1990s for truth and reconciliation commissions was the choice between amnesty and justice.

Any nation having to deal with a recent past of human rights' abuses and dealing with perpetrators, could either grant amnesty to all perpetrators, or hand them over to the justice system.. With the hindsight granted by the experiences from earlier commissions, any similar commission would have to deal with the issues raised by by the demands for justice. An alternative was to involve the international community as El Salvador did in its truth commission, or simply to establish criminal tribunals, as in Yugoslavia and Rwanda.[65]

However practical political concerns, including the eminently practical one of actually getting the military regime to step down, meant that justice was in fact compromised. The rationale being that amnesty is the price to be paid for social stability or perhaps even for national reconciliation. According to José Zalaquett, the best practical attainment is for the truth to be known, and only that justice which is (practicably) possible.[66] Yet, the political consequences of lenient amnesty decisions raise questions for this approach.

Nevertheless, it has become clear that the 'justice' (in either its retributive or restorative forms) option while it might work in a situation where there is a foreign

---

63 Rotberg, Robert I. & Dennis Thompson. *Truth V. Justice. The Morality of Truth Commissions.* Princeton: Princeton University Press, 2000.

64 On an early study on reparations see Willa Boesak, *God's Wrathful Children. Political Oppression & Christian Ethics* (Grand Rapids, MI: William B. Eerdmans Publishing, 1995), but post the TRC report, see Charles Villa-Vicencio and Willem Verwoerd (eds) *Looking Back, Looking Forward. Reflections on the Truth and Reconciliation Commission of South Africa* (Cape Town: University of Cape Town Press, 2000).

65 Richard Goldstone, 'Justice as a Tool for Peace-making: Truth Commissions and International Criminal Tribunals', *New York University Journal of International Law & Politics* 28/3 (1996), 485–503.

66 Charles Harper (ed.), *Impunity: an Ethical Perspective. Six Latin American Case Studies*, x.

victor and a defeated opponent, does not offer great possibilities of success when the conflict is internal. In fact evidence from the post-Second World War Germany, and even a formerly occupied territory such as the Netherlands, indicates that justice was very unevenly applied, with harsh penalties (including the death penalty) being imposed upon perpetrators immediately after the war, but shortly later, imposing prison sentences for similar offenses. In Germany a further complication was the almost total involvement of the police and judicial system in the previous regime. Thus total denazification of the civil service had to be balanced by the need for services in the present and the inability to try all those who were, presumably, guilty. Consequently, the arguments against the justice option can be summarized in the following four points. First, the formidable legal and constitutional issues involved in trying members of a previous regime under newly formulated laws include questions of due process, ex post facto law-making, statutes of limitations, and equal protection.[67] Second, there is the problem of the capability of a national legal system to deal with such cases. Third, any pragmatic approach to national reconciliation, based on 'realpolitik', seeks a moderate approach to justice that will ensure a stable transitional government and lower the possibility of a coup. Fourth, and finally, in contexts where guilt or complicity has been widespread, national reconciliation is not served by settling past scores but rather by accepting some measure of truth-telling, acknowledging crimes, and seeking a new beginning. These arguments can be countered by observing that, first, justice must be upheld otherwise there is no justice for the victims, and, secondly, trials that seek justice provide greater legitimacy to emerging democracies and the human rights of all citizens. Finally, such processes indicate in a very public manner that no one is above the law and that no regime has the right to self-legislate impunity or amnesty for its own actions. Thus, trials and the quest for justice serve to hold all governments up to standards of international law and in fact their own legal obligations. These four arguments for and three arguments against are used in varying combinations by most analyses of the cases outlined above.[68]

Yet by downplaying the demands of justice, those without power, precisely the victims or the survivors, are neglected. This is where the call for justice remains critical. It sets a norm, and by that norm, can help in exposing the truth (or what truth can be reached) about the past. Whether this is attained by a war crimes trial or a truth commission, justice that reveals truth becomes critical not just for revealing past atrocities, but also in the ways briefly summarized above. In addition, the

---

67 What of the oft-made claim by subordinates that they were following then legitimate orders? The accused subordinate claims that he acted to prevent greater harm to the national good. What of the influence of the then dominant ideology? See the examination of these issues in Robert L. Rotberg and Dennis Thomson (eds), *Truth V. Justice. The Morality of Truth Commissions* (Princeton: Princeton University Press, 2000).

68 See previous note as well as works by Charles Harper (ed.), *Impunity*; Priscilla B. F. Hayner 'Fifteen Truth Commissions – 1974 to 1994: A Comparative Study', 597–655; and John Dugard, 'Dealing with Crimes of a Past Regime. Is Amnesty Still an Option?' *Leiden Journal of International Law* 12/4 (2000), 1001–1015.

focus on justice does emphasize individual guilt and thus has the advantage of not burdening whole communities with collective guilt. This is not to deny that such communities have benefited from past abuses committed by others, but merely to remind readers that the Western legal systems operate on the premise of individual guilt or innocence.[69] This explains the trend in such national commissions to focus on human rights' abuses as the most basic criterion of whether a violation has occurred or not, and then only to select the most severe abuses for investigation, amnesty procedures or criminal prosecution. This is well illustrated by the South African TRC decision only to examine 'gross human rights' violations'.[70]

## Reparations (as Reconciliation)

The all too often missing element in national truth and reconciliation commissions is the issue of reparations, so essential to 'restor[e] justice' as John De Gruchy subtitles his recent work on reconciliation.[71] The truth provides the basis not only for justice and possible amnesty, but also for reparations. However this must not be thought of only in individualistic, but also in broader social, terms. People and especially participants need to recognize truth and reconciliation commissions as but a beginning. If these commissions only deal with crimes of the past and fail to address the existing structural social and economic inequalities that led to civil unrest, then they fail to deal with causes that led to military coups in the first place (such unrest was not all due to communist threats), or, in the South African context, fail to address societal inequalities based on racial classification.

The earlier Latin American commissions did not achieve a great track record in limiting military powers, limiting amnesty for perpetrators, and thereby providing the truth, justice, and reparations for victims (and/or their families). Some of these elements were remedied through subsequent legislation, as occurred in Argentina and Chile where amnesty decrees were limited or even revoked, and generous reparations paid out to survivors. So when the South African TRC was establishing its future procedures, conferences were held with Latin Americans who had participated in their own national commissions, so that the South African one might learn from its predecessors. The most well-known result of this inter-continental

---

69 Robert Dorsman, Hans Hartman and Lieneke Noteboom-Kronoemeijer (eds), *Truth and Reconciliation in South Africa and the Netherlands* (Utrecht: Studie-en Informatiecentrum Menschenrechten, 1999); José Zalaquett, 'Balancing Ethical Imperatives and Political Restraints. The Dilemma of New Democracies Confronting Past Human Rights Violations', *The Hastings Law Journal* 43/6 (August 1992), 1425–1438.

70 TRC *Report*, Vol. I, 12–14, 70–90. It must be noted though that such an approach does have the effect of lessening the scope of the crimes committed against a population. For example, if a commission only examines cases where death resulted, what about all the others, involving torture, abuse, and life-long damages?

71 John W. De Gruchy, *Reconciliation: Restoring Justice* (Cape Town: David Phillips, 2002).

cooperation was the TRC's decision to only grant amnesty to perpetrators if the full truth was told. However, on the issue of reparations, while the TRC could hear testimonies, gather material, subpoena witnesses, and even grant amnesty or remand for criminal prosecution, it could only advise the South African Parliament on the matter of reparations. Reparations then were subject to parliamentary action and the subsequent payments were limited and provoked much criticism of the TRC itself. Perhaps of more significance was that the TRC revealed more fully the social structures and practices that required dramatic change and the alteration of these would be a form of social reparations.

### Reconciliation, Churches and Theologies

In the beginning of military rule in Latin American nations, the churches, apart from individual, prophetic voices, were either silent or expressed support for the new regimes and their anti-communist stance. The South African case was slightly different, with the Afrikaner Dutch Reformed Churches supporting apartheid as a theological and political policy, and the so-called 'English Churches' (Anglican, Congregational, Methodist, Presbyterian, and Roman Catholic) opposing apartheid theologically, but in practical terms largely acquiescing in the political developments. This initial acceptance changed in both contexts as the social situation worsened, public opposition to the regime increased, and the Church itself became a target, as occurred as early as 1973 for the Roman Catholic Church in Brazi,l, .and after 1961 for the 'English Churches' in South Africa.

As the nation divided along social, political, ideological, or racial lines, the Church typically also divided. While in South Africa the churches were divided along predictable historical lines, in Latin America the divisions were generally internal to the Roman Catholic hierarchies of each nation. If a generalization may be permitted, the hierarchy tended to view the Church as the traditional keeper of the national genius and thus as the preserver of national identity. So it was loath to oppose any regime claiming to protect the patrimony from communism, as the military rulers indeed claimed. However, at the same time the hierarchy was also seeking to implement the social and economic principles that had been endorsed by Church Social Teaching (for example as early as the 1950s with Paulo Freire's work in North East Brazil) and through international (Vatican Council II) and continental bishops' conferences (Episcopal Conference of Latin America, CELAM) such as those at Medellin (1968) and Puebla (1979). National hierarchies adopted an ameliorist approach, seeking improved living standards through reform and development projects. In a predominantly Roman Catholic context, the role of the Vatican as a trans-national actor has to be factored into an analysis of national Churches. Likewise, even in largely Protestant contexts, the role of international organizations such as the World Council of Churches (WCC) and the World Alliance of Reformed Churches (WARC) must be noted. For example, in the South African situation, apart from numerous WCC meetings and declarations, there was the role played by the 'Program to Combat Racism', the Lutheran World Federation, and the WARC decision in 1982 to declare theological support of apartheid a heresy and to suspend membership of the Dutch Reformed Churches.[72] Thus international links placed pressure on national churches to modify specific contextual stances.

A more radical stance to reform and development was taken by a new current of Roman Catholic theologians who developed a new way of doing theology in the early 1970s. Emerging from the work pioneered by the Brazilian Presbyterian Rubem Alves and in particular the Peruvian Roman Catholic Gustavo Gutiérrez, in his *A Theology of Liberation*,[73] such a theology was sharply opposed to development schemes and sought not so much individual reform and social, amelioration, but the transformation of the social economic, and political system from below through the organization of the poor. Likewise, any programme of reconciliation, unless it addressed existing structural inequalities, simply accepted the status quo. This was unacceptable to the progressive sectors of the Church.[74]

The Latin American national churches, largely immobile after the imposition of military or authoritarian rule, were spurred to criticism and action only when the regime turned upon its clergy, and religious, or prominent laity. Thus, given its prior tacit support of such regimes, the Church somewhat reluctantly found itself in opposition to the ruling powers. However, paradoxically, when regime transition came about, in many cases this precise reluctance led to the national Church becoming a trusted broker between opposing forces. This is precisely what happened, with varying decrees of involvement, in Argentina, Chile, El Salvador, and Guatemala, though in Argentina, Brazil, and Chile the Churches were accused of either supporting a repressive regime or of not doing enough to remove such a regime.

In general it might be stated that the national Churches took a mediating role while opposition and (particularly during democratic transition periods) government parties urged the Church to support only one position. The Church, caught between these diverging political options, and urged to adopt specific political platforms by liberation theologians, desperately sought to avoid taking, or to be seen to be taking, a partisan political party position. This stance only earned further criticism from these parties.

In each national context, both the political powers and the church hierarchies sought peace, stressed national unity, dialogue, forgiveness by all, and national reconciliation. Such reconciliation, as the history of individual nations has shown,

---

72  John de Gruchy and Charles Villa-Vicencio (eds), *Apartheid is a Heresy* (Grand Rapids, MI: Wm B. Eerdmans Publishing, 1983). Consult this volume for information on differing Churches' positions on apartheid up to the 1980s. See also G. D. Cloete and D. J. Smit (eds), *A Moment of Truth. The Confession of the Dutch Reformed Mission Church 1982* (Grand Rapids: Wm. B. Eerdmans Publishing, 1984).

73  See Rubem A. Alves, *A Theology of Human Hope* (Washington, DC: Corpus Books, 1969); and Gustavo Gutiérrez, *A Theology of Liberation. History, Politics and Salvation* (Maryknoll, NY: Orbis Books, 1973).

74  This point is succinctly expressed in José Comblin's contribution to this volume.

can only begin when there have been genuine and successful attempts at establishing the truth, limiting amnesty, upholding justice, and employing reparation programmes both as immediate attempts at restoring individual justice and as long-range programmes of national reconstruction.

It is interesting to speculate on the origins of such religious language in Latin American politics. While the present author has not been able to locate an exact link it is surely suggestive that, in a predominantly Roman Catholic continent, notice would have been taken of the new Vatican directives on confession drawn up in 1983.[75] Further, not only did the call for reconciliation come from the national Churches, but, in the Argentine case, from the side of the outgoing military government. The papal visits to Argentina in 1983 and to Chile in 1984 included calls for all sectors of society to work for reconciliation.[76]

Further, national churches also became the recorders of crimes of the military regimes, in addition to preserving the memories of opponents and providing martyrs in the national liberation struggles, as happened with Archbishop Oscar Romero of El Salvador. The Churches also became the source of legal and other aid for those targeted by regimes, and so, as in Brazil and elsewhere, served as the 'voice of the voiceless'. In these and similar ways, they became, in some ways unwillingly, the midwife to new structures of civil society, so critical to empowerment of citizens of democratizing nations. A classic example of recording state crimes is provided by the work that led to the publishing of *Brasil Nunca Mais* (1985) under the auspices of the Roman Catholic Archdiocese of São Paulo and the World Council of Churches. This publication, which provided a dramatic insight into previously unknown activities, was the work of an ecumenical group that secretly recorded all the military cases of torture from 1968 to 1979 from the military's own records.[77]

In addition to preserving the memory of the past, individual case studies of the role of the Churches under military rule in Latin America and under apartheid in South Africa reveal a number of common themes. The three most striking of these themes may be briefly noted below. First, the Church had laid down moral guidelines for best promoting the common good of society, and so provided both a critique of the present state of affairs as well as an alternative (for example, in Argentina, Chile, South Africa, and El Salvador). Second, the national Church served as a mediator or open space for differing parties to converge (for example as happened in Chile and El Salvador, though it did so in an ambiguous manner in the Argentine case). Finally, through its support of voluntary societies during years of repression, and its

---

75  John Paul II, *Post-Synodical Apostolic Exhortation RECONCILIATION AND PENANCE of John Paul II to the Bishops, Clergy and Faithful on Reconciliation and Penance in the Mission of the Church Today* (Rome: Vatican, December 1984).

76  For the Argentine case see Tito Garabal, *El Viaje comienza ahora: Juan Pablo II en Uruguay, Chile y la Argentina* (Buenos Aires: Ediciones Paulinas, 1987), 227; and for Chile, see Jeffrey Klaiber, *The Church, Dictatorships and Democracy in Latin America*, 62.

77  Arquidiocese de São Paulo, *Brasil Nunca Mais. Um Relato para a história* (Petropolis: Editora Vozes, 1984).

support for the poor, the national Churches mobilized (and in many cases created) new civil societies.

However the Church often found itself in tension between the competing demands of a liberal democratic polity and preserving other moral imperatives of Church Social Teachings. It was perhaps the liberation theologians (for example, Jong Mo Sung, Clodovis Boff, Leonardo Boff, Jose Comblin in Brazil, Gustavo Guttierrez in Peru, and Jon Sobrino and the late Ignacio Ellacuria in El Salvador) who continued to stress the universality of sin as separation and as both individual and structural (the issue of individual versus collective guilt, repentance, and forgiveness) and who called governments to account for their actions. The need for the truth to be known was maintained through the testimony of the martyrs such as Archbishop Oscar Romero of San Salvador. The Church, and in particular, liberation theologians, by their advocacy and empowerment of the poor, not only preserved the memory of the past but developed in the poor the sense of personhood so critical for civil involvement in the present.

In South Africa, while on one level the TRC was a political compromise, the idea of such a commission can be traced back beyond the release of Nelson Mandela and the freeing of proscribed political organizations in 1991, to numerous and repeated ecclesiastical calls for national reconciliation noted above. Thus from the outset there existed a convergence of political and ecclesiastical interest in setting up a commission to examine the recent South African past and to consider the issue of amnesty and its role in future national reconciliation. Consequently, the TRC clearly understood itself as a 'bridge', using the words of the Interim Constitution, between a divided past 'of untold suffering and injustice' and a future 'founded on the recognition of human rights, democracy, peaceful co-existence, and development opportunities for all'.[78]

The theoretical centre of the TRC Report is to be found in the brief excursus on the concept of *ubuntu*, one often associated with the thought and ministry of the Chairman of the TRC himself, Archbishop Desmond Tutu.[79] The term *Ubuntu* itself means 'people' in numerous Southern African languages and is known particularly from the proverb *umuntu ngumuntu ngabantu* which can be translated as 'one only is a person through other persons'.[80] This relational understanding of the person and personhood through the community plays a central role in Archbishop Desmond Tutu's theology, as will be noted below. In addition such an understanding of relationality is supported not only by the Southern African indigenous traditions, but also by the Judaeo-Christian tradition.[81] The Report also understands *ubuntu* as 'a commitment

---

78  TRC, *Report*, Vol. 1/5, Section 1.

79  TRC, *Report* Vol. I/5, Sections 80–88. See also Michael Battle, *Reconciliation. The Ubuntu Theology of Desmond Tutu* (Cleveland Ohio: Pilgrim Press, 1997).

80  See TRC, *Report* Vol. I/5, Section 80; Battle, *Reconciliation* (1997), 39.

81  The theme of relationality runs through the concept of *ubuntu*. However the concept needs further precision as it has typically been used in 'occasional' contexts such as sermons, pastoral settings, and so forth. Apart from Battle's book and brief discussions by Augustine Shutte (see his *Ubuntu: An Ethic for a New South Africa* (Pietermaritzburg: Cluster Publications, 2001) there

36     *Reconciliation, Nations and Churches in Latin America*

that included the strengthening of the restorative dimensions of justice'.[82] Such a restorative justice is defined in a fourfold manner as justice that seeks 'to redefine crime ... to a perception of crime as violations against human beings, 'to be based on reparation instead of vengeance', to include victims, offenders, and the community in conflict resolution, and finally, to be a form of justice that supports a criminal system that aims at offender accountability, full participation, and reparations. Thus what is presupposed on this understanding of human being-in-relationship, is a society that is responsible, comprising individuals taking on responsibility for themselves, for others, and indeed for society itself.

Archbishop Tutu's emphasis on the concept of *ubuntu* is clear in the Report. The relational focus in this concept seeks to correct the Western overemphasis on atomic individualism. Thus the individual is not a given, but rather a product of a community, which then becomes vital to individual self-identity. Such an understanding leads to Battle's summation that: 'The sumum bonum here is not independence but sharing, interdependence. And what is true of the human person is true surely of human aggregations.'[83] According to Battle, Tutu's '*Ubuntu* theology' contains four critical elements. First it presupposes (and proposes to build up) an interdependent community in which, secondly, persons are recognized as distinctive in their identities, and which seeks, thirdly, to combine the best in European and African theologies. All this originally aimed at providing an alternative to the separatedness assumed by apartheid as a social ordering. Thus, according to '*Ubuntu* theology' the crime of apartheid lay not only in the separation of peoples, but in the hubristic claim to self-sufficiency. The Report expresses this *ubuntu* approach powerfully when it declares that the:[84]

> emergence of a responsible society includes more than direct perpetrators, but the whole community. This moral responsibility goes deeper than political or legal accountability. Such individual and shared moral responsibility cannot be adequately addressed by legislation or this commission. What is required is that individuals and the community as a whole must recognize that the abdication of responsibility, the unquestioning obeying of commands ... are all essential parts of the many-layered spiral of responsibility which makes large-scale, systematic human rights' violations possible in modern states. Only this realization can create the possibility for the emergence of something new in South African society. In short what is required is a moral and spiritual renaissance capable of transforming moral indifference, denial, paralyzing guilt and unacknowledged shame, into personal and social responsibility.

---

is little discussion of this quite powerful concept. The feminist theologian Denise Ackermann has sought to relate this concept to philosophical and feminist understandings of relationality and mutuality. Perhaps the concept needs to be related to other (African) philosophical traditions. I think here (with some reservations) of J. Smuts' early work which in fact gave us the term *Holism* (London: Macmillan, 1926).

82   TRC, *Report*, Vol. I/5, Section 82.
83   Michael Battle, *Reconciliation*, 38.
84   TRC, *Report*, Vol. I/5, Section 85.

Other South African theologians, most notably Charles Villa-Vicencio, Willa Boesak and Tinyiko Maluleke, in their admittedly differing theological trajectories and divergences on how reconciliation should be understood, nevertheless all emphasize this common humanity and common responsibility presupposed by this anthropological concept. In quite Niebuhrian terms, though to differing degrees, they all emphasize that to be a creature is to be responsible to God and to the neighbour. This is a typical Augustinian approach to the human and indeed human society. Thus Karl Barth understood such relatedness or participation with the other as a critical step in full humanity, the character of which is *Mitmenschlichkeit*, for indeed, 'humanity is co-humanity'.[85] Thus the human, Barth argues, is a social being and capable of behaving ethically and being humanized. The social consequence of this is that Barth, following on Calvin, understands the Christian life as including responsibility for the social order. Faith is not restricted or limited only to an individualistic relationship to God, but necessarily includes the neighbour, and thus includes concern and responsibility for the social and indeed the political dimensions of life. So the concept of *ubuntu* serves as the functional African equivalent to the traditional Christian concept of the *imago Dei*. Like Barth's understanding of humanity, Tutu's *ubuntu* theology begins with the relational (and indeed with God) and not with the atomistic individual of much Enlightenment social and political thought, with its subsequent difficulties in relating the individual to others, to the social, and indeed in relating religion to the public arena.

Charles Villa-Vicencio, who served as the TRC's Research Director, is a well-known theologian who has presented a critical reading of liberation theological approaches to society. Recognizing and accepting their prophetic role, he nevertheless faults liberation theologies for failing systematically address positive agendas for national reconstruction. Hence the title of his earlier work, *A Theology of Reconstruction: Nation-Building and Human Rights*.[86] His positive emphases on reconstruction and 'restorative justice' are certainly consonant with, if not part of, the TRC. However, democratization (as experience has already shown in Latin America and Eastern Europe) and structural change are not enough by themselves to guarantee community and a functional society. Such an approach needs the emphasis on individual dignity and being-in-relation which Tutu's relational approach provides.

The South African population is overwhelmingly Christian and the largest churches are Protestant. Most of these churches willingly made submissions to the TRC at a public hearing specifically dedicated to religious institutions and their stances and practices during the years of apartheid.[87] However these honest and

---

85 Karl Barth, *Kirchliche Dogmatik* (Zurich: Evangelischer Verlag, 1948) III/2, 319, 344.

86 Charles Villa-Vicencio, *A Theology of Reconstruction: Nation-Building and Human Rights* (Cambridge: Cambridge University Press, 1992).

87 See the study on this by James Cochrane, John W. De Gruchy, and Stephen Martin (eds), *Facing the Truth: South African Faith Communities and the Truth & Reconciliation Commission* (Cape Town: David Philip Publishers, 1999).

courageous stances do not fully address the even more challenging issues raised by religious pluralism. The failures of the Churches and their ambiguous role in national politics remain as theological and ethical challenges. While the case studies outlined above have provided numerous examples of both individual and social or 'structural' sin, further reflection is needed on the ethical issues raised by the abused practice of granting amnesty and the weaknesses of many reparations programmes. In addition, the question of forgiveness still remains with its troubling reminders of who may offer and who may receive forgiveness.[88]

Further, both the Latin American and the South African cases outlined above reveal the importance not only of ecumenical, but also of inter-religious cooperation, which becomes more central as societies become increasingly pluralistic. Finally, recent studies of truth and reconciliation commissions indicate that such commissions represent only the start of a process which must be institutionalized if national reconciliation is to provide hope for a better future.[89] To do so, the process of reconciliation requires not just amnesty, justice, and truth, but also restitution and reparations for individuals, groups, and indeed all, so that the whole society, being reconciled, might live and work for a better future.

## Conclusion

Is reconciliation then possible? Complete reconciliation that includes forgiveness, reparations, justice, truth, restored memories and a renewed and just society, remains, as the cases outlined above indicate, a future hope. Yet, the more the critical elements noted above are present, the stronger and more secure is the hope that such might actually come to be. As Michael Ignatief describes this process,

> Truth commissions have the greatest chance of success in a societies that have already created a powerful political consensus behind reconciliation, such as in South Africa. In such a context, Tutu's commission has the chance to create a virtuous upward spiral between the disclosure of painful truth and the consolidation of the political consensus that created his commission in the first place.[90]

---

88 A fine work that however, does not deal with more recent truth and reconciliation commissions, remains Donald W. Shriver, Jr., *An Ethic for Enemies: Forgiveness in Politics* (New York: Oxford University Press, 1995) and the issue of forgiveness is examined further in the political sphere by P. E. Digeser's *Political Forgiveness* (Ithaca: Cornell University Press, 2001) and the specifically theological work of Miroslav Volf.

89 Apart from the work by Charles Villa-Vicencio already mentioned, see those by Mark Hay, *Ukubuyisana: Reconciliation in South Africa* (Pietermaritzburg: Cluster Publications, 1998) and José Zalaquett, *The Ethics of Responsibility: Human Rights, Truth and Reconciliation in Chile* (Washington: Washington Office on Latin America, 1991).

90 Quotation from Michael Ignatief ('Truth, Justice, and Reconciliation' Lecture to the Canadian Bar Association, Toronto, 30 August 1996).

An ongoing process in which all religious traditions are called to participate. The Christian Churches that have so powerfully moulded, negatively and positively, Latin American and South African cultures, must continue to exercise their callings by continual repentance and actions of penance as they seek to build a future better than the possible present.

Chapter 2

# The *Mesa de Diálogo* and the Fate of the Disappeared in Chile 1999–2000: National Forgiveness Without Political Truth?

Mario I. Aguilar

In October 1998 Augusto Pinochet Ugarte, at that time Senator (for life) and previously head of the Chilean military government (1973–1990) was arrested at the London Clinic in the United Kingdom. His arrest featured prominently in the international media as the first former head of state to be arrested under provisions of International Law related to the International Conventions on Torture and Enforced Disappearance.[1] In March 2000 the British Home Secretary, Jack Straw, allowed Pinochet to return to Chile on humanitarian grounds related to ill-health and Pinochet's inability to stand trial.[2] Nevertheless, his stay in Britain provided a different scenario for human rights' discussions in Chile that had previously been dominated by his refusal to co-operate with the Chilean government and the Chilean human rights' organizations.

Nevertheless, Pinochet's arrest and his stay in Britain polarised Chileans to the extent that while most Chileans were convinced that Pinochet was guilty of human rights' violations and crimes, some wanted him to be extradited to Spain, while

---

1 'Any person alleged to have perpetrated an act of enforced disappearance in a particular State shall, when the facts disclosed by an official investigation so warrant, be brought before the competent civil authorities of that State for the purpose of prosecution and trial unless he has been extradited to another State wishing to exercise jurisdiction in accordance with the relevant international agreement in force. All States should take any lawful and appropriate action available to them to bring to justice all persons presumed responsible for an act of enforced disappearance, who are found to be in their jurisdiction or under their control'. Article 14 UN Declaration on the Protection of All Persons from Enforced Disappearance, adopted by the UN General Assembly in Resolution 47/133 of 18 December 1992, in Amnesty International, 'The Case of general Pinochet: Universal jurisdiction and the absence of immunity for crimes against humanity', London, 19 January 1999.

2 Joanna Bale, Melissa Kite, and Richard Beeston, 'Pinochet Flies Out a Free Man', *The Times* (3 March 2000), 1.

others wanted him to stand trial in Chile.[3] The position of the Chilean government was clear. They wanted Pinochet back and they did not want a foreign legal Court to intervene in domestic affairs.

To sustain such a parameter of repatriation President Frei's Minister of Defence, Edmundo Pérez Yoma, invited a number of personalities in order to discuss pending problems and themes related to human rights' abuses that had taken place from the day of the military coup in Chile, 11 September 1973 (the '*Once*') till the end of the military government in March 1990. Those participating in this governmental initiative, i.e. the *Mesa de Diálogo* (table of dialogue) met for the first time on Saturday 21 August 1999 at the Diego Portales Building in Santiago.

This paper explores the debates and interventions by members of the *Mesa de Diálogo* and the repercussions of such exercises in political diplomacy within the recent political history of Chile. The paper concludes by suggesting that the *Mesa de Diálogo* provided the first instance of an open conversation about such 'human rights' matters within Chilean society.  However it also provided a political engineering of social control that by excluding victims of such violations also excluded the possibility of a social catharsis and forgiveness. Following the *Mesa de Diálogo* and by the summer of 2001 it was clear that very few bodies of those who had been made to disappear by the security forces had been recovered. It has become clearer since that without such social truth and without finding those bodies there will never be reconciliation and unity within the Chilean nation.

## National Efforts at Reconciliation and the Chilean Truth Commission

During the military government's rule, the arrest and torture of political opponents became a social norm of national unity. By the time that the first democratically elected president, Patricio Aylwin, took over from Pinochet in 1990 a round number of 3,000 disappearances had still to be investigated.

President Aywin asked a group of jurists and lawyers led by Raúl Rettig Guissen to investigate human rights' abuses and report to him. The *Comisión de Verdad y Reconciliación* was legally constituted on the 9 May 1990 and was given till the 9 February 1991 to produce a report.[4] The Commission had four specific tasks:

(1) To prepare a full picture of the extent of human rights' violations, its details

---

3    After Pinochet's return to Chile 57 per cent of the Chilean population agreed that Pinochet should stand trial even when he was ill. 'Encuesta Mori: 57 porcent de los chilenos cree que Pinochet debe ser juzgado', *La Tercera*, 29 March 2001.

4    Decreto Supremo 335, Ministerio del Interior, 25/4/90, *Diario Oficial* 9/5/90.

and circumstances.

(2) To collect information concerning individual victims, their fate and location.

(3) To recommend just reparation and necessary retribution.

(4) To recommend legal and administrative measures in order to prevent future serious violations of human rights in Chile.[5]

The Commission examined 3,400 cases presented to them, in order to decide if there had been a violation of human rights that could be recorded. Organizations and associations submitted lists of their members who died violently between the 11 September 1973 and the 11 March 1990.

On the 4 March 1991 President Aylwin announced the results of the Rettig Report, as it was subsequently known, to the nation. The lengthy report included 2,279 cases that were accepted, divided broadly into victims of political violence (164) and victims of violations of their human rights (2,115). Four categories of victims were described:

(1) Killed by state agents or those under their command (war tribunals 59, killed during public protests 93, executed after being accused of trying to escape 101, executed or killed under torture 815).

(2) Arrested by state agents and then made to disappear (957).

(3) Killed by civilians with political motives (90).

(4) Cases that were not concluded and their investigation continued (641).

The Rettig Report can be considered a Truth Commission that provided open information to the Chilean nation on abuses against citizens with their name and their stories.[6] The Report triggered further investigations and the submission of other cases by relatives and national organizations (see for example, Agrupación de Familiares de Detenido Desaparecidos [AFDD] 1992).

In 1996 a further Report was published by the *Corporación Nacional de Reparación y Reconciliación (CNRR)*, created in 1992 by the Chilean Government in order to continue the work of the National Commission of Truth and Reconciliation.[7] The *Corporación* made enormous progress on advising relatives of other cases of human rights' abuses, influencing public opinion in Chile and abroad, co-operating with other Truth Commissions, and advising payments and material reparations to relatives of the victims (CNRR 1996).

At the same time hundreds of legal cases were filed at the Courts in order to investigate the fate of the disappeared, to request the arrest and incarceration of

---

5 *Informe de la Comisión de Verdad y Reconciliación*, Primera Parte, Capítulo I, 'Métodos de trabajo y labor desplegada por la Comisión Nacional de Verdad y Reconciliación para la elaboración de este informe', 'Los objetivos de la Comisión'.

6 While the Rettig Report was officially published as a bound volume it was also available as a supplement by the daily official newspaper *La Nación*.

7 Law 19123, published in the *Diario Oficial*, 8 February 1992.

the perpetrators of human rights' abuses and to deal with human remains located at different locations all over the country.

Already in 1992 the Catholic Church closed the *Vicaría de la Solidaridad*, an administrative body of the Santiago Archdiocese that had been active in the protection of human rights, the support of victims' relatives, and the dispenser of food, education, medical help, and shelter for the poor, the dispossessed, and those persecuted by the military regime. The *Vicaría* had been the recipient of international awards and over the years its legal section collected testimonies and documents of all those who needed legal help and could not get it anywhere else. The documents were moved to the buildings of the Archbishopric under the office of the *Fundación Archivos de la Vicaría de la Solidaridad* and continued providing human rights' lawyers with legal evidence on cases that had been followed by lawyers working for the *Vicaría* from 1976 to 1992.[8]

### Background to the *Mesa de Diálogo*

By 1998 the fate of the disappeared and the impossibility of recovering bodies continued to impede a full closure of the Pinochet regime. President Aylwin provided the necessary mechanisms for an initial investigation. However, by the time that President Frei took over it was clear that a couple of thousand people still remained unaccounted. Pinochet had remained Army commander-in chief and later had also become Senator for life. There had been attempts to pass an Amnesty Law so as to allow the political closure of the transition into democracy, however this proposal was not successful. Nevertheless, it had already suggested that democratic forces were looking for a political solution to the problem of the disappeared.

With the arrest of Pinochet in London in October 1998 the Chilean government eased its foreign policy predicament by suggesting that Pinochet's trial in Chile was possible, if not necessary. Further, while the national truth of suffering and disappearance was known to the general public the military had never agreed to cooperate with politicians and civilians in the search for bodies and the trial of armed forces members suspected and accused of human rights' abuses.[9]

The arrest of Pinochet provided the space to negotiate political formulae between the government and the military, previously unthinkable while Pinochet was in Chile. In the past and whenever the government had gone too far in reductions on

---

8    Current address: Arzobispado de Santiago, Fundación Documentación y Archivo de la Vicaría de la Solidaridad, Erasmo Escala 1884, piso 3o. Santiago, Chile.

9    It is clear that the military did not agree with any human rights' investigations, that they destroyed prisoners' files in notorious detention centres such as the Villa Grimaldi and that they helped some of their personnel previously involved in illegal activities so that they could leave Chile and be economically supported abroad. See Mario I. Aguilar, 'El Muro de los Nombres de villa Grimaldi (Chile): Exploraciones sobre la Memoria, el Silencio y la Voz de la Historia', *European Review of Latin American and Caribbean Studies* 69 (October 2000), 81–88.

military expenditure or had asked questions about army officers' involvement in human rights' abuses Pinochet had declared a red alert and had recalled all troops to barracks. With Pinochet in London and with the Chilean Army in need of support in order to bring their 'military icon' home, conversations started about national unity, reconciliation, forgiving and forgetting. A few months after Pinochet's detention the Chilean government was ready to move in order to try to bridge the national disunity created by the Pinochet affair and to try to be seen by both the military and human rights' organizations as proactive and effective.

The Defence Minister Edmundo Pérez Yoma, and the Office of the President Secretary, General José Miguel Insulza, suggested to the Interior Minister the formation of a presidential commission that would discuss the pending themes and political difficulties related to human rights' abuses that had taken place after the 1973 military coup. Chilean personalities were invited onto this commission in order to try to unite voices that had been divided by their own interest in matters related to human rights' abuses.

## The Participants and their Calling

Initial criticisms to the constitution and objectives of the *Mesa de Diálogo* pointed to the fact that earlier investigations on human rights' abuses, for example the Rettig Report, had been successful because of the presidential involvement of Patricio Aylwin. At that time the Minister of the Interior Raúl Troncoso had been encouraged by an initial report by two human rights' lawyers had been working with armed forces' personnel. Later on, Troncoso withdrew his support for such a negotiation table and it was finally President Frei who agreed to Pérez Yoma's initiative.

By the time that Pinochet had been arrested, the armed forces were not willing to co-operate and wanted an investigation that emphasized the armed forces' role in 'saving Chile from Communism' and that compelled the Chilean judiciary to implement quite forcefully the 1978 Amnesty Law.[10] The human rights' lawyers on the other hand wanted to pursue the Rettig Report and the judicial cases filed by victim's relatives till they could find out what actually happened to those who disappeared and those who were responsible for their disappearance. According to the human rights' lawyers only after such investigations were carried out and guilt established, the Amnesty Law could be applied.

In summary, while the military saw such an initiative as providing a political end to the transition of military power to civilians (*transición*), human rights' organizations perceived this forum as a fresh start for investigations and legal processes related to human rights' abuses during the period of military government. The Chilean government suggested instead that there were too many political fora

---

10 Decreto Ley 2,191 that covered the period between the 11th of September 1973 and the 10th of March 1978 and absolved those involved in crimes under the state of siege and those condemned by military courts after the military coup.

where the problem was being discussed and therefore a single political space was going to help preventing further 'disorder and indecision'.[11]

As a result of those different expectations the start of the *Mesa de Diálogo* was difficult. Edmundo Pérez Yoma presided over their first meeting at the Diego Portales Building on Saturday 21 August 1999.[12] The initial meeting started at 11:20am and lasted for forty minutes. In that meeting Pérez Yoma explained the objectives of the presidential initiative, as comprising three goals:

1. To build up a confidential climate of trust.
2. To generate dynamics of co-operation related to truth, justice, reparation and forgiveness; and,
3. To avoid setting dates, conditions or particular circumstances to the group's conversations.[13]

After that start in the presence of the journalists all other meetings were held in private, while limited information was given to the press. Roberto Garretón challenged such confidentiality. However the Chilean government made it quite clear that open deliberations in public were not the norm in Chilean society as was the case in South Africa within the context and the work of their Truth Commission. The Church, personified by Bishop Valech, continued its support for any social mechanism that could help to find the truth and he offered blessings for the deliberations to come. Pamela Pereira, a lawyer, did not shake hands with the military representatives throughout the meetings and explained that as the daughter of somebody who was arrested and disappeared she could not shake hands with them.

The following Chilean personalities had been chosen to take part in the round table deliberations and participated in one or more of the sessions:

1. **Luciano Fouillioux**. Assistant minister for the Carabineros, i.e. the uniformed police, he studied law at the Chilean University Law School where he began studies in 1973 together with classmates such as Alberto Espina and Roberto Osandón of the Renovación Nacional (RN) and Jorge Burgos of the Christian Democrats (PDC). Throughout his career he maintained an open dialogue with the militaries, while criticising them harshly if needed. In 1989 he acted as a consultant lawyer for the *Vicaría de la Solidaridad* of the Archdiocese of Santiago, defending opponents of the military regime such as Andrés Palma,

---

11 Objetivos de la mesa de diálogo', http://www.tercera.cl/casos/mesa/datos/dato02.html.

12 Formerly known as the UNCTAD Building, it was built in order to host the 1972 international meeting of the UNCTAD in Santiago. After the military coup the building was renamed as Diego Portales and used by the military junta as its headquarters due to the destruction within the La Moneda Palace caused by the military assault that took place on 11 September 1973.

13 'Qué es la mesa de diálogo?' *La Tercera* at http://www.tercera.cl/casos/mesa/datos/dato01.html.

Tomás Jocelyn-Holt and Felipe Sandoval.

2. **Sol Serrano**. Historian, she received her doctorate in history from the Catholic University and till June 1999 she represented the Christian Democrats at the National Council for Television. Together with Jaime Gazmuri and Mariana Aylwin she produced a series for the Chilean National Television based on her book *Chile en el Siglo XX*. Sol Serrano is married to the lawyer Jorge Correa Sutil, secretary to the *Comisión de Verdad y Reconciliación* that produced the first national report on human rights' abuses (the so-called Rettig Report) in 1991.

3. **José Zalaquett**. Lawyer, a member of the *Partido por la Democracia* (PPD) Zalaquett was one of the juridical brains behind the *Comité Pro Paz*, an ecumenical organisation that defended human rights from 1973 to 1975. He was world president of Amnesty International (1978–1982) and a member of the Rettig working group. Zalaquett is respected by all sections of Chilean society, including the military and the right-wing politicians.

4. **Jorge Carvajal**. Master of the Masons. All founders of the Chilean armed forces belonged to the Masonic lodge and an important number of top officers have also been Masons.

5. **Pamela Pereira**. Lawyer, she joined the *Mesa de Diálogo*, even when her Socialist Party and the Association of Relatives of Agrupación de Familiares de Detenidos Desaparecidos (AFDD) had objected to any dialoguing with the armed forces. She became a lawyer at the *Vicaría de la Solidaridad* after her father Andrés Pereira disappeared. She still suspects that her father is buried in plot 29 of the Santiago General Cemetery.

6. **Edmundo Pérez Yoma**. Minister of defence during the Administration of Eduardo Frei (he served from 1994–1998), and later Ambassador to Argentina. In June 1999 he returned to Chile as Minister of Defence. He was to propose a *Mesa de Diálogo* that would meet once a week with one session for each one of the groups involved in the human rights' investigations, i.e. armed forces, human rights' lawyers, civil society and those involved in science and culture.

7. **Mario Fernández**. Minister of defence in the administration of President Ricardo Lagos.

8. **Sergio Valech**. Auxiliary bishop in the Archdiocese of Santiago, he was the last vicar of the Vicariate of Solidarity, the church organisation that helped those in need of legal and general assistance during the military government. While he had the task of closing down this organisation, he continued supporting legal processes involving human rights for two years after the end of the military government (1990–1992).

9. **Alex Waghorn Jarpa**. Admiral and a close friend of the Navy commander-in-chief admiral Jorge Patricio Arancibia, at the time of the *Mesa de Diálogo* he was Admiral-in-charge of the First Naval Zone of the Navy, including the ship Esmeralda, where many people were tortured in 1973 (see the case of Fr.

Michael Woodward)[14] in Aguilar 2002; Crouzet 2001; Jordá 2001). Formerly he was the Navy's director of intelligence.

10. **Héctor Salazar Ardiles**. A lawyer, he was involved in the *Comité Pro-Paz* in 1974, and later he joined the legal team of the *Vicaría de la Solidaridad*. He continues working for human rights at the *Fundación de Ayuda Social de Iglesias Cristianas* (FASIC). He undertook important cases of human rights' abuses such as the burning of Carmen Gloria Quintana and Rodrigo Rojas Denegri (July 1986), the case of Mario Fernández in relation to the killing of Tucapel Jiménez (February 1982) and the case of those who were killed after the attempted assassination of Pinochet (September 1986). In 1994 he was arrested and accused of sedition against the armed forces.

11. **Dany Simonsohn**. Jewish community representative and member of the B'Nai B'rith, an organisation that aims at promoting human rights and is present in 57 countries world-wide.

12. **Mario Fernández**. He worked in the Ministry of Defence and was advisor to the minister of defence, Edmundo Pérez Yoma.

13. **Angel Flisfisch**. Lawyer, political scientist and member of the *Partido por la Democracia*. He was assistant minister for the Air Force and he was the link with that particular branch of the armed forces. During the military government he worked at Flacso, an institution of social research in Santiago.

14. **Guillermo Blanco**. Writer and journalist, he was the recipient of the National Prize for Journalism in 1999. He was surprised at his nomination to the *Mesa de Diálogo*, however he considered it a duty to participate.

15. **Reinaldo Ríos**. General of the *Carabineros* and graduate in political science. He was director of the police section on drugs.

16. **Roberto Garretón**. A lawyer, Garretón has served in the human rights' commission of the United Nations, having been head of the *Vicaría de la Solidaridad*'s legal section between 1974 and 1990. His experience with militaries all over the world, for example, Indonesia, Peru, Mexico, Democratic Republic of Congo, and Timor, was suggested as useful for this kind of negotiation. During the case against Pinochet in the UK he wrote a legal report to the House of Lords arguing that Pinochet's trial could not take place in Chile.

17. **Juan Carlos Salgado**. Army general and political scientist, General Salgado was the director of the *Centro de Estudios e Investigaciones Militares* (Cesim) and the direct contact between Augusto Pinochet and the Army Commander-in-Chief Ricardo Izurieta. Salgado spent most of his time with Augusto Pinochet in the UK while the Spanish extradition process was being considered. He

---

14 Mario I. Aguilar, Current Issues on Theology and Religion in Latin America and Africa (Lampeter: Edwin Mellen Press, 2002); Edward Crouzet, Sangre sobre la Esmeralda: Sacerdote Miguel Woodward, Vida y Martirio (Santiago, Chile: Ediciones Chile-América – CESOC, 2001); Miguel Jordá Sureda, Martirologio de la Iglesia Chilena: Juan Alsina y Sacerdotes Víctimas del Terrorismo de Estado (Santiago, Chile: LOM Ediciones, 2001).

belongs to a generation of army officers sent by Pinochet to study abroad to acquire relevant academic degrees.

18. **Jaime Castillo Velasco**. A lawyer and president of the Chilean Human Rights' Commission he has become a respected mediator in different political and social conflicts.

19. **Claudio Teitelboim**. Scientist and winner of the National Prize for Science he is the son of the former Secretary General of the Chilean Communist Party Volodia Teitelboim. Since 1995 he was president of the Consultative Commission on Scientific Matters (*Comisión Asesora en Materias Científicas*) and worked hard on linking scientific knowledge with industry and business.

20. **Víctor Aravena**. Bishop of the Lutheran community.

21. **Ignacio Concha**. Air Force general, at that time third in the line of command of the Air Force. With a Masters Degree in Political Science he was Air Force attaché in London and commander of the Grupo 10 squadron. He was at the time of the *Mesa de Diálogo* Air Force chief of personnel and commander of the second Air Force Brigade in charge of the Metropolitan Region. He was the highest-ranking military officer at the round table.

22. **Gonzalo Vial**. Historian and lawyer at the Catholic University, Vial was a member of the *Comisión de Verdad y Reconciliación*. In 1973 he was one of the authors of the written justification of the military coup, the so-called *Libro Blanco de la Junta Militar*. Vial is a conservative who wrote a column in *The Times* newspaper praising Augusto Pinochet. The inclusion of Vial gave confidence to the right-wing political sectors and also gave the round table the possibility of looking at the political history and historical processes that took place in Chile over the past fifty years.

23. **Elizabeth Lira**. Psychologist, she worked for ten years with victims of human rights' abuses at the *Fundación de Ayuda Social de las Iglesias Cristianas* (Fasic). She worked for another nine years at the Latin American Institute for Mental Health and Human Rights and she lectures at the Alberto Hurtado University in Santiago. Her research on reconciliation processes has been published as *Las Suaves Cenizas del Olvido*.[15] Lira presented interesting points to the parliamentarian commission that studied the accusation against Augusto Pinochet in the UK.

24. **Jorge Manzi**. Psychologist, elected co-ordinator of the round table. He has been professor of psychology at the Catholic University since 1982 after getting a Ph.D. in Social Psychology from UCLA. Manzi also served as director of the Projects Department of the National Commission for Scientific and Technological Research (CONICYT) between 1992 and 1993 and as Director of the School of Psychology of the Catholic University between

---

15 Elizabeth Lira, *Las Suaves Cenizas Del Olvido Vía Chilena De Re-conciliación Política 1814–1932*. Santiago: LOM-DIBAM, 1999.

1995 and 1999.

**25. Gonzalo Sánchez García-Huidobro**. Lawyer, named co-ordinator of the *Mesa de Diálogo*, he completed a PhD in Law at the University of Toulouse, France. He worked in the Catholic University of Valparaíso and is currently Secretary General of the Alberto Hurtado University in Santiago.

## The Sessions

The *Mesa de Diálogo* met nine times: 31 August 1999 (Session I), 7 September 1999 (Session II), 14 September 1999 (Session III), 24 September 1999 (Session IV), 5 October 1999 (Session V), 2 December 1999 (Session VI) and 22 December 1999 (Session VII). Sessions in the year 2000 started on the 13 January (Session VIII).

The format of the sessions was structured by individual addresses that opened further discussions in a formalised way. Indeed, formality was the rule for a social engineering of dialogue and possible communal agreement. Those representing the armed forces had set pieces that delivered an official line:

(a) The armed forces and the Carabineros were not involved in the politics that preceded the military coup, however they were forced to intervene;

(b) What followed the coup took longer than expected and was a response to an ongoing violent internal strife;

(c) The armed forces did not have a concerted policy of extermination towards any political opposition as the armed forces were not part of the political spectrum;

(d) If there were excesses those were not part of an institutionalised policy but they were the result of individuals who exceeded their orders and their role within the situation of internal strife;

(e) It is important to remember that there were also military personnel whose human rights were violated;

(f) The armed forces recognised that the main obstacle for any reconciliation was the situation of the disappeared. However, it is clear that they do not have any information about them, such as archives or official records;

(g) The armed forces would be willing to cooperate with the search for information about the disappeared if they were to be assured anonymity.

The participants closer to the human rights' organizations contested the nationalistic myth of origin of actions and people who were called 'to save the Nation'. Instead they pressed for a total recognition of International Law, i.e. treatises signed by the Chilean state such as the Geneva Convention on prisoners of war and those concerning torture and genocide. Following such legal premise their main propositions were the following:

(a) The military coup was not a nationalistic instance that provided a temporary solution to national economic problems. Instead it was a concerted effort to implement economic policies that were based on class-related issues;

(b) The military used all the state machinery in order to implement such a socio-economic model, a model suitable for a segment of Chilean society, thus a localised model rather than a universal one;

(c) The military misused the legal idea of *estados de excepción* (emergency legal powers) in order to abolish democratic institutions instead of protecting them;

(d) Due to the fact that 'state terrorism' was the norm it was an arbitrary decision to deal with the problem of the disappeared only within a larger context of systematic human rights' violations;

(e) It is unacceptable to respond to ideological calls for national unity without visible signs of contrition on the part of the military and the subsequent availability of archives with information regarding the fate of the disappeared;

(f) Thus, there is a need to rethink and to implement a just social order and to re-build ethical and moral foundations for social life rather than accept a militaristic ideological foundation of national unity.

It was clear that such an ideological narrative of national unity had come from Pinochet himself, at that time a prisoner in the United Kingdom. It was only in their meeting of 29 February 2000 that the Pinochet situation was mentioned. Further meetings generated by the *Mesa de Diálogo* were interrupted due to the release of Pinochet and the subsequent public demonstrations of support at Santiago airport by the Army's commander-in-chief General Ricardo Izurieta and the armed forces in general.[16] Therefore the meeting scheduled for 6 March was cancelled due to pressure by human rights' lawyers. At that time a working document of agreement was being negotiated and it never came to completion. Subsequently, Minister Yoma gave the volumes with the transcription of the sessions to President Frei who passed them to the newly elected President Lagos.

In the following months Lagos proceeded to negotiate a public agreement by all participants so that a decree with legal power could be suggested to the Senate in order to request anonymity for armed forces' witnesses and to find further information about the disappeared. The working document with the presidential proposals was agreed upon on the 13 June 2000 and it quickly moved through the appropriate legislative mechanisms of the Chilean executive.

The negative propositions within the agreement related to two areas that were finally ignored: (a) there was no action taken in order to clarify and record torture and intimidation by the armed forces and the security forces, and (b) there was no public admission of guilt by the Chilean armed forces. The positive side of the agreement expressed the good will of the armed forces to find the truth and thereafter every commander of a military unit explained the agreement to the armed

---

16 Gabriella Gamini, 'Pinochet is Fit Enough to Leave Hospital', *The Times* (4 March 2000), 4.

forces' personnel and provided an anonymous channel for gathering sensitive and confidential information.

While in principle this was a step forward by the *Mesa de Diálogo* toward a final agreement, some of its legal elements were controversial and 'conduced directly to the most open impunity' as suggested by thirty lawyers who condemned the agreement.[17] They argued that:

(a) Those who were more concerned with the disappeared, i.e. the human rights' organizations and the human rights' lawyers, were excluded.
(b) The agreement violated principles of law and justice due to the fact that those who perpetrated the abuses were commissioned to find out the facts of the crimes through witnesses that were not accountable to a tribunal thereafter;
(c) The appointment of judges (*Ministros en Visita*) to investigate information provided by anonymous witnesses resembled an archaeological search whereby judges were to inform the relatives of those found about their location, however they could not investigate what actually happened to them;
(d) Further, they suggested that the ulterior motive of such an agreement was to apply the same anonymous procedures of investigation in the Pinochet case;

## The Armed Forces Report

In order to aid the anonymous witnesses programme of the armed forces the Chilean parliament approved a legal mechanism whereby those witnesses who helped legal investigations on the fate and location of the disappeared were granted anonymity. Despite the opposition by human rights' organizations, particularly the *Agrupación de Familiares de Detenidos Desaparecidos* and the *Agrupación de Ejecutados Políticos*, the law was passed by the Chamber of Deputies on 20 June (for the motion 104, abstentions 4) and by the Senate on 21 June (for the motion 43, against 1).[18]

The law had one single article containing six points and suggested that pastors, priests and ministers of churches, religious institutions and confessions approved by law, Masons, members of the Chilean B'nai B'rith and members of the armed forces should keep confidential information about those individuals who helped

---

17 'Declaración conjunta de 30 abogados de Derechos Humanos sobre el acuerdo de la Mesa de Diálogo', in Hernán Vidal, *Chile: Poética de la Tortura Política* (Santiago, Chile: Mosquito Editores, 2000), 268–269.

18 Discussions in the Senate lasted for 34 hours and the representatives from the human rights' organizations were expelled from the Chambers for constant disorder. See 'Cámara aprobó proyecto sobre secreto de identidad para informantes', *La Tercera*, 21 June 2000 and 'Senado aprobó proyecto sobre secreto de identidad para informantes,' *La Tercera*, 22 June 2000.

with information regarding the location and fate of the disappeared mentioned in the previous law 19/123 that continued the work of the Rettig Commission.[19]

On the 5 January 2001 the armed forces gave their report to President Lagos. They had asked all their members to cooperate and the report looked very hopeful. It indicated the fate of 200 disappeared, particularly the location of their bodies or how their bodies had been disposed.[20] President Lagos spoke to the nation on Monday 8 January. Lagos praised the armed forces for their gesture of co-operation and requested further information on many other cases of the disappeared. The data provided by the armed forces expanded the information available on 171 cases of disappeared that had been resolved since 1973. However, the report concentrated on cases between September 1973 and March 1974 avoiding a public condemnation of the systematic work of kidnapping and torture carried out by the DINA from 1974 onwards.[21]

Eight months later enormous doubts had arisen about such information. In summary, three bodies had been found and identified, two major mistakes had been detected in the armed forces information and a major legal investigation related to one of the sites of assassination and disappearance (the Cuesta Barriga near Santiago) was close to completion. The bodies of Horacio Cepeda and Fernando Ortiz were partially identified after their remains were found at the Cuesta Barriga, while the body of Juan Luis Rivera Matus was located at the Fuerte Artega.[22] While the armed forces had indicated that Rivera's body and that of Samuel Lazo had been thrown into the sea, Lazo's body was found in the Patio 29 of the Santiago General Cemetery.[23] It is possible that informants gave the right information, however in all locations there was evidence that bodies had been previously removed, a strategy that was used by the armed forces at the end of the military government in order to cover and destroy physical evidence related to human rights' abuses.[24]

Further, since the submission of the armed forces report in January 2001 there had not been any legal procedures to find out who were responsible for the kidnapping, torture, and death of those termed 'disappeared' and whose bodies had been found. The results of the *Mesa de Diálogo's* initiative were disappointing and

---

19 'Las modificaciones legales que ha propuesto la Mesa de Diálogo deben tener por objeto establecer el secreto professional para quienes reciban o recaben información sobre el paradero de los detenidos-desaparecidos', Texto del proyecto de ley sobre secreto profesional 4 (a).

20 (Fundación Documentación y Archivo de la Vicaría de la Solidaridad (FDAVS), 2001. *Informe de Derechos Humanos del Primer Semestre de 2001* (Santiago, Chile: Arzobispado de Santiago Fundación Documentación y Archivo de la Vicaría de la Solidaridad, 2001).

21 'Desaparecidos: Lagos valora los datos y pide más', *La Tercera*, 8 January 2001; Jonathan Franklin, 'Chilean Army Admits 120 Thrown into the Sea', *The Guardian* (9 January 2001), 14.

22 'Encuentran osamentas en el Fuerte Arteaga', *La Tercera*, 19 July 2001.

23 'Próximo cierre de caso Cuesta Barriga pone en jaque informe de FF.AA.' *La Tercera*, 20 August 2001.

24 'Cuesta Barriga: Juez admite remoción de cuerpos', *La Tercera*, 16 July 2001.

the legal initiative had created in practice a new legal amnesty for those responsible for kidnapping, torture and murder.

## Conclusions

According to human rights' lawyers and human rights' organizations the Chilean situation of impunity continues. In their perception of legal realities those who committed and those who covered human rights' abuses have not been punished. The case of Augusto Pinochet supports such assumptions as he was released from his London arrest on humanitarian grounds and was also considered too ill ('insane') to stand trial in Chile,[25] despite the fact that in November 2000 Pinochet had admitted all responsibility for the political actions by the Chilean armed forces during his regime.[26]

However, the investigations of the Truth Commission led by Raúl Rettig made significant progress on social truths and the facts related to human rights' abuses during the military regime. The truth is known, though the legal processes against perpetrators of human rights' abuses did not produce the massive arrests requested by the relatives of the disappeared and those thousands of Chileans who were arrested, tortured, and released without an explanation or a later legal process.

The *Mesa de Diálogo* constituted the first time that the armed forces recognised their public involvement in the disappearance of many Chileans. If the *Mesa de Diálogo* can be considered a success it is because it brought to the public sphere those who took part in the history of Chile, the torturers and the tortured, the oppressors and the oppressed. However, the *Mesa de Diálogo* became a governmental failure because most of the information on the disappeared gathered by the armed forces and conveyed to the government was inaccurate and in some cases false. The *Mesa de Diálogo* helped to create a national social consciousness on terrible events, though it failed to secure a historical and social truth on human rights' abuses that had not been solved by previous commissions.

Six months after the armed forces' report only a couple of bodies had been recovered, enormous amounts of resources had been invested, and the errors in information and the search for bodies had created distrust and animosity among those who sat at the *Mesa de Diálogo*. There is no doubt that judge Guzmán will ask

---

25 'Corte Suprema desaforó a Pinochet por 14–6', *El Mercurio*, 8 August 2000 and 'El sobreseimiento de Pinochet: Fallo pone fin a la vida pública del general', *La Tercera*, 9 July 2001.

26 As the Archbishop of Santiago led a liturgy of forgiveness for the past sins of the Catholic Church at the Santiago Cathedral and in the presence of President Lagos, Pinochet addressed his supporters of the Pinochet Foundation on the occasion of his eighty-fifth birthday. On that occasion he assumed responsibility for all actions of the armed forces as an ex-President of the Republic: 'Por eso puedo decirles, señores, que acepto como ex Presidente de la República, todo lo cometido por el Ejército y las Fuerzas Armadas', *La Tercera*, 25 November 2001.

further historical and legal questions in the future. Without such historical and social truths there will be no reconciliation and no national unity within a country that has suffered political fragmentation and apathy on the part of the youth and that in the future could forget the painful lessons of disunity and social concern for others.

Truth and reconciliation as human responses to violence are still central to the Chilean transition to democracy, a process that is far from completed. Recent events such as the nomination of retired members of the Chilean armed forces as candidates to the Chilean Senate suggest that the political transition most probably will never occur as originally intended by Presidents Aylwin and Frei.

Further, it is possible that the Catholic Church that during the Pinochet regime insisted on legal processes so as to clarify penal responsibilities via the *Vicaría de la Solidaridad* will favour an end to the search for the disappeared. Such risk was highlighted in March 2001 when the newly invested Cardinal Francisco Javier Errázuriz arrived in Chile. At a government reception at La Moneda Palace the Cardinal addressed the topic of reconciliation in Chile reminding those present that there was still a deep wound among Chileans that impeded a more hopeful view of the nation's future. Following the report produced by the Chilean armed forces he suggested that 'truth and justice are not everything, only through forgiveness there will be reconciliation, so that the only road to peace is forgiveness'.[27]

The *Mesa de Diálogo* as a pragmatic instance facilitated such civilian dialogue. It is difficult to see how truth, reconciliation and legality will be discussed outside other forms of democratic inclusion. The legal investigations will continue, though as the protagonists of those events pass away, the urgency of such reconciliation will become less apparent. Nevertheless, it is also clear that due to her influence the Catholic Church will continue playing some kind of intermediary role between the political past and present. After all, and in the words of José Comblin, 'reconciliation can be seen as a political project' that involves a theological and a political reality.[28]

---

27 'Cardenal Errázuriz llegó a Chile llamando a la unidad', *La Tercera*, 3 March 2001; 'Cardenal Errázuriz: "la verdad y la justicia no son todo"', *La Tercera*, 5 March 2001.

28 See José Comblin, *Reconciliación y Liberación* (Santiago, Chile: CESOC, Ediciones Chile y América, 1987), 13.

Chapter 3

# Unspeakable Violence:
# The UN Truth Commissions in El
# Salvador and Guatemala

David Tombs

> *The ordinary response to atrocities is to banish them from consciousness. Certain violations of the social compact are too terrible to utter aloud: this is the meaning of the word unspeakable. Atrocities, however, refuse to be buried. Equally as powerful as the desire to deny atrocities is the conviction that denial does not work ... Remembering and telling the truth about terrible events are prerequisites both for the restoration of the social order and for the healing of individual victims.*

Judith Herman[1]

In the last few decades many countries have adopted investigative 'truth commissions' to examine and document past abuses in attempts to deal with a painful past.[2] As a result, the politics of truth-telling and its significance for social reconciliation after periods of political violence has received unprecedented attention from political scientists, lawyers, ethicists, and other interested parties. Whilst extra-judicial commissions have many limitations and are certainly not a straightforward or universal remedy for social healing, their potential value in providing a new start based on truth rather than denial has been widely acknowledged, especially in countries where other ways have not been practical.

In carrying out their mandates to document human rights' abuses, truth commission reports offer insights into the dynamics of terror and mechanics of repression. In reviewing the lessons to be learnt from the reports a striking feature of reports after the mid-1990s has been their attention to gender violence whereas earlier reports had little to say on this. It seems that prior to the conflict in the former Yugoslavia (1992–95), which highlighted the political use of rape as a war crime, the reports did not include abuses against women and sexual violence as a distinctive and essential

---

1 Judith L. Herman, *Trauma and Recovery: From Domestic Abuse to Political Terror* (London: Pandora, rev ed 2001), 1.

2 For a very helpful overview of recent truth commissions and their reports, see Priscilla Hayner, *Unspeakable Truths: Confronting State Terror and Atrocity* (New York and London: Routledge, 2000). See also her earlier surveys, 'Fifteen Truth Commissions – 1974–1994: A Comparative Study', *Human Rights Quarterly* 16/4 (1994), 597–655, and 'Commissioning the Truth: Further Research Questions', *Third World Quarterly* 17/1 (1996), 19–29.

part of the quest for truth.[3] Rape and other sexual violence during conflicts were usually either unacknowledged or presented as a marginal or secondary issue. To illustrate this change, this chapter examines the very different approaches to sexual violence taken by the UN investigatory commissions in El Salvador (1992–93) and Guatemala (1997–99).

When these two reports are explored in the light of each other, they reveal the 'unspeakable' nature of sexual violence. In the process, they also point to the major barriers that sexual violence poses for reconciliation processes based on truth-telling. From a theological perspective, what the two Commissions show about sexual violence might help theologians to analyse political violence more clearly and confront 'unspeakable' atrocities more openly.[4]

## The Peace Process in El Salvador and Guatemala

During the 1970s and 1980s, El Salvador and Guatemala were convulsed by political violence and counter-insurgency wars sponsored by the US. In both countries, Cold War geo-politics were used to justify waves of extreme violence against innocent communities. Civilians and the poor – especially women, children, and the elderly – bore the brunt of this terror.[5]

In El Salvador, the military fought a full-scale civil war (1980–91) with the Farabundo Marti National Liberation Front (FMLN) in which an estimated 80,000 people were killed.[6] In Guatemala, the armed resistance movement was relatively

---

3    Hayner, *Unspeakable Truths*, 78–79.

4    This includes the challenge to address the extremes of sexual violence in recent Central American conflicts, and also to recognise the sexual humiliation and possible violence in the Gospel accounts of Jesus' crucifixion. Although I do not pursue these issues here, I have examined them in more detail in David Tombs, 'Crucifixion, State Terror and Sexual Abuse', *Union Seminary Quarterly Review* 53 (Autumn 1999), 89–108.

5    On US support for the Salvadoran and Guatemalan militaries, see M. McClintock, *The American Connection: State Terror and Popular Resistance in El Salvador* (London: Zed Books, 1985); the exact level of US responsibility for the torture techniques that were adopted is unclear but the US claims that its training included lessons on respect for human rights needs to be treated with some scepticism. In 1996 the Pentagon finally admitted that manuals used at the School of Americas in Fort Benning Georgia for training Latin American militaries included instructions on torture and many of the worst abuses were committed by graduates of the School. Furthermore, US training of Brazilian security services in torture techniques in the 1960s has been documented and commentators have suggested that in the 1970s many of these techniques passed from Brazil through Chile, Uruguay, and Argentina and onto El Salvador and Guatemala. On Argentine involvement in counter-insurgency training in El Salvador (1979–81) and Guatemala (1978–82), see A. C. Armony, *Argentina, the United States and the Anti-Communist Crusade in Central America 1977–1984* (Athens, OH: Ohio University Press, 1997), 83–93.

6    The literature on the conflict is considerable, but see especially: Tommie Sue Montgomery, *Revolution in El Salvador: From Civil Strife to Civil Peace* (Boulder, CO and

small throughout the entire thirty-six year conflict (1960–96). Nonetheless military repression was so fierce that the death toll may have reached 200,000 deaths.[7] The wave known as *La Violencia* (1978–85), which began under General Lucas García (1978–82), and peaked during the brief rule of General Efrain Ríos Montt (1982–83), amounted in some places to genocide of indigenous communities.

Despite intermittent peace talks during the 1980's there had been little real progress towards settling the conflict in either country. However, the fall of the Berlin Wall on 9 November 1989, which symbolised the ending to the Cold War, opened the way for new initiatives. Three months later, on 25 February 1990, the surprise political defeat of the Sandinistas after a decade in government (1979–90) signalled an equally significant end to the US-sponsored Contra war.[8] With the international and regional political situation in rapid flux, there was a renewed seriousness in the stalled Guatemalan and Salvadoran peace processes. In the first months of 1990 both the US and the UN exerted new political pressure for a resolution to the conflict in both countries and both governments had at least start to appear to be taking the process seriously.[9]

On 30 March 1990 talks between the Guatemalan National Reconciliation Commission (CNR) and the opposition National Revolutionary Union of Guatemala (URNG) led to the Oslo Accord, which committed the participants to the 'search for peace by political means'. A few days later, UN Secretary General Pérez de Cuéllar

---

Oxford: Westview Press, 2nd edn. 1995); Hugh Byrne, *El Salvador's Civil War: A Study of Revolution* (Boulder, CO and London: Lynne Rienner, 1996); William Stanley, *The Protection Racket State: Elite Politics, Military Extortion, and Civil War in El Salvador* (Philadelphia: Temple University Press, 1996).

7　See Robert M. Carmack (ed.), *Harvest of Violence: The Maya Indians and the Guatemalan Crisis* (Norman, OK: University of Oklahoma Press, 1988); Ricardo Falla, *Massacres in the Jungle* (Boulder, CO and Oxford: Westview Press, 1995); Susanne Jonas, *The Battle for Guatemala: Rebels, Death Squads, and U.S. Power* (Boulder, CO and London: Westview Press, 1996).

8　Furthermore, UN monitoring of the Nicaraguan elections pointed to the major contribution that the UN was soon to make in both El Salvador and Guatemala. See esp., Cynthia J Arnson, *Crossroads: Congress, the President and Central America, 1976–93* (University Park, PA Penn State Press, 2nd edn. 1993), 218–64; Thomas Carothers, *In the Name of Democracy: U.S. Policy Toward Latin America in the Reagan Years* (Berkeley: University of California Press, 1991).

9　Public opinion in the US had been particularly horrified by the massacre of six Jesuits, their housekeeper and her daughter, carried out by soldiers belonging to an elite US-trained Salvadoran battalion on 16 November 1989 during the FMLN offensive; see Teresa Whitfield, *Paying the Price: Ignacio Ellacuría and the Murdered Jesuits of El Salvador* (Philadelphia: Temple University Press, 1994); Martha Doggett, *Death Foretold: The Jesuit Murders in El Salvador* (Washington, DC: Georgetown University Press & Lawyers Committee for Human Rights and Americas Watch, 1993). At the UN, Javier Pérez de Cuéllar (UN Secretary General from 1 January 1982 to 31 December 1991) took a close personal interest in assisting the Central American Peace Process.

brokered a joint declaration by the Salvadoran government and the FMLN in Geneva on 4 April 1990, which expressed the desire to end the ten-year conflict.[10]

Although progress continued to be slow – especially in Guatemala – a protracted series of further UN-sponsored negotiations eventually led to national Peace Accords in both countries, signed in El Salvador in 1992 and in Guatemala in 1996.[11] During these negotiations, it was also agreed that the UN would have a role after the signing of agreements to oversee compliance and actively help the democratic transition and building of peace.[12] As part of this process, at the insistence of the FMLN and URNG, both settlements included provisions for official UN commissions to investigate, document and report on cases of political violence during the conflict.

The 'Commission on the Truth for El Salvador' – usually referred to simply as the Truth Commission (TC) – began its formal work on 13 July 1992.[13] It included three commissioners – Belisario Betancur (an ex-President of Colombia), Reinaldo Figueredo Planchart (ex-Minister for Foreign Relations of Venezuela) and Thomas Buergenthal (Professor of Law at George Washington University and ex-President of the Inter-American Court) – who were supported by a professional staff.[14] After approximately six months of investigation in El Salvador, and a further three months of compilation and writing in New York, they presented their findings entitled *From Madness to Hope: The 12-Year War in El Salvador* in New York on 15 March 1993.[15]

---

10  See Reed Brody, 'The United Nations and Human Rights in El Salvador's Negotiated Revolution', *Harvard Human Rights Journal* 8 (Spring 1995), 153–78.

11  For good overviews of the two Peace Processes and their wider context, see the relevant chapters in Cynthia Arnson (ed.), *Comparative Peace Processes in Latin America*, including Antonio Cañas and Héctor Dada, 'Political Institutionalization in El Salvador' (69–95); Dinorah Azpuru, 'Peace and Democratization in Guatemala: Two Parallel Processes' (97–125); and Teresa Whitfield, 'The Role of the United Nations in El Salvador and Guatemala: A Preliminary Comparison' (257–90).

12  The shift in policy towards 'peace-building' reflected a new direction in UN strategy under Boutros Boutros-Ghali, who succeeded Pérez de Cuéllar as UN Secretary General. Boutros-Ghali's term in office (1 January 1992 to 31 December 1996) spanned the implementation of the Salvadoran Accords and the prolonged negotiations in Guatemala. The conclusion of the Guatemalan negotiations on 29 December 1996 (in the last days in office for Boutros-Ghali) gave an interesting historical echo to the Salvadoran process, because the crucial New York Agreement on 31 December 1991 was signed in the very last hours of Pérez de Cuéllar's term; see especially Teresa Whitfield, 'The Role of the United Nations in El Salvador and Guatemala', 259.

13  Its Spanish title was 'Comisión de la Verdad para El Salvador', often abbreviated to 'CVES' or simply 'CV'.

14  All three commissioners were named on 10 December 1991. They elected Betancur as their chair.

15  The report's Findings were made public in New York on 15 March 1993 but the official text (in the original Spanish and in English translation) was not released until two weeks later as an annex of 251 pages (dated 1 April 1993) to a one-page letter from UN Secretary Boutros Boutros-Ghali to the UN Security Council (UN Document S/25500, dated

In Guatemala the full title of the Commission was 'The Commission to Clarify Past Human Rights Violations and Acts of Violence that have caused the Guatemalan Population to Suffer' but they were widely referred to by the abbreviated title, *Comisión de Esclarecimiento Histórico* (Commission of Historical Clarification), or simply by the Spanish acronym, CEH. The absence of the word ·'Truth' in the Commission's title reflected a sensitive political compromise. The Guatemalan military – which had been in a much stronger position than its Salvadoran counterpart – had fiercely resisted the notion of a 'Truth Commission' but the URNG had been equally firm on insisting that any settlement include a Commission to investigate past abuses. In June 1994 both sides finally agreed to a UN-sponsored Commission of Historical Clarification as the best way forward.

The CEH chair was Christian Tomuschat, a German law professor (and expert on human rights). The other two commissioners, Edgar Alfredo Balsells Tojo and Otilia Lux de Cotí, were both Guatemalan.[16] The CEH started work on 1 August 1997 and continued to 31 January 1999. It presented its report *Guatemala: Memoria de Silencio* in February 1999 and published it in June 1999.[17] The extra months between presentation and publication meant that the work for the final report stretched over two years and the resources available to the commissioners made it a very lengthy document.[18]

---

29 March 1993). Whilst it is common to simply refer to the published Findings as the report, the full report actually consists of three volumes, the Findings plus two annexes of supporting material. Annex I contains the texts of the Salvadoran Peace Accords plus the full findings of the forensic scientists who investigated El Mozote. Annex II details statistical information on the testimony presented to the Commission and lists the names of individual victims. The annexes were deposited in the UN library but have not been translated or published. The page numbers for quotations given here refer to the version published as S/25500.

16 The appointment of two Guatemalan commissioners (and the many Guatemalans who served on the investigative staff) was in marked contrast to the Salvadoran Truth Commission, which had had no Salvadoran personnel.

17 Comision para el Esclaracimiento Histórico *Guatemala: Memoria del Silencio* (Guatemala: United Nations, 1999). The full Spanish text of the 12 volume report is also available on CD-Rom published by the American Academy for the Advancement of Science or as PDF at http://hrdata.aaas.org/ceh/index.html. An English Translation of the Prologue (from Vol. 1), the Conclusions (from Vol. 5) and the Recommendations (also from Vol. 5) is available as *Guatemala: Memory of Silence: Summary* at http://hrdata.aaas.org/ceh/report/english. In what follows below, quotations from the Prologue, Conclusions and Recommendations are from this translation (and referenced to it as *Guatemala: Memory of Silence*). All other quotations are my own translation from the Spanish (and referenced to it as *Guatemala: Memoria del Silencio*). The PDF and CD-ROM are subdivided slightly differently but in each case the paragraph sections run on consecutively (Vol. 1, §§1–737; Vol. 2, §§738–2349; Vol. 3, §§2350–3882; Vol. 4. §§3883–4594). I am grateful to Cath Collins, Institute of Latin American Studies, University of London, for assistance with some of the translation.

18 The period from mid-April 1997 to July 1997 was a particularly productive preparation period and the Commission received a six-month extension to its original six-to-twelve-month term for investigations.

Neither the overall success of the political transition in El Salvador and Guatemala nor the role of the truth commissions within the process should be overstated.[19] Despite the economic benefits that arose from ending the conflict, both countries continue to face very serious economic and social pressures.[20] Despite the important legislative and political reforms of the 1990s, the ironic term 'Low Intensity Democracy' remains an apt description for both societies. Nonetheless, the two Truth Commissions have generally been seen as constructive parts of the process and welcomed as important new landmarks of progress in human rights work in Latin America.[21]

Both Commissions faced national militaries that would have preferred for the past to be forgotten. In both countries the military sought wherever possible to restrict the Commissions' mandates and powers, frustrate their investigations, dismiss their conclusions, and ignore their recommendations. Despite these serious obstacles, both *From Madness to Hope* and *Guatemala: Memoria del Silencio* provide authoritative statements on the political violence and terror that afflicted the two countries. Both reports confirm that the military and related para-militaries were responsible for the vast majority of abuses.[22] In the process, they document many similar patterns of violence in the two countries and point to state terror policies behind them. The Salvadoran Truth Commission notes that:

> The main characteristics of this period [1980–83] were that violence became systematic and terror and distrust reigned among the civilian population. The fragmentation of any opposition or dissident movement by means of arbitrary arrests, murders and selective

---

19 On the challenges still facing the two countries, see especially, Margaret Popkin, *Peace Without Justice: Obstacles to Building the Rule of Law in El Salvador* (University Park, PA: Pennsylvania State University Park, 2000); Jack Spence *et al.*, *Chapultepec: Five Years Later: El Salvador's Political Reality and Uncertain Future* (Boston: Hemispheres Initiative, 1997); Rachel Sieder (ed.), *Guatemala after the Peace Accords* (London: Institute of Latin American Studies, 1998).

20 See Rachel Sieder (ed.), *Central America: Fragile Transition* (Basingstoke: Macmillan Press, 1996).

21 The most significant reservations usually relate to issues of justice, especially on the intractable issue of truth at the price of justice. For a helpful comparative evaluation of how this was handled differently in El Salvador, Gautemala and Honduras, see Rachel Sieder, 'War, Peace and Memory Politics in Central America', in Alexandra Barahona De Brito, Carmen González-Enríquez and Paloma Aguilar (eds), *The Politics of Memory: Transitional Justice in Democratizing Socities* (Oxford: Oxford University Press, 2001), 161–93.

22 The Salvadoran Commission noted that: 'those giving testimony attributed almost 85 per cent of cases to agents of the State, paramilitary groups allied to them, and the death squads. Armed forces personnel were accused in almost 60 percent of complaints, members of the security forces in approximately 25 percent, members of military escorts and civil defence units in approximately 20 per cent, and members of death squads in more than 10 per cent of cases' (TC, *From Madness to Hope*, 43). The CEH stated that state forces and paramilitary groups were responsible for 93 per cent of the violations that they documented. This included responsibility for 92 per cent of the arbitrary executions and 91 per cent of the forced disappearances. CEH, *Memory of Silence: Conclusions*, §15.

and indiscriminate disappearances of leaders became common practice ... Organized terrorism, in the form of the so-called 'death-squads', became the most aberrant manifestation of the escalation of violence'.[23]

The CEH is equally emphatic when it states:

[T]hroughout the armed confrontation the Army designed and implemented a strategy to provoke terror in the population. This strategy became a core element of the Army's operations ... A high proportion of the human rights' violations known to the CEH and committed by the Army or other security forces were perpetrated publicly and with extreme brutality, especially in the Mayan communities of the country's interior.[24]

Most significantly of all the CEH Conclusions confirm that:

... agents of the State of Guatemala, within the framework of counterinsurgency operations carried out between 1981 and 1983, committed acts of genocide against groups of Mayan people ...[25]

However, despite the many similarities, one area in which the reports differ markedly is their attitudes to sexual violence as an integral part of state terror strategy. The systematic rape of women prisoners in detention centres and rural massacres was commonplace in both countries.[26] Standard operating procedures in torture sessions in both countries included physical and/or psychological sexual abuse of both men and women.[27] Yet, whilst the CEH provides graphic documentation of the sexual violence, the Salvadoran Truth Commission is entirely silent on it.

23 TC, *From Madness to Hope*, 27.

24 CEH, *Guatemala: Memory of Silence. Conclusions*, §§44–46. See further, *Guatemala: Memoria del Silencio*, §§3897–4003.

25 CEH, *Memory of Silence: Conclusions*, §§108–23 (122).

26 Elizabeth Shrader Cox reports that interviews with Central American refugees by social workers in Texas and California suggested that rape was virtually a universal experience for refugee women over the age of twelve (Cox, 'Gender Violence and Women's Health in Central America', in Miranda E. Davies (ed.), *Women and Violence*, 118–33. For a personal testimony, see Robin Ormes Quizar, *My Turn to Weep: Salvadoran Refugee Women in Costa Rica* (Westport, CT and London: Bergin & Garvey, 1998), 4–6 and 14; see also Beatriz Mariz, *Refugees of a Hidden War: Counterinsurgency in Guatemala* (Albany, NY: State University of New York Press, 1988).

27 On the variety of tortures inflicted on women in El Salvador and Guatemala, see A. Aron *et al.*, 'The Gender Specific Terror of El Salvador and Guatemala: Post-traumatic Stress Disorder in Central American Refugee Women', *Women's Studies International Forum* 14 (1991), 37–47.

## The Salvadoran Truth Commission

In their report *From Madness to Hope* the Salvadoran Truth Commissioners affirm the principle that is central to truth-telling investigations, when they say that 'One bitter but unavoidable step is to look at and acknowledge what happened and must never happen again.'[28] In many ways the report offers a frank and outspoken record of serious human rights' abuses between 1980 and 1989.[29] Yet reading *From Madness to Hope* in the light of *Guatemala: Memoria del Silencio*, one of the most notable issues is that *From Madness to Hope* makes virtually no mention of rape or other sexual violence against men or women. Throughout the entire Salvadoran Truth report, the most unspeakable truth remains unspoken.

The silence on sexual violence is particularly striking in cases where sexual violence had already been widely reported by human rights' agencies and the press. For example, when documenting the notorious case of the four US churchwomen who were raped and murdered in December 1980, the Truth Commission makes no mention of the rape, despite it being widely reported at the time.[30] Likewise, in its account of the notorious massacre at El Mozote – which the report highlighted as an 'illustrative case' – the Truth Commission failed to mention the systematic rape of approximately twenty-five young women and girls.[31] *Tutela Legal* (the Archdiocesan Legal Aid office) had already documented that, after the soldiers had separated the men and women of the village, the soldiers took about twenty-five of the younger women and older girls to the nearby hill known as Cerro La Cruz – Hill of the Cross – where they repeatedly raped and then executed them.[32] However, although the

---

28 Commission on Truth for El Salvador, *From Madness to Hope: The 12-Year War in El Salvador* (Report of the Commission on Truth for El Salvador; New York: United Nations, 1993), 185; reprinted in United Nations, *The United Nations and El Salvador, 1990–1995* (The United Nations Blue Books Series, 4; New York: United Nations, 1996), 290–415 (384).

29 The Salvadoran Truth Commission presented just thirty-two cases of the violence. These were chosen either because they specially outraged Salvadoran society or the international community, or because as individual cases they illustrated a systematic pattern, or both (see TC, *From Madness to Hope*, 19). For each case, the report offers a 'Summary of the Case', a 'Description of the Facts', and the Commission's 'Findings'.

30 The 'Description of the Facts' simply records: 'Shortly after 7 p.m. on 2 December 1980, members of the National Guard of El Salvador arrested four churchwomen as they were leaving Comalapa International Airport. Churchwomen Ita Ford, Maura Clarke, Dorothy Kazel and Jean Donovan were taken to an isolated spot where they were shot dead at close range', (TC, *From Madness to Hope*, 62). Nor is there mention of rape in the 'Summary of the Case' or the 'Findings'.

31 See Mark Danner, *The Massacre at El Mozote: A Parable of the Cold War* (New York: Vintage, 1994), 71, 78–79; and Leigh Binford, *The El Mozote Massacre: Anthropology and Human Rights* (Tuscon: University of Arizona Press, 1996), 21.

32 Tutela Legal, *Investigación sobre la masacre de centenares de campesinos en los caseríos El Mozote, Ranchería y Jocote Amarillo del cantón Guacamaya, en los cantones La Joya y Cerro Pando, de la jurisdicción de Meanguera y en el caserío Los Toriles de la jurisdicción de Arambala, todos del departamento de Morazán, por tropas del BIRI Atlacatl*

Truth Commission mentions that the men and women were separated it does not give details on what happened to the women before they were killed. It confirms that the men were 'tortured and executed' but only states that 'the women were executed'.[33]

Elsewhere, such as the 'Attack on an FMLN hospital and execution of nurse' (15 April 1989), the report gives details that strongly suggest rape but it does not name rape as part of the atrocity.[34] The case summary states that members of a Salvadoran air force unit captured the French nurse Madeleine Lagadec alive and executed her, alongside José Ignacio Isla Casares (an Argentine doctor) and Clelia Concepción Díaz (a Salvadoran literacy instructor). Later, in the description of the facts and the investigation, it says: 'The soldiers questioned the three captives and screams were heard, the loudest being those of Madeleine Lagadec. Next, some shots rang out …'. That same day, FMLN members found the bodies at the scene. According to two of them, Madeleine Lagadec's trousers were below her knees and she did not have any underwear on under them.[35] It also reports that in addition to the potentially lethal shots to the head and shoulder she was shot at close range in the pelvic area, thighs and right breast. In addition it notes that her left hand had been severed at the wrist.[36] However, it offers no comment on her loud screams, her state of undress or on the practice of Salvadoran security forces to deliberately target the pelvic area of the body in their executions.[37]

The one partial exception to the Truth Commission's silence on sexual violence is in the account of the massacre at El Junquillo, Morazán. Here the 'Summary of the Case' records that:

On 12 March 1981, soldiers and members of the Cacaopera civil defence attacked the population, consisting solely of women, young children and old people. They killed the inhabitants and raped a number of the women and little girls under the age of 12. They set fire to houses, cornfields and barns.[38]

However, even in the El Junquillo case, the report downplays the role of sexual violence in the atrocity. The unambiguous statement presented in the 'Summary

---

*durante operativo militar los días 11,12 y 13 de Diciembre de 1981: Hechos conocidos como 'Masacre de El Mozote'* (San Salvador: Tutela Legal, 1991).

33  TC, *From Madness to Hope*, 114–15 and 120.

34  TC, *From Madness to Hope,* 87–89. Whether or not the literacy instructor Clelia Concepción Díaz was also raped is left unclear. An unfortunate feature of the report – in this case and elsewhere – is that international victims of the violence were given more prominence than Salvadoran victims.

35  Subsequent analysis of the French autopsy reports confirmed that she could not have been wearing her brassiere, briefs and trousers when executed; see TC, *From Madness to Hope*, 89.

36  Salvadoran death squads commonly severed the hands from their victims' bodies to signify that they had been executed as 'leftists'.

37  Similar injuries to the pelvic and thigh areas in the case of Jesuit housekeeper and her daughter go unmentioned in the report of the Jesuit assassinations; see TC, *From Madness to Hope*, 45–54.

38  TC, *From Madness to Hope*, 67.

of the Case' is more tentatively qualified in the 'Description of the Facts' to read *'According to testimony*, some of the women and little girls had been raped'.[39] Then when it comes to the part of the case dealing with 'Findings', there is no mention of rape at all. It simply reads:

> There is substantial evidence that on 12 March 1981, units of the Military Detachment at Sonsonate and members of the civil defence unti at Cacaopera indiscriminately attacked and summarily executed men, women and children of El Junquillo canton in the district of Cacaopera, Department of Morazán.[40]

Given its silence on sexual violence against women it is no surprise that the Salvadoran Truth Commission likewise makes no reference to sexual violence against men in any of the cases it documents in which men were disappeared, tortured or killed. Yet there is good evidence that the Salvadoran security forces subjected their male prisoners to sexual torture, sexual assaults with foreign objects, rape, and genital mutilation.

A wide variety of sexual abuses as part of torture had already been clearly documented during the military dictatorships in Chile (1973–89), Uruguay (1973–85), and Argentina (1976–83).[41] The report by the Uruguayan Peace and Justice Service (SERPAJ) in 1989 explicitly included the sexual torture and rape of men as well as women.[42] It recorded that 7 per cent of male prisoners interviewed testified to being raped – the same percentage for men as for women – and noted that the figure could be much higher.[43]

The report on *Torture in El Salvador* from the non-governmental Human Rights Committee of El Salvador (CDHES-NG) provides evidence that sexual violence against male prisoners was relatively common. Based on research on 433 of the 434 prisoners remanded to Mariona men's prison between January and August 1986, it indicates that eighty-five men suffered blows to their testicles during physical torture. Furthermore, sixty-six men reported being threatened with rape and two

---

39  TC, *From Madness to Hope*, 68 (emphasis added). There is no such qualification in recording other details in this section – such as setting fire to the houses and cornfields, stealing some of the stored corn, or killing some of the animals – although presumably these also relied on similar testimony from survivors.

40  TC, *From Madness to Hope*, 69.

41  See esp. Frank Graziano, *Divine Violence: Spectacle, Psychosexuality, and Radical Christianity in the Argentine 'Dirty War'* (Boulder, CO and Oxford: Westview Press, 1992); Ximena Bunster-Burotto, 'Surviving Beyond Fear: Women and Torture in Latin America', in Miranda E. Davies (ed.), *Women and Violence*, 156–76.

42  SERPAJ, *Uruguay: Nunca Más: Human Rights Violations, 1972–1985* (Montevideo: Servicio Justicia y Paz, 1992 [Spanish orig. 1989]), 99.

43  SERPAJ, *Uruguay: Nunca Más*, 99. A further reason for under-reporting of rape can be that some tortures – such as rape with objects and instruments or even with animals – might be classified by the victim or by the interviewer under headings other than rape.

testified that they had actually been raped.[44] On top of this, news reports and other writing from El Salvador referred to bodies being openly dumped by the roadside with mutilated genitals or other signs of sexual assault.[45] Yet there is no hint to this dimension of the conflict in *From Madness to Hope*.

## The Guatemalan Commission for Historical Clarification

In the Prologue to their report the CEH commissioners recall that prior to their investigation none of them had imagined the full horror of what had happened.

> When we were appointed to form the CEH, each of us, through different routes and all by life's fortune, knew in general terms the outline of events. As Guatemalans, two of us had lived the entire tragedy on our native soil, and in one way or another, had suffered it. However, none of us could have imagined the full horror and magnitude of what actually happened.[46]

This was probably nowhere more true than in their investigations of sexual violence summed up in their conclusion that: 'Sexual violence was a widespread and systematic practice carried out by agents of the state as part of their counterinsurgency strategy'.[47] Volume III Section 13 of the report, entitled 'Sexual Violence against

---

44  CDHES-NG, *Torture in El Salvador* (San Salvador: CDHES-NG, September 1986), cited in Leigh Binford, *The El Mozote Massacre*, 158–59. The under-reporting of rape cases has been extensively documented and since the stigma of male rape is particularly strong it is widely assumed to be even more of a problem in cases of male rape.

45  The Salvadoran novelist Manlio Argueta includes a passage in his famous work *One Day of Life* (trans. W. Brow; London: Chatto and Windus, 1984 [Spanish orig. 1980]), 30, which describes the discovery of a naked priest by the roadside with a stick still stuck up his anus. Joan Didion's book *Salvador* (London: Chatto & Windus, 1983) records sightings of male corpses left with their genitals hacked off during her visits in the early 1980s. As the decade progressed and the Salvadoran government came under increasing pressure to improve human rights – or at least appear to be doing so – these public displays became less common. Evidence from Joya Martínez (a death squad member in 1988–89 who fled El Salvador in 1989 and sought asylum in the US) suggests that by the late 1980s greater care was taken to eliminate all traces of victims. One way to do this, using techniques well-known in Argentina and Chile, was by throwing them into the sea or large lakes; see Human Rights Watch, *El Salvador: Extradition Sought for Alleged Death Squad Participant* (New York: Human Rights Watch, August 1991), 3.

46  Commission for Historical Clarification, *Guatemala: Memory of Silence. Prologue* (Guatemala: United Nations, 1999). See also Hayner's reference to a Commissioner on the Chilean National Commission on Truth and Reconciliation who reported after the release of the Chilean report 'What I know now, I would not have imagined' (Hayner, *Unspeakable Truths*, 37). The Chilean confession is especially telling because the Commissioner had himself led a human rights commission during the Pinochet era.

47  CEH, *Guatemala: Memoria del Silencio*, §2351: 'La violación sexual fue una práctica generalizada y sistemática realizada por agentes del Estado en el marco de la estrategia

Women', gives a frank and shocking insight into the unimaginable cruelty of many of these practices. [48]

The majority of the abuses were concentrated in the period 1980–83 when the violence against indigenous communities was at its peak under Lucas García and Ríos Montt.[49] The violence often included the public humiliation of victims to maximise the terror and trauma. During massacres mass rapes were common and often included assaults with foreign objects. For example:

> The most usual practice was to strip women and insert objects into their vaginas or drive stakes into their wombs. The soldier said that when the women were dead they lifted up their skirts and put a stick in their vagina … they hung one elderly woman with a noose around her neck. She was naked with a banana in her vagina.[50]

Some of the worst violence was deliberately directed against pregnant women.[51] In some cases this included the sadistic destruction of the unborn. For example:

> They opened the womb of a pregnant woman and pulled out the child and pushed a stick up the child's behind, until it came out through the child's mouth.[52]

---

contrainsurgente'. In compiling their report, the CEH benefited greatly from the 1998 report of the Guatemalan Archdiocesan Recovery of Historical Memory project (Recuperación de la memoria histórica) usually known by the Spanish acronym REMHI; REMHI/ODHAG, *Guatemala Nunca Más* (Informe proyecto interdiocesano de recuperación de la memoria histórica; 4 vols; Guatemala: Oficina de Derechos Humanos del Arzobispado de Guatemala [ODHAG], 1998). An abridged single volume version has been published in English as REMHI/ODHAG, *Guatemala: Never Again!* (The Official Report of the Human Rights Office, Archdiocese of Guatemala; trans. G. Tovar Siebentritt; Maryknoll, NY: Orbis Books; London: Catholic Institute for International Relations and Latin America Bureau, 1999). Some of the testimonies from REMHI are also included in the CEH report. On sexual violence in the REMHI report, see esp. REMHI, *Never Again!*, 76–85, 170–71, 298. For background to the REMHI report, see Marcela López Levy, 'Recovery: The Uses of Memory and History in the Guatemalan Church's REMHI Project' in M. A. Hayes and D. Tombs (eds), *Truth and Memory: The Church and Human Rights in El Salvador and Guatemala* (Leominster, Herefordshire: Gracewing, 2001), 103–17.

48  CEH, *Guatemala: Memoria del Silencio*, §§2350–2485. Very little of the detail from this part of the report is included in *Guatemala: Memory of Silence. Conclusions*, but see §28 on Children, §§29–30 on Women, and §91 on rape.

49    CEH, *Guatemala: Memoria del Silencio*, §2392.

50  CEH, *Guatemala: Memoria del Silencio*, §2412: 'El más usual fue la desnudez y la introducción de objetos en la vagina de las mujeres o estacas que clavaban en sus vientres. "El soldado … contaba que cuando estaban las señoras muertas les subía la falda y les metía un palo en la vagina … a una anciana la ahorcaron con un lazo en el cuello. Estaba desnuda con un banano en la vagina'.

51  CEH, *Guatemala: Memoria del Silencio*, §2352.

52  CEH, *Guatemala: Memoria del Silencio*, §2412: 'Abrieron la panza de una mujer embarazada y sacaron el nene y al nene le pusieron un palo por atrás hasta que salió de su boca.'

Elsewhere the CEH describes other particularly misogynistic and degrading executions of women. For example, 'They raped the women, they put them on all-fours, and then they shot them putting the gun in the rectum or in the vagina'.[53]

The CEH notes that the army tried to classify such atrocities simply as 'errors'.[54] However, it would be entirely mistaken to assume that the abuses were an unfortunate by-product of military action and restricted to cases where troops got out of control. The CEH shows that the sexual violence was systematic and part of a strategy.[55] The frequency and extremity of the violence suggests that these were not just 'excesses' or 'errors' committed by untrained troops but a recognised part of a political strategy. The CEH concludes:

> Based on the extensive and systematic form in which the army perpetrated the sexual violation of women, the CEH arrives at the conviction that these were not isolated acts or sporadic excesses but were above all a planned strategy.[56]

On some occasions, the violence was clearly organised and the result of very explicit orders.[57] As one witness explains:

> Each officer had his own little band of killers, and he would tell them what methods to use. 'Today you are going to cut their throats, or hang them up with wire; rape all the women today'. They often gave instructions beforehand like this.[58]

---

53 'Violaban a las mujeres, las ponían a cuatro patas, luego les disparaban metiendo el arma en el recto o en la vagina' CEH, *Guatemala: Memoria del Silencio*, §2404. Close parallels are clear in the following story reported from El Salvador: 'One night Brenda's co-worker was dragged from her apartment and brought to national guard headquarters where she was gang raped and tortured. In the morning the soldiers led her into the town square and forced her to bend over. Then a soldier inserted a machine gun into her rectum and pulled the trigger. She was three months pregnant'; R. Golden and M. McConnell, *Sanctuary: The New Underground Railway* (Maryknoll, NY: Orbis Books, 1986), 65, cited C. Smith, *Resisting Reagan: The U.S. Central America Peace Movement* (Chicago: Chicago University Press, 1996), 53.

54 CEH, *Guatemala: Memoria del Silencio*, §2413.

55 CEH, *Guatemala: Memoria del Silencio*, §§2389 and 2398.

56 'Con base en la forma masiva y sistemática con la que el Ejército perpetró las violaciones sexuales de las mujeres, la CEH llegó a la convicción de que no se trató de actos aislados y excesos esporádicos sino sobre todo de una planificación estratégica'; CEH, *Guatemala: Memoria del Silencio*, §2398, cf. §2214.

57 Whether US advisers played an active role in encouraging sexual violence is unclear. However, there is no doubt that the US bears a very heavy responsibility for much of the political repression in Guatemala since the CIA-led coup of 1954. The CEH explicitly acknowledges the support given by the US government and the CIA to the Guatemalan security forces.

58 'El oficial tiene sus grupitos de asesinos y les dice cómo tienen que matar. Hoy van a degollar o a guindar con alambres, hoy violan a todas las mujeres. Muchas veces las órdenes las dan antes'; CEH, *Guatemala: Memoria del Silencio*, §2404.

On other occasions the organisation was less direct but no less significant. The soldiers shared a *macho* culture of sexual aggression rooted in norms and values of wider society and reinforced by the distinctive ethos of military institutions.[59] As the CEH notes, *machismo* would have encouraged and appeared to justify acts of sexual violence and humiliation in warfare.[60] The CEH points to aspects of military training that were intended to channel this and make sexual atrocities more likely even when they were not directly ordered.[61] For example, according to testimonies, recruits were provided with prostitutes to acclimatise them to sexual violence.[62]

In addition to physical suffering, frequent injury, and a woman's risk of pregnancy, a single rape could traumatise not just the immediate victim and but whole families and others in the community.[63] To increase the humiliation sexual abuses were often conducted in public rather than in secrecy.

Whilst the focus of the CEH report is on sexual violence directed against women, it also makes clear that sexual torture was widely used against men as well. It states that: 'The direct victims were principally women and girls, but in addition, there were sexual abuses of boys and men'.[64] Violence against men included sexual violation with animals or bottles, and physical blows or electrical current applied to the genitals.[65] It also confirms that the mutilation of the sexual organs of male victims – along with the eyes and tongue – was a systematically applied practice.[66]

---

59 See further, David Tombs, 'Honour, Shame and Conquest: Male Identity, Sexual Violence and the Body Politic', *Journal of Hispanic/Latino Theology* 9 (May 2002), 21–40.

60 CEH, *Guatemala: Memoria del Silencio*, §2395. It should, however, be emphasised that sexual violence in warfare is not in any way a distinctively Latin America phenomenon. Whilst the specifics of sexual violence might vary human rights abuses against women have been a typical feature of many conflicts across the world. For a helpful summary of major abuses committed in earlier twentieth-century wars – including World Wars One and Two, Vietnam and Bangladesh – see Susan Brownmiller, *Against Our Will: Men, Women and Rape* (London: Secker and Warburg, 1975), 31–113.

61 At a number of points the CEH makes explicit reference to the training methods used by the *Kaibiles* (specialist counter-insurgency forces responsible for many of the massacres); see esp. *Guatemala: Memory of Silence. Conclusions*, §42.

62 See CEH, *Guatemala: Memoria del Silencio*, §2397. The soldiers' tendency to describe indigenous women as 'meat' reflects this brutalization; see esp. §§2389 and 2421.

63 Along with other physical and psychological injuries, contracting venereal diseases from the soldiers could add to the women's distress; CEH, *Guatemala: Memoria del Silencio*, §2234.

64 'Las víctimas directas fueron principalmente mujeres y niñas, pero también fueron ultrajados sexualmente niños y hombres'; CEH, *Guatemala: Memoria del Silencio*, §235.

65 'La tortura sexual consistía en violencia directa en los órganos genitales, en la forma de violación sexual por animales, con botellas o porras, y golpes o corriente eléctrica aplicada a los órganos genitales. Se aplicaba tanto a hombres como a mujeres'; CEH, *Guatemala: Memoria del Silencio*, §2232, see further, §§2237 and 2247.

66 'La mutilación de los órganos sexuales de los hombres fue aplicada sistemáticamente;' CEH, *Guatemala: Memoria del Silencio*, §2251.

David Tombs 71

For all victims, the shame and the stigma were invariably much longer lasting than the physical suffering. For male victims, the psychological burdens of sexual violence could be especially hard. In the eyes of *machista* society, sexual violation of a male prisoner signified his loss of manhood whilst simultaneously reinforcing the 'manly' status of the torturers. Torturers could therefore take a particular 'pride' in male rapes or penetrations with objects and might even boast of them.[67] For example, after three days of various violations, the body of one dumped victim was left with a note that read: 'He had never met a real man before'.[68]

## Breaking the Silence on Sexual Violence

Given the prevalence of sexual abuses in the Central American conflicts, the failure of the Salvadoran Truth Commission to address sexual violence as an obvious 'pattern of abuse' is a serious omission.[69] The silence on sexual violence is all the more striking given the report's recognition that atrocities need to be understood in terms of a policy of systematic terror. Only a policy of systematic terror could make sense of the sexual violence, and there is no real understanding of the terror without addressing its sexual element. However, the Salvadoran Truth commission did not see it this way – or at least, they did not believe that there was sufficient direct evidence for it. Part of the reason may have been sheer revulsion at the atrocities of the crimes but other factors were also significant.

For example, in the case of the four US churchwomen it appears that the commissioners concluded that the rapes had occurred. However, as there was no direct evidence that they had been ordered from above, they were therefore not seen as 'politically' motivated.[70]

One factor in this was that the Commissioners were determined to focus on the responsibility of individuals rather than institutions.[71] Establishing explicit

---

67 See David Tombs, 'Honour, Shame and Conquest: Male Identity, Sexual Violence and the Body-Politic', 27–33.

68 CEH, *Guatemala: Memoria del Silencio*, §2235.

69 For further elaboration of the Commission's work and the thinking behind it, see Thomas Buergenthal, 'The United Nations Truth Commission for El Salvador', *Vanderbilt Journal of Transnational Law* 27 (1994), 497–544.

70 See Patricia Hayner, *Unspeakable Truths*, 79. Furthermore, Hayner also notes (79 n. 20) that the unpublished appendix to the Salvadoran Truth Commission Report lists many incidents of rape and that commissioners never explained the apparent discrepancy between the Report and the appendix.

71 TC, *From Madness to Hope*, 13–14. The Salvadoran Truth Commission's approach was explicitly intended to protect institutions whilst punishing individuals. The Commission therefore rejected the argument for institutional responsibility. The report notes: 'A situation of repeated criminal acts may arise in which different individuals act within the same institution in unmistakably similar ways ... This gives reason to believe that institutions may indeed commit crimes, if the same behaviour becomes a constant of the institution and, especially, if clear-cut accusations are met with a cover-up by the institution to which the accused belong and the

orders in individual cases certainly gives the most clear-cut grounds for assigning responsibility. However, whilst the focus on individuals had legal advantages, it also carried significant disadvantages in presenting a complete record of why certain patterns of violence were especially prominent. Explicit orders were often very hard to document. Regrettably, on matters of sexual violence, the Commission ignored the equally significant and obvious responsibility of those who failed in their duty to make any attempt to stop the atrocities and/or helped cover them up. Thus in the case of the four US churchwomen, the Truth Commission highlighted the complicity of superiors in attempting to cover up the National Guard's responsibility for the murders. It also accused the Salvadoran government of failing its obligations under international law to investigate the case.[72] Yet even though the evidence of complicity was also clearly relevant to the rapes (the military attempted to deny responsibility for the entire incident, not just the murders) the Truth Commission drew no attention to this.

In 1993 the political status of rape and other forms of sexual violence as war crimes was only just starting to be internationally recognised. The 1949 Geneva Convention lays out internationally agreed humanitarian protocols during conflicts (which forbid torture and cruel and inhuman treatment) but before the early 1990s little international attention had been given to rape and sexual violence as 'war crimes'.

The conflict in the former Yugoslavia (1992–95) dramatically raised international awareness of the issues. The use of rape (and the threat of rape) to terrorize families and whole communities into flight was widely reported.[73] The role of rape in 'ethnic cleansing' made clear that rapes could be part of a deliberate political strategy.

---

institution is slow to act when investigations reveal who is responsible. In such circumstances, it is easy to succumb to the argument that repeated crimes mean that the institution is to blame. The Commission on the Truth did not fall into that temptation ... the Commission believes that responsibility for anything that happened during the period of the conflict could not and should not be laid at the door of the institution'. Within the framework of individual responsibility the Commission was much stronger in ascribing responsibility for abuses, which were explicitly ordered, rather than patterns of violence that were tacitly condoned or encouraged indirectly. The Commission stated that its intention was to lay responsibility at the door of 'those who ordered the procedures for operating in the way that members of the institution did and also of those who, having been in a position to prevent such procedures, were compromised by the degree of tolerance and permissiveness with which they acted from their positions of authority or leadership or by the fact that they covered up incidents which came to their knowledge or themselves gave the order which led to the action in question'. However, as far as sexual violence was concerned, the Commission focused entirely on the lack of clear evidence for knowing what was explicitly ordered (thereby virtually excluding it from the report) rather than condemning the failure of those responsible to stop a clearly widespread pattern.

72 TC, *From Madness to Hope*, 66.

73 On rape in Bosnia, see Alexandra Stiglmayer (ed.), *Mass Rape: The War Against Women in Bosnia-Herzegovonia* (trans. Marion Faber; Lincoln: University of Nebraska Press, 1993); Beverly Allen, *Rape Warfare: The Hidden Genocide in Bosnia-Herzegovonia*

International law reflected this increased awareness in the Statutes adopted in May 1993 for the UN International Criminal Tribunal for the former Yugoslavia (ICTY).[74] Statute 5 (on Crimes Against Humanity) specifically names rapes during the conflict as one of the 'crimes against humanity' for which it would prosecute.[75] Furthermore, because mass rapes could disrupt the very basis of a community and destroy its future, Statute 4 of the ICTY (on Genocide) also provides scope for prosecutions for rapes intended as part of ethnic-cleansing.[76]

Meanwhile, and much closer to Central America, atrocities during the military regime of Lt. Gen. Raoul Cédras in Haiti (September 1991–September 1994) highlighted the use of rape in internal political repression.[77] Haiti's National Commission for Truth and Justice included specific attention to sexual crimes committed against women during the Cédras regime.[78]

In 1995 the New York-based Human Rights Watch drew attention to the integral role of rape in war and political repression in their *Global Report on Women's Human Rights*. Drawing on their investigations in the former Yugoslavia, Peru, Kashmir, and Somalia they noted that rape was used for a wide variety of different political purposes in different situations. This included 'terrorizing civilian communities', conducting 'ethnic cleansing', avenging historical disputes, and rewarding mercenary soldiers.[79]

The Salvadoran and the Guatemalan reports stand on either side of an important watershed in human rights' work during the 1990s. After 1993 there was a growing

---

(Minneapolis: University of Minnesota Press, 1996); Ivana Nizich, *War Crimes in Bosnia-Hercegovina,* vols I–II (New York: Human Rights Watch, 1992–93).

74 The Tribunal's full title was 'International Tribunal for the Prosecution of Persons Responsible for Serious Violations of International Humanitarian Law Committed in the Territory of the Former Yugoslavia since 1991'.

75 The ICTY 1993 statutes are available at http://www.un.org/icty. On ICTY prosecutions for crimes against women, see Kelly Askin, *War Crimes Against Women: Prosecution in International War Crimes Tribunals* (The Hague: Martinus Nijhoff, 1997); Liz Philipose, 'The Laws of War and Women's Human Rights', *Hypatia* 11/4 (Fall 1996), 46–62. On 22 February 2001 the ICTY convicted three suspects accused of the Foca abuses. This was the first time in history that an international tribunal prosecution had been based solely on crimes of sexual violence against women.

76 Serb forces were accused of deliberately impregnating Bosnian Muslim women with 'Serb' babies to destroy future community relations.

77 Human Rights Watch and National Coalition for Haitian Refugees, *Rape in Haiti: A Weapon of Terror* (New York: Human Rights Watch, July 1994). Terry Rey discusses the unprecedented scale of rape during the Cédras era in terms of widespread social attitudes and Haiti's earlier history of conquest rapes (including rapes committed by US marines during the occupation of Haiti 1915–34); Terry Rey, 'Junta, Rape, and Religion in Haiti, 1993–94', *Journal of Feminist Studies in Religion* 15/2 (1999), 73–100 (esp. 79–85).

78 Commission national de verité (CNVJ), *Si M Pa Rele* (Port-au-Prince: Minstère Nationale de la Justice de la République d'Haiti, 1996).

79 Human Rights Watch, *Global Report on Women's Human Rights* (New York: Human Rights Watch, 1995).

recognition of the significance of sexual violence. In contrast to the Salvadoran Truth Commission, the CEH (which worked in the second half of the decade) was much better placed to acknowledge the wider consequences of sexual violence and see its political role.[80]

By breaking the silence on sexual violence, the CEH made a major advance on its Salvadoran predecessor. It is an important model for future reports.[81] There can no longer be any justification for assuming *a priori* that widespread sexual violence during conflicts is only a side effect of political violence.[82] Rather it is often an integral part of political violence. Even where there is no evidence of deliberate planning and organization, apparently 'random' atrocities have political consequences and reflect political values that are relevant to the conflict.

These insights provide a new dimension to past and present conflicts. They contribute to a clearer understanding of the layers of 'truth' that are to be acknowledged. However, this 'progress' also shows how difficult attempts at reconciliation based on truth are likely to be. Even when there is a wish to discover

---

80  The CEH has a section in Vol. 3 on 'International Human Rights and the Rights of Women in Situations of Armed Conflict' (*Guatemala: Memoria del Silencio*, §§2363–2374) and makes explicit reference to the precedents set by Tribunals for the Former Yugoslavia and Bosnia (§§2372–73). In particular, it cites the observation by Elizabeth Odio (Vice-President of the Tribunal for the Former Yugoslavia) that 'The rape of women is not a more or less inevitable or unavoidable consequence of an armed conflict but is a systematically applied political strategy to destroy collective groups of people in addition to the immediate victim' (§2363 n. 2).

81  It may also be significant that the CEH took the opposite stance to the Salvadoran Truth Commission by naming institutions but not individuals. This was a condition imposed by the Guatemalan military to protect military personnel from possible prosecutions. Preventing consideration of individual responsibility may have encouraged the CEH to look more critically at how the institutions themselves actually contributed to the violence.

82  The concern of this chapter with sexual violence during periods of state terror and armed political conflicts is to be distinguished from more 'everyday' sexual violence in societies that are supposedly at 'peace'. However, whilst preserving this distinction is important (in order to examine the special circumstances created by armed conflicts), it should not disguise the fact that sexual violence in 'peace' times can sometimes be so widespread and intense that it approximates to a political conflict in its own right. For example, on the day before this paper was first presented, the *New York Times* carried a story from Johannesburg on the trial of six men for the rape of a 10-month-old baby, which it headlined as an 'Unthinkable Attack'. Even though the atrocity was not part of a political conflict in the usual sense, the article raises questions about when civil violence against women should be seen as part of a systemic conflict. Mpho Thekiso (the Program Manager of the national Network on Violence) is quoted as saying: 'There is a civil war in this country and it's a war against women's bodies.' The 'unthinkable' makes more sense when viewed in terms of patriarchal sexual attitudes that have no concern for female victims. When these include the belief that sexual intercourse with a virgin is a cure for AIDS, the unthinkable becomes as possible in 'peace' as it is during conflicts. See Rachel Swarns, 'Unthinkable Attack Jolts a Crime-Weary Country', *New York Times* (16 November 2001), A3.

the truth, it can often remain hidden. Silence and self-censorship amongst victims can seriously impede a Commission's ability to document the full truth. The reluctance of victims to speak of rape was one of the principal difficulties that the CEH says it faced in documenting the atrocities.[83] Feelings of extreme shame kept survivors and communities silent. When rape was mentioned in testimonies, survivors often only referred to what happened with euphemisms. Very few victims named what happened as 'rape' or 'violation'.[84]

According to the CEH, few women spoke of their experience of rape with other people. They did not even tell other women who had been victims of similar violence.[85] In many cases even the closest family member of a victim might be unaware of what had happened. As one woman testified:

> Never before have I told of how the soldiers raped the women, even less have I said that they also abused me ... I am going to die with this ... nobody can know ... my children do not know, my husband does not know ... nobody knows.[86]

The traditionalist values of Mayan culture created an additional pressure on the women. The report notes: 'It is not easy for a woman to dare to say that they raped her, and it is even more difficult for an indigenous woman'.[87] Some women feared that they themselves would be blamed.[88] In some cases, the stigma from what happened was so strong that survivors preferred to leave their own communities and live elsewhere because they could not bear to live with others knowing.[89] The reluctance of male survivors in *machista* societies to testify to what happened is just as strong.

Confronting unspeakable truths is a deeply painful process. Some victims may never be able to face some of the things that they suffered. Others might only refer to them only indirectly. In such cases the 'truth' can only ever be partial and provisional. However, a sensitive investigator can help victims to disclose their experiences. Perhaps the Guatemalan woman who said that she would tell nobody about what happened to her shows how complex this can be. Even as she says she will not tell anybody about what happened to her, she tells the depth of her experience to the

---

83  See CEH, *Guatemala: Memoria del Silencio*, §2383. Sections 2379–2387 of the report are subtitled 'El dolor en silencio' (Grieving in Silence).

84  'Las víctimas o testigos usan las palabras *"pasar"* o *"usar"* en vez de violar (los soldados *pasaron* con ellas, las usaron). Muy pocas identifican el hecho como "violación", es decir como aggression'; CEH, *Guatemala: Memoria del Silencio*, §2381.

85  CEH, *Guatemala: Memoria del Silencio*, §§2379–2387 (2380).

86  CEH, *Guatemala: Memoria del Silencio*, §2380.

87  CEH, *Guatemala: Memoria del Silencio*, §2380.

88  CEH, *Guatemala: Memoria del Silencio*, §2384. Cox notes that some men become abusive against their wives when they learn that they have been sexually assaulted; Elizabeth Shrader Cox, 'Gender Violence and Women's Health in Central America', 125.

89  CEH, *Guatemala: Memoria del Silencio*, §2384.

world – and perhaps to herself – reaching a level that could not be expressed by any amount of words.

## Truth and Reconciliation

Neither the Salvadoran nor the Guatemalan Commission had the word 'reconciliation' as part of their official titles. However, the mandates for both commissions made clear that their work for truth was understood in a broader context of national reconciliation.[90] The mandate of the Salvadoran Commission stated that: 'The Commission shall have the task of investigating serious acts of violence that have occurred since 1980 and whose impact on society urgently demands that the public should know the truth'.[91] In carrying out this task it was agreed that it must take account of:

> The exceptional importance that may be attached to the acts to be investigated, their characteristic and impact, and the social unrest to which they gave rise; and the need to create confidence in the positive changes that the peace process is promoting and to assist in the transition to national reconciliation.[92]

The CEH makes the link even more directly in its Preface with the statement that:

> Despite the shock that the Nation could suffer upon seeing itself reflected in the mirror of its past, it was nevertheless necessary to know the truth and make it public. It was their

---

90 The Chilean National Commission on Truth and Reconciliation and the Truth and Reconciliation Commission South Africa are perhaps the two best-known Commissions that explicitly linked Truth and Reconciliation in their titles and mandates. See Chilean National Commission on Truth and Reconciliation, *Report of the Chilean National Commission on Truth and Reconciliation* (2 vols; trans. Phillip E. Berryman; Center for Civil and Human Rights, Notre Dame Law School; Notre Dame, IN and London: University of Notre Dame Press, 1993 [1991]); Truth and Reconciliation Commission South Africa, *Report* (5 vols; Cape Town: Juta and Co, 1998; London: Macmillan, 1999).

91 Cited in TC, *From Madness to Hope*, 18. The mandate was agreed during the Peace process as Section 4 (Commission on the Truth) of the 27 April 1991 Mexico Agreement. The Mexico agreement is re-printed as Document 29 in United Nations, *The United Nations and El Salvador*, 167–74 (for Section 4, see p. 168). The characteristics, functions and powers of the Commission (along with other related matters including the Parties agreement on co-operation with it and acceptance of its recommendations as binding were set out in a corresponding annex to this section (173–74). Subsequently, Section 5 ('End to Impunity'), of the 16 January 1992 Chapultepec Agreement added to this initial mandate a further responsibility for the consideration and resolution of any indication of impunity on the part of officers of the armed forces. The entire Chapultepec Agreement is reprinted as Document 36 in United Nations, *The United Nations and El Salvador*, 193–230 (with Section 5 on page 196). The Commissioners helpfully summarise the Mandate and explain their interpretation of it as a preliminary section in the Report; see TC, *From Madness to Hope*, 18–19.

92 TC, *From Madness to Hope*, 18.

hope that truth would lead to reconciliation, and furthermore, that coming to terms with the truth is the only way to achieve this objective.[93]

Both Commissions believed that documenting the truth of what happened in political conflicts could make important contributions to long-term healing at both an individual and a political level. The Introduction to *From Madness to Hope* indicates some of the ways in which the truth might contribute to reconciliation and a new political order:

> Learning the truth and strengthening and tempering the determination to find it out; putting an end to impunity and cover-up; settling political and social differences by means of agreement instead of violent action: these are the creative consequences of an analytical search for truth.[94]

It would be naïve to believe that this healing process occurs in some magical way as soon as the truth becomes known. Survivors often need long-term help and support in rebuilding their personal identities and their social confidence. The physical scars and psychological wounds of sexual violence may leave a permanent mark. For some victims, proclaiming the truth about sexual atrocities might at first seem to be an additional punishment rather than an affirmation of their dignity. Nonetheless, survivors and relatives often attest to the importance of breaking the silence about atrocities.

Anthropologist Judith Zur (who studied the impact of terror on Guatemalan war widows) notes that terror brings about shared denial in a population. Knowing what not to know is a common coping mechanism.[95] Speaking the truth reverses this culture of denial and involuntary complicity. This is necessary for the well-being of society. Likewise, for the healing of individuals, therapists who have worked with torture victims who suffered extreme traumatization in Chile suggest that sometimes the past must be 're-experienced' in order to make new futures possible.

In other words, the more victims try to forget and leave their terrible experience in the past, the more they tend to reproduce it in the present in the form of emotional illness. But once they begin to confront the past directly, the past, present, and future can be adequately discriminated. To achieve this, we have found that the person or the family needs to recount the traumatic experience in detail, and express the emotions it produced.[96]

---

93 CEH, *Guatemala: Memory of Silence*, Preface. See also Supreme Decree 355 establishing the Chilean Commission, which states: 'That only upon a foundation of truth will it be possible to meet the basic demands of justice and create the necessary conditions for achieving true national reconciliation'; cited Chilean National Commission on Truth and Reconciliation, *Report of the Chilean National Commission on Truth and Reconciliation*, 5.

94 TC, *From Madness to Hope*, 11.

95 Judith Zur, 'The Psychological Impact of State Terror', *Anthropology Today* 10/3 (June 1994), 12–17 (15).

96 David Becker, Elizabeth Lira, Maria Isabel Castillo, Elena Gómez and Juana Kovalskys, 'Therapy with the Victims of Political Repression in Chile: The Challenge of

William Cavanaugh, a North American theologian who has studied torture in Chile, puts it succinctly:

> Years later, many victims are incapable of expressing significant parts of the horror they underwent; the tortures remain, in a word, unspeakable. The experiences are remembered vaguely, as those of another, repressed into a hidden corner of the fragmented self ... This is why therapy for torture victims is centred on recovering their voices, allowing them to conceptualise and verbalize their anguish.[97]

Truth commissions can help victims to realise that what happened to them happened to many others and relatives can feel that the record has been put straight about their loved ones. In some cases, the actual process of investigation and testimony can be as important as the publication of the findings. In testifying to a commission, survivors document their story. Sometimes this is the first time that they have been able to officially record it. To have their testimony formally acknowledged in this way often provides a strong sense of vindication, especially if it follows on years of systematic denial by the authorities and wider society, and even self-denial by the victims.

Many of Latin America's political reconciliation processes reflect the need to break the silence on what happened to initiate a process of individual and social healing. However, survivors and relatives can feel that even the positive aspects of a truth process can ring hollow if they are not accompanied by other measures including admission of responsibility by those responsible for the abuses. The political trade-offs that are often involved in establishing Truth Commissions can undermine the sense of acknowledgement that survivors and victims' families might feel.[98]

In many Latin American countries, amnesty and impunity laws raise questions about how seriously the suffering of victims is seen in wider society. Survivors and victims' families are often disillusioned by the failure to bring perpetrators to trial.[99] Only Argentina managed to carry through the momentum from its National

---

Social Reparation', *Journal of Social Issues* 46/3 (1990), 133–49 (142).

97  William T. Cavanaugh, *Torture and Eucharist: Theology, Politics and the Body of Christ* (Oxford: Basil Blackwell, 1998), 40 and 42.

98  See M. Popkin and N. Roht-Arriaza, 'Truth as Justice: Investigatory Commissions in Latin America', *Law and Social Inquiry: The Journal of the American Bar Foundation* (1995), 79–16; J. M. Pasqualucci, 'The Whole Truth and Nothing But the Truth: Truth Commissions, Impunity and the Inter-American Human Rights System', *Boston University International Law Journal* 12/2 (1994), 321–70. For an excellent comparative analysis of El Salvador, Guatemala and Honduras see Rachel Sieder, 'War, Peace and Memory Politics in Central America', in Alexandra Barahona de Brito, Carmen Gonzalez-Enriquez and Paloma Aguilar (eds), *The Politics of Memory and Democratization: Transitional Justice in Democratizing Societies* (Oxford Studies in Democratization; Oxford: Oxford University Press, 2001), 162–93.

99  See Carlos Santiago Nino, *Radical Evil on Trial* (New Haven and Yale: Yale University Press, 1996); Jaime Malamud-Goti, *Game Without End: State Terror and the Politics of Justice* (Norman, OK and London: University of Oklahoma Press, 1996).

Commission into trials of high-ranking military leaders. Even there, despite partial success in convicting some of the leading figures responsible for the Dirty War the civilian government eventually backed down when faced by intense pressure from the military.

When the Truth Commission report was released in El Salvador neither the military nor the government of Alfredo Cristiani were willing to acknowledge responsibility or express any remorse for what had happened. Three days after publication, Cristiani addressed the nation. He urged that, in the interests of reconciliation, there should be no further actions because 'What is most important now is to see what has to be done to erase, eliminate and forget everything in the past'.[100] On 20 March, just five days after the Truth Commission report became public, the Salvadoran government pushed through a sweeping amnesty law, which ended any hope of trials.[101]

In Guatemala, by contrast, neither the Guatemalan military nor the government publicly criticized the report. Nonetheless, they did not distance themselves from those in the private sector who felt no such need for restraint. Furthermore, on 26 April 1998, three days after presenting the hard-hitting REMHI report, Bishop Gerardi (chair of the Archdiocesan Human Rights Office) had been brutally murdered. Despite the military's attempts to shift the blame elsewhere, it was widely – and rightly – believed that they were responsible and the murder was intended as a warning that things had not changed that much.[102] In any case, the amnesty provisions included in the Law of National Reconciliation – agreed in December 1996 – already gave absolute protection to those guilty of all abuses, expect the internationally proscribed crimes of torture, genocide and forced disappearance.[103]

In these circumstances it is easy for victims to question the value – and even the sincerity – of a truth commission. The Guatemalan CEH countered this danger by recommending prosecutions for abuses excluded by the amnesty.[104] It also

---

100 Presidential Address to the Nation (18 March 1993), quoted in Popkin, *Peace Without Justice*, 150.

101 Given the supposedly binding nature of the Salvadoran Truth Commission's recommendations, some critics point to its failure to recommend against an amnesty as making life too easy for the ARENA government.

102 After a prolonged investigation and trial process, three officers from the Military High Command were finally convicted of Gerardi's murder on 8 June 2001. See esp. Judith Escribano, 'The Cook, the Dog, the Priest and His Lover: Who Killed Bishop Gerardi and Why?', in M. A. Hayes and D. Tombs (eds), *Truth and Memory*, 59–80; Francisco Goldman, 'Murder Comes for the Bishop', *The New Yorker* (15 March 1999), 60–77.

103 The amnesty was agreed during the peace negotiations between the government and URNG, despite the active opposition of Human Rights groups and others who formed the 'Alliance against Impunity' to oppose it.

104 On 2 December 1999 Nobel Laureate Rigoberta Menchú Tum and various human rights' organizations filed a case in Spain against eight Guatemalan ex-military officers, including former-Presidents Generals Lucas García (1978–82), Efrain Ríos Montt (1982–83), and Oscar Humberto Mejia Victores (1983–85). Both the CEH and REMHI reports were submitted in evidence of the argument that because of the genocide, the case could be tried in

recommended an extensive system of reparations, compensations and victim support.[105] The Salvadoran Truth Commission also made recommendations on reparations – arguing that this is where the need for justice could best be served.[106] However, the Salvadoran provisions were less comprehensive than in Guatemala and – despite their supposedly binding nature – much less carefully observed by the government.[107] Inevitably in such instances, meaningful reconciliation remains a distant hope.

## Challenges for Christian Theology

*From Madness to Hope* and *Guatemala: Memoria del Silencio* are secular documents. At times, however, they touch on religious themes. This is particularly marked when they address reconciliation and it is notable that when speaking of reconciliation the reports sometimes draw on religious terms. For example, *From Madness to Hope* states that: 'The process of reconciliation is restoring the nation's faith in itself and its leaders and institutions'.[108] A little later, it describes El Salvador as a 'society of sacrifice and hope'.[109] Such religious language invites theological analysis and critiques of how the concepts of reconciliation, faith, sacrifice (and others that might be related to them such as forgiveness and justice) are understood in the reports and the assumptions that shape their use. However, perhaps an even more important task is to explore what significance the reports might have for theology rather than vice-versa. To phrase the question this way round – starting with what theology might learn from Truth Commissions, rather than what Truth Commissions might learn from theology – is to adopt the approach pioneered in Latin America by liberation theologians after the Medellín conference of Latin American Bishops in 1968.[110] In this light, the two reports address issues of power and violence, gender and domination, truth and reconciliation, acknowledgment and forgiveness, and memory and amnesia that are rooted in the Central American contexts but are also relevant

---

Spain under international law. However, on 13 December 2000 the Spanish court announced that it did not have jurisdiction, since there was insufficient proof that the plaintiffs had first been denied justice in the Guatemalan courts. Meanwhile in Guatemala, on 3 May 2000 the Center for Human Rights Legal Action (known by the Spanish acronym CALDH) filed a genocide case against General Romeo Lucas García and his military high command. On 6 June 2001 CALDH added a second genocide case, against Ríos Montt and members of his military high command.

105 See *Guatemala: Memory of Silence. Recommendations*, §§7–21.

106 TC, *From Madness to Hope*, 186.

107 Margaret Popkin, *Peace Without Justice*, 134–36.

108 TC, *From Madness to Hope*, 14.

109 TC, *From Madness to Hope*, 17.

110 The literature on liberation theology is now far to extensive to mention but for the classic advocacy of theology as a 'second step' rather than the first step, see G. Gutiérrez, *A Theology of Liberation: History, Politics and Salvation* (trans. and ed. C. Inda and J. Eagleson; Maryknoll, NY: Orbis Books; London: SCM Press, 2nd edn., 1988 [ET 1973]), 9–12.

to many other contexts as well. This chapter can hardly begin to address the many theological issues they help to raise as they highlight both the dignity and potential depravity of the human person but it can at least point to the importance of the work to be done.

First and foremost, there is the supreme importance of seeking the truth, even when the truth is full of pain. John's gospel records the promise that 'you will know the truth and the truth will set you free' (Jn 8:32). In John's gospel the truth is an 'uncovering' of what is hidden. However, as the gospel shows this is not an easy or comfortable process. Truth can be full of pain and when it is it is usually avoided or set aside. It is only those who actively seek truth and accept the difficulties this involves who are likely to 'discover' it. In Christian terms, as the rest of the verse shows, the truth comes in following Christ's words and actions. This should be the mission of the church. Yet too often the churches avoid rather than confront the disturbing realities of the world. In affluent societies cultural pressures to conform to wider society have compromised the prophetic heritage of the church. Instead of taking a courageous lead to speak on painful issues as an integral part of proclaiming the gospel, the churches tend to avoid issues that might raise disquieting questions. Alternatively, they address them only in an abstract way that tends to erase, obscure, or at least sanitise, the true nature of the problem.[111]

The sexual violence that was part of the state terror in El Salvador and Guatemala is a salutary reminder of the depths of evil that Christian theology must confront. It challenges theologians to deepen their understanding of God's presence in the world and in human suffering. A Christian witness to truth must confront the realities of political violence and its legacies. A Christian ministry of reconciliation must recognize the full range and intensity of suffering and shame. A Christian theology of redemption can only be credible if the human experiences that the cross is supposed to redeem are not systematically sanitized or excluded altogether.

Read alongside the gospels the two reports from Central America can help to root theological discussion of Jesus' crucifixion in a more concrete awareness of state terror and its abusive mechanisms. They show why questions relating to Jesus of Nazareth's treatment as a political prisoner need to be examined with the same careful critical scrutiny that is commonly shown for other parts of the text. Crucifixion was an abusive torture that involved the extreme humiliation of victims and was associated in many cases with mutilation or other form of sexual violence.[112] Yet New Testament scholars have done little to explore the significance of the repeated stripping of Jesus, the display of his humiliated body, or the sexually suggestive

---

111 Unfortunately the churches have an especially poor record on gender and sexuality justice issues. Traditional church teaching has often reinforced rather than challenged the patriarchal foundations on which sexual violence is based.

112 See David Tombs, 'Crucifixion, State Terror and Sexual Abuse', especially pages 100–109; see also *idem*, 'Crucifixion, Rape and the Body-Politics of Power in the Roman Empire', unpublished paper presented at the Society of Biblical Literature International Meeting, Rome, 9 July 2001.

elements of crucifixion as a form of execution. These historical questions may at first seem very disturbing, even offensive, to Christian faith. However, if the cross is taken seriously as a message of hope and not despair, understanding and confronting the true nature of crucifixion is a necessity. At a theological level, recognizing the unspeakable violence of crucifixion ensures that theology is honest to reality. This can help guard against sacralizing the evil which Jesus suffered.

The painful truth of the cross points to the significance of resurrection in affirming human dignity. There is no shame or stigma that puts human beings outside of God's love. There is no trauma or despair that is unknown to God.[113] The cross reveals God as intimately present with victims of abuse, sharing in all their suffering and standing in open protest against it. Christianity as a religion is founded on these 'scandalous' affirmations yet they have often been too scandalous for Christian theology to address.

## Conclusion

Both the Commission on Truth for El Salvador and the Guatemalan Historical Clarification Commission believed that reconciliation had to be built on truth not denial. Despite considerable resistance from those who preferred the past to be forgotten, *From Madness to Hope* and *Guatemala: Memoria del Silencio* are important records of what really happened during the years of terror.

However, the reports also show that some parts of the truth are often so painful that they are 'unspeakable'. The Salvadoran report repeatedly passes over sexual atrocities in silence, because their political significance was beyond the Commission's imagination. The Guatemalan report (written in the aftermath of widely publicized and recent sexual violence in the former Yugoslavia, Rwanda, Haiti, and elsewhere) documents many testimonies to sexual violence with unspeakable frankness, but also recognises that the silence of many victims of sexual violence was one of the biggest challenges that it faced in recording the truth.

There is good reason to believe that breaking the silence on abuses and confronting the truth is a vital first step for individual healing and social reconciliation. Any meaningful reconciliation process is likely to begin this way, although other steps may also be necessary if it is to carry forward successfully. Christian theologians therefore have much to learn about truth and reconciliation from concrete experiences in El Salvador and Guatemala and from the UN Commissions that became part of this history. For theological reflection in relation to sexual violence, the reticence of the Salvadoran Truth Commission shows how strong the urge to silence can be. At the same time, the frankness of the Guatemalan CEH shows how brutal the truth often is when the silence is broken. Both aspects are important for a reading of the

---

113 Flora Keshgegian's work on theology and trauma offers a particularly thought provoking suggestion on how Jesus's followers experienced Jesus's death as a trauma and how they struggled to respond to it; see Flora A. Keshgegian, *Redeeming Memories: A Theology of Healing and Transformation* (Nashville: Abingdon Press, 2000), esp. 166.

crucifixion and challenge Christian theology to confront the realities of the world, to imagine the unimaginable, and speak of the unspeakable in bold witness to God's painful presence in the world.

Chapter 4

# The Maya 'Greening Road' of Reconciliation: the Pan-Maya Movement in Guatemala

Brett Greider

The indigenous Maya communities of Guatemala and Southern Mexico vividly manifest the 'reconciliation' process as a '*camino*' or road to restoration and reparation of cultures surviving the ravages of colonialism and the forces of globalization in order to create a sustainable future. These communities must pass through historical memories of their origins and their struggles to survive as they travel this *camino* bearing their broken hearts and agonizing losses. The colonial structural forces disrupted their cultural continuity by systematically dismantling integral and vital relationships with ancestral lands. 'Reconciliation' is the path to repairing these tattered communities, restoring the strength of their connection to the land, and affirming their cultural survival into the new millennium. The revitalization and resurgence of indigenous cultures in Latin America is well illustrated by a journey to Guatemala.

## The Recovery of Memory as Horizon for a New Dawn

Guatemala is the vital heartland of Maya civilization: a verdant country of more than twenty pre-conquest traditional languages, communities with complex social hierarchies, festivals with costumed dancers and ceremonial religious practices, and thousands of archaeological sites. Today in Guatemala I am an international traveller leaving the capital city by a public bus that crawls through the fumes of morning traffic. I am struck by the glistening structures and signs of global corporations along the route leading out to the Maya Highlands, soon climbing into forested mountains. Half an hour, later in Antigua, I wander up cobblestone streets to the lively colonial plaza of the former capital, stopping by a cyber-café for cappuccino, browsing the *New York Times*, and checking E-mail. Then, catching a bus winding through the mountains and pine trees into the historic Maya town of Chichicastenango, I meander up an ancient pathway and warm myself by an altar fire at the shrine of Pascual Abaj, later staying the night in a traditional adobe *huespedaje* overlooking the sacred landscape of the Cuchumatane Mountains. I have entered the sacred zone of the *Popol Vuh*'s mythic topography, and a night punctuated by ritual fireworks, in the town where the text of the *Quiche Maya Book of the Dawn of Life* was transcribed in the seventeenth century from hieroglyphs into Spanish.[1] In the course of travelling little more than two hundred kilometers I have crossed centuries in cultural traditions: from the globalized concatenation of a Latin American urban zone; to a Spanish colonial capital populated by colorful Maya, international students, and Ladino merchants; and ascended into an indigenous Quiche´ Highland market town, swirling with copal incense to the rhythms of trade and ceremonial rituals.

The *Popol Vuh* is the unifying text of the Maya-world's topography that expands from its southern extension at Copan in Honduras to the Northern region of Chiapas in Mexico: the vast region of the ancient Maya peoples unifying Guatemala and southern Mexico in a living cultural nexus. The *Popol Vuh* is the alphabetic Quiche´ version of their mythic origins, the 'Maya book of the Dawn of Life' recorded by priests in *Kumarkaj* (Santa Cruz el Quiche), transmitted from ancient origins inscribed on hieroglyphic stones and temples, and illustrated in murals and ceramics among thousands of archaeological sites. Modern Maya festivals still tell their stories of a world grown from the abundance of natural affinities and struggles between earth and sky, life and death, humans and animals, living together in a world of dangerous beauty. Numerous deities of the natural world and cosmos, joining within one unifying deity (known by various names, for example, Hanap'ku), still animate the Maya worlds today. Theirs is a civilization surviving over two thousand years, still building upon the legacies of thousands of diverse kingdoms whose brilliance and mystery are still emerging from archaeological sites, and whose secrets are still kept by their elders and councils in defiance of cultural colonization. Yet the Maya cultural transformations caused by surviving a half-millennium of colonization still are embodied in numerous dialects and the continuity of their ancestral 'cosmovisions' (Sp. *cosmovisiones*)[2] rooted in the mythical narratives that were later recounted in the *Popol Vuh*.

Guatemala is a case in which religion is rooted in sacred relationships to the land that are the key elements of cultural survival and social change. The revitalization of Mayan religious identity involves reconstructing complex social identities within their

---

1 See Dennis Tedlock, trans., *The Popol Vuh: The Definitive Edition of the Mayan Book of Life and the Glories of Kings* (New York: Vintage, 1985), 218–222. Also see Dennis Tedlock, *Breath on the Mirror: Mythic Voices and Visions of the Living Maya* (New York: HarperCollins, 1993) for a description of the cultural topography of 'Rotten Cane' or *Kumarkaj*.

2 The term *cosmovisión* (pl. *cosmovisiones*) is used by Latin American scholars to describe the complex indigenous world view, including its socio-political reality, environmental relationships, mythic consciousness, orientation to time, and *mestizaje* (mixing) with colonial cultures. My use of it here distinguishes the Maya *cosmovisión* from the colonial, Westernized and globalized secular 'world view' that threatens the Maya with cultural genocide. For discussion of indigenous *cosmovisiones* see: Angel Rama, *Transculturación narrativa en America Latina* (Mexico: Siglo Veintiuno Editores 1982); also Braulio Munoz, *Sons of the Wind: The Search of Identity in Spanish American Indian Literature* (New Brunswick, NJ: Rutgers University Press 1982).

sacred topographies, while equally engaged in the political struggle to repair ravaged communities, restore ancient traditions, and navigate into the future. The reparation of lands in the reconciliation process recognizes the significance of religious land rights and sites, their land-based symbol systems, ceremonial activities in sacred spatiality, and the importance of land in cultural reconstruction. The sacred geography woven into Maya religion serves as a cohesive element in the re-fabrication of a society torn by war: refugees returning from Mexico and abroad; entire communities displaced by the war returning to their lands; transitional and liminal Mayan refugees who fled to the cities straddling the urban and agrarian realms; demobilized soldiers and ex-guerrillas coming home; still others of the 'resistance' communities who tenaciously held ground – in many cases at the cost of 50 per cent of the population. Refugees who fled the Highland region for southern Mexico and beyond in the 1980's during military counter-insurgency operations have returned to their communities to rebuild their lives. Reconciling these disparities in the midst of social transition is a crucial factor in the historical development of modern Guatemala. Religious ceremonies and sacred arts are vitally linked to land rights and sacred sites in the context of contemporary political resistance. The reinvention of Mayan *cosmovisiones* assures the survival of indigenous cultures and vital spirituality in the post-colonial struggle for contemporary Pan-Mayan self-determination rooted in the traditional cultural sacred topography.[3]

For the indigenous Maya of Guatemala, the colonial disruption of 'Globalization' began in 1524 with the arrival of the Spanish conquistador Pedro de Alvarado.[4] It was a clash of *cosmovisiones* (sacred world views) that persists today in the conflicting social and political movements of contemporary Guatemala. Pedro de Alvarado defeated the Mayan general from Kumark'aj, Tecun Uman – near the present-day Mayan city of Xelaju´ – known as Quetzaltenango. Ten thousand Maya

3 Enrique Dussel argues that Spain's expansion westward to 'Amerindia' constitutes the first *world* system and *world* hegemony, and that modernity emerges from the Eurocentric colonial system which views all other systems as 'peripheral', and 'eccentric' to the Eurocentric cultures, such as Latin America, indigenous, and slave communities. He says that the opposing paradigm is *planetary*, the perspective from the *periphery* or *planetary horizon* where the three 'limits' of Eurocentric modernity are viewed as: environmental degradation, despoiled humanity, and the liberating re-emergence of cultures (the 'impossibility of their subsumption'). For this reason, he says that liberation ethics – a factor in indigenous activism – is *Transmodern*, toward an integral yet variegated sustainable future, as opposed to *Postmodern* in which the Eurocentric paradigm views the planet as a unitary *object* for exploitation. This terminology comes from the brilliant work of Enrique Dussel in *The Invention of the Americas: Eclipse of 'the Other' and the Myth of Modernity* (New York: Continuum, 1995) and other works. My study is indebted to his framework of analysis in an attempt to interpret the Pan-Mayan's contribution to reinventing Guatemala, and the discussion of globalization and religion.

4 Pedro de Alvarado, *Cartas de relacion,* BAE, Vol. XXII (Madrid: M. Rivadeneyra, 1863); Miguel Leon-Portilla, *El reverso de la Conquista. Relaciones aztecas, mayas e incas* (Mexico City: Joaquin Mortiz, 1964).

were slaughtered in battle in that first encounter. Alvarado's army went on to plunder the Maya Highlands, ravaging the villages of Lake Atitlan, then capturing the sacred ceremonial city of Kumark'aj (Utatlan).[5] The Spanish troops plundered the Highlands and incinerated the library of Uspantán (in the present-day 'Ixil Triangle'), the greatest repository of indigenous texts in the Western hemisphere. Mayan priests anticipating the pillaging of all things sacred, fled into hiding with their most sacred texts. Among them was the hieroglyphic source of the *Popol Vuh*, a 'bible' of the Mayan people that re-emerged in 1703 transcribed to an alphabetic version, and translated by Catholic priests in Chichicastenango.[6]

The dynamics of a bloody colonial history continue to seep into contemporary issues through other avenues of modernity. The Mayan kingdoms were subjugated and colonized by Europeans, and continue today suffering the oppressive socio-religious conflicts caused by five hundred years of colonization in new guises of exploitation. The human forces of destruction today are little different than the Spanish Conquistadors described in 1542 by the Archbishop of Chiapas, Bartolome de las Casas:

> Their reason for killing and destroying such an infinite number of souls is that the Christians have an ultimate aim, which is to acquire gold, and to swell themselves with riches in a very brief time and thus rise to a high estate disproportionate to their merits. It should be kept in mind that their insatiable greed and ambition, the greatest ever seen in the world, is the cause of their villainies. And also, those lands are so rich and felicitous, the native peoples so meek and patient, so easy to subject, and that our Spaniards have no more consideration for them than beasts.[7]

Bartolome's description of the 'insatiable greed and ambition' of the European colonizers was amplified in the last decade of the twentieth century by the acceleration of globalization: transnational investing and corporate exploitation of labour markets, multinational plundering of natural resources and ecological environments wherever they are not tenaciously defended.

The threat to extinguish the indigenous cultures of the Americas accelerated during the last fifty years of the twentieth century beyond all the atrocities experienced in the first Mayan encounters with colonial armies. Environmental destruction and economic exploitation accompanied the modern military's genocidal counter-insurgency campaigns of the 1980s and rival the destructive impact of the first wave of European colonialism in the sixteenth century. Approximately 36 million indigenous people live today in the Western hemisphere, the highest numbers being: 10.5 million in Mexico (12.4 per cent of total population); 5.4 million in

---

5   See Dennis Tedlock, trans., *The Popol Vuh*, 27–33.

6   Quoted in David Maybury-Lewis, *Millennium: Tribal Wisdom and the Modern World* (New York: Viking, 1979), 16. See also Enrique Dussel, *The Invention of the Americas*, 14–15 for placing this within the discussion of globalization.

7   Kay Warren, *Indigenous Movements and their Critics: Pan-Maya Activism in Guatemala* (Princeton, NJ: Princeton University Press 1998), 8–9.

Guatemala (60.3 per cent of total population today); and 5 million in Bolivia (71.2 per cent of total population). For comparison and perspective: less than 2 million American Indian indigenous citizens in the United States comprise 0.8 per cent of the population.[8] Guatemala is a case study of how indigenous people survived and continue to determine their cultural survival after the holocausts they have endured.[9] The social consequences of globalization for those who are not mobile, affluent, and 'connected' with communications technology, are 'social deprivation and degradation', says Zygmunt Bauman. The new war on indigenous people as the result of the colonial paradigm of modernity in Guatemala is an 'economic war' waged by perpetual poverty, ecocide of sacred lands, and alienation of Maya people from their enduring origins.[10]

The Guatemalan Mayan Highlands are a vital landscape of living Mayan culture recovering from this colonial legacy. The Maya of contemporary Guatemala are currently engaged in a struggle for *'Pan-Maya Revindication'* in a cultural resistance movement that includes re-invention of their ancestral religious and spiritual practices. Pan-Mayanism is a 'social adhesive' that brings together individuals from various subcultures and languages, restoring and preserving ceremonial elements of traditional Mayan agrarian communities, and straddling the urban realities of contemporary society. Maya agrarian cultures entering the new millennium in a surprising resurgence have survived colonization and repressive military dictatorships. The spectrum of Maya religious culture ranges from traditionalist practitioners of pre-Colombian rituals such as the *Daykeepers*, to contemporary *Pan-Mayanists* who propose a de-colonized, re-invented, trans-lingual Maya identity. As Demetrio Cojti Cuxil, a leading Maya intellectual at the University of San Carlos in Guatemala City, says, 'The Mayanist movement is at once predominantly conservative on the cultural plane and predominantly innovative and revolutionary on the political and economic plane. For that reason, it is said that the Maya movement's path leads not only to Tikal (traditionalism) but also to New York and Tokyo (modernism)'.[11]

---

8  See chapters 2 and 3 in James Loucky and Marilyn M. Moors, (eds), *The Maya Diaspora: Guatemalan Roots, New American Lives* (Philadelphia: Temple University Press, 2000): Christopher H. Lutz and W. George Lovell, 'Survivors on the Move: Maya Migration in Time and Space', 11–34; and Catherine L. Nolin Hanlon and W. *George* Lovell, 'Flight, Exile, Repatriation, and Return: Guatemalan Refugee Scenarios, 1989-1998', 35–55.

9  Zygmunt Bauman, *Globalization: The Human Consequences* (New York: Columbia University Press, 1998), 2. It follows the pattern observed by Bauman: 'localities are losing their meaning-generating and meaning-negotiating capacity' and are increasingly surrendering their communities to the cultural imperialism of transnational corporations – 'so much for the communitarianist dreams/consolations of the globalized intellectuals'.

10  Demetrio Cojti Cuxil's significant translated work includes 'The Politics of Maya Revindication', in Edward Fischer and R. McKenna Brown (eds), *Maya Cultural Activism in Guatemala* (Austin: University of Texas Press 1996), 19–50; see Kay Warren, *Indigenous Movements and Their Critics*, 3.

11  Demetrio Cojti Cuxil, 'Global Fragments: a Second Latinamericanism', in Frederick Jaemson and Masau Miyoshi (eds), *Cultures of Globalization* (Chapel Hill: Duke University

Guatemala's indigenous Mayan cultures are currently struggling for self-determination and a nascent democracy within a pluralistic society brutalized by a globalized national security state. The spectrum of Mayan religious cultures is variegated: 'traditionalist' practitioners revitalizing pre-Colombian rituals (for example, the 'Daykeepers' of Momostenango); syncretistic and cross-hybridizing Catholic Maya social groups; and contemporary 'Neo-Mayan' cultural activists seeking post-colonial Pan-Mayan unification and 're-invented' Maya identity. Religious groups are struggling with the issues of indigenous survival, and are increasingly critical of evangelistic and colonial forms of Christianity. Evangelical and charismatic Christian movements insert into this complex social weave conflictual cultural and political challenges. Religious ceremonies, sacred arts, land rights, sacred sites, and the reinvention of Mayan *cosmovisions* signify the survival of indigenous cultures and their vital spirituality in the post-colonial struggle for self-determination.

Mayan cultural identity is complexified by the diverse range of participants in the Pan-Maya movement: faces of 'localized' community activists and 'traditionalist' religious leaders; the returned refugee groups and traumatized villages recovering from war; those torn between worlds by assimilation; the young urbanized Mayan intellectuals navigating new political waters; the international exile and refugee communities still abroad in the Americas and Europe; the solidarity of international activists and scholars networking through the World Wide Web; and the trans-border revitalization of indigenous communities mutually assisting each other in the assertion of their political and legal rights. Their combined momentum is a 'counterhegemonic response to globalization', as Alberto Moreiras describes 'solidarity politics', because its focus is solidarity with the dead and dying, with remembering and revitalizing a culture, and with reconstructing an identity that originated in regional traditions and sacred ecology, in a Mayan *cosmovision*.[12] Following Moreira's discussion of neotraditionalist practices, we may consider Pan-Mayanism as an example of 'a deliberate political and collective choice', in a situation in which 'little remains of a past that must be completely reinvented'.[13] Yet the tenacity of Maya culture demonstrates that more of the cultural memory remains than at first appears, as their roots are embedded in the foundations of history and tenacious religious practices.

---

Press, 1998), 90–92. The Pan-Mayan movement presents an example of 'the preserving and effecting of a Latin American singularity that would arrest "the total closure of the world by the dominant order", as Moreiras frames it. In this sense, the Pan-Mayan movement is "the repository of a cultural difference that would resist assimilation by Eurocentric modernity".'

12  Demetrio Cojti Cuxil, 'Global Fragments: a Second Latinamericanism', in Frederick Jameson and Masau Miyoshi (eds), *Cultures of Globalization* (Chapel Hill: Duke University Press, 1998).

13  Fredric Jameson, *The Seeds of Time* (New York: Columbia University Press, 1994), 20.

## The Greening Road to Truth and Reconciliation

'The orgy of violence of the early 1980s caused a demographic, social and cultural holocaust of the Maya people, on a scale similar to the devastation wrought by the Spanish Conquest in the sixteenth century,' says Antonio Otzoy.[14] Yet it was during this period of violence that a determined surviving Maya community was deepening its commitment to an alternative Pan-Mayan resistance movement projecting a strategy of survival. A struggle for Mayan leadership and unity emerged when the government's brutal counter-insurgency forced Mayan people to transcend their localized politics and regional market economies by experiencing intolerable injustices, displacement, exile, revolutionary resistance, and international political solidarity and resistance. Awareness on a global scale of the Guatemalan military's genocidal brutality also grew from the outcry of international solidarity, social workers, and travellers. Violence in the 1980s escalated to a scale of genocide by the military and intensified a coordinated guerilla revolutionary war. Condemnation of the Guatemalan regime pressured a national outcry for democratization, and led to the first election of a nominal 'civil' government in the mid-1980s. Although the Generals remained in control of the government, the political discussion widened, if only for appearances to international observers. Scholars and activists continued to work within the country while international solidarity through human rights' networks and the exile community continued to organize a revolutionary political unity. Mayan intellectuals and a broad range of Mayan organizations emerged under the watch of international observers, until in the early 1990s over two hundred various Mayan organizations represented a range of specific issues to the national conversation. The presence of the United Nations lent further security to the organizations, and the possibility of engaging in national politics emerged. The Pan-Mayan movement took form in vocal 'cultural-activism' on behalf of diverse interest groups as a negotiated peace settlement was brokered in 1997 and 1998.

The Pan-Mayan movement in Guatemala is emerging from the ashes of civil war and military counter-insurgency campaigns to seize the opportunity for an authentic cultural revolution to protect indigenous rights. Many of the issues of cultural determination were addressed in the United Nations 'Conmigua' brokered Peace Accords between the Guatemalan military regime and leaders of the URNG (the Unified Revolutionary National Guatemalan political opposition) in 1996, in negotiations to end almost twenty years of counter-insurgency and genocidal war. The Peace Accords guaranteed certain rights to the indigenous peoples, addressing demands for recognition of human rights and development of a national constitution to include a Mayan voice in politics and economics.[15] Following the negotiated peace settlement in 1996, Mayan cultural activists continue struggling to revitalize not only the villages ravaged by the government's counter-insurgency campaign,

---

14 See Antonio Otzoy, 'The Struggle for Maya Unity', in *NACLA Report on the Americas*, Vol. XXIX/5 (March–April 1996), 33–35.

15 See Kay Warren, *Indigenous Movements and Their Critics*, 211f.

but also the culture that is the heart of their history. The reconciliation and tension between these worlds is anguishing with birth pangs, yet the Pan-Mayan movement prophetically confronts profoundly crucial concerns as visionaries of a potential common and sustainable future.

Indigenous leaders surprised the negotiation proceedings by asserting their demands, including rights to religious practices and ceremonial sacred sites. The participation of indigenous leaders in the United Nations brokered Peace negotiations resulted in a significant *Accord on the Identity and Rights of Indigenous People* in the Peace Accords signed in 1996.[16] Today the indigenous Maya of Guatemala are recovering from civil war and military occupation by the National Army that claimed the lives of over two hundred thousand people since 1979, the majority (83 per cent) of whom were indigenous, according to *The Guatemalan Historical Clarification Commission* (1999).[17] A million of Guatemala's population of eight and a half million became international refugees; one hundred and fifty thousand fled to Mexico as political and economic refugees; and over two hundred thousand fled to the United States, Canada, and Europe.

The recovery of cultural memory in the reconciliation process for Maya peoples involves the substantially painful task of responding to two 'Truth Commissions' in the 1990s documenting the violence that claimed over two hundred thousand lives in twenty years. The rationale for the commissions was to investigate abuses, to clarify the actual events, identify perpetrators and victims, and prevent further human rights abuses and initiate conditions for reconciliation. On the one hand there is the 'official' *Comisión de Esclarecimiento Histórico* (or CEH, the acronym for the Guatemalan Historical Clarification Commission), a national entity administered by the United Nations established on 23 June 1994, anticipating the Peace Accords process

---

16 *The Guatemalan Historical Clarification Commission* (hereafter CEH) provides extensive data and investigative reports on the violence (online: http://shr.aaas.org/guatemala/ceh/report/english/toc.html). According to the commission, 'Eighty-three per cent of fully identified victims were Mayan and seventeen per cent were Ladino'.

17 From the Prologue to *Guatemala: Memory of Silence. Report of the Commission for Historical Clarification* (CEH). 'For nearly thirty-six years, Guatemala suffered a violent internal armed confrontation that profoundly affected almost every sector of society. The conflict officially came to an end with the signing of the Guatemalan Peace Accords on 29 December 1996 by the Guatemalan Government and the Unidad Nacional Guatemalteca [URNG]. The Accord of Oslo, signed as part of the Peace Process in 1994, provided for the establishment of the Guatemalan Historical Clarification Commission (CEH), charged with investigating and elucidating the human rights violations and violence connected with the armed confrontation and recommending measures to promote peace and national harmony. The Guatemalan Historical Clarification Commission has now completed its work and has handed over its report to the Parties to the Peace Accords and to the Secretary General of the United Nations'. Quoted from the Science and Human Rights Data Center of the American Association for the Advancement of Science, 1200 New York Avenue, NW, Washington, DC 20005 (http://hrdata.aaas.org). All of the principal text of *Guatemala: Memoria del Silencio* is online: http://hrdata.aaas.org/ceh/report/english/prologue.html.

between the Guatemalan government and the unified revolutionary organizations (URNG) in 1995–1997. The purpose of CEH was to 'clarify with all objectivity, equity and impartiality the human rights violations and acts of violence that have caused the Guatemalan population to suffer connected with the armed conflict'.[18] On 25 February 1999 the UN released the truth commission's report *Memory of Silence*, condemning the Guatemalan government stating that 'agents of the State committed acts of genocide against groups of Mayan People'. The report does not hedge the blame, holding the military responsible for 93 per cent of the war's violence, more than 200,000 deaths, 400 massacres and destroying 400 Indigenous villages, 40,000 rapes and acts of torture, and causing over 1 million indigenous people to flee their homes. However the official report made a gesture in exchange for cooperation: specific officials were not identified or charged with crimes.

On the other hand, the second and more amplified 'truth commission' was initiated in 1995 by a network of inter-diocesan Catholic clergy whose involvement in Guatemalan society often included the arbitration of justice and concern for human rights. The Bishops believed that the 'truth' must be known for reconciliation to begin in the wake of violence. The investigation was preemptively ordered by Catholic officials in 1995 during the United Nations brokered political negotiations as they expected the anticipated CEH investigation to narrow the focus, purging the CEH report of perpetrator's names to avert bringing military officers to justice. *Guatemala: Nunca Mas* ('Never Again'), the report of the 'Recovery of Historical Memory' (REMHI) project of the Catholic Archbishop's Human Rights Office (ODHA) is far more substantial and provocative than the report of the Guatemalan Historical Clarification Commission. It is a comprehensive investigation collated from the human rights' violations documented by ten Guatemalan dioceses and culminating in a three-year process of reported results for the project. It is amplified to cover violations committed over the course of 34 years of civil war, and the modus operandi of the government's apparatus of repression, with a wide network of reliable corroborating sources.

Bishop Gerardi Conedera was head of the REMHI project who envisioned the report ten years earlier, and he delivered a moving homily at the special Mass held on 24 April 1998 to unveil the report. During the liturgy the attending Bishops of Guatemala distributed copies of the four-volume report to representative of indigenous, human rights and other civil society organizations. It cited names and locations of atrocities, giving descriptions of specific events, placing responsibility on the military for 87 per cent of the two hundred thousand deaths and disappearances. The document includes the religious contexts of many human rights' violations in relationship to land issues, including the desecration of sacred sites and disposal of victims' bodies to despoil ritual sites, including more than three hundred mass graves across the country which the army kept hidden. Many of these sites have

---

18  See *Guatemala: Never Again! Recovery of Historical Memory Project Official Report, Human Rights Office, Archdiocese of Guatemala* (Maryknoll, NY: Orbis Press, 1999).

also now become important as religious 'exhumations' grounds where victims were identified and ritually reburied after consecration by Mayan priests. Two days after the release of the report, on 26 April 1998, Bishop Gerardi was bludgeoned to death with a cinderblock while returning home from a family dinner.

The publication of the truth commission reports for the purpose of reconciliation was both agonizing and cathartic for the Mayan communities, a
passageway to healing from the pain of the past by raising the most anguishing of questions:

> Why did the violence, especially that used by the State, affect civilians and particularly the Mayan people, whose women were considered to be the spoils of war and who bore the full brunt of the institutionalized violence? Why did defenseless children suffer acts of savagery? Why, using the name of God, was there an attempt to erase from the face of the earth the sons and daughters of Xmukane', the grandmother of life and natural creation? Why did these acts of outrageous brutality, which showed no respect for the most basic rules of humanitarian law, Christian ethics and the values of Mayan spirituality, take place?

The *Guatemalan Historical Clarification Commission* recommendations to promote peace and national harmony conclude:

> Given that the relationship between the State and the indigenous population of Guatemala – particularly the Mayan people – has subsisted within an environment of racism, inequality and exclusion, and that this is one of the historical causes of the armed confrontation, measures guaranteeing the protection of the individual and collective rights of the indigenous population, respect for cultural plurality and promotion of intercultural relations, become vital.[19]

In Guatemala this means that the intentions of the Peace Accords and the aspirations of Maya people are in conflict with the economic function of the elite who govern – as it has been since Pedro de Alvarado's arrival.

### Revitalizing the Way of 'Mayan Knowing'

The Guatemalan Peace Accords included provisions for protection and development of indigenous core culture, which includes the development of indigenous language in schools. This issue is addressed in the third section of the Peace Accord which focuses on indigenous people's right to control their own cultural destiny. Due to the importance of historical Mayan artifacts, the third section of the *Accord on Identity and the Rights of Indigenous Peoples* addresses the concern over conservation of temples, ceremonial centres and archaeological sites. There is now an effort to

---

19  See *Guatemala: Never Again! Recovery of Historical Memory Project Official Report, Human Rights Office, Archdiocese of Guatemala* (Maryknoll, NY: Orbis Press, 1999).

involve indigenous peoples in all stages of conservation and the excavation of their cultural heritage.

Distinguishing themselves from the various forces of Christian groups, this 'renascimiento' or rebirth of Mayan spirituality represents a movement to re-interpret the more traditional pre-Columbian and pre-Christian spiritual teachings and practices in constructing a national Maya identity in Guatemala, while internationally asserting their self-determination to the global community. The oral transmission of traditional Mayan religion has continued unbroken (according to Demetrio Cojti Cuxil, Dennis and Barbara Tedlock, and others), practiced clandestinely in the mountains by priests and their councils.

One of the signs that the Pan-Mayan movement is rooted in pre-Columbian religious origins is their renaissance in languages and hieroglyphics' workshops. A crucial sign of indigenous vitality is the practice of languages: in the case of the Maya over twenty dialects and several hieroglyphic and transliterated alphabetic scripts are currently in usage. 'The modern use of Maya hieroglyphic writing is an expression of self determination and political resistance against non-Indian hegemony'.[20] This issue is addressed in the third section of the *Peace Accords* which focuses on indigenous people's right to control their own cultural destiny.

> The production and control of history and prehistory are of central importance to the [Pan-Mayan] Movement's cultural promotion because of the widely held view, found in early Western scholarship and influential today among Maya and non-Maya alike, that 'true' Maya culture consists only of those features surviving from the precontact period. [21]

The traditional resistance movement can be traced back through 500 years of colonial rule and has been the constant backbone of the resistance movement in Guatemala.

> Modern Maya who use the glyphs are reclaiming their past, with the hope of encouraging greater autonomy in the Maya's future. The past that they 're-appropriate' and 're-sacralize' helps to build a larger pan-Mayan identity based on a common pre-Columbian history … This blurring of historical and geographic detail becomes a practical and powerful tool with which to subvert non-Indian hegemony and construct a sense of pan-Mayan community' says Crice Sturm.[22]

It is these efforts and intentions that allow for a stronger cultural identity while increasing social cohesion within the Mayan community.

## Religious Resurgence and the Spectrum of Syncretism

It seems clear that a syncretistic religion hybridized between indigenous traditions and Christian theology was never the intention of those who sought to rule Latin

---

20  Crice Sturm in Fischer and Brown, *Maya Cultural Activism*, 114.

21  Crice Sturm in Fischer and Brown, *Maya Cultural Activism*, 13.

22  Crice Sturm in Fischer and Brown, *Maya Cultural Activism*, 117.

America. 'Nevertheless, in the clarity/obscurity of everyday practices a syncretistic religion formed, which not even the purest Inquisition could have snuffed out', says the philosopher Enrique Dussel.[23] Within a syncretized religion there is never an equal balance between both traditions that, if once achieved, can be maintained with any consistency. There is a constant vacillating between an 'indigenizing of Christianity and the Christianizing of indigenous beliefs'.[24] This interplay has continued since the first encounter with Spanish missionaries. Yet, as Rigoberta Menchu says in *500 Years of Evangelization*: 'As a Maya I am not offended by the word evangelization; however, we have to ask who should evangelize whom. Evangelization between the missionary and the indigenous can work both ways. If history were to judge, who stands in more need of evangelization: the missionaries or the indigenous?'[25]

Mayan culture has been shielded by the 'mask-making' of *syncretism* within the boundaries of Catholicism that represents a large per centage of post-colonial Maya cultural forms. The Spanish missionizing of Mayan Indians was a double-edged sword, acculturating to accommodate Maya cultural practices, yet also unbending on issues of authority and structure. Mayan Catholicism transmits the impulse of Mayan spirituality, affirms cultural identity, and yet remains conservative in commitment to a protective Church. Yet the necessity of survival, facing the fear of cultural genocide by the Spanish military, required wearing the mask of Christian religion, with the possibility of transmitting deeper Mayan cultural values. There is still an element of subversion in some of the popular religion, even humour, for example, in the *combite* dance when Mayas wear masks of the Spanish elite. Most importantly, even in their acculturation to Christianity the Maya have maintained their obligations to sacred sites and rituals, and cultivating their maize, demonstrating the centrality of land issues in Mayan cultural continuity.

In Chichicastenango there are diverse examples of syncretism permeating Guatemalan culture, and the ceremonies at Chichicastenango follow the Mayan calendar as well as the liturgical calendar of saints' feast days. '*Santos*' are brought from the old Cathedral of Santo Tomas in a procession through town, with drums and flutes, stopping to set off *cojetes* (exploding rockets) at cardinal points. They stop to enter the courtyards of *cofradia* host families where everyone is served '*atol*' (a corn drink) while the *cofradia* pray inside. Meanwhile, the presence of the *Santos* are a blessing to the household and all guests, and the social gathering is a time of reaffirming associations and cultural values, and welcoming outsiders.

The Church therefore extends culturally into the community in folk traditions beyond the control of the priest and other religious while still maintaining catholic tradition. Membership in the *cofradia* or Mayan Catholic brotherhood is considered

---

23  Enrique Dussel, *The Invention of the Americas*, 55.

24  Richard Wilson, *Maya Resurgence in Guatemala: Q'Eqchi Experiences* (Norman, OK: Univeristy of Oklahoma Press, 1995), 304.

25  Rigoberta Menchu, '500 Years of Evangelization and Colonization' (Washington, DC: EPICA, 2003). Available on EPICA webpage http://www.epica.org/library/indigenous/menchu2.htm.

a community prestige and family heritage that includes service obligations, and often the expenditure and distribution of wealth. For this and other reasons, it has meant conservative political commitments that functioned both to preserve the traditions, but also to raise the suspicions of Mayan cultural activists. The younger generation of Mayan religious leaders may have broader experience with refugees, politics, education, and diverse groups, and actively practice 'decolonized' Mayan ceremonies.

The history of the Church Diocese of El Quiche is bloodied with martyrs (a theme throughout Latin American liberation theology) yet deeply rooted in Mayan Catholicism. During the 1980s many clergy members and religious were murdered due to their involvement in, or sympathy for, the indigenous movement. The priest serving Chichicastenango, Padre Axel Mencos, is the only active Catholic priest in the region who remained throughout the repression of the 1970s and 1980s when many priests were either killed by right wing death squads (such as Father Stan Rother) or fled with the refugees. Although he received numerous death threats for his work with the *Indigenas*, Padre Mencos remained to give sanctuary and the transmission of religious ritual, with an *indigenista* (indigenous active) theological vision.

The cathedral as a center of community activities is a cultural bridge, and the mass is a good example of syncretistic ritual, or blending of religions. This cathedral is the site of the transmission into Spanish of the most significant Mayan sacred text, the Popol Vuh, in 1703. In this famous church can be seen all the elements of Mayan and Catholic rituals, people in prayer amidst a myriad of candles and billowing Copal incense (a mythic symbol of Mayan ritual sacrifice), a Maya choir and sacred marimba music, once the ceremonial instrument of Mayan priests.

The Catholic Church has also issued public statements and documents strongly affirming indigenous identity and self-determination.[26] The latest development in Christian 'liberation theology' includes the affirmation of ethnic indigenous orientation toward a '*cosmovision*' which is distinct from the official church doctrine. Theologians and clergy are recognizing the spiritual authenticity in the 'Indian face of God' through *syncretism,* and other forms of Amerindian cultural interpretations of Christianity.[27] 'Syncretism' and other forms of '*mestizaje*', or hybridizing of religious practices among Catholic Maya, have long functioned as survival strategies since the arrival of the Spanish missionaries.

The inter-religious weaving worn for protection and survival for centuries of colonialism was torn into by more extreme forms of colonial missionizing to degrade Maya culture. In the 1980s Army repression against Mayan Catholics in the

---

26 Conferencia Episcopal de Guatemala, '*500 años sembrando el Evangelio*' (1992). See *Conferencia Episcopal de Guatemala, Al Servicio de la vida, la justicia y la pax: documentos de la Conferencia Episcopal de Guatemala*, 1956–1997.

27 See for example the recent works by Gustavo Gutierrez, *Las Casas: In Search of the Poor Jesus Christ* (Maryknoll, NY: Orbis Books, 1993) and M. Marzal et al. *The Indian Face of God in Latin America* (Maryknoll, NY: Orbis Books, 1996).

Quiché province became so intense that many Mayas 'converted' to the evangelical sects and civil militia units to escape persecution. Many of their communities remain splintered by evangelical groups that required the shedding of all Maya cultural vestiges.[28] Mayan evangelicals seem to avoid the conflicts of cultural activism by shedding traditional languages, clothing, and social associations, and seeking baptism in economic development or the delusions of sectarian churches that divide former communitarian Mayan villages.

The Pan-Mayan movement is an opportunity for critical questioning of this 'colonized' form of Maya identity that has hidden behind the Church for centuries. Intellectual critics such as Demetrio Cojtí Cuxil affirm the need for adapting and revitalizing ancient practices distinct from the colonial culture's hegemony, while others such as Victor Montejo consider the new religious movements as invented forms of hybridization contributing to Guatemala's pluralistic society. But for many younger Mayan cultural activists emerging in a fractured Maya-Christian society, 'husking the corn' to remove the outer coverings of the Church is an authentic sign of revitalization, returning to their *milpas* (corn plots) as the 'hombres de maize'.

### Glimpses of the Mayan *'Greening Road'*: the *'Oxlajuj Ajpop'*

> *They were reverent, they were givers of praise,*
> *givers of respect, lifting their faces to the sky*
> *when they made requests for their daughters*
> *and sons:*
> *'Wait!*
> *Thou Maker, thou Modeler,*
> *Look at us, listen to us,*
> *Don't let us fall, don't leave us aside,*
> *Thou god in the sky, on the earth,*
> *Heart of Sky, Heart of Earth*
> *Give us our sign, our word,*
> *As long as there is day, as long as there is light.*
> *When it comes to the sowing, the dawning,*
> *Will it be a greening road, a greening path?'*
>
> *Popol Vuh*

The *'Oxlajuj Ajpop'* (*'Ministerio de espiritualidad maya'* or 'Ministry of Mayan Spirituality') serves hundreds of Maya organizations within the umbrella *Council of Mayan Organizations of Guatemala*, many of which are involved in religious

---

28 See Robert M. Carmack (ed.), *Harvest of Violence: The Mayan Indians and the Guatamalan Crisis* (Norman, OK: University of Oklahoma Press, 1998) and David Stoll, *Between Two Armies in the Ixil Towns of Guatemala* (New York: Columbia University Press, 1993).

issues, in addition to legal, educational, medical, language, and development groups. Growing out of the early 1990s Mayan activist organization *Majawi'l qui'j*, the *Oxlajuj Ajpop* celebrates Mayan spirituality through the training of *Ajq'ij* or *sacerdotes Mayas* (priests), and organizes significant ritual events corresponding to the Mayan calendar at such sacred sites as Tikal and Kumarka'aj (Uspantan).[29] *Oxlajuj Ajpop* is dedicated to revitalizing ancient ceremonial practices in the context of Guatemala's post-revolutionary and pluralistic social environment. The actual function of this organization, its role in the Peace Accords, its value in constructing a contemporary Maya social identity, and its religious orientation, are four major aspects of *Oxlajuj Ajpop*.

The Mayan Calendar (shaped like a multicoloured Maltese cross) is the central visual scripture of the movement, and the *Oxlajuj Ajpop* publishes the vivid calendar with each of the Gregorian calendar's months interpreted into Mayan days and glyphs. The Four directions also correspond with the tree of life, with fifth and sixth directions – sky and earth – represented in blue and green (the centre road). The Four cardinal directions with their traditional colors are represented, in a way similar to the Tibetan *Kalachakra* Wheel of Time *Mandala*, a *cosmogram* that 'maps' the multidimensional universe. Comparative studies of *Mesoamerican* calendars, including the Aztec calendar, demonstrate widespread knowledge of *archaeoastronomy*. The inspiration for this contemporary *visual sacred text* draws on the pre-Columbian *Codex Fejervdry-Mayer*.[30] This counter-hegemonic symbol re-appropriates an ancient orientation to the Mayan cosmovision as a countermeasure to the colonial chronological orientation, to reinvent the 'greening road' passage through the Mayan past into the future.

Within the *Oxlajuj Ajpop* are a spectrum of smaller organizations and Mayan councils. The *Accion Cristiana Guatemalteca* (ACG), based in Santa Cruz del Quiche near *Kumar'kaj*, is an example of the revitalization of Mayan identity. A smaller organization of around a hundred members, they are now in the process of 'decolonizing' their faith, reconsidering their Christian influences (and name), and are training in the *Oxlajuj Ajpop*. ACG has a history of religious involvement in 'Communities of Popular Resistance' (CPRs) during their refugee years in the Ixcan region, as children in communities migrating constantly to escape the counter-insurgency.[31] The younger generation raised during the years of repression are questioning the religious affiliation of their Catholic Catechist parents now that hiding behind the Church may no longer be necessary. They practice Mayan ritual according to the Mayan calendar, represented by the *Pastoral del Pueblo Maya* calendar, and honor their roots in cultural resistance. 'Juan' has received training from a Mayan priest of *Oxlajuj Ajpop* named Nikolas, and is himself an experienced *Daykeeper*

---

29 For documentation/images see Greider, *Heart of Sky* website online. http://www/uwec.edu/greider/hos/.

30 See: http://pages.prodigy.com/GBonline/awborgia.html.

31 As described by Ricardo Falla in *The Story of a Great Love* (New York: Epica, 1998) Online at http://www.igc.org/epica

and practitioner of ceremonies. With his spiritual participation, and the intelligent leadership of their current president, 'Luis', and his sister's work with women's issues, this organization exemplifies Mayan spirituality and cultural activism from within the dynamic social transformation of contemporary social issues.

## New Questions: 'Look at Us, Listen to Us'

As indigenous movements emerge in the twenty-first century the Pan-Mayan movement raises many intriguing questions: How do contemporary Mayan cultural dynamics and 're-vindication' political trajectories involve traditional religious revitalization? To what extent is Mayan religious spirituality reforming the 'historical imagination' into a unifying element for Guatemala's pluralism of Mayan populations? How substantial and integral are the vestiges of the Maya historical culture (for example, mythico-religious cosmovisions, ceremonial practices, hieroglyphic texts and oral transmission of ancient teachings) transmitted in religious revitalization? As indigenous Mayan people re-interpret their heritage, to what extent are they 'inventing' new traditions in the construction of their identity? How can we understand the many movements under one umbrella as a complex, heterodox, multi-vocal and diverse cultural dynamic, representing a plurality of views? Will there emerge in this century a foundational 'collective wisdom' from indigenous origins that can resist and challenge a materialist, transnational, globalized civilization? What framework can bring these disparate forces into a sustainable planetary paradigm that can withstand the destructive forces threatening their future? Can we imagine a map for the road ahead that shows a way into the undiscovered topography on the horizon where diverse cultures and their sacred lands and traditions may yet spiritually flourish? Can such a paradigm of liberation nourish the integral vision of a sustainable planetary future? Can the 'Greening Road' beyond reconciliation lead into a sustainable future, showing a passage-way to a more integral 'planetary' framework?

## Maya Revindication and Globalization

The tension between contemporary Mayan experience of recent history and the legacy of a profound cultural memory frames the problematic issues facing the Pan-Mayan movement. The resurgence of Mayan spirituality in Guatemala is the emergence of a culture long kept hidden behind the mask of Catholic syncretism and grinding rural poverty under military control. The emergence of indigenous movements in Guatemala have national and global implications showing that indigenous '*cosmovisiones*' (integral traditional world-views) are a crucial factor in the survival, transmission, and re-invention of traditional identities and localized cultures resisting the dynamics of globalization. The contemporary Maya of Guatemala and Chiapas in Southern Mexico exemplify complex historical and contemporary examples of how traditional indigenous people confront the effects of globalization for self-determination, community identity, and cultural survival. It is this specificity of localized self-determination movements among indigenous peoples in opposition to the universalizing influences of an emerging transnational market economy that defines the tension of contemporary cultural realities. In the emerging freedom to negotiate their political contract and their relationship to the 'marketplace' the Pan-Maya movement celebrates the vitality and the history of their culture.[32]

Maya cultural identity is 'problematized' by the diverse range of participants in the Pan-Maya movement: faces of the impoverished and devastated campesinos and refugees recovering from counter-insurgency campaigns and war; faces of 'localized' community activists and traditionalist religious leaders facing repression; artisan cooperatives and organizations of urbanized Maya intellectuals navigating new political waters; the presence of international solidarity activists and scholars using World Wide Web sites; in the post-modern international exile and refugee communities of the Americas and Europe; and the emergence of trans-border 'planetary' global networking and revitalization of indigenous activists mutually assisting each other in the assertion of their international human rights and environmental activism.

### Indigenous Planetary *Cosmovion*: A Countermeasure to Globalization

Is there an emerging indigenous world-view, a cosmovision, comprehensive and critical enough that could point us beyond the excesses of the globalized elite toward a sustainable planetary economics projected by localized communities? Indigenous cultures are by definition 'localized' and their cultures' origins rooted in ancestral lands. Globalization, on the other hand, is mobile, ready to up-root corporate business and move it elsewhere, wherever the labour pool is compliant, and to abandon local worker communities for higher profits. Politically-organized labour and indigenous cultural activism are the very social situations global corporations shun. Yet the governing elite see it in their own interest to have a 'modern' economic environment attractive to new economic development. The polarization experienced at the level of indigenous communities is that the landlords may have changed business, but the economic effect is increasing poverty, degradation, and exclusion from the privileges of the top culture.[33] Is the Pan-Mayan movement capable of organizing a unified Maya society, and still advancing economically beyond the crushing poverty of post-colonialism following civil war?

---

32 See Frederick Jameson's Preface, and 'Global Fragments: a Second Latinamericanism', in Frederick Jameson and Masao Miyoshi (eds), *The Cultures of Globalization* (Durham and London: Duke University Press, 1998), xiii.

33 'Neo-tribal and fundamentalist tendencies, which reflect and articulate the experience of people on the receiving end of globalization, are as much legitimate offspring of globalization as the widely acclaimed "hybridization" of top culture – the culture at the globalized top,' writes Zygmunt Bauman, in his *Globalization: The Human Consequences* (New York: Columbia University Press, 1998), 3.

Guatemala has long been living under military rule (especially the dictatorships from 1955 to 1989), and the transition to civil rule has meant a transition to a globalized economy managed by a military elite. A younger generation of military leaders has found it more profitable to invest in international banking than to wage low-intensity conflict and counter-insurgency operations against self-determination resistance movements. Traditionally, landowners and corporations have exploited such national resources as coffee, bananas, cotton, and sugar production by military repression of labour forces. Urbanization and the feminization of the labour-pool in maquiladoras (assembly plants) coincided with the penetration of transnational companies seeking cheap labour for the production of consumer products such as clothing and electronics.[34]

Could there emerge, at the beginning of the Third Millenium, a pertinent 'planetary' economic model that counters the immense power of transnational corporations and globalization? The Peace Accords appear to bring Guatemala into the twenty-first century with a new pluralistic and multicultural society that will accommodate the indigenous sectors, recognizing their culture and means of production. However, the dominant paradigm of the colonial past forms the framework of the national economic, political, and judicial system. In Guatemala's post-military economy, international market forces have transferred wealth to multinational corporations that have established themselves in Guatemala City, drawing upon cheaper urban labour and economic incentives. International banking has slowly replaced the traditional national production with a globalized elite: the former military elite trading masks for transnational power. The policing of labour movements continues, but the new economy has dictated nominal recognition of human rights for appearances in order to enter the globalized economy.

The creative and communitarian vitality of indigenous economics, such as the cooperatives movement of the 1970s and 1980s, represents a renewed threat to the dominant paradigm. Can the Maya develop an indigenous model of 'global economics', or are these mutually contradictory? In the 1980s over 250,000 Guatemala Maya *cooperativos* – productive collectives – originated a 'communitarian economics' that was seen as a threat by the Guatemala military who crushed the movement. Today Guatemalan cooperatives are taking their products to global markets using the World Wide Web, creating a cyber-co-operativism that transcends their national and political boundaries.[35] Resistance to the destruction and degradation of indigenous

---

34 See Mark Lewis Taylor, 'Transnational Corporations and Institutionalized Violence', in David Batstone (ed.), *New Visions for the Americas: Religious Engagement and Social Transformation* (Minneapolis: Fortress Press, 1993), 109–110.

35 Enrique Dussel says that economics has a 'non-substitutable pertinence, because in it the *practical* (politics, erotics, pedagogy, anti-fetishism) and the *productive* relations (ecological, semiotic-pragmatic or linguistic, poietic-technological or, of design, aesthetic or of art) are made *concrete* … Earth and poor humanity are exploited and destroyed simultaneously, by a capitalism whose criterion of the subsumption of technology is the growth of the rate of profit, and … the growth of the rate of production, both of which are anti-ecological and anti-

cultures and ecological regions now accesses the global communications' network to extend a form of 'planetary' solidarity with a one-world ethic.[36] Simultaneously, resistance takes the form of traditional sustainable agriculture cooperatives and 'communitarian permaculture' and self-sufficient communities in Guatemala – fending off for at least the time being the renewed invasion of communities by international corporate interests.

Indigenous cultures around the planet face twenty-first century globalization with divergent trajectories toward survival, yet most are in the perilous process of modernization, assimilation, and degradation of traditional identities.[37] Emerging from the weight of centuries of colonialism constitutes a kind of social resurrection, a form of cultural revitalization and resurgence involving complex strategies of resistance and survival. Indigenous cultures are often considered by dominant groups as hopelessly marginalized and destined to marginalization by contemporary political and economic developments. Indigenous peoples around the world have commonly experienced impoverishment and social oppression as the voiceless, anonymous, and tragically rejected peoples of the earth while the transnational economic tides of history bury them.

Opposition to the struggles of indigenous cultures around the world in general have meant the following: cultural genocide, human rights abuses, declining populations, environmental degradation of sacred lands, exploitation of human labour and natural resources, catastrophic diseases, economic hardships and disruptions, foreign military occupations and oppression, and assimilation under colonial expansion. Democratization and liberalization of former military regimes only began to open avenues for expressing indigenous issues and concerns at the end of the second millennium. Yet military motives were often masked in the subterfuge of co-opted 'democracy movements' controlled by powerbrokers, with

---

human systems', in his chapter, 'Liberation Philosophy from the Praxis of the Oppressed'; in Eduardo Mendieta (ed.), *The Underside of Modernity* (New Jersey: Humanities Press, 1996), 13. 'As a reference to the conditions of possibility, Dussel's transcendental economics refers to the conditions of the preservation of life as such, the one true condition of possibility for everything else', writes Mendieta in the Introduction. It is Mendieta's use of the term 'planetary' (not universal) which gives context to my use. *The Underside of Modernity* is a collection of essays on Dussel.

36 See, for example, *The Declaration of a Global Ethic* by the 1993 Parliament of the World's Religions, 4 September 1993, in Chicago, Illinois; online: http://www.earthspirit.com/Parliament/parliamentstat.html.

37 For a definition of globalization, see Frederick Jameson's emphasis on the tension and antagonism between 'the poles of particularization of the universal, and universalization of the particular'; the binary relations to the exclusion of cultural differences and 'Imaginaries'; of transnational domination on the one hand, and the freedom of local cultures on the other; of global communication and mobility, versus local isolation and marginalization; of the binary relationships between indigenous cultures and transnational global powers. See Jameson and Miyoshi (eds), *The Cultures of Globalization* (1998), xi.

military waiting in the wings to re-emerge in civilian suits as the rotating 'heads of state'. The 'Truth Commissions' of Guatemala and El Salvador in the early 1990s revealed the terrible realities of decades of military counter-insurgency campaigns and terrorization of populations. In the wake of the twentieth century the Mayan revitalization movements face considerable obstacles to their objectives.

In the 1990s there were a number of remarkable indigenous resurgence movements around the planet that addressed critical issues facing emerging cultures in the age of postcolonial globalization. Indigenous movements in Africa, the Pacific, Canada, the United States, Mexico, Central America, and South America have surprised political observers and scholars alike. The worldwide criticism of the 1992 'Columbus Quincentennial' celebrations of 500 years of Spanish colonial expansion demonstrated global political solidarity of scholars, cultural activists, and localized indigenous cultures. The historical perspective from indigenous groups influenced conferences, international resolutions, demonstrations, and media attention. Self-determination movements in countries as diverse as Nigeria, Canada, Mexico, and Guatemala made significant political headway in the last decade of the century. The United Nations emphasis on Human Rights, environmental issues and monitoring international refugee issues encouraged previously censored voices to emerge. Second-generation Christian 'liberation theologies' in Latin America, Africa and the Philippines affirmed the humanity of the voiceless and anonymous, and seriously approached the 'cosmovisiones' of indigenous people with respect and solidarity.[38]

The surprising emergence of these movements at the end of the twentieth century was viewed cynically by many observers. Many Euro-American culture critics doubt that indigenous groups will emerge in the twenty-first century with any viable power to control their own destinies following the postcolonial fragmentation of cultures, international diaspora of refugees and exile communities, and the shift from localized to global politics. Some academic scholars and observers have discounted the viability of successful indigenous resurgence and self-determination movements. Scholars of indigenous 'revitalization' and authentic 'transmission' of indigenous 'worldviews' are criticized as 'orientalists' romanticizing unviable cultures, paternalistic toward weaker groups, ideologically polemical and marginal as scholars in the 'real' socio-political world. Intellectuals who study contemporary indigenous movements are astounded by the vehemence of critical opposition to their committed 'solidarity' scholarship. Critics of indigenous movement scholars warn of 'Balkanization' and 'ethnic intensification' in their academic work to validate and document indigenous resistance movements.[39] Indigenous cultures, bluntly dismissed by their critics, are 'road-kill' beneath the tank tracks of modern history.

Indigenous intellectuals are suspicious of the invisible loyalties of 'Eurocentric' postmodern and essentialist scholars who absolve themselves of commitment to

---

38  See, for example, M. Marzal, E. Maurer, X. Albo, B. Melia, *The Indian Face of God in Latin America* (Maryknoll, NY: Orbis Books, 1996).

39  See Kay Warren, *Indigenous Movements and Their Critics*, 18–20. This text provides a 'thick description' of contemporary indigenous Mayan movements.

political solidarity with cultural movements. Eurocentric critics of Latin America's indigenous movements must examine their own contextualized 'meta-racism' and 'neo-Latinamericanism' (a form of 'Orientalism') and its 'co-optation of difference'. Alberto Moreiras challenges his readers to recognize that 'historically reconstituted Latinamericanism' is an ideological formation at the service of 'globalized technopolitics' that selectively includes and hierarchically organizes the distribution of planetary resources'.[40] Kay Warren, in her study of Mayan indigenous movements, warns of ideologically tainted academics within 'the multiplicity of social cleavages, identities, and cross-cutting identifications imputed and practiced by all subjects – insiders and outsiders alike'.[41] Approaching the complex dialectical interplay of Eurocentrism and globalization in conflict with indigenous movements and a sustainable planetary future opens the discussion of alternative frameworks for scholars to reconcile their own origins and commitments.

Indigenous movements and those in academic solidarity with them oppose their 'Eurocentric' critics with a new framework of thinking: 'transmodern' in critical opposition to 'postmodern' globalization; post-Eurocentric and anticolonial in method; and 'planetary' in affirmative scope of potential solutions.[42] Enrique Dussel, an Argentinean philosopher at the Universidad Autonoma of Puebla in Mexico, documents and examines the emergence of 'modernity' out of the Eurocentric colonial expansion and subjugation of 'Amerindians' in relation to globalization. Religious traditions that sustained unique cultural visions for surviving in their bioregional habitats were forcibly suppressed by the imposition of colonial religious systems. Whether missionized and converted to the colonizer's religious system, or syncretized into new forms of religious world-views, indigenous cultures have suffered rapid and alienating changes in the colonial period. Dussel's 'Pan-Amerindian paradigm' framework and terminology offers an approach for recognizing the significance and potential alternative framework for discussion of indigenous cultures and globalization, with an indigenous historiography from the periphery.

In Dussel's elaborate yet lucid analysis, Spain's expansion into *Amerindia* constitutes the beginning of the 'world-system' and the first 'modernity':

---

40 Demetrio Cujti Cuxil, 'Global Fragments: a Second Latinamericanism', in Frederick Jameson and Masao Miyoshi (eds), *The Cultures of Globalization*, 99. He examines, as one case in point the negative criticism leveled at activist Jennifer Harbury for her committed work with Mayan human rights. Her critics, accusing her of 'delusionary orientalism of the heart', show the 'neo-racist subtext' of 'neo-Latinamericanism'. A similar case for scrutiny is the work of David Stoll, whose efforts to discredit Nobel Laureate Rigoberta Menchu is a neo-Latinamericanism argument saying that no clear demarcations exist between indigenous and *mestizo* mainstream cultures. See Kay Warren's discussion, *Indigenous Movements*, 8–10, 20–22. Mayan activists have distanced themselves from international Mayan scholars and activists and their disputes.

41 Kay Warren, *Indigenous Movements*, 19.

42 Enrique Dussel in *The Invention of the Americas: Eclipse of 'the Other' and the Myth of Modernity* (New York: Continuum, 1995) and other works cited herein.

'European in its center, capitalist in its economy', and 'planetary' in its scope. The Latin American indigenous experience also delineates the limits of globalizing modernity: environmental destruction, massive destruction of humanity itself, and 'the impossibility of the subsumption of the populations, economies, nations, and cultures that it has been attacking since its origin and has excluded from its horizon and cornered into poverty'.[43] Enrique Dussel's approach provides a framework for considering the contribution of Amerindian self-determination movements in opposition to Eurocentric postmodernity. Dussel argues that Spain's expansion westward to *Amerindia* constitutes the first *world* system and *world* hegemony, and that modernity emerges from the Eurocentric colonial system which views all other systems as peripheral (for example, Latin America, indigenous, and slave communities). He also proposes that the opposing paradigm is *planetary*, the view from the *periphery* with a *planetary horizon*, where the three *limits* of Eurocentric modernity can be recognized as environmental degradation, despoiled humanity, and the liberating re-emergence of cultures (the impossibility of their subsumption). For this reason, he says that liberation ethics – a factor in indigenous activism – is *Transmodern* and constructive of a *planetary* framework, as opposed to *Postmodern* globalization which originates in the Eurocentric paradigm that consumes the planet as *object* for exploitation. Out of the indigenous *cosmovision* emerges a framework for reconciling differences and constructing a sustainable cultural trajectory for survival and ecological restoration.

Globalization has ironically spawned the emergence of global networking in cyber-solidarity with local communities. Undoubtedly, many of the factors employed by the global elite for colonizing and exploiting cultures – instant communication, information, mobility, international banking and economics, and the lawlessness of corporations – have steamrolled against all resistance into the twenty-first century with a vengeance for local cultures. Yet the same instruments used by the elite to oppress have been taken in hand by activists for defending the oppressed, for networking in solidarity with the marginalized, and forming economic communities of resistance. The medium of the World Wide Web incorporates textual and visual elements vital to Pan-Maya cultural objectives, crossing the former boundaries that hindered communication. The 'fax-resistance' movements of the 1980s in China and the Soviet Union, and monitoring of human rights' violations through television and radio, were transcended by the Maya 'lap-top' revolution of Sub-Comandante Marcos smoking his pipe in the mountains of Chiapas, Mexico in the 1990s. The Zapatistas wielded the website to broadcast 'Zapatista' *comuniques* and digitized audio-video disseminating international press releases and publications, confronting the Mexican government by international forum. Diane M. Nelson makes the observation that Maya Hackers are

---

43 See Enrique Dussel, 'Beyond Eurocentrism', in Eduardo Mendieta (ed.), *The Underside of Modernity*, 21; also 'Amerindia ... constitutes the fundamental structure of the first modernity' in Jameson and Miyoshi (eds), *The Cultures of Globalization*, 11.

decoding and reprogramming such familiar binary oppositions as those between past and future, between being rooted in geography and being mobile, between being traditional and being modern, between manual labor and white-collar technology/information manipulation, between mountain shrines and mini-malls, and between unpaved roads and the information superhighway. Thinking of the site of this reprogramming work as the cyberspatialized nation-state foregrounds the importance of information and representation in the work of the Mayan activist and in the production of an imagined community like the Guatemalan nation.[44]

Guatemala's Mayan activists and local organizations have proliferated websites for networking at the ground-level, crossing the former divisions of rural and urban, national and global, and the distances over rough roads. Communities and organizations often share their computers, crossing the 'digital divide' by making them accessible to diverse constituencies. The inventiveness of indigenous movements ('Hay que inventar') in adaptation to conditions requires drawing deeply from the wells of their cultural memories, yet envisioning a better world beyond the unimaginative and destructive forces of our postmodern civilization.

### Vignette: A Contemporary Face of Pan-Mayan Spirituality

I have a clandestine meeting with a Maya council member named Mario in an empty upstairs room at a corn depot on a cobblestone street coincidentally named 'Popol Vuh'. He is young and strong, dressed in blue jeans and tee shirt, with long black hair to his shoulders framing a face carved like a Tecun Uman mask. He is watchful and careful, reverent and wise, well educated through international travel and seasoned by permanent resistance in the mountains. Traditional Mayan councils of twelve members called *consejos*, each member selected for their calendrical astrological attributes and community connections, have transmitted a living flame of their traditional *cosmovision* for generations in hiding from centuries of colonial and military forces. The young *consejo* member asks for my birth date, swiftly calculates the Mayan calendar symbols, and accurately nails my personal history. He says the 'mind' is the powerful computer of the Maya, and then we talk about getting portable computers and scanner hardware for the Pan-Mayan movement cultural projects. We discuss his training by Elders in hieroglyphics, traditional mountaintop prayer ceremonies, and the need for graphics-intensive laptop computers to scan ancient hieroglyphic texts. Their dream is for the new generation of the 'hombres de Maize' to flourish once again in the sacred mountains and forests of Guatemala. He is an ancient Mayan flame of the ancestors, yet a *transmodern* face of the *consejos* of the *Ojlajuc' Ajpop*, a council member of the 'Greening Road' in the horizon.

---

44 Diane M. Nelson, 'Maya Hackers and the Cyberspatialized Nation-State: Modernity, Ethnostalgia, and a Lizard Queen in Guatemala', *Cultural Anthropology* 11/9 (1998), 287–308, quote from page 289.

The author wishes to acknowledge the invaluable research support of grants from the National Endowment for the Humanities, and especially for the N.E.II. 'Maya Worlds' Institute 2002 and its members, in collaboration with the Community Colleges Humanities Association.

**Selected Bibliography: The Pan-Mayan Movement in Transmodernity**

Archdiocese of Guatemala. *Guatemala: Never Again! Recovery of Historical Memory Project Official Report, Human Rights Office. Archdiocese of Guatemala.* Maryknoll, NY: Orbis Press, 1999.

Batstone, David, Eduardo Mendieta, Lois Ann Lorentzen, and Dwight Hopkins (eds). *Liberation Theologies, Postmodernity, and the Americas.* New York: Routledge, 1997.

Bauman, Zygmunt. *Globalization: The Human Consequences.* New York: Columbia University Press, 1998.

Burnett, Virginia Garrard. 'Identity, Community and Religious Change Among the Maya of Chiapas and Guatemala'. *Journal of Hispanic/Latino Theology* 6/1 (August 1998), 61–79.

Carmack, Robert M. (ed.). *Harvest of Violence: The Maya Indians and the Guatamalan Crisis.* Norman: University of Oklahoma Press, 1988.

Carmack, Robert M. *Rebels of Highland Guatemala: The Quiché Mayas of Momostenango.* Norman: University of Oklahoma Press, 1995.

Cojti Cuxil, Demetrio. *Configuracion del pensamiento politico del pueblo Maya.* Quetzaltenango: Associacion de escritores Mayenses de Guatemala, 1995.

Cojti Cuxil, Demetrio. *Configuracion del pensamiento politico del pueblo Maya, 2ndo parte.* Guatemala: SPEM/Editorial Cholsamaj, 1995.

Dussel, Enrique. *The Invention of the Americas: Eclipse of 'the Other' and the Myth of Modernity.* New York: Continuum, 1995.

Falla, Ricardo. *The Story of a Great Love.* New York: Epica, 1998.

Fischer, Edward, and R. McKenna Brown. *Maya Cultural Activism in Guatemala.* Austin: University of Texas Press, 1996.

Gutiérrez, Gustavo. *En busca de los pobres de Jesuscristo: El pensamiento de Bartolome de Las Casa.* Lima: Ediciones Siquerre, 1992.

Gutiérrez, Gustavo. *Las Casas: In Search of the Poor of Jesus Christ.* Marynoll, NY: Orbis Books, 1993.

Jameson, Frederick and Masao Miyoshi (eds). *The Cultures of Globalization.* Duke University Press, 1998.

Loucky, James and Marilyn M. Moors (eds). *The Maya Diaspora: Guatemalan Roots, New American Lives.* Philadelphia: Temple University Press, 2000.

Marzal, M., E. Maurer, X. Albo, B. Melia. *The Indian Face of God in Latin America.* Maryknoll, NY: Orbis Books, 1996.

Mendieta, Eduardo, (ed.). *The Underside of Modernity.* New Jersey: Humanities Press, 1996.

Perera, Victor. *Unfinished Conquest: The Guatemalan Tragedy*. Berkeley: University of California, 1993.

Stoll, David. *Between Two Armies in the Ixil Towns of Guatemala*. New York: Columbia University Press, 1993.

Schele, Linda, and David Freidel. *A Forest of Kings: The Untold Story of the Ancient Maya*. New York: William Morrow, 1990.

Tedlock, Barbara. *Time and the Highland Maya*. Albuquerque: University of New Mexico Press, 1982; Revised 1992.

Tedlock, Dennis, trans. *The Popol Vuh: The Definitive Edition of the Mayan Book of Life and the Glories of Kings*. New York: Vintage, 1985.

Tedlock, Dennis, trans. *Breath on the Mirror: Mythic Voices and Visions of the Living Maya*. New York: HarperCollins, 1993.

Warren, Kay. *Indigenous Movements and Their Critics: Pan-Maya Activism in Guatemala*. Princeton: Princeton University Press, 1998.

Wilson, Richard. *Maya Resurgence in Guatemala: Queqchí Experiences*. Norman, OK: University of Okalahoma, 1995.

Chapter 5

# Reinventing Life and Hope: Coming to Terms with Truth and Reconciliation Brazilian Style

Margaret Eletta Guider

> 'A vida só é possível
> reinventada'.
> Cecília Meireles[1]

The thesis of this chapter is a simple one: in the aftermath of torture and terror, there need to be as many ways to truth and reconciliation as there are obstacles and desires. In a number of countries around the world, truth and reconciliation commissions have made significant contributions to national processes of recovery and reconstruction. In some cases, they also have provided a larger world with instructive lessons about their potential as well as their limits. Lessons about their limits underscore the importance of paying attention to other vehicles that may be in a position to function as alternatives or complements to commissions. These alternative or complementary approaches warrant investigation for at least two reasons. First, the study of alternative vehicles may be instructive with regard to strategies for getting around the impasses that preclude the establishment of formal commissions. Second, such study may be instructive with regard to assessing the comparative merits and outcomes of various vehicles in the short term and over the long term.

Using the country of Brazil as a point of reference in the study of alternative vehicles, the first section of this chapter offers an overview of some suppositions about truth and reconciliation commissions as well as the role of the religious sector in such commissions that serves as the pretext for this study. The second section briefly reviews the historical-political context of Brazil since 1964. This section also includes some culturally-specific reflections on obstacles to the establishment of a Brazilian truth commission, noting in particular the constraints inherent in the 1979 Law of Amnesty.[2] The third section of the chapter presents an overarching narrative about the life and works of the retired cardinal archbishop of São Paulo, Dom Paulo

---

1  Cecília Meireles, 'Reinvenção' – Translation: 'Life is only possible, reinvented'.

2  For a complete text of the law, see http://www.dhnet.org.br/direitos/brasil/.leisbr/lexdh9.htm.

Evaristo Arns, OFM.[3] Within the context of Brazil, Dom Paulo serves as a noteworthy figure in the creation, development and promotion of alternative vehicles to truth and reconciliation. Through his efforts and the efforts of his collaborators, Dom Paulo found ways of supporting victims of torture and political repression in their struggle for justice, sustaining the efforts of those committed to the defense of human rights, and raising the socio-political and historical consciousness of the Brazilian people. In the absence of a formal national commission, these alternative vehicles of spirit,[4] characterized by their power of *jeito* and their capacity for *reinvenção*,[5] exercised substantial influence on Brazil and the quest of its people for truth and reconciliation.

### The Pretext: The Role of the Religious Sector in Truth and Reconciliation Commissions

Throughout the world, the establishment of truth and reconciliation commissions has been advanced by both governments and non-governmental agencies, often under pressure from proponents of human rights and social justice. Such commissions have been viewed as necessary, indispensable and non-negotiable ways of proceeding in democratic efforts to rebuild countries after years of repressive authoritarian regimes, popular resistance, civil wars, violent revolutionary struggles, and genocide.[6] Theoretically speaking, the foundational conviction guiding such commissions is the belief that coming to terms with horrific memories of the past is essential for restoring the dignity of victims and preventing violations of human rights in the future. In practice, it means bringing to light the truth and creating the conditions for reconciliation, including the seeking of reparations in the form of compensation and justice, sometimes retributive, sometimes restorative. Ideally, commissions contribute to redemocratization through processes of truth-telling

---

3    For a more detailed explanation of the significance of narratives in the transformation of consciousness, see Jerome S. Bruner, *Making Stories: Law, Literature and Life* (Cambridge: Harvard University Press, 2003).

4    This concept of spirit signifies what the existentialist philosopher Gabriel Marcel referred to as a fundamental openness to the spirit of truth, the courage to face the facts of life, and preparedness to challenge the life-lie as it is lived by those who exist in a state of non-awareness, not seeing reality by shutting out what they would otherwise know or come to realize. See Margaret Eletta Guider, *Daughters of Rahab* (Minneapolis: Fortress Press, 1995), 158.

5    *Jeito* may be described as the Brazilian way of finding a creative and, at times, a surreptitious way through any impasse so as to get what one wants or what another needs. *Reinvenção* corresponds to its English equivalent reinvention. It also may be translated as re-creation.

6    Priscilla B. Hayner, 'Fifteen Truth Commissions – 1974 to 1994: A Comparative Study', *Human Rights Quarterly* 16:4 (November 1994), 597–655; and Neil J. Kritz (ed.), *Transitional Justice: How Emerging Democracies Reckon with Former Regimes*, 3 vols, (Washington, DC: US Institute of Peace Press, 1995).

that open the way to confession and remorse, restitution and forgiveness, healing and reconciliation, deterrence and an unwavering commitment to 'never again'. In reality, they provide a formal forum for accounts of torture and terror to be told and recorded, for victims and their loved ones to confront abusers, and for those accused of violations to acknowledge responsibility for their offenses. For posterity, the findings of commissions hold citizens of their respective nations as well as other nations accountable for remembering atrocities that many would sooner forget, deny, or minimize.

In a number of contexts, commissions have looked to religious sectors of society for both guidance and support, even in those situations where religious leaders and communities were themselves politically polarized and morally compromised. Without negating the fact that some Christian leaders and church-based organizations have impeded or repudiated the efforts and outcomes of commissions, it is fair to say that scores of others have played very significant roles in the organization, facilitation and development of such commissions.[7] Their contributions cannot be underestimated, especially in countries and regions where the Christian tradition is a major cultural influence.

Building on these observations, two questions emerge that go to the heart of this particular chapter: What role can the religious sector play in the quest for truth and reconciliation in countries where commissions have yet to be established? And precisely what particular powers of *jeito* are representatives of the religious sector in a privileged position to exercise in the effort to reinvent life and hope in circumstances of death and desperation? The response of Cardinal Arns to the military regime's legacy of torture in Brazil provides a case in point.

## The Context: Brazil's Law of Amnesty – Implications for Truth and Reconciliation

With the coup d'état of 1964, Brazil entered into a twenty-year period characterized by historians as the Anos de Chumbo – the leaden years. A military regime was set in place to combat the threat of communism. Brazil became a national security state. Democratic freedoms were suspended. In an atmosphere of political repression, citizens were subjected to surveillance, intimidation, arrest, imprisonment, torture, exile, and assassination. By the time the dictatorship came to end, more than 300 people had lost their lives as a direct consequence of political repression by government forces and over 136 are counted among the disappeared,[8] 200 had been held as political prisoners,15,000 people, some of whom had been banished from

---

7   See Raymond G. Helmick, S.J. and Rodney L. Peterson (eds), *Forgiveness and Reconciliation: Religion, Public Policy and Conflict Transformation* (Philadelphia: Templeton Foundation, 2001).

8   The precise number of those who were killed or who are counted among the disappeared continues to be adjusted. These estimates nevertheless reveal significant differences between Brazil and countries such as Chile (with approximately 3,200) and Argentina (with

Brazil, had gone into exile (of which approximately 10,000 returned), the mandates of 774 elected officials had been annulled, 15,000 workers had lost their jobs as a consequence of political persecution, and 300,000 people had been voluntarily or involuntarily investigated by the Serviço Nacional de Informações (SNI).[9]

In 1979, in response to a broad social consensus and in anticipation of a gradual process of redemocratization, the military government, amnesty movements, and the Brazilian people, with the support of religious leaders and institutions, chose the pragmatic, paradoxical, and ultimately problematic route of amnesty as a national way of proceeding.[10] There was a precedent for this choice inasmuch as Brazil had opted for amnesty at other moments in its political history.[11] In the short term, amnesty created the conditions for rebuilding a divided nation and restoring some measure of national unity.[12] Over the long term, however, it proved to be an impediment to justice and an ongoing source of national controversy and contention.[13] While the Law of Amnesty facilitated the recovery of Brazil's national treasure, namely, the two-sided coin of honor, its original design, intent and promulgation, excluded the possibility of holding the military governments accountable for violating the human rights of Brazilian citizens or bringing to justice those responsible for torture. Unlike many other Latin American countries, Brazil's initial efforts to deal with the aftermath of military rule (1964–1984) were not the result of commissions established by the government or international human rights organizations. Initially, the option for general amnesty precluded such a possibility.[14] As a consequence, the quest for truth in Brazil was dependent upon alternative vehicles.

---

approximately 30,000). See Angelo Priori, 'Memória, Esquecimento e Violência Política', http://www.aduem.org.br/artigo017.htm.

9  A number of these statistics are calculated estimates, some of which are at variance with one another. See Nilmário Miranda, 'A Lei da Anistia', http://www.dhnet.org.br/direitosmilitantes/nilmario/Novos/lei-anistia.htm; and Ana Guedes 'História da Luta: 25 Anos da Anistia Política no Brasil', http:/www.vermelho.org.br/diario/2004/0828/0828_anaguedes-anistia.asp.

10  See José Inácio Ferreira, *Anistia: Caminho e Solução* (Vitória: JANC, 1979); Therezinha Godoy Zerbine, *Anistia: Semente da Liberdade* (São Paulo: Escolas Profissionais Salesianas, 1979); João Baptista Herkenhoff, 'A Cidadania no Brasil Contemporâneo: O Povo como Construtor da Própria História', http://www.dhnet.org.br/direitos/militantes/herkenhoff/livro2/brasil2/html.

11  See Homero de Oliveira Costa, 'Incursões na História das Anistias Políticas no Brasil', http://www.dhnet.org.br/direitos/anthistbr/Redemocratizacao1988/homeroanistia.html.

12  See Senador Teotônio Vilela, 'Discurso proferido por ocasião da posse na Presidência da Comissão Mista da Anistia em 2 de agosto de 1979', and 'Discurso proferido no Congresso Nacional, sessão de 22 de agosto de 1979', http://www.intelecto.net/anistia/teo1.htm and http://www.intelecto.net/anistia/teo2.htm.

13  See 'Anistia Parcial e Restrita', http://www.desaparecidospoliticos.org.br/anistia/20anos.html.

14  It could be argued that with the 1995 Law of Indemnity (Lei n. 9.140/95) processes were set in place for giving government compensation in the form of monetary reparations to individuals who were victims of the Repression from 1961–1979 (or their family members).

The option for amnesty revealed much about the social organization and cultural character of the nation.[15] Brazilians tended to be more socio-centric than ego-centric, more collectivistic than individualistic. People invested themselves in belonging, social cohesion was valued as were relationships of interdependence. The predominating orientation to life was short-term, living in the present moment and making choices that were best in terms of the here and now. Saving face was not only critical for individuals and families, but also for leaders and institutions. Honour mattered, as did certainty about being in full possession of the truth. Power distance tended to be high, meaning that inequalities were viewed as a fact of life. High power distance also contributed to the creation of heroes and heroines popularized by the forces of culture and social location. Authoritarian ways of proceeding were in evidence in every stratum of society.

Socially, culturally, politically, and religiously, the rationality of amnesty seemed to make a great deal of sense. In the estimation of those committed to a vision of order,[16] amnesty was perceived as a vindication of the military's action to use of every means possible to accomplish the end of dismantling the threat of a communist revolution. In the estimation of those committed to a vision of progress, amnesty gave rise to the hope for a brighter future through the release and return of a persecuted and exiled generation of committed social, political, economic, cultural, and religious leaders. Though many would agree that in the short term the socio-political pact of amnesty did get the country moving in the direction of redemocratization, there is a diversity of opinion on the Right and the Left regarding its long-term advantages and disadvantages.

In the estimation of contemporary critics committed to advancing the status and welfare of Brazil's most vulnerable, exploited and expendable citizens, the conditions of amnesty ended up serving the bourgeois interests and aspirations of those who had access to power – Right, Left, and Centre. Ultimately, the conditions of amnesty left the poor behind, no matter what their politics, in a downward spiral of regress and chaos characterized most dramatically by the 'torture of hunger'.[17] In terms of redressing and preventing the shape-shifting insidiousness of violence, victimization, and revenge, the present-day reality of Brazil suggests that amnesty alone was of little consequence in containing or curtailing the devastating effects

---

In the estimation of some, this approximates a formal acknowledgement of responsibility on the part of the government for the loss of employment, imprisonment, torture, deaths, and disappearances of Brazilian citizens.

15 For more detailed information on comparative cultural analysis, see Fred E. Jandt, *Intercultural Communication: An Introduction* (Thousand Oaks, CA: Sage Publications, 1998).

16 For a chronology of the history of the Law of Amnesty (1964–1995), see http://www. fpa.org.br/especiais/anistia/anistia.htm. See the treatment of the brazilian concept of order in Gilberto Freyre's *Order and Progress: Brazil from Monarchy to Republic*, edited and translated from the Portuguese by Rod W. Horton (Westport, CT: Greenwood Press, 1980).

17 Frei Betto, 'Anistia para o Povo Brasileiro', http://www.correiocidadania.com.br/ed157/opiniao.htm.

of unresolved tensions and divisions of the recent past. Not only was amnesty of little help in addressing these tensions and divisions, but the very conditions of amnesty actually hindered the possibility. Under the law, amnesty forestalled efforts to bring those responsible for state violence to justice thereby allowing the continued use of torture by police and other security forces to go unchecked. It is argued by some that this problematic aspect of amnesty led to decades of delay in securing the necessary conditions for recognizing, treating, healing, and preventing the open and unattended wounds of repression and resistance from festering in ways that over time exacerbated violence, tolerated corruption, and compounded misery.

Still, from the perspective of its advocates, the argument continues to be made that early on in the process of abertura – the opening of the country to the process of redemocratization, Brazilians had good reason to be hesitant and anxious about the renegotiation of socio-political relationships. People were cautious about the ways in which any aspect of their lives, beliefs, actions, or possessions might be controlled, manipulated, or distorted. Concerns regarding the potential for acts of vengeance and retaliation were grounded in reality. Under these circumstances, opting for amnesty in exchange for truth and justice was a trade-off that Brazilians who had something to gain from this pact initially were willing to make given the fact that normative judgments regarding truth and justice were still under the control of the military regime. Exiles wanted to return home. Political prisoners wanted to be released. The military and civilian police wanted immunity. The people wanted to be free to live, to love, to work, and to dream. The promise of amnesty, however, could only be fulfilled if the conditions of amnesty were met. Meeting these conditions meant forgetting, denying, excusing, or hiding the truth of people's participation in, knowledge of or victimization by repressive forms of violence and their consequences.

While valuing many aspects of amnesty, not all Brazilians agreed with its conditions, among them Dom Paulo Evaristo Arns (b. 1921), who before and after the Law of Amnesty, endeavoured to engage the moral imaginations of Brazilians as an advocate for the victims of torture. Relying on his own power of *jeito*, he set in motion alternative vehicles for arriving at truth and reconciliation. These vehicles permitted him to communicate in no uncertain terms that the possibility of national redemocratzation and reconciliation could not be uncoupled from the struggle for truth and justice predicated on the defense of human rights and dignity. From his perspective, the only abertura that could bring about the *reinvenção da vida* – the reinvention of Brazil's life – was an openness on the part of every Brazilian to the truth about torture and a broad social consensus against its use and justification.

### The Text: 'Torture, Never Again?' – Cardinal Arns and the Use of Alternative Vehicles to Truth and Reconciliation

Prior to becoming archbishop of São Paulo in 1970, Dom Paulo served as an auxiliary bishop in Santana, the northern region of the archdiocese, where various jails and detention centers were located. As part of his ministry, he was called upon to visit numerous political prisoners, including Dominican friars and a Franciscan sister, who were being held and tortured. According to his own memoirs, this experience was a turning point in his life after which he would never be the same.[18] Getting at the truth behind this life-altering experience requires a brief consideration of four individuals whose lives and memories capture in many ways the complex reality of the years of heightened repression: Sergio Paranhos Fleury, Carlos Marighella, Frei Tito de Alencar Lima, and Madre Maurina Borges Silveira.

**Entering into the Truth of Torture and Its Aftermath**

Police detective Sergio Paranhos Fleury (1943–1979) was the most powerful police agent in Brazil and among the most notorius of torturers.[19] In the stories of countless detainees, political prisoners, and exiles, living, dead, and disappeared, encounters with Fleury were a constant. Whether heralded or denounced by Brazilian citizens, acts of brutality and torture by groups or individuals affiliated with the military, secret police, intelligence officers, or other civil security forces, were fused with the actions of Fleury. For some he symbolized the ultimate defender of national security, for others the ultimate violator of human rights. A harrowing mastermind of police violence against those who would threaten to destabilize the government of Brazil through non-violent protest or armed militancy, the reputation of Fleury elicited fear throughout country and beyond.[20] Fleury died prematurely in a questionable drowning accident in May 1979.

Carlos Marighella (1911–1969),[21] the most internationally recognized of Brazil's militant leaders, believed that Brazil's future was to be found in socialism. Marighella was regarded by some as a charismatic revolutionary patriot and by others as Brazil's most wanted criminal. His efforts to bring down the military dictatorship through armed struggle and terrorist activities signaled a turning point in the use of guerrilla warfare in Brazil. Ambushed by police, his body, riddled by bullets, was put on

---

18  Dom Paulo Evaristo Arns, *Da Esperança à Utopia: Testemunho de Uma Vida* (Rio de Janeiro: Editora Sextante, 2001), 145–152.

19  Percival de Souza, *Autópsia do Medo – Vida e Morte do Delegado Sérgio Pasranhos Fleury* (São Paulo: Editora Globo, 2000). See also Douglas Tavolaro, 'História macabra', Isto É Independente, http://www.terra.com.br/istoe/1626/brasil/1626_historia_macabra.htm.

20  See Thomas Skidmore, *Brasil: de Castelo a Tancredo* (Rio de Janeiro: Paz e Terra, 1988), 425.

21  Carlos Marighella, *The Terrorist Classic:Manual of Urban Guerrillas*, trans. Gene Hanrahan (Chapel Hill: Documentary Publications, 1985); and *Porque Resisti à Prisão*, 3rd edn. (São Paulo: Editora Brasiliense, 1995). For more background on Carlos Marighella, see Frei Betto, *Batismo de Sangue: A Luta Clandestina Contra a Ditadura Militar – Dossiês Carlos Marighella e Frei Tito*, 11th edn. (São Paulo: Editora Casa Amarela, 2000), 21–54; 169–215.

photographic display in the media for the world to see. Marighella died both as an assassinated hero and executed criminal.

Fleury is remembered for torture as well as for suppressing subversion and communist insurgency. Marighella is remembered for terror and for advancing revolutionary acts of armed resistance to liberate and unite the poor and oppressed masses of Brazil. Viewed in tandem, they serve as symbolic representations of the competing ideological claims that contributed to the legacy and justification of violence, torture and terror in Brazilian society. From the foreground of this historical backdrop the images of two of the tortured religious who left such a deep impression on Dom Paulo emerge. The first is the image of a young exiled Dominican friar, Frei Tito Alencar Lima (1945–1974), hanging from a tree in France.[22] The second is that of a middle-aged exiled Franciscan sister, Madre Maurina Borges Silveira (b. 1926), recuperating in a Mexican convent. Viewed in tandem, they serve as symbolic representations of the plight of tortured political prisoners caught in the crossfire of national security and revolutionary activity.

Tortured by Fleury and tortured for Marighella, Frei Tito became a symbol of all the victims of torture, whose dedicated and hope-filled spirits were lacerated beyond recovery and recognition by the dehumanizing effects of torture. Consigned indefinitely to a broken body he no longer experienced as his own, Tito joined the company of fragmented souls for whom 'death was to be preferred over losing one's life'.[23] His letters, poems and reflections reveal the depth of his passion, his commitment and his agony. Arrested for subversion and held for four torturous months at the Tiradentes prison, he was released and banished from Brazil on 17 February 1970 as part of a negotiated exchange for Switzerland's kidnapped ambassador. His suicide in France four years later was viewed as a martyrdom of the human spirit caused by acts of torture and their lasting effects. His legacy has been memorialized by film-makers, poets, playrights and novelists. [24]

Madre Maurina was the director of the Lar Santana, an orphanage for young children in the city of Riberão Preto. She was taken prisoner, accused of subversion, and tortured in connection with the arrest of a university student who had held meetings at the orphanage where she worked. Another victim of Fleury, Madre Maurina became a symbol of those survivors of torture whose declarations of innocence were disregarded, whose stories may never be known in their entirety, and for whom the details of the truth remain unspeakable as they themselves endeavour to forgive and to forget. She was banished from Brazil in 1970, along with other

---

22   See Frei Betto, 'Tito, a Paixão', in *Batismo de Sangue*, 255–289.

23   'É melhor morrer do que perder a vida'. See Frei Betto et al., *Frei Tito: Resistência & Utopia* (São Paulo: CEPIS, 1994), and *Batismo dé Sangue*, 257–289.

24   See the film documentary *Frei Tito* directed by Marlene França (1985), the play by Licínio Rios Neto, 'Não Seria o Arco de Triunfo um Monumento ao Pau de Arara?', in Murilo Días César, Licínio Ries Neto and Jaci Bezerra, *Teatro Social: Três Dramas* (Rio de Janeiro: Ministério da Cultura- Instituto Nacional de Artes e Cênicas, 1986); and Madeleine Alliens, *Le Désert et la Nuit* (Paris: Cerf, 1981).

political prisoners in exchange for the release of the kidnapped Japanese Consul.[25] She eventually returned to Brazil in frail condition and has remained in relative seclusion. Over the years, human rights advocates and journalists have recounted Madre Maurina's story in articles, plays and novels. [26]

As Dom Paulo recounts in his own memoirs, these particular stories, along with those of countless other victims of torture, profoundly affected him, intensifying his commitment to bring an end to torture by bringing to light the truth of its use, its perpetrators and its victims. In the absence of official or formal processes where justice could be served prior to the Law of Amnesty and after its enactment, Dom Paulo relied on alternative vehicles, making the most of his power of *jeito* in overcoming obstacles and impasses. Some of these included: the secret Bipartite Commission, various liturgical events and public demonstrations at the Cathedral in São Paulo, the establishment of numerous commissions and networks, and the project Brazil, Never Again. These selected alternative vehicles do not account for all of his activities or efforts on behalf of victims of torture. They do highlight, however, the significance of inter-related interventions made by one representative of the religious sector at critical moments during the years of military rule and the gradual return to a civilian government.

### Becoming a Witness and an Advocate: The Alternative Vehicle of the Bipartite Commission

Using the power of his reputation, authority, and integrity, Dom Paulo became involved in secret dialogues carried on with high-ranking military officers known as the Bipartite Commission.[27] The Bipartite was an effort on the part of key Roman Catholic bishops and military generals to overcome Church-State conflict during the military dictatorship. The dialogues took place in secrecy from 3 November 1970 to 26 August 1974. The Bipartite focused intensely on the politics of human rights, the struggle over proof and denial of the existence of torture, the tension between power

---

25 According to one of the kidnappers who negotiated the exchange, Madre Maurina was chosen instead of Frei Betto, who initially was on the list of prisoners to be released See Luis Eblak, 'Madre Maurina, uma vítima da ditadura', *Jornal do Commercio* (7 junho 1998) http://www2.uol.com.br/JC/_1998/0706/br0706g.htm; 'Lembranças compartilhadas da tortura', *Jornal do Brasil* Online (16 November 2003), http://jbonline.terra.combr/jb/papel/brasil/2003/11/16/jorbra20031116003.html.

26 Using personal interviews and official documents, they have attempted to sew together pieces of information with the threads of conjecture. Madre Maurina, for her part, has held fast to her own version of her imprisonment, torture and exile, negating rumors that she was raped, that she became pregnant, and that she gave birth to a child while in Mexico. See Matilde Leone, *Sombras da Repressão: O Outono de Maurina Borges* (Petrópolis: Vozes, 1998); Jacob Gorender, *Combate nas Trevas*, 5th edn. (São Paulo: Editora Atica, 1998); and Jorge Andrade, *Milagre na Cela* (Rio de Janeiro: Paz e Terra, 1977).

27 See Kenneth P. Serbin, *Secret Dialogues: Church-State Relations, Torture, and Social Justice in Authoritarian Brazil* (Pittsburgh: University of Pittsburgh Press, 2000), ix ff.

and faith, and the polarization of institutions and ideologies. In these meetings, Dom Paulo acquired information from military sources regarding the whereabouts of the disappeared and presented evidence to the generals regarding the treatment and actual conditions of political prisoners. A significant number of lives were saved as a consequence of these dialogues the full story of which has only come to light in recent years.

### Becoming the Pastor of a Nation and a Voice of Conscience for the World: The Alternative Vehicles of Rituals of Solidarity and Proclamations of Truth

The pastor of a nation divided, Dom Paulo made the Cathedral of São Paulo and its surrounding praça an ecumenical and inter-religious sanctuary of truth, remembrance, consolation, solidarity, hope and freedom.[28] In this Cathedral, an arena of sacred space worthy of the trust of victims, several dramatic events took place. Finding a way through the impasse of censorship, in the name of God, Dom Paulo brought to the attention of the nation the truth of about the torture of victims as he called for accountability on the part of perpetrators.

Among these events was the funeral liturgy celebrated for the student leader Alexandre Vannucchi Leme.[29] Alexandre was tortured to death on 17 March 1973. Defying riot troops, three thousand people, university students and pastoral workers, gathered to hear Dom Paulo challenge the government during a liturgy held in the Cathedral on 30 March 1973. Referring to the story of Cain and Abel, Dom Paulo's words: 'Where is your brother? The voice of your brother's blood is crying out to Me from the ground', echoed within and beyond the borders of Brazil.[30]

A second event was a Jewish memorial for the well-known journalist Vladmir Herzog.[31] On 31 October 1975, Rabbi Henry Sobel, joined by many religious leaders from various faith traditions and 10,000 mourners, presided over a moving ritual of remembrance and resistance. Herzog was a victim of torture by beating, electric shock, and drowning. When he died unexpectedly at the hands of his torturers, his captors staged a suicide by hanging. The public's refusal to accept the government's official story regarding Herzog's cause of death was demonstrated at his burial

---

28  It is important to note the close relationship that developed between Dom Paulo and Presbyterian minister Rev. Jaime Wright, along with Rabbi Henry Sobel, *Da Esperança à Utopia*, 217–221. Also, an unprecedented ecumenical solidarity emerged with the Conselho Nacional de Igrejas Cristã (CONIC) and the World Council of Churches (WCC) under the direction of Phillip Potter. It was this connection that helped to bring together Dom Paulo and the exiled Paulo Freire, who was working for the WCC in Geneva.

29  See K. Serbin, 'Anatomy of a Death: The Case of Alexandre Vannucchi Leme', in *Secret Dialogues*, 200–218.

30  In November 1975, following the death of Vladmir Herzog, Dom Paulo and the bishops of São Paulo issued a declaration denouncing and condemning torture following this theme entitled 'Não oprimas teu irmão' – Do not oppress your brother.

31  See Dom Paulo Evaristo Arns, *Da Esperança à Utopia*, 302.

which took place in the centre of the Jewish cemetery rather than at its walls, the usual place of burial reserved for victims of suicide.

A third event occurred in the Cathedral in April 1979. On this occasion, Dom Paulo made arrangements for the first celebration of the Missa da Terra Sem Males written by Dom Pedro Casaldáliga, the persecuted missionary bishop of São Felix de Araguaia. The message of the Mass for an Earth without Evils resounded for all the world to hear, reaching people throughout Brazil as well as other countries.[32] Dom Paulo, in the company of forty other bishops, used this liturgy of protest and hope as an occasion for uncovering the hidden truths of Brazil's legacy of torturous violence against the indigenous peoples and their lands. By drawing particular attention to the interconnectedness and lasting effects of all crimes of violence against humanity and the earth, the Mass signaled a new moment in consciousness as it issued a call for 'Memory, Remorse and Commitment' in solidarity with all martyrs and victims of violence, past and present.

A fourth event to take place at the Cathedral was another funeral liturgy celebrated for Santo Dias da Silva. More than 30,000 mourners were in attendance for the service. A steelworker, union activist and leader in the formation of basic Christian communities, Santo Dias was assassinated by police on 30 October 1979, in front of the factory where he worked. Six months later, following the arrest of numerous factory workers by military police, Dom Paulo arranged for another prayer service to take place at the Cathedral. The call to prayer for the release of all those arrested was scheduled for 21 April 1980, a national holiday commemorating Tiradentes, a martyr and symbol of Brazil's struggle for freedom. Once again, Dom Paulo's message echoed throughout Brazil and around the world.[33] Coming a month after the assassination of El Salvador's Archbishop Oscar Romero, Dom Paulo was all too aware of the dynamics of violence and repression taking their toll throughout the continent and indeed throughout the globe. He also was aware of the power of solidarity, a movement of spirit, manifested especially by workers united in the struggle for justice, dignity and freedom.

On 25 March 1983, the Feast of the Annunciation, in another event Dom Paulo brought to the attention of the nation once again, the memories of the lives and deaths of Frei Tito de Alencar and Alexandre Vannucchi Leme. Officiating at a special liturgy, after which the mortal remains of Tito and Alexandre were finally laid to rest,[34] Dom Paulo drew attention, historically and symbolically, to the fate of the dead and disappeared, in Brazil and everywhere. In this courageous liturgical act he held up the memory of all victims of torture whose bodies would never be

---

32  See Dom Pedro Casaldáliga, *Missa da Terra Sem Males* (São Paulo: Edições Paulinas Discos, 1980).

33  Dom Pedro Casaldáliga, *Missa da Terra Sem Males*, 303–305.

34  Frei Tito's remains were exhumed from the Dominican cemetery in France and returned to Brazil for burial. The remains of Alexandre were among the skeletons found in the cemetery of Perus, identified forensically and recovered by his family for burial. See Vala de Perus, Um Símbolo de Resistência below.

recovered for burial and whose families would continue to suffer immeasurably from the loss of their loved ones as well as the unrevealed circumstances surrounding their deaths and disappearances. This sacramental and symbolic gesture was manifested again in a related event. On 2 November 1990, Dom Paulo celebrated a liturgy with the families and friends of the 'disappeared' whose skeletal remains were discovered among the 1,049 bones found in a mass grave, hidden clandestinely in the Vala de Perus, in the municipal cemetery of Dom Bosco.[35]

Through these rituals, Dom Paulo reiterated his appeal for truth and justice for all victims of torture. Each of these events communicated in the strongest and broadest terms possible the interconnectedness of all forms of violence and destruction, urging all those that would listen to undertake the work of reparations and reconciliation. As a result of the many events, ranging from liturgical celebrations to demonstrations of solidarity, that took place at the Cathedral and the Praça da Sé, Dom Paulo deeply touched the social consciences of Brazilians through his incomparable *jeito* for communicating truth with courage and integrity.

As people came to express their longings for justice, peace, hope, and freedom, all that took place in these sacred spaces in forms of prayer, song, reflection or call to action, had a rippling effect by way of repetition, imitation and symbolic re-presentation throughout and beyond Brazil. Nowhere was this more obvious than in the memorial liturgies and rituals that reaffirmed the power of life, solidarity and goodness over the forces of death, violence and evil. These dramas of solidarity, resistance, and hope encouraged people in their struggle to reinvent their lives. In the face of unimaginable horror, unsupportable grief, and prevailing uncertainty, these events kept the quest for truth and justice in the forefront of the people's consciousness.

These particular events, along with many others, disclosed the truth of torture, dramatically and emotionally raising the cry of the people and symbolizing their resistance to the forces of violence and repression. The sentiment was captured in a single word – 'enough!' – enough torture, enough death, enough denial, enough silence, enough injustice, enough amnesia.

**Becoming an Ambassador for Truth and Human Rights: Alternative Vehicles of Pastoral, Ecumenical and International Organizations**

Unrelenting in his efforts to sustain hope and create the conditions for ever-greater solidarity among a people struggling to use the compelling power of truth to disarm the forces of oppression, repression and destruction, Dom Paulo endeavoured to make clear that the struggle was both one and many. To this end, he extended himself publicly and privately in organized efforts to draw upon and contribute to the resources

---

35 See 'Vala de Perus: Um Símbolo de Resistência', http://www.resgatehistorico.com.br/doc_06.htm.

of international and ecumenical working in the service of truth and justice and the building up of a world free of torture, hunger, and all forms of dehumanization.[36]

In 1972 Dom Paulo established the Comissão de Paz e Justiça – the Commission of Peace and Justice, a pastoral initiative focusing on the defence of human rights and the struggle for justice.[37] Through the commission's vigilance and intervention the suffering, abuse, torture, and death of hundreds of individuals were mitigated or prevented. The commission served as a model for similar types of commissions in Latin America and other places around the world.[38] In subsequent years, he established the Archdiocesan Pastoral Commission on Human Rights and the Marginalized, which in December of 1978 issued the challenging and controversial document 'Humildes contra a Violência'.[39]

Creating the conditions for movements and organizations to network more effectively, Dom Paulo's highly profiled work for victims of dictatorships within and beyond the borders of Brazil was furthered in 1977 when he made available in his metropolitan curia an office for the United Nations High Commission on Refugees. In 1978, he helped to organize the Comitê de Defesa dos Direitos Humanos no cone Sul (CLAMOR) – the Defense of Human Rights Committee of the Southern Cone. Strengthening ties with the WCC, and helping to organize numerous ecumenical and inter-religious groups in Latin America, Dom Paulo worked to unite leaders and people of various faith traditions in creating alternative vehicles for confronting the use of torture and redressing violence.

## Becoming an Investigator and Protagonist for the Sake of Memory and Justice: The Alternative Vehicle of the 'Projeto Brasil, Nunca Mais'

In continuity with his previous efforts in the service of truth and the possibility of reconciliation, Dom Paulo set in motion a daunting project that once again initially involved secret efforts to bring about a more complete understanding of the government's use of torture. Given his personal presence at trials and in jails, along with his presence in the media as a journalist and as a broadcaster, Dom Paulo signaled a commitment to truth as he unmasked hypocrisy, uncovered lies and gave

---

36 For more detailed information, see Dom Paulo Evaristo Arns, 'Biografia', http://www. dhnet.org.br/direitos/militantes/arns/dpaulo_notasbiograficas.html.

37 In 1972, the bishops of the State of São Paulo issued 'Testemunho de Paz' – (Testimony of Peace), the first of many challenging documents dealing with the Church and the Defense of Human Rights. See Episcopado de São Paulo, 'Testemunho de Paz', SEDOC (Servico de Documentacão), 5, 1972, 107–109.

38 See Don Paulo Evaristo Arns, *Da Esperança à Utopia*, 181. See also Thomas C. Fox, 'Arns is a Symbol of Human Rights in Latin America', *National Catholic Reporter* (14 September 2001), 24 and Margaret Hebblethwaite, 'Brazil's Moral Giant', *The Tablet* (26 January 2001).

39 Comissão Pastoral dos Direitos Humanos e dos Marginalizados da Arquidiocese de São Paulo, 'Violência contra os Humildes', SEDOC 10 (1978), 961–983.

people a reason for their hope. Among his many efforts in this regard, the most significant alternative vehicle was that of the Projeto Brasil Nunca Mais (BNM),[40] which Dom Paulo Evaristo Arns set in motion with the collaboration of Presbyterian minister Rev. Jaime Wright, and a small group of courageous researchers.[41] Aided financially by the support of the World Council of Churches, Brazil's most stunning effort in bringing to light the truth of torture was, comparatively speaking, informal, unconventional, and without precedent. Bordering on the miraculous and subsequently serving as a precedent for formal commissions in other countries, the findings and publication of BNM in 1985 gave rise to an echoing global cry of 'torture, never again'.

The book was ranked number one on the Brazilian best-seller list two weeks after its publication. It remained on the list for ninety-one weeks, becoming one of the all-time best-selling non-fiction works published in Brazil. BNM effectively overcame the impasse of amnesty and required the country to come to terms with the truth about torture.[42] Over the course of five years, a handful of daring and committed researchers gained access to archives of Brazilian military court records documenting in minute detail routine torture, deaths, and disappearances between April 1964 and March 1979.[43] The original copies of documents were removed, copied, and returned to their shelves, folders, and binders. Described as a quixotic effort of full disclosure, Dom Paulo was successful in responding to the need for bringing to light the memories of torture that the shadows of repression endeavoured to conceal.

Translated into other languages and published in other countries, it is an irony of history that Brazil, in the absence of a formal truth and reconciliation commission, provided the prototype from which in later years countries such as Argentina, Uruguay and Paraguay would pattern their respective truth commission reports. An even more important to underscore as researcher Joan Dassin has observed, 'BNM was able to achieve something that neighboring groups did not – to establish official responsibility for politically motivated human rights abuses on the basis of military records'.[44]

To victims and perpetrators alike, BNM gave the faceless faces and the nameless names. Denial was impossible, the revelations were uncontestable, and the response of silence on the part of the government was to be expected. To this day, the narrative

---

40  See Archdiocese of São Paulo, *Torture in Brazil: A Shocking Report on the Pervasive Use of Torture by Brazlian Military Governments, 1964–1979*, trans. Jaime Wright. Edited with a new preface by Joan Dassin (Austin: University of Texas, 1998). See also Archdiocese of São Paulo, Brasil: *Nunca Mais* (Petrópolis: Vozes, 1985).

41  Rev. Jaime Wright ([+]1999) was the son of US Presbyterian missionaries to Brazil. In 1973 his younger brother Paulo Stuart Wright, a founder of 'Popular Action' and a legislator, was abducted and disappeared.

42  See Joan Dassin, Preface to Archdioces of São Paulo, *Torture in Brazil*, xiv.

43  See Lawrence Weschler, *A Miracle, A Universe: Settling Accounts with Torturers* (New York: Penguin, 1991).

44  Joan Dassin, in prefarce to Archdioces of São Paulo, *Torture in Brazil*, xvi.

history of those who obtained the documents of the BNM project continues to captivate readers in the same measure that the revelations of BNM continue to haunt them. The factual events detailed in the proceedings have proven to be more unbelievable than fiction, characterized as they are by the seemingly miraculous achievement of this undertaking and the shear magnitude of official archival records detailing verifiable acts of terror, brutality, and torture.[45] Perhaps even more amazing is the ongoing development of projects and movements in Brazil and beyond that BNM set in motion.

For more than two decades, individuals involved in movements inspired by or modeled after BNM have dedicated themselves to the ongoing struggle for social justice and the defense of human rights by creating dossiers and reconstructing the details of individual cases of imprisonment, torture, death and disappearance. In recent years, the discovery of hidden graves and the use of forensics in identifying skeletal remains have brought some resolution to numerous cases and repudiated with evidence the 'official' stories regarding the fate of the disappeared.

In 1979 no one could have anticipated the impact of internet technology on consciousness-raising, the preservation of national memory, and the struggle for truth and justice. Cyberspace has now become a new site of demonstration, protest, and education that is occupied with the same passion, conviction, tenacity, and creativity as the cathedrals and *praças* of the past. Making information accessible to Brazilians as well as people throughout the world, these movements have provided detailed resources and multiple research tools in a variety of forms including such things as biographies, testimonies, historical chronologies, legal processes, photo galleries, and so on. In cyberspace, the memories and legacies of the deceased and the disappeared have been handed on in ways previously unimagined. The following examples offer a few illustrations.

In 1985 the Grupo Tortura, Nunca Mais (GTNM/RJ) was established in the state of Rio de Janeiro by ex-political prisoners and family members of deceased and disappeared political prisoners.[46] In addition to working for human rights, GTNM/RJ has forced the resignation of former torturers from public office. It also has succeeded in placing pressure on the government to revoke the licenses of medical professionals who collaborated in torture by falsifying records and failing to report cases. GTNM/RJ is actively involved in bringing to justice and denouncing past and contemporary cases of torture. Committed to remembering the names and stories of those who died, GTNM/RJ is a contributor to various Latin American and international organizations dedicated to combating torture and redressing impunity. Other state chapters of the

---

45 The BNM included the complete proceedings of 707 political trials and dozens of incomplete proceedings. This amounted to over one million pages. The BNM team had two projects: Project A produced a report of 7,000 pages. The book version of *Brasil* Nunca Mais is a summary of Project A. The project also includes 10,000 political documents appended to the military court proceedings. The denunciations made in military courts include the name of torturers, the places where torture took place, the murderd, the disappeared, and other harrowing details. See *Torture in Brazil*, 4–8.

46 http://www.torturanuncamais-rj.org.br.

organization exist throughout Brazil, including *Movimento Tortura Nunca Mais* of Pernambuco founded in 1986,[47] *Grupo Tortura Nunca Mias de Bahia* founded in 1995,[48] along with those in Brasília, São Paulo, Minas Gerais, and Porto Alegre, among others. In addition to these groups, the Agência de Informação Frei Tito para América Latina (ADITAL) also serves as a centre of documentation and social action in defense of human rights, preserving the memory and legacy of Frei Tito.[49]

The Comissão de Familiares dos Mortos e Desaparecidos Políticos and the Centro de Documentação Eremias Delizoicov organized and developed a web site to make available information regarding investigations into the death of victims of the dictatorship. The commission also is involved in the localization and identification of their human remains, the identification of those responsible for crimes of torture, homicide, and the hiding of corpses during the years of dictatorship (1964 to 1985).[50] In 1993, it founded the Instituto de Estudos sobre a Violência do Estado (IEVE) which led to the opening of the *Vala de Perus* in the municipal cemetery of Dom Bosco in São Paulo where the remains of political prisoners, indigents and victims of death squads were discovered.

Direitos Humanos Net was established in 1994 by a group of human rights activists and researchers. Working in virtual reality and cyberspace, DHNet went on line for the first time on 1 May 1995. Funded by Centro de Estudos, Pesquisa e Ação Cultural (CENARTE) - it has as its main objective the use of means of communication to promote the democratization of communication and the broad-based understanding of human rights.[51]

Impunidade, Nunca Mais[52] is an organization of documentation, research, and solidarity dedicated to the struggle for justice in various cases of violence against journalists committed to the reporting of highly politicized articles, many of which address directly violations of human rights. It also seeks to demonstrate ways of combating impunity in order to preserve the freedom of the press and the inalienable right of the people to information. It is under the direction of the Sociedade Interamericana da Imprensa and sponsored by the John S. and James L. Knight Foundation. The memory of Vladmir Herzog serves as point of reference, particularly for Brazilian journalists. From 1988–2004, twenty-four Brazilian journalists were assassinated or have disappeared for engaging in the dangerous exercise of freedom of expression. As of 2004, eighteen cases were under investigation.

Though divergent in its political orientation from the previous groups, a final example that warrants mentioning is Ternuma – Terrorismo, Nunca Mais – Terrorism, Never Again.[53] Established in 1998 by a group of civilians and military,

---

47  http://www.torturanuncamais.org.br.
48  http://www.grupotorturanuncamaisbahia.org.br.
49  See http://www.adital.org.br.
50  http://www.desaparecidospoliticos.org.br.
51  http://www.dhnet.org.br.
52  http://www.impunidad.com/toplevel/indexP.htm.
53  http://www.ternuma.com.br.

it is anti-communist in its historical orientation. It stands in defense of the national security policies of the Brazilian Armed Forces and characterizes the activities of Brazil's political left during the years of military rule as acts of terrorism. It also takes issue with the 1979 Law of Amnesty, which in its opinion allowed for the return and release of exiled and imprisoned terrorists and over time resulted in their occupation of significant government positions. Ternuma criticizes what it refers to as the 'false politics of human rights'. Through the internet it seeks to provide future generations with the history of those who defended democracy in Brazil from communist insurgency.

As the final example reveals, Brazil's quest for truth and reconciliation is far from over. Interpretations of history are contradicted or repudiated and much continues to remain hidden. Yet even in the midst of ideological controversy, the witness of Dom Paulo Evaristo Arns and the mandate of Brazil's own Federal Constitution held out for the ideal of 'torture, never again'.[54]

## Interpreting the Significance of Dom Paulo's Alternative Vehicles to Truth and Reconciliation

As a representative of the religious sector of Brazilian society, Dom Paulo is but one of many leaders of spirit who contributed to the uncovering of truth, the creating of conditions for the possibility of reconciliation, and the reinvention of Brazil's life and hope as a nation. As this brief and impressionistic narrative reveals, the quest for truth and reconciliation during and after the years of military rule was a complex endeavor that took place at many levels and from many perspectives. Yet the truth remains incomplete and much of Brazilian society remains unreconciled. For those interested in studying the nature, function and achievements of alternative vehicles, the narrative offers numerous insights.

First, as the hell of torture was reinvented during the years of military rule, no one affected by this reinvention could avoid being dehumanized and demonized – by someone or some group – not Fleury, not Marighella, not Tito, and not Maurina. As the violence spun out of control and the loss of lives and legacies became incalculable, both Tito and Maurina, along with others who shared their experiences of torture, had to estimate how much violence to the self would be required in order to interrupt the cycle of violence? In their respective efforts to dispel the life-threatening forces of violence so as to restore their own human dignity and recover the lives that were taken from them, Tito and Maurina ended up finding very different escapes from the hell of torture. Their memories, however, communicated the same message to Dom

---

54 On 28 September 1989, Brazil ratified the United Nations' Convention Against Torture and Other Cruel, Inhuman and Degrading Treatment or Punishment of 1984. According to Article 5 of the 1988 *Constitution of the Federal Republic of Brazil*, the rights upheld by international treaties ratified by Brazil are guaranteed to its citizens. See Relator sobre a Tortura da Comissão DH – ONU 05/03/2003 http://www.midiaindependente.org/eo/blue/2003/03/249039.shtml.

Paulo, to the people of Brazil and to the world: 'tortura, nunca mais – torture, never again'.

Second, anyone familiar with the legacy of Church of Liberation in Brazil knows that the narrative of Dom Paulo offers but a sampling of the courageous ability of ecclesial leaders of spirit to creatively seek alternative vehicles in the quest for truth and reconciliation.[55] The narrative is a reflection of those leaders willing to pay the price of solidarity with the poor and powerless regardless of the cost. It serves by way of example as a testimony to the ongoing efforts of other heralds of truth and agents of reconciliation, shepherds who have taken seriously the laying down of their lives for their sheep. These leaders embody the *jeito* of hope, a way of proceeding as if tomorrow could be different from yesterday.

Third, in the case of Brazil, leaders such as Dom Paulo, have functioned symbolically as lightening rods for bringing about truth and reconciliation using alternative approaches to disclosing truth and creating the conditions for the possibility of reconciliation. The narratives of their lives and legacies hold great appeal. Building upon an incredible network of multiple relationships of the first and second degree, their actions, understood symbolically, engaged and continue to engage the culture of Brazil on its own terms. Leaders like Dom Paulo were able to make the most of alternative vehicles, in part because of personal charism, but also because they knew how to make the most of collectivism through invitations to consciousness and solidarity. They tapped into Brazil's short-term orientation to life by intensifying mindfulness about the present moment and accentuating the fragility and preciousness of life, so often in circumstances that required them to make meaning of death and evil, while holding out hope for life and goodness. They made the most of high power distance, personally, politically, and spiritually, by placing representative symbols of Brazil's national honour and shame in the quotidian weighting of individual integrity as well as in the internationally measured scale of human rights and the divinely judged balance of good and evil. With their gifts of *jeito* and *reinvenção*, they reinvented the symbols of leadership, thereby creating one set of conditions for putting in motion a broader cultural understanding of leadership in the service of truth and reconciliation.

## Conclusion: The *Jeito* of Hope and the Reinvention of Life – The Ongoing Role of the Religious Sector in the Work of Truth and Reconciliation

So how, in the judgment of political scientists and social historians, and even more importantly, in the estimation of Brazilians themselves, will the alternative vehicles used by Dom Paulo and his companions be judged comparatively? Did they succeed in helping Brazil as a country to become less violent, more truthful, more just, less divided, more conscious, less corrupt, more accountable?

---

55 The Church of Liberation refers to the progressive sectors of the Brazilian Catholic Church. For details, see John Burdick, *Looking for God in Brazil*, chapters 2 and 7 as well as Iain Maclean, *Opting for Democracy?*, chapters 4 and 7.

There are a number of indicators to suggest that these alternative vehicles did make a difference. At the level of government accountability, Brazil ratified the United Nations' 1984 Convention Against Torture and Other Cruel, Inhuman and Degrading Treatment or Punishment on 28 September 1989.[56] Another significant indicator is the Law of Indemnity (Law 9.140 enacted on 5 December 1995) which defined the Brazilian Government's responsibility for the death and disappearance of political dissidents from 1961 through 1979.[57] Another noteworthy indicator is the *Anistia, Comissão de Paz* – Amnesty, Commission of Peace, established by the Ministry of Justice on 28 August 2001, in accord with the 1988 Federal Constitution, and subsequently regulated by Law 10.559 of 13 November 2002. The purpose of the commission is to consider and grant requests for reparations from individuals who, during the period ranging from 1946–1988, lost employment for political motives.[58] Among the more than 40,000 individuals initially making such requests, a number were victims of torture.

At the level of Brazil's historical memory from 1964–1985, alternative vehicles set in motion by Cardinal Arns contributed to the survival of multiple social constructions of reality. This reorientation of historical consciousness set a different course for truth and reconciliation in Brazil.[59] A history that might have been written exclusively from the perspective of the military has been written as well from the perspective of the exiles, the imprisoned, the tortured, the disappeared, the censured, the intimidated, the grief-stricken, the defeated, and the dead. Theoretically, this consolidated view of history is contributed to the understanding and development of the 1988 Constitution with its emphasis on the defense of human rights and dignity. However, despite the emergence of these positive indicators, a look at the contemporary Brazilian reality suggests a growing disparity between the articulation and enactment of principles and laws and their enforcement in practice.[60]

In the light of this disparity, the limitations of alternative vehicles also must be acknowledged. Admittedly, the non-existence of official governmental proceedings to acknowledge human rights violations in Brazil from 1964–84) until the 1995 Law of Indemnity continues to be viewed as a lost opportunity to curb Brazil's long-standing and unabated reliance on strategies and tactics associated with the ideology of national security. As institutionalized violence reflected in acts of brutality,

---

56 According to Article 5 of the 1988 *Constituition of the Federal Republic of Brazil*, the rights upheld by international treaties ratified by Brazil are guaranteed to its citizens. This ratification, at least in theory, signaled Brazil's repudiation of torture.

57 See http://www.fpa.org.br/especiais/anistia/anistia.htm.

58 See http://www.mj.gov.br/anistia/default.htm.

59 As was demonstrated in the case of the *Projeto Brasil, Nunca Mais*, where key narratives used to prove government responsibility for torture were not only the narratives of victims and survivors, but narratives taken directly from the archives of military judicial hearings.

60 See Relatório sobre a Tortura no Brasil, Por Relator sobre a Tortura da Comissão Direitos Humanos, ONU 05/03/2003, http://www.midiaindependente.org/eo/blue/2003/03/249039.shtml.

torture and de facto execution by Brazilian military, civilian police and death squads continues to draw the attention of the world,[61] the landless,[62] the street children,[63] the incarcerated,[64] and the marginalized of Brazil remain caught in a vortex of human rights violations.[65] Finally, it is important to not lose sight of the ideological reversals, religious shifts, and ecclesiological ruptures that have taken place in the religious sector of Brazil as reflected in the current priorities and profiles of a number of current leaders. While members of the previous generation, such as Cardinal Arns, continue tirelessly to provide leadership and continuity between the past and the present, they are not immortal.

Without negating analyses of Brazil's seeming inability to break the cycle of violence, poverty, and curruption, it nonetheless is important to acknowledge a few of the ways in which the legacy of Dom Paulo's *jeito* of hope and his ongoing *reinvençao* of life sustained – and continue to sustain – the will of the people united in the struggle against every form of dehumanization.

First, in the absence of a formal truth and reconciliation commission earlier on in the redemocratization process, other vehicles enabled the Brazilian people to succeed in achieving some of the ends of such commissions using alternative strategies and methods, many of which were informal in terms of authority and structure. Second, Brazilians did arrive at some measure of truth and reconciliation despite obstacles and impassses. Third, Brazilians of all political persuasions, including representatives of the religious sector such as Dom Paulo, anticipated the problems often associated with bringing offenders to justice and securing justice for the offended. Aware of the lessons of national and international history, Brazil's way of proceeding involved a bricolage of social pacts, which only future generations will be able to assess

---

61  See Asma Jahanger, Report of the Special Rapporteur, 'Civil and Political Rights, including the Questions of Disappearances and Summary Executions – Mission to Brazil', Sixtieth Session of the U.N. Commission on Human Rights (28 January 2004), http://www. unhchr.ch/huridocda/huridoca.nsf; Theo van Boven, Report of the Special Rapporteur, 'Civil and Political Rights, including the Questions of Torture and Detention', Sixtieth Session of the U.N. Commission on Human Rights (20 December 2003), http://www.unhchr.ch/huridocda/huridoca.nsf; and US Department of State Human Rights Report for 2000, 59th Session of the UN Commission on Human Rights, 'Brazil', http://www.humanrights-usa.net/reports/brazil.html.

62  See Amnesty International, Brazil: Corumbiara and Eldorado de Carajás: Rural Violence, Police Brutality and Impunity (1 January 1998), http://web.amnesty.org/library/print/ENGAMR190011998; Amnesty International, 'Brazil: Eldorado de Carajás – Hopes Betrayed', http://www.amnesty.org.yk/deliver?document=12904.

63  See Anthony Swift, 'The Street Kids Who Took on a Government', *Guardian* London (18 November 1995), 31. http://pangaea.org/street_children/latin/guard.htm.

64  See Amnesty International News, 'Brazil: Carandiru Trial – A Clear Message To Those in Charge', http://www.amnesty.org.uk/news/press/12903.shtml; see also the film *Carandiru*, Hector Babenco, director, Columbia TriStar (2004).

65  See Celma Tavares, 'Anistia: O Brasil Após Vinte Anos', http:www.torturanuncamais.org.br/mtnm_pub/pub_artigos/pub_art_celma12.htm.

comparatively in terms of their historical consequence and political significance in the short term and the long term.

As eternal values and temporal interests compete for primacy in the arena of social consciousness, the protagonists and antagonists of human history are determined in large measure by the paradoxical processes of consensus building. Citizens in search of truth and reconciliation must be capable of understanding, withdrawing and coming to terms with their projections and experiences of good and of evil. Brazil's quest for truth and reconciliation continues in 2004 – forty years after the military revolution of 1964, twenty-five years after the 1979 Law of Amnesty, nineteen years after the return to civilian rule in 1985, sixteen years after the approval of the 1988 Federal Constitution, nine years after the 1995 Law of Indemnity, and two years after the presidential election of Luís Inácio 'Lula' da Silva. Threatened by the unbridled forces of violence, poverty and corruption, popular appeals for non-violence, sustainability, and transparency remain in evidence.

It goes without saying that the reality of Brazil is complex and paradoxical. No single theory of causality can account for the illegal but ongoing abuse and disregard of human rights in both urban and rural areas, just as no single theory can account for Brazil's ongoing contribution to national and international efforts in the promotion and defense of human rights. Given this reality, the example of Dom Paulo, and the ongoing role of the religious sector at this moment in time, some open questions remain. How are current representatives of the religious sector responding to the present-day incidences of police and gang violence,[66] the unattended claims of victims, and the corrupt legalities that protect perpetrators? How are they dealing with the direct or indirect consequences of Brazil's difficulties and failures in bringing an end to torture and impunity? How are they contributing to the creation of alternative vehicles in the absence of formal commissions needed to redress these contemporary violations of human rights? And ultimately, how are they carrying forward Brazil's legacy of raising up leaders of spirit from the religious sector who are capable of inspiring, educating and leading the world community by means of governmental and non-governmental initiatives in the advancement of life through the defense of human rights and by witnessing to the power of hope in the face of seemingly insurmountable odds?

---

66 Martha Huggins et al., *Violence Workers: Police Torturers and Murderers Reconstruct Brazilian Atrocities* (Berkeley: University of California Press, 2002).

# PART II
# Churches and Religious Reconciliation

Chapter 6

# The Theme of Reconciliation and Theology in Latin America[1]

José Comblin

## Introduction

During the past year (1985) at a regular meeting of CELAM, the President of CELAM made a most interesting proposal for theologians: he suggested that theology should study the theme of reconciliation and develop a 'theology of reconciliation'. In this brief study I wish to respond to the wish of the Council's President. It will not be possible within the limits of a short article to present a complete outline of a theology of reconciliation. I simply wish to open some paths and to indicate some interesting perspectives.

Certainly, in making this proposal the President of CELAM was inspired by the document which the Holy Father sent to the Catholic world as a conclusion to the Roman Synod (1983). (The Apostolic Exhortation *Reconciliatio et Paenitentia* of 2 December 1984). In Latin America the theme of reconciliation responded and indeed still responds to the problems of the political realities, above all in certain countries such as Chile and Colombia. In Chile, where for some years now the episcopacy has assumed leadership of a political movement of 'national reconciliation', the theme of reconciliation expresses the direct involvement of the Chilean Bishops in the politics of the nation. In Chile, the Bishops assumed a direct political role: fostering a change in the political regime. In Colombia, the conservative government of President Betancur was involved in reconciliation with the guerilla movements which had disturbed the political life of the country for two decades. The Church is interested also in the politics of 'national reconciliation' of the government. In Central America the fundamental problem is that of peace in the sense of the cessation of hostilities. It is only after this step has been taken that one is able to speak of 'national reconciliation'. In each case the struggles and the ruling tensions manifest the existence of destroyed societies or perhaps not yet really developed:

1  Originally published in *Revista Eclesiástica Brasileira*, (REB) Volume 46, Fasc. 182 (June 1986), 272–314, as 'O Tema da Reconciliacáo e a Teologia na Américan Latina'. Translated and reproduced by kind permission of the author, Padre Prof. João Comblin, and Padre Piva, the editor of REB. The editor of this volume, and translator, wishes to thank Sr. M. Guider and Carlos Viana, S.J., who checked the translation.

the theme of reconciliation thus questions the whole of Latin America. The problem is, what does reconciliation signify for Latin America? What are the demands for an authentic reconciliation in Latin America? Finally, what are the paths to reconciliation in Latin America and in what sense is the Church able to contribute to authentic reconciliation?

Viewed from another perspective, reconciliation has a political as well as a biblical-theological meaning. In the question of reconciliation we must study how the Church and politics are related, where lies the autonomy of the political and the specificity of the Church, both acute problems in the contemporary period.

A theology of reconciliation ought to begin with the state of the evolution of both philosophical and theological reflection in the real world. Fortunately we do not need to begin from square one. Though the theme of reconciliation was not studied much by Catholic theology across the centuries, we can nonetheless discern powerful and interesting reference points.

In the Old Testament the theme of reconciliation is not treated explicitly. However a certain concept of reconciliation can be inferred from the drama of the covenant between God and His people. The events of the covenant, concluded, broken, restored, leave place for a certain concept of reconciliation. Nevertheless, the Old Testament does not elaborate on a theology of reconciliation: it prepares the ground. Beginning with the Old Testament, we understand that reconciliation is above everything else a social fact: It deals with reconciliation between God and His people, between God and humanity. Individual reconciliation occurs within the context of social reconciliation, but that interpretation is primarily within the biblical perspective. Like the covenant which restores, reconciliation is collective.

The gospels do not explicate a doctrine of reconciliation. Nevertheless, the theme of the covenant is clearly presented and is presented in context of the text as an extension of the trajectory of the Old Testament. A true theology of reconciliation appears in the Pauline epistles, though it does not occupy a central place in Pauline theology (though it does not cease to be important): if it is compared to the theme of justification or that of grace. It forms part of a wider Pauline synthesis. The proper theme of Pauline reconciliation is indeed synthetic. Consequently there is no doubt: the Pauline doctrine of reconciliation is the fundamental referent for any Christian doctrine of reconciliation.

Neither the patristic fathers not the scholastics emphasize the theme of reconciliation. This was probably largely connected to Jewish origins and the Jewish mindset. The scholastics stressed the themes of redemption, vicarious satisfaction, and sacrifice. The article that St Thomas Aquinas dedicated to reconciliation in the III part of the *Summa Theologica* was not commented upon nor recovered by subsequent scholastics because they did not perceive the subject to be of interest.

In the controversies of the Reformation, the themes of justification and grace prevailed and have predominated right through to the contemporary epoch. In the contemporary epoch Protestant authors have given much more prominence to the theme of reconciliation than have the Catholics: it is in the center of the soteriology of Karl Barth. Protestant theological dictionaries contain the entry 'reconciliation'.

However, in the traditional Catholic theological manuals, the term 'reconciliation' has no place at all. For example, consult the classic text of B. Bartmann, which was translated into Portuguese as *Dogmatic Theology* (1962).[2]

In reality, the theme of reconciliation was early on reserved to the sacrament of penance: it treated of the 'reconciliation' of the sinner with God and with the Church through confession, by public penance, and later private penance. The term 'reconciliation' became a technical and juridical term in sacramental usage. It was not developed theologically, but rather as a canonical juridical term.

Though the Second Vatican Council did not create a theology of reconciliation, the term was used various times in ways that were not common in the tradition of the Church: It was used in the context of the dialogue between the Church and the world and all those sectors more or less separated from the church. In this manner then it set the bases for possible future development.

The 1983 Synod of Bishops had as its subject reconciliation and penitence and the subsequent apostolic exhortation addressed the same theme. More than anything else, it was a theological elaboration of reconciliation within the context of the sacrament of penance. Generally speaking, the elaboration of the theme of reconciliation is typically directed to the consideration of the sacrament of penance. Conciliar themes were not taken up. The Pauline texts were cited, but the Pauline synthesis was not recovered. Above all, the concern was centered around the sacrament of penance, in accord with the sacramental tradition of the Latin Church.

Besides, reconciliation was a theological theme taken up by German Idealism. The romantic poets launched the theme of humanity divided within itself and of the aspiration for a reconciliation of the human being within itself. This theme was assumed theologically and philosophically by Hegel who laid much stress upon it. From Hegel the theme was picked up by Marx and in fact the theme of reconciliation is fundamental in Marxist philosophy. If we did not know the president of CELAM so well, we might have been led to conclude that, in proposing a theology of reconciliation, he was suggesting and stimulating dialogue with Marxism. Unfortunately, this hypothesis needs to be disposed of immediately. It does not fit at all with the actual concerns of the presidency of CELAM. In any case, the German idealists opened up a perspective. Henceforth, it would not be possible to develop a theology of reconciliation without reference to Hegel and Marxism.

On the other hand, reconciliation is also able to signify a certain kind of political project. In Latin America we already say that this term covers varying projects: the transition to democracy in Chile; the re-integration of the guerillas into national society in Colombia; the eventual cessation of hostilities in Central America. It also implies attempts to obtain amnesty for members of the military implicated in the contravention of human rights in Argentina- however we must pause as we do not wish to prolong the list in an article that is not political.

Inasmuch as the term reconciliation designates a theological reality and a political reality, any theology of reconciliation exposes itself to the danger of 'reductionism'.

---

2   B. Bartmann, *Teologia dogmática*, 3 vols (São Paulo: Ed. Paulinas, 1962).

That is, of deriving from a religious legitimation a definitive political stance. Such a danger is able to be avoided, but it is necessary to take into account the possible conditions for a non-reductionist theology. There exists a connection between the salvation of God and earthly conditions: such salvation indeed begins already in this world. However there must be agreement on what exactly this connection is and where exactly it is located. Not every political project can bear the name of reconciliation, or merit inclusion in theology. Divine reconciliation is not necessarily incarnated in any project to which humans give the name reconciliation. It is not sufficient to adopt this name to receive theological cover.

Some persons, somewhat maliciously, have suggested that a theology of reconciliation was proposed as an alternative to the theology of liberation which had developed in Latin America. But it is impossible to imagine that the president of CELAM would be so ingenuous and simplistic, since the theme of reconciliation is included obviously, within liberation theology. This involves all the biblical and theological themes: it is not a limited conjunction of themes, but rather a new understanding of all themes. Reconciliation will have a different interpretation in a theology of liberation, than in a bourgeois theology. In no way could reconciliation function as an alternative to liberation, as far as the fear of Marxist contamination goes, reconciliation is more affected by Marxism than liberation, in virtue of the the the Hegelian tradition to which Marx is indebted.

These considerations lead us to propose in this article some considerations of the following points: a] a Pauline theology of reconciliation, b] the development of the theme of reconciliation in the Church through to the present, c] the theology of reconciliation of the Second Vatican Council, d] reconciliation and Marxism, e] reconciliation as a political project and as a theology, and finally, f] reconciliation in the Latin American context.

## a. The Pauline Theology of Reconciliation

Saint Paul understood reconciliation on three levels: a Christological level in which Christ is the mediator through whom God reconciles Godself with humanity; an ecclesiological level in which Christ reconciles the Jews and the Gentiles; and a cosmic level in which Christ reconciles in himself all powers in heaven and on earth. Paul relates these three levels; in fact the three are related; there is in all of them a planned unity. The same divine design, the same 'mystery' of the Father, unites in a single image the three levels. The same divine design is encountered in all three. The three mutually illumine each other. If we separate one of the three levels from the other two, the specificity of the Pauline theology disappears.

### 1. Reconciliation between God and Humanity

Saint Paul does not often use the language of reconciliation. He uses the term *katallasso* (to reconcile) six times, the word *katallege* (reconciliation) four times, and the word *apokatallasso* (to reconcile) three times. The majority of times this usage refers to reconciliation between God and humanity: five times the word *katallasso* (Rom. 5:10 twice; 2 Cor. 5:18, 19, 20), while the sixth case does not have a specific theological significance, referring to reconciliation between a man and his wife (1 Cor. 7:11).

In the Captivity Epistles, Paul uses the term *apokatallasso* three times: twice with reference to reconciliation between Jews and Gentiles (Eph. 2:16; Col. 1:20) and once to reconciliation between Christ and the powers of heaven and of the earth (Col.1:20). As far as the substantive noun *katallege* is concerned, it is used three times to refer to reconciliation between God and humanity (Rom. 5:11; 2 Cor. 5:18, 19) and once to reconciliation between the Jews and the Gentiles (Rom.11:15). These few uses of the vocabulary of reconciliation are significant because they are localized in important sections of the epistles. They reveal an elaborate theology even though less important in the thought of Paul than the theology of justification, with which it is closely associated. We just wish to call attention to some items from this paragraph of reconciliation between God and humanity

[a] The author of reconciliation is God. The word reconciliation is drawn from the language of human relationships. It is not a word drawn from religious vocabulary. Amongst humans there are friendships and enmities. Enemies are to be reconciled. Amongst humans, reconciliation is a reciprocal action. Therefore the verb is used as a reflexive: two persons are reconciled. Eventually a third person intervenes in order to reconcile two enemies. Between persons, reconciliation presupposes two actions, two processes from the two adversaries which draw the one closer to the other. The two adversaries change their personal dispositions, and become friends. The change subjectively and their relationship changes because they have changed their subjective dispositions.

Between God and humanity it does not happen like this. God does not change his subjective dispositions. Neither do humans. There is no relationship of equality. Thus no accord results between the two. Pauline reconciliation refers to an objective fact. Before God humanity remains hostile and is transformed into friendship. This occurs through a divine act. Humans can effect nothing to result in this action. This rather is the result of a free and gracious disposition of the Father. The subject of reconciliation is not two, God and humanity, but rather God alone. Humanity is reconciled but does not reconcile. Humanity does not return to God seeking reconciliation. Everything comes from God.[3] From there then is the formulation of the Pauline texts. 'While we were yet enemies, we were reconciled to God ... once reconciled we shall be saved ... since we have received reconciliation'. (Rom. 5:10-11), and 'God reconciled us to himself through Christ and entrusted to us the ministry of reconciliation. Since then God was in Christ reconciling the world to himself, not imputing to humanity

---

3    John Paul II, *Reconciliation and Penitence in the Mission of the Church Today* (1984) Nos 5, 6, 10; J. Dupont, *La reconciliation dans la Théologie de Saint Paul* (Lovaina-Bruges-Paris, Publications Universitaires de Louvain, 1953), 6–19.

their faults and placing amongst us the word of reconciliation' (2 Cor. 5:18–19). We were enemies. Now we are friends, reconciled. We can say nothing. Everything comes from God. The subject of reconciliation is God. God altered our situation. God removed from us our sins and made us God's friends.

In this way reconciliation is presented as the core of the gospel: It is good news. It is the following: We do not have to preoccupy ourselves about sin. We no longer have to fear God because of our sin. There is no room for anxiety, or a sense of culpability, nor even that modern aggression against a God who reprimands and punishes.

Now, either by virtue of a very ancient cultural atavism, or by virtue of a systematically culpable preaching, many of our contemporaries perceive God as a great master who reprimands and punishes. In earlier times our ancestors indeed feared and accepted such a repressive God. Today humanity has rebelled and has become incredulous because it seeks to rebel against such a God who implacably reprimands and punishes. Indeed the gospel of Paul declares the contrary. Even before we knew that we were sinners, we learn that we are reconciled. The gospel announces that we are at peace with God, without the necessity of fear, indeed reconciled. From this reconciliation we understand that we are sinners. But our sin appears to us at the same time as our pardon. The Christian conscience of sin is part of the awareness of reconciliation. The gospel announces that we are pardoned, before we had the time necessary to enter into a state of culpability.[4]

We know well that this gospel of reconciliation is still far away from the religious mentality of Latin America's peoples. In fact the Latin American people were subjected to a guilty conscience in two senses: first, as the destination of a culpabilifying message which had developed from the end of the Middle Ages in Europe; and secondly, because as Blacks and Native American Indians they were pagans and were always suspected of wishing to return to their paganism. Blacks, Indians, Mestizos, were always greater sinners than others. This attitude was also behind the denial of priestly ordination to most of these individuals. For centuries, the Latin American Church convinced itself that Blacks, Indians or assimilated, mixed castes did not possess the conditions for the priesthood or for religious life (the state of perfection). After all, they were members of races less perfect than the race of the conquistadors. The message of reconciliation was not announced. In fact, reconciliation should have been doubly the object of evangelization.

That reconciliation should be the object of evangelization is noted in the words of the apostle, when he speaks of 'the ministry of reconciliation' (2 Cor. 5:18) and of 'the word of reconciliation' (2 Cor. 5:19). It expresses the ministry of the apostle

---

4   See John Paul II, *Reconciliation and Penitence in the Mission of the Church Today* (1984), no. 13. In the past, the Church's pastoral work advocated indiscriminately human culpability, and for many this past is still the only experience of the Church they had. Thus the revolt of the masses is a silent revolt which is manifested by absence. See the classic work by J. Delumeau, *Le péché et la peur. La culpabilisation en Occident. XIII–XVII siècles*. (Paris: Fayar, 1983).

who proclaims reconciliation and by doing that he makes it real. So this word of reconciliation is powerful and produces its effect: it produces faith and constitutes a new humanity, renewed in faith.[5]

God is not conditioned by anything to reconcile humanity with Godself. God does not expect an expiation, nor reparations, nor satisfaction. God freely takes the initiative and makes it gratis too. God does not depend on any prior condition.[6] Our part is 'to receive reconciliation' (Rom. 5:11). In this sense then we must reinterpret a possible misinterpretation of 2 Corinthians 5:20, 'reconcile yourselves with God'. It does not mean the establishment of the prior conditions of reconciliation. The Greek text clearly states the contrary. What we ought to do is to actively receive pardon from God, accept it and make it our own.[7] For the reconciliation of God does not turn us into passive recipients. It makes us new creatures, new human beings, and therefore, active and free (2 Cor. 5:17).

[b] God's reconciliation was made as a function of the final judgment. By virtue of reconciliation, what we await on that last day is not the 'wrath' of God, but indeed 'salvation' (Rom. 5:9–10).

The object of reconciliation is the final accomplishment of our lives. Reconciliation is thus a promise of accomplishment. It turns us from destructive anguish. Reconciliation is a promise for the final point of life. The judgment will be favorable. The sentence will be positive. We do not need to seek for guarantees, to make calculations, to attempt to guest the future, or to wonder about the final resolution of our existence. We are able to commit ourselves to the present moment because, if we are reconciled, we will be saved (Rom. 5:10).

The wrath of God does not refer to the sentiments or subjective dispositions of God. It is the description of a matter of fact, the state of separation between God and humanity. Such was the condition of humanity. Not that we knew this before. We learn about this situation when we have already been saved from it. [8]

Reconciliation that removes from us the threat of future wrath has indeed an effect in present life. Thanks to it, we are able to begin a new life. Our earthly existence is, through partial failures, always resuming and renewing, a process of repeated phases of renewal. Already now there is no sin or failure that would be an impermeable barrier, an insuperable obstacle. Everything is surmountable. Reconciliation is not offered a single time or for a single moment, but rather occurs throughout our whole life as a permanent source of renewal.

---

5    J. Dupont, *La reconciliation dans la Théologie de Saint Paul*, 22f; H. G. Link, entry 'Reconciliación', in *Diccionario Teológico del Nuevo Testamento*, vol. IV (Salamanca: Ed. Sígueme, 1984), 46f. [Translation of Lothar Coenen, E. Bayreuther and H. Bietenhard (eds), *Theologisches Begriffslexikon zum Neuen Testament* (Wuppertal: Brockhaus, 1971)].

6    The gratuitousness of reconciliation is the parallel to the gratuitousness of justification. C. F. J. Dupont, *La reconciliation dans la Théologie de Saint Paul*, 29–33.

7    J. Dupont, *La reconciliation*, 10–18.

8    J. Dupont, *La reconciliation*, 24–28.

[c] God reconciles humanity with Godself through Jesus Christ and, most specifically, through the cross, death, and the blood of Jesus. Jesus's blood and death have value of a propitiatory sacrifice, they destroy sin and the hostility between God and humanity.[9] The Pauline texts explicitly expose the connection between Jesus's blood and God's reconciliation.

'We were reconciled with God through the death of God's son' (Rom. 5:10); 'We now rejoice in God through our Lord Jesus Christ, through whom we have now received reconciliation' (Rom. 5:11); 'God who reconciled us to Godself through Christ' (2 Cor. 5:18); 'God who in Christ has reconciled the world to Godself' (2 Cor. 5:19);' He who knew not sin, God made sin for our sake' (2 Cor. 5:21); 'to reconcile both with God in one body, through the cross' (Eph. 2:16); 'He reconciled us in his body of flesh by his death' (Col. 1:22).

These texts are similar to others which present the death and the blood of Christ as a propitiatory sacrifice, as an expiation for sins (Mk. 10:45; Rom. 3:25; Heb. 9–10). In order to understand them, we should take into account the meaning of expiation and of propitiation in the Old Testament.[10]

From the Middle Ages on, Latin theology, deeply influenced by Saint Anselm, understood the biblical ideas of expiation and propitiation in a pagan religious sense. In the modern period this damage worsened even more. It created a monstrous representation of the death of Jesus. Now it was understood that the pardon of God was subordinate to punishment. God was not able to pardon before someone had suffered punishment. The prior punishment was thus a condition of reconciliation with God. It was claimed that Jesus had accepted the punishment: his death had been the punishment demanded by the wrath of God in order to pardon the sin of humanity. Still today, such ideas permeate the thought of many among our people. How can they reconcile this vision of a cruel and implacable God with the biblical themes of the goodness and mercy of God? Probably what happened was that people recited the catholic doctrine as they recited a sacred text without fully understanding it. Being a sacred text, it was not questioned. It was accepted as such, no matter how absurd. After all, throughout human history, people have accepted such absurd and even monstrous religious doctrines. No one understands but everyone accepts it because they ought to accept it: for if they do not accept it they are condemned as heretics. In order not to be treated as a heretic a person is disposed to say anything.

In any case in the Scriptures, there is an absolutely fundamental reference: God is not determined by anything nor by anyone. God does not need to punish in order to forgive. God pardons without punishment. God always takes the initiative. God's mercy has no limits and does not depend upon any prior condition. So then, how must we understand 'expiation'?

In the Scriptures, expiation does not have the meaning which is typically found in our dictionaries. For the Israelites had an objective conception of sin. Sin

---

9    Cf. John Paul II, *Reconciliation and Penitence*, vol. 1, no. 7, 254–71.

10   Cf. G. Von Rad, *Theologie des Alten Testaments* (Munich: Kaiser Verlag, 1958), vol. 1, 264–271; H-G Link, entry 'Reconciliation', 39ff.

is the entrance of an evil into human society. Sin is simply a subjective reality as understood by medieval and modern society. Sin is more like a contagious sickness. As in a contagious sickness a bacteria enters and creates a danger for all, so sin is a reality that introduces a principle of destruction into society. It does not only create a danger, but also unleashes a succession of destructive consequences. Sin drives people to destruction. In order to remove this ill that has entered the world, only God is able to intervene. Only God can save us from this sin.

God intervenes to destroy the sin which has entered the world. God decides to do it in a visible and material way. Thus the sacrifice: the sacrifice is not offered to God. On the contrary, who offers the sacrifice is God. The priests are representatives of God to perform the sacrifice which will remove sin. The sacrifice is like a serum which works against the sin which has entered humanity, it is the means by which God saves humanity. To expiate sin does not mean to endure a punishment, but on the contrary, to perform a protective act that overcomes the danger of sin, which removes the evil of sin from this world. Therefore the one who expiates sin is God. The subject of expiation is God. Humanity is the beneficiary, the recipient of expiation.[11]

So expiation is a means given by God in order to destroy human sin and in this way save humanity from destruction and death. In the New Testament, the inability of the sacrifices of the Old Testament to accomplish this is shown. They were given as a preparation only. But it was not through such means that God expiated sin. Jesus is the means used by God. The personal death of Jesus that the Father accepted (and did neither wish nor decree) is the means given by God. The blood shed by Jesus is the means used by the Father to expiate sin, that is, to destroy the sin in our midst. Jesus' death was not a punishment: it was an act of faith, of confidence in the Father, and of love. For whoever killed Jesus was certainly not the Father, but rather the unbelievers.

The reconciliation of God is accomplished by means of this sacrifice of Jesus. There was no punishment. God, wishing to give a sign of pardon to humanity, sent God's son to them. Humanity murdered him. Despite that, God did not give up, but made the very death of the Son the sign of God's pardon and the means for the gift of pardon. Jesus's death was not the necessary condition in order that God might pardon. If God accepted that, it is the sign that God was disposed to pardon all by any manner and that nothing was able to stop God's will to pardon. Not even the terrible reception by God's people was able to prevent God pardoning and saving humanity from the disease of sin. There cannot be a more evident testimony of pardon.

---

11 The book of Leviticus, which speaks of expiation, reveals that the best translation is not so much expiation but rather purification. It deals with it as an act given or established by God as a means of purification. God gave blood to the Israelites in order that they could make purification – expiation with it. This blood did not represent any privation, suffering, or 'penitence', since the blood contained the life and was given by God as a means of redemption. It is a means of purification because it contained the life and not because it is a privation, an act of death (Lev. 17:10 ff.).

## 2. Reconciliation between Jews and Pagans

*[a] The texts:*

Reconciliation between God and humanity has a 'horizontal' aspect within the history of humanity. In a single movement, God reconciles humanity with Godself and with each other. Hostile peoples are reconciled to each other through the same act by which they were reconciled with God. How is it that this happens?

We start from the opposition between Jews and pagans. For the Jews, they deal with the most fundamental facts of humanity and their history. No opposition is as radical as the opposition between Israel and the rest of humanity, all pagan. For in Israel's mind there existed a covenant between God and Israel and there did not therefore exist any covenant with the other peoples. Israel is the elect people and so the rest are the rejected peoples. Israel has all the privileges enunciated in Romans 9:4–5. The other peoples have nothing. Israel is the friend of God. The other peoples are the enemies of God.

For the Jews this situation was so self-evident that it underlies whatever religious arrangement. Noone felt the necessity of explaining this because for everyone the existence of the people of Israel was a most obvious certainty. Besides, Paul made it the centre of his own considerations. According to Paul, with Christ something radical happened in the history of the world because the ancient and traditional opposition between Jews and pagans had been removed. With that the history of the world had radically changed. According to Paul, Christ achieved two reconciliations at the same time and both had profound implications for the other. Christ reconciled the Father with humanity and reconciled the pagans with the Jews.

How are both these events connected? Since Christ became the means of reconciliation with God, all the other means claimed by the Jews have been eliminated. The whole system of beliefs, rituals and preconceptions which constituted the people of Israel were revealed not only as useless but as prejudiced. The whole system kept the pagans separated. Once the system disappears the opposition also disappears. The Jewish system no longer represents the mediation of the Father. Christ is that mediation.

However, the case is more difficult for the Jews. Paul perceives that God now prefers the pagans as far they do not have the Jewish system and are not bound to it. The fact of being a pagan now seems to be a privilege. God now prefers those who do not have any system of reconciliation, because they appear to be poorer before God, receiving everything from God. The pure and gratuitous mercy of God becomes more evident in the case of the pagans: it is made clear that they do not merit anything, that they cannot reach, or have any right to, salvation. In their case then it becomes evident that in salvation, everything proceeds from God.[12]

---

12  J. Dupont, *La reconciliation dans la Théologie de Saint Paul*, 42–46; R. Schnackenburg, *Der Brief an die Epheser* Evang.-Katholischer Kommentar zum Neuen Testament, X. (Zurich-Einsiedeln: Benzinger-Neukirchener, 1982), 116–122; Norbert Hugedé, *L'Epître aux Colossiens* (Geneva: Ed. Labor et fides, 1968), 78–84; also of value is the essay by E. Peterson

Conversely, with their religious system, the Jews claim merit and think that they deserve salvation. They think that they acquire or are able to acquire rights to it. The Jews are invited to return to the source of their condition. Their people were and ought to be a witness of gratitude of God's love. Instead they have replaced this message by a message of trust in themselves. In order to re-establish the system of the absolute mercy of God the Jews are invited to abandon their presumed privileges, acknowledging that the only mediator of reconciliation is Jesus.

For the Jews then, reconciliation through Jesus means the renunciation of their religious system. For the pagans God's reconciliation means that they are no longer obligated to the Jewish system. Jews and pagans encounter each other in Christ as equals. This equality is precisely what scandalizes the Jews and rejoices the pagans. Reconciliation between Jews and pagans does not demand of everyone the same thing: it precisely demands reversed behaviors.

The equality between Jews and pagans is now the great sign that God is the only author of reconciliation. It is the evidence that everything comes from God and that human religious systems do not help, but rather hinder. Placing the pagans on an equal footing with the Jews, Christ manifests the true nature of reconciliation, a gracious act of the Father.

> He is our peace, who has made us both one, and has broken down the dividing wall of hostility, by abolishing in his flesh the law of commandments and ordinances, that he might create in himself one new man in place of the two, so making peace, and might reconcile us both to God in one body through the cross, thereby bringing the hostility to an end. And he came and preached peace to you who were afar off and peace to those who were near, for through him we both, Jews and gentiles, have access in one spirit to the Father (Eph. 2:14–18).

Enmity came from the law, and Jesus overcame the law and abolished it. Indeed nothing separates Jews and Gentiles. All are equally reconciled with God and form a single body in Christ. Forming a single body, they are reconciled. Neither the Jews, nor the Greeks have anything to contribute to this reconciliation. It was accomplished by God through the abolition of the law. Nothing is asked of the Jews to do in order to reconcile themselves with the pagans, nor is anything asked of the pagans to reconcile themselves with the Jews. God accomplishes all through Christ. The law is abolished and forming a single body in Christ, all has been done: everyone has been reconciled with God and with each other.

'You who once were estranged and enemies, by your thoughts and by your actions, He now, through his death, has reconciled you through his body of flesh, by his death'. (Col. 1:21–22.) In reality, this plan of God's presented in the Captivity Epistles, is a plan that he accomplished entirely alone at the end of time. The Jews were invited, but did not accept. They placed themselves outside the plan of God. Nevertheless, Paul awaits a future reconciliation at the end of time (Rom. 11:25–

---

published in 1933 in Salzburg and re-edited much later. See E. Peterson, 'Die Kirche aus Juden und Heiden', in *Theologische Traktate*, Vol. V (Munich: Kosel, 1951), 239–292.

32). The new man who unites the two peoples now is a hope. Until now only the gentiles accepted the Father's reconciliation and the Jews have remained outside. Those who had been 'the elect' now are 'the rejected'. In Romans chapters 9 to 11 Paul explains at length this mystery of the wisdom of God. 'Their rejection resulted in the reconciliation of the world' (Rom 11:15). God desires to reconcile the world, pardoning the gentiles and lifting the barrier which separated them from the Jews. They however did not accept this and ended up outside the way of salvation. Thus the reconciliation between the gentiles and the Jews yet remains a project. On the side of the gentiles nothing lacks. Paul, however, is persuaded that the Jews shall return in the end of time.

*[b] The Dialectic between Jews and Pagans in History*
Is it so that the reconciliation between Jews and Gentiles still constitutes a significant reality for us today? Are we not dealing with an event that was definitely dealt with in the past?

Our reply is provided through patristic exegesis. It proposes a typological interpretation of the Bible.[13] The events of the Bible have typological value. They help us to understand the events of contemporary life and of all time. What occurred in biblical times is a type, an image of that which has happened since then in the history of the world which is embedded in Christianity. What the Bible shows from the past illumines that is happening now.

Typology provides the basic principles for a theology of history. Medieval theology and the Latin theology that was derived from it, ignored history and were not able to provide any meaning to the history of Christianity. They left aside the typology of the Bible and adopted the fundamentals of Greek philosophy which did not have any principles for interpreting history. Thus even Saint Thomas became radically allergic to history: the *Summa Theologica* absolutely lacks historical reference or even any interpretation of history. Apart from some allusions in support of the Crusades, it could have been written in any period of history.

Patristic typology offers a solution that the scholastics neglected because of their lack of interest and because of the prestige of the Greek philosophers. Indeed Origen teaches that the dialectic of the Jew, of the pagan and of the Christian still exists in the present. For a Jew, a pagan and a Christian continue to live inside us. In fact, dialectic reflects an internal process within every Christian.[14]

In the modern and contemporary periods, in general, exegetes have not given much attention to the dialectic between the Jews and the pagans. For their part, theologians who had been in search of a theology of history, poorly understood the Pauline dialectic. Nevertheless, without a doubt the Pauline dialectic between Jew and pagan occupies a central place in Pauline theology. But it was not sufficiently

---

13  Cf. P. Grelot, *Sens Chrétien de L'Ancien Testament* (Tournai-Paris: Desclée, 1962), 209–248, 286–326.

14  Cf. J. Daniélou, *Origène* (Paris: La Table Ronde, 1948), 166f.

valued. Until the time of the Second Vatican Council, Judaism little interested Christians.

The one who drew together Pauline exegesis and the theology of history was the French Jesuit Gaston Fessard. He dedicated various books and articles to the subject of the dialectic between the Jews and the pagans, and these constitute the core of his thought.[15]

For Fr. Fessard, the Jewish, pagan, and Christian dialectic is a primary key principle for the theological interpretation of history. He in his own work applied it to contemporary history. He discovered the Jewish – pagan opposition operating in a similar fashion in the actual opposition of the two great systems that struggled against each other in an implacable war this century: Communism and Nazism. The Communists are the Jews and the Nazis are the pagans. Since in Communism one encounters a temporal Messianism typical of Judaism and an attachment to law which ought to be the matrix of the messianic kingdom. In Nazism one encountered the incarnation of a pagan spirit, of the adoration of the creature, the exaltation of struggle and of force.[16] However, Fessard insisted more in describing the two opposed systems, than in describing their reconciliation with Christianity. From a theological point of view, he used the dialectic to identify and to judge the great ideologies our time, rather than to improve historical Christianity.

Fessard also used the Jewish-pagan dialectic to judge and to denounce the well-known 'progressivism' then being debated in France between 1945 and 1955 and finally resolved by Pope Pius XII.[17] The progressivist movement was on the side of the Communists and can be judged, according to Fessard, by the same method. The author mixed his condemnation of progressivism with critical comments on the role of the Dominicans, notably of Chenu, in the debates surrounding progressivism and the worker-priests. He attributed to the Thomism of Dominicans their historical naïveté which made them victims of the seductions of contemporary philosophies of history. This controversy with the Thomists deeply fractured this author's potential audience.

However, the idea of the Jewish-pagan dialectic as a key to the interpretation of Christian history is worth being reformulated. We will not apply this dialectic to the debate within each Christian, as Origen did, although this application also could be valid, worthwhile for the Christian spiritual journey. Rather we shall be rather faithful followers of Paul by applying it to the Church, so as the Church in its origins was confronted by the Jews and the pagans, and, in a certain way arrived at its historical expression through confrontation between these two poles, so also it has been challenged throughout history by the resurgence of these two poles even though in differing ways. There has always been within the Church a 'Jewish' pole and a 'pagan' pole. The Church always is the reconciliation of God accomplished

---

15  Most importantly, see the essays collected in Gaston Fessard, *De L'Actualitè historique* (Paris: Desclée de Brouwer, 1960).

16  Cf. G Fessard, *De L'Actualitè historique*, volume I, 25–56, 121–241.

17  G. Fessard, *De L'Actualitè historique,* volume I, 27–147.

according to the rule defined by Paul. Reconciliation is accomplished not through a synthesis but rather through the rejection of the 'Jew' and through the acceptance of the 'pagan'. This is not the acceptance of paganism, it is rather the total transformation of the pagan in Christ, but without paying the high price that the Jews wish to exact

In his dialectic, Fessard opposed above all two complete systems, the Jewish and the pagan. In his dialectic Saint Paul did not give such attention to two systems, but rather to the relations between the two poles. The characteristic of the Jew is the rejection of the pagan. For the Jew, God rejects the pagan and the true believer must follow God in this stance. The pagans are not characterized by any system, but above all by rejection. The pagans are sinners and being sinners are worthy of rejection by God and by the Jews. The moment of reconciliation comes. It produces the reverse of these roles. God chooses the pagans and overturns the exclusivism of the Jews. The Jews are still called and chosen, but do not accept the invitation made to the pagans, a shameful invitation in their view. The Pauline dialectic deals not so much with a synthesis between two opposed poles as rather with an inversion. Reconciliation is an inversion of the relationships. The pagans, who were afar off, now come near, and the Jews who were near, are now afar off.

From this perspective we can ask who today in the church represents the role played by the pagan, and that played by the Jew. Who was treated with rejection and now is chosen by God? Who did want to be the incarnation of God's fidelity and the incarnation of the truth, and ended up being rejected for not accepting the company of the pagans?

In historical material we arrive at nothing with absolute certainty. The sciences of history are made of approximations. Each fact is unique. Nevertheless there are between the facts continuities, reformulations, repetitions adapted to new contexts. There are similarities. There are no absolute laws, but comparisons which illumine situations. Historical reality never is totally rational. Neither is it purely irrational. Consequently we are able to suggest comparisons and to consider rationally that they have a basis, but we are never able to identify with absolute certainty one or numerous events as being a repetition of past events. This uncertainty in theological reflection however, does not diminish its value. The Bible itself offers an interpretation of history based upon comparisons: namely typology. The return from the Babylonian exile is compared with the Exodus from Egypt even though there are not perfect similarities and the two events are indeed different. What the Bible shows is the equal value and content of the revelation of various events which are linked through typology. The facts are diverse, but the theological content, the message, the teaching, is the same.

Today there does not exist within or without the Church a pure Jew or a pure pagan, according to the Pauline view. But the theological value, the meaning of his opposition, still exists. There are situations in the Church today to which apply the 'Pauline' dialectic of Jew and pagan and of the concept of reconciliation.

Here are some suggestions. In Latin America the pagan, always rejected as an irredeemable sinner, is the Native American Indian. The Native American Indian has to jump thousands of years of culture in order to be a 'Christian'. The 'Jews' impose upon him all the culture of the 'Latin' Church with its liturgy, its right, its theology, all of this being the fruit of 4,000 years and more of cultural evolution. The Native American Indian has to accept all of this at once. In the midst of this cultural confusion, will he/she still be able to understand the Gospel's voice? Will he/she be able to fully hear the voice of the Gospel in the midst of such voices which suddenly cry out at the same time? Facing this situation, what does reconciliation comprise according to Saint Paul?

What does 'reconciliation' signify for the Blacks in Brazil? If reconciliation signifies a reversal of situations, would not the Blacks be the primary ones privileged by reconciliation? In the Catholic Church, what is the participation in black culture? What is the participation of Blacks in the episcopate, the clergy and in religious institutions? What is their participation in theology, in canon law? Everything is white.

The same inversion of situations that is reconciliation is able to be proposed by women confronted by a patriarchical Church and by workers in industrial society confronted by an ecclesiastical institution formed in medieval rural conditions. The problems are more acute even for separated Christians. From the sixteenth century onwards never have so large a number of catholics crossed over to reformed Protestantism as has occurred in Latin America during the twentieth century. Can we reckon that the thirty or forty million catholics who discovered the gospel of Christ in Pentecostal Churches will ever return to the Catholic Church in the form they knew it? Impossible. They are the new pagans rejected by an institution attached to a moribund past that did not offer them any help when they were seeking the Gospel.

All these categories, which unite at least 90 per cent of baptized Latin Americans, are the pagans who are in the Church. They are the pagans who demand true 'reconciliation', that is, the inversion of the contemporary situations. The Church in order to truly be the Church, shall have to consider these pagans. Otherwise it shall have the fate of the 'Judaizing Christians' of the first century.

*3. Reconciliation of the World*

Some texts of Saint Paul speak of a reconciliation that extends to the world, to everything, to all beings that are in the heavens and upon the earth. There does not exist unanimity regarding the interpretation of these texts. Some think that reconciliation refers uniquely and always to human beings, and that all these texts thus refer to human beings. Others think that Saint Paul desires to say something more. First then let us examine the texts.

*[a] The Texts*
'For their rejection resulted in the reconciliation of the world'. (Rom. 11:15) Here 'the world' can signify simply the nations of the world, the inhabitants of the world, the totality of humans (except the Jews). It does not impose an extension to the meaning of the world save that of humanity. Now here is the text which is the origin of the problem: 'and through Him to reconcile to Himself all things, things on earth

and things in heaven'. (Col. 1:20). 'All things', in Greek *ta panta*, so 'everything', does still not demand an extension beyond that of humanity. In biblical usage, 'everything' can refer to the human world, the only one which directly concerns God. The addition however 'things on earth and things in heaven', seems to open a broader perspective. Throughout the preceding verses, Col. 1:15-16, the expressions 'everything' and 'things on earth and things in heaven' receive a more detailed content. Christ is described as 'first-born of all creation' (Col. 1:15), and not only of humanity. 'For in Him all things were created, in heaven and on the earth, visible and invisible, whether thrones, or dominions or principalities or authorities, all things were created through Him and for Him' (Col. 1:16). Here 'everything' clearly refers to powers which are in the heavens. In relation to creatures of the earth, is it limited to humans? Are the powers of heaven just the powers that govern human beings, their nations and religions? Or was Paul also thinking of the whole of the material world?[18]

In the Epistle to the Ephesians there is a similar text: 'God has a plan to unite all things in Christ, those things in the heavens and those things on the earth' (Eph. 1:10). The word 'unite' (or 'recapitulate') corresponds to the word 'reconcile' of Colossians, and the theme is similar.[19] In the Epistle to the Romans Paul affirms that the entire creation is touched by the freedom of Christ: 'the creation was subject to futility ...in hope the creation itself will be set free from the bondage of corruption in order to enter into the liberty of the glory of the children of God. Since we know that the whole creation groans and suffers in travail until now' (Rom. 8:20ff). Here there seems to be a clear distinction between humanity and the material world.

Interpretation depends in part on what precise meaning is given to the 'heavenly powers'. We are not able here to make either a full exegetical study of the cited texts, nor present an exposition on the problem of the powers in Saint Paul.[20] So we will just cite the facts that apply to the interpretation of the texts of the union of the powers and of the whole material world in the redemption of Christ.

There are two important schools of interpretation: The first reckons that the Pauline concept of the powers derives entirely from Judaism: and in this case the powers are the angels. In late Judaism the angels occupy the role of intermediaries between God and His people. They are the mediators of the law. The angels are also able to effect the material world, but normally in benefit for and in dependence upon

---

18 Cf. The extensive discussion in the commentary by Eduard Schweizer, *Der Brief and der Kolosser Evangelisch-Katholisch Kommentar zum Neuen Testament* (Zurich-Neukirchen: Benzinger-Neukirchener Verlag, 1980), 192–205.

19 Cf. H–G. Link, article 'Reconciliación', in *Diccionario teològico del Nuevo Testamento*, Volume IV (Salamanca: Sigueme, 1984), 44–48; R. Schnackenburg, *Die Brief an die Epheser*, Evangelisch-Katholisch Kommentar zum Neuen Testament (Zurich-Neukirchen: Benzinger-Neukirchener Verlag, 1982), 57–60.

20 See the article 'Puissances', by M. Cambe in Louis Pirot (ed.), *Supplément au Dictionnaire de la Bible* (Paris: Letouzey et Ané, 1926).

the chosen people. Besides Judaism is not interested in the evolution of the material world in itself. The world is centred in the people of Israel.[21]

The other school thinks that Paul is inspired by a concept largely drawn from the pagan world of his time. In Greek culture there was always curiosity regarding the composition of the world and a search for its 'elements'. The idea dominated that the world was made from a combination of a few simple elements. There was also the conviction that disorder and chaos ruled between the elements and that such disorder was the cause of problems, of the conflicts between human beings. The creation or the world was thus immersed in disorder. The better spirits aspired to a reconciliation of the world's forces in a state of internal struggle. War was thus part of the constitution of the world: from here it would be necessary to reconstitute order.

In the Greek world there gradually prevailed the idea that the visible and material elements of the world were governed by spirits, and by the way, this conviction was shared by many peoples in many cultures. There was struggle between the visible elements because there was struggle between the invisible powers. Thus this concept urges reconciliation of this world of heavenly powers and thus they will control the earthly elements. The Pauline message of the reconciliation of the creation must then be a response to this anxiety of the pagan world.[22]

We are not able here to settle this question. Naturally if the powers are of Greek inspiration, then in the first place they refer to the whole cosmos, for the Greeks, humanity was part of the whole cosmos. If the powers are rather just the Jewish angels, it is not so obvious that they include the material world. It is not probable that a decisive argument to this question will ever be reached. Therefore the whole problem of the reconciliation of the powers remains suspended. However we will have to take into account what tradition has to say.

At any rate, the reconciliation of the powers has to be examined from two points of view.

On the one hand the powers ought to be reconciled with God because they are rebels. Paul views them as associated with the enslavement of humanity. They are forces that enslave and dominate. They are separated from God. They draw to themselves what is owing to God. Therefore the work of Christ amongst them is an act of victory. Christ 'despoiled the principalities and powers, and made a public example of them, taking them in triumphant processional' (Col. 2:15). They were rebels. They return to discipline, subordinating themselves to Christ.

On the other hand, the powers have to be reconciled amongst themselves. This aspect would be clearer if the powers were of Greek origins and not just Jewish angels, who would not manifest such internal struggles. However, the very word reconciliation applied to the powers, seems to have very broad meaning.

---

21  See the article cited above by M. Cambe, wherein he strongly defends this point.

22  See the excursus by Eduard Schweizer, 'Die kolossische Philosophie', in his *Der Brief an die Kolosser*, 100–104.

Reconciliation in general normally signifies reconciliation with God and between each other, in accord with the common usage of this word in the epistles.

If the powers are of Greek provenance, reconciliation directly affects the cosmos, the material world comprising the heavens and the earth. For the powers do not just govern heaven (stars), but also the earth. If the powers are reconciled, it is a sign that the material world is also going to be reconciled. If the powers are Jewish angels, then Paul does not clearly speak of a reconciliation of the world, distinct from humanity, at least in the texts that speak of the powers.

Now we have to consider the texts that speak of 'all' (all things), or all creatures. In addition to the Pauline texts, the prologue of the Gospel of John also refers to the creation of everything by Christ.

In conclusion we can say that the texts do not require (with complete evidence), a reconciliation of the material cosmos as a result of reconciliation in Christ. It is understood however, that in the patristic tradition there were illustrious voices who understood the Pauline theology in this way. Today the problem has been presented anew.

### [b] The Problem of Universal Reconciliation

The doctrine of Colossians 1:20 on the reconciliation of all things and of all powers deeply interested the fathers of the first centuries. They interpreted it in the sense of the complete integration of the whole universe, of the entire material creation in Christ and in the freedom of Christ. Thus Justin, Irenaeus, Hippolytus, and above all, Origen.[23] Now Origen was beyond this. For he understood universal reconciliation in a radial sense: at the end of time everything, including the damned and the very demons, would be reconciled. It would be a final eschatological re-establishment of the cosmos (*apokatastasis*).[24] The subsequent school of Origen vigorously defended this doctrine of their founder. Gregory Nazianzus, Gregory of Nyssa, Didymus the Blind, Evagrius, Diodore of Tarsus, and Theodore of Mopsuestia all followed Origen.

Notwithstanding such authorities' support, the doctrine of *apokatastasis* was condemned by the Church's Magisterium.[25] It has had a long history through to the present.[26] We will not give more attention to this because what actually interests us

---

23  See the references in Eduard Schweizer, *Der Brief an die Kolosser*, 193–197.

24  See the references in Eduard Schweizer, *Der Brief an die Kolosser*, 197–202; C. Andresen and P. Althaus, 'Widerbringung Aller', in Hans Frhr von Campenhausen (ed.), *Die Religion in Geschichte und Gegenwart* (Tübingen: J. C. B. Morh, 1962), Vol. VI, columns 1693–1696.

25  The condemnation of *apokatastasis* was contained in the anathemas against the errors of Origenism adopted by the Synod of Constantinople in 543, nos 7 and 11. See Henricus Denzinger and Adolfus Schönmetzer (eds), *Enchiridion symbolorum. Definitionum et Declarationum de rebus fidei et morum.* Edition xxxii, (Barcelona: Herder, 1963), 409 and 411.

26  Numerous authors refer to Origen, mediated through the Abbot Joachim of Fiore, whose Messianism was secularized during the modern and contemporary periods, according

is the reconciliation of the whole world, of the creation as a totality beyond human limitations. The problem of *apokatastasis* passionately occupied the Fathers and the medieval Church. The moderns however seem less interested in the final fate of the condemned and the demons and more interested in the fate of the material world, the objective world which is 'the human's companion through their mundane existence'.

The modern problem was succinctly expressed by Teihard de Chardin. This was an interesting phenomenon. He was prohibited from publishing on theological materials throughout his life. Up to his death nothing was cited. But well before his death his ideas were present in many theological problems. It is possible to state that the problematic of *Gaudium et Spes* proceeds in large part from his thought. Everyone implicitly refered back to his thought, but no one mentioned him by name. Teilhard was the interpreter of the modern world formed by science, and living from and for science, and passionate about the material world. What is the destiny of this world? Is what is done in this world of any worth or not?

Theologically, the problem was formulated in the following manner: Does Christ only work in the Church and through the Church, or also in the world, in the history of the world, in the history of human societies which is linked to the history of science and of technology? Is Christ also involved in the principle of domination and development of the world?[27]

A theology of reconciliation could not prescind totally from the problematic posed by Teilhard. Today, even more so than in the time of Teilhard, science is in the centre of modern Western culture, now also virtually world-wide. Is there (or not) a cosmic Christology?[28]

The Second Vatican Council was inspired by the 'Teilhardian movement' and gave a sufficiently general response that suggested rather than properly taught. It thus left the theological problem open, though it expressed a visible sympathy. The conciliar judgments are expressed in paragraph 45 of *Gaudium et Spes*:

'For God's Word by whom all things were made, was Himself made flesh so that as perfect man he might save all men and sum up all things. The Lord is the goal of human history the focal point of the longings of history and of civilization, the center of the human race...' (see also the Brazilian edition produced by Editora Vozes, paragraph 343) . The text ends with the explicit citation from Ephesians 1:10, while the text itself is comprised of citations from both Colossians and Ephesians. Nevertheless, the Vatican Council increases its use of certain words such as history and civilization. If these words are taken in the sense of the contemporary world, then they include the material world, the objective world worked upon by humanity. Thereby the Vatican Council suggests a reconciliation of the material world within the

---

to Karl Löwith. Likewise Henri de Lubac, *La postérité spirituelle de Joachim de Fiore*, 2 vols (Paris: P. Lethielleux, 1979, 1981).

27  See Henri de Lubac, *La pensée religieuse du Père Teilhard de Chardin* (Paris: Aubier, 1962), 168–183.

28  See Eduard Schweizer, *Der Brief an die Kolosser*, 202–205.

totality of the creation. In what sense then ought we to understand this reconciliation of the whole world? This is a question that a theology of reconciliation is not able to avoid.

### b. The Destiny of the Pauline Doctrine of Reconciliation in the History of Theology

In the West at least, the Pauline doctrine did not develop. In fact it was marginalized. The principal objection to it was probably the strong dualism of Saint Augustine. Nevertheless, in the course of history there appeared isolated voices that attempted to resuscitate in some manner the Pauline and Patristic themes of universal reconciliation. In the contemporary period the theme re-appeared with greater force until it was assumed by the Second Vatican Council and by various General Assemblies of the Protestant Churches.

*1. Reconciliation In Scholastic Theology*

From its beginnings, Latin theology focused on the means of redemption rather than on the final goals. It thus devoted itself to concepts of satisfaction and of merit. Saint Augustine reinforced this tendency. Saint Anselm turned the idea of satisfaction into the center of scholastic exposition. The Anselmic school prevailed both in Protestant as well as in Catholic tradition.[29]

In the *Summa Theologica*, Saint Thomas Aquinas still dedicated an article to the theme of reconciliation (see IIIA, Q. XLIX. a. 4). 'Whether we were reconciled to God through Christ's Passion?' In practical terms, Saint Thomas reduced the theme of reconciliation to the most fundamental theme of sacrifice. He cites Romans 5: 10, but he does not cite the Pauline Captivity Epistles. For him, reconciliation does not add anything to the theme of satisfaction and of sacrifice. It is understandable that his successors could many times overlook a theme considered so insignificant.

As would be expected, his great rival John Duns Scotus valued what St. Thomas had disregarded. He went back to the texts of the Epistles of Captivity. John Duns Scotus envisions the reconciliation and redemption (for lack of a better term in the sense that recapitulacão is being used here) of all of mankind in the New Jerusalem, along with the reconciliation of the entire universe.

By its insistence on divine initiative, the Protestant reformation could have given more emphasis on universal reconciliation. However Melanchton's conservative tendency prevailed, with its scholastic insistence on human action. The most heterodox Protestant theologians were going to insist on the reconciliation of the world. In general then, those who give more emphasis to the plan of God, to the sovereign initiative of God, give also more attention to total reconciliation. Conversely, those

---

29 See F. H. Kettler, 'Versöhnung', in Hans Frhr. von Campenhausen (ed.), *Religion in Geschichte und Gegenwart*, Volume VI (Tübingen: J. C. B. Morh, 1962), columns 1373–1378.

who emphasize more human action and freedom, give more value to the theme of satisfaction and focus on the salvation around that part of humanity which fulfills all demands.[30] Viewed from another perspective, the Augustinian theme of the '*massa damnata*' made acceptable the idea that the redemption of Christ and the work of God resulted finally only in the salvation of a small number of the faithful. In this was seen not the defeat of God but rather the victory of His justice.

The Council of Trent used the term reconciliation a few times in the context of the doctrine of redemption. It was used in the third canon of the decree regarding original sin, but in an implicit citation, and in a form totally subordinate to the concept of 'merit' of Christ, which is the actual object of the canon (DS 1513).[31] The fundamental concept of Trent was that of justification, with its connections to those of satisfaction and of merit (DS 1529). Indeed, the decrees of Trent totally orient modern Catholic theology, and explain thus the subsequent silence concerning the theme of reconciliation in dogmatic theology.

## 2. Reconciliation in the Sacrament of Penance

In the Patristic period in order to reintegrate a sinner back to church two acts were distinguished: penance and reconciliation through communion. Penance did not necessarily lead to admission to communion. This was in fact a second juridical act. The texts make a distinction between penance and reconciliation. For reconciliation is the admission to communion. So they write, for example, Pope Innocent I in his epistle *Consulenti tibi* of 405 (DS 212), and Pope Leo I in his epistle *Sollicitudinis quidem tuae* of 452 (DS 308–310). Saint Augustine makes the same distinction in his letter 153.3.7,[32] or in his treatise *De adulterinis coniugiis* 2,16,16.[33] The word reconciliation is linked to communion and not directly to penitence.

In the scholastics, reconciliation does not fall under the effects of penitence. The predominance of the themes of contrition and of satisfaction did not allow space for the theme of reconciliation. Much later though, to the extent that penitence opened the door to the eucharist, the term reconciliation was attached to penitence proper: It fell under the effects of the sacrament of penitence, and it became part of the sacrament of penance itself.

In the decrees of the Council of Trent, reconciliation with God appeared effectively as part of the sacrament itself: 'Res et effectus huius sacramenti, quantum ad eius vim et efficacium pertinet, reconciliatio est cum Deo'. (Decreto de Paenitentia,

---

30 See W. Joest, 'Versöhnung', in Hans Frhr. von Campenhausen (ed.), *Religion in Geschichte und Gegenwart*, Volume VI, column 1378.

31 'DS' followed by a paragraph number refers to official church decrees, in Henricus Denzinger and Adolfus Schönmetzer (eds) *Enchiridion symbolorum. Definitionum et Declarationum de rebus fidei et morum*. Edition xxxii (Barcelona: Herder, 1963).

32 Marie Joseph Rouët de Journel, *Enchiridion patristicum: Loci ss. Partum , doctorum, scriptorium ecclesiasticorum quos in usum scholarum collegit M. J. Rouët de Journel*. 24th edn (Barcelona: Herder, 1969), 1435.

33 Marie Joseph Rouët de Journel, *Enchiridion patristicum*, 1864.

caput 3 [DS 1674]). But the Council did use most frequently the words 'remissio peccatorum' to evoke the effect of the sacrament. Thus there did not really exist, in the mind of the Council, a true theology of reconciliation linked to the sacrament of penance. After Trent the 'remission of sins' was used many more times than 'reconciliation' to express the effects of penitence.

The real introduction of the term 'reconciliation' in its theological sense within the theology of the sacrament of penance is owed to the liturgical movement of the twentieth century, which prepared Vatican Council II. This movement emphasized the theme of reconciliation as much as with God as with the Church through the sacrament of penance. *Lumen Gentium* states that the sacrament of penance reconciles with the Church (paragraph 11b). The decree *Presbyterorum Ordinis* teaches that the priests 'by the sacrament of penance reconcile sinners with God and the Church' (paragraph 5). From this then, the theme of reconciliation came to be much more closely linked to the sacrament of penance than it had before. This even came to be called the sacrament of reconciliation. The *Apostolic Exhortation* of Pope John Paul II on reconciliation and penitence in the mission of the Church today joins the two terms: 'the sacrament of penance and of reconciliation'.

*3. The Resurgence of the Theme of Universal Reconciliation in the Contemporary Epoch*

Contemporary exegesis considers Pauline theology with far more attention than before. In fact it is possible to say that it has re-discovered the Pauline theology of reconciliation and simultaneously with the patristic doctrine taught by Saint Irenaeus and Origen. Further, the biblical exegesis besides, did not develop in a world divorced from contemporary culture. It experienced the effects of the dominant themes of the civilization, notably of its philosophy. The German romantic and idealistic philosophy of the nineteenth century could not let it be without its particular influence like any in any other theology. German Protestant theology and German Protestant exegesis were the first ones to react to it. Little by little all areas of Christian theology were affected. The theme of reconciliation came into prominence.[34]

In the twentieth century there occurred a rapprochement between the world and the Gospel. The theologians more aware of the world context, sought support on the Pauline Captivity Epistles and rediscovered the theme of total universal reconciliation with God. They sought to bind these themes with the other Pauline themes of the reconciliation of humanity with God, in order not to fall into the Gnostic tendencies which frequently threatened the heterodox of the past who had maintained a memory of the Pauline theme, but had undervalued it. Thus it is not without reason that the theologian who most concentrated on the theme of reconciliation was Karl Barth in his *Church Dogmatics*.[35]

---

34 See the bibliography of the article 'Reconciliation', in Volume IV of *Diccionario teológico del Nuevo Testamento*.

35 See Heinz Zahrnt, *Die Sache mit Gott* (Munich: Piper, 1966), 115–123.

In the Catholic world the person who had the most impact was naturally Teilhard de Chardin. He sought to link, in the most intimate manner possible, the destiny of the universe studied by scientists with the redemptive work of God in Christ. In many instances the commentators referred Teihard's proposition to the Captivity Epistles, as if he had proposed an actualized reading of the Pauline hymns in the light of the contemporary sciences. Teilhard's orthodoxy was attacked many times. He appeared suspicious in the eyes of authority, which prohibited him from publishing in the religious sphere. However, theologians of great importance, such as Cardinal de Lubac, took up the defense of the orthodoxy of this great Jesuit.[36] Leaving to one side the controversial question of his orthodoxy, it is possible to discuss the range of reconciliation of all things in Christ according to Teilhard. What was most controversial about his thought was his Christology. This though, is not indispensable for a doctrine of the reconciliation of the universe. It is possible to conceptualize this without an integration into a great cosmic Christ.[37]

The great question for Teilhard was the following: 'Is or is there not convergence between the terrestrial functions of humanity in which culminate all the evolution of the earth, and the redemptive work of Christ?' In other words: Human works in the universe, through science, through technology, and through labour, do they or do they not serve the Kingdom of God? The classic Latin theology did not understand this question. The classical theology of the Latin Church sees the history of the world and redemption as two independent histories, separate and without connection. Was it able to sustain this approach? Was it possible to sustain the contrary? In a certain way Vatican Council II responded though in a very general manner. In reality the Churches are now in doubt and the subject continues to be debated with some passion.

A theology of reconciliation is not able to leave aside the explicit formation of questions raised by Teilhard de Chardin and to seek a reply. Modern scientists, technicians, workers, all await a response. It is evident that the Gospel proposed to modern humanity ought necessarily to touch on this subject.

### c. Vatican Council II's Doctrine of Reconciliation

In the documents of the second Vatican Council the word reconciliation appears thirteen times. Should there be more or less? There are not enough since it is possible to say that the theme of reconciliation is a fundamental theme of the Council's message. But it is more than in the Council of Trent and in other more such important places that, if one compared the two Councils, one can say that the second Vatican Council effected a rehabilitation of the Pauline theme of reconciliation.

---

36  Henri de Lubac, *La pensée religieuse du Père Teilhard de Chardin*. During this period the lack of confidence in Teilhard's orthodoxy reigned in many contexts.

37  See the discussion of the problem in Eduard Schweizer, *Der Brief an die Kolosser*, 202–205.

Almost all the Vatican Council texts which deal with reconciliation refer to Pauline texts, but do not take reconciliation in the Pauline sense.

One can say that the majority of the Vatican Council texts concerning reconciliation are dependent upon a very general theme of dialogue: dialogue with the world in the texts that speak of the integration of the world in Christ; dialogue with separated Christians, dialogue with the Jews, dialogue with humanity in general. Only three texts are referred to the sacrament of penance, certainly with the goal of approaching this sacrament from a more global doctrine of reconciliation, seeking to attract to the sacrament of penance some of the theology of dialogue.

Two texts from the Vatican Council's *Gaudium et Spes* use the term reconciliation, each in a very broad sense, quoting implicitly Paul and within a context of the dialogue between Christ and the world. 'In Him God reconciled us with Godself and with each other' (GS 22), with reference to 2 Cor. 5:18–19 and Col. 1:20–22. The context is that Christ gives to humanity its significance. The idea is that Christ makes the unity and the integration of the human race and not only that of the Christians.

In the chapter on the construction of peace, *Gaudium et Spes* recalls the Christological hymns of the Captivity Epistles. 'Since the incarnate son [by His cross] prince of peace, reconciled all men with God'. (GS 78). There is here no theological elaboration, but a desire to valorize the hymns of the Captivity Epistles and to introduce them to the confrontation between Church and world.

Further, in a general sense, the *Constitution on the Liturgy* uses the word reconciliation drawn from the *Sacramentarium Veronense*: 'in Christ occurred the perfect satisfaction for our reconciliation' (SC 5).

In the Decree *Ad Gentes* on the Church's missions there is a paragraph that contemplates the mission of the Son as the foundation of the evangelistic mission of the Church in the midst of the nations. In this summary of the mission of the Son, the editors compiled a text comprised of implicit New Testament citations, amongst them the Christological texts from the Captivity Epistles. Here also one senses the desire to valorize the Pauline texts which associate Christ and the universe: 'He sent His own Son in a human body, in order that He might deliver us from the power of darkness and from Satan through Him and to reconcile the world to Himself' (CAG 3, see the Brazilian translation by Ed. Vozes, No. 867, p. 353).

Most specific is the adopted in the *Decree on Ecumenism*. Reconciliation applies to the relations between the separated Churches. The first text appeals to 'actualize the reconciliation of Christians both Eastern and Western' (*Unitatis Redintegratio*, 15). In the conclusion of the Decree, the conciliar Fathers used the word reconciliation to express their intent: 'The Council declares that it realizes that this holy objective – the reconciliation of all Christians in the unity of the one and only Church of Christ, transcends human powers and gifts' (*Unitatis Redintegratio*, 24. In Brazilian Edition, Ed. Vozes, no. 829, p. 331).

In the beginning of the Decree it made a quick allusion to reconciliation in the canonical sense: the sense of return of individuals from the separated Churches to the Catholic Church: 'the reconciliation of those individuals who desire the full Catholic communion' (*Unitatis Redintegratio*, paragraph 4, in Brazilian Edition, Ed.

Vozes, no. 768, p. 315). Here there was no theology but just a pious and juridical expression.

Twice, the Council alludes to reconciliation between Jews and Christians, in referring to Pauline theology. Nevertheless, the Council did not recover appropriately the Pauline theology of the Church comprised of Jews and the pagan nations. It rather addresses the dialogue between Jews and Christians which is similar to the dialogue with the separated Christians or between Christians and non-Christians.

The Decree *Lumen Gentium* makes an enumeration of all the titles and images of the Church. It alludes to Romans 11:13–26, 'the reconciliation of the Jews and the Gentiles', but without any explication (*Lumen Gentium*, 6). In the Declaration on the relations with non-Christian religions, the Council notes that 'God reconciles all to Himself', citing clearly 2 Cor. 5:18–19 (*Nostra Aetate*, 2). In what it states concerning Judaism, the same Declaration says that 'Christ, our peace, through the cross, reconciled the Jews and the peoples and united both in Himself', citing Eph. 2:14–16 (*Nostra Aetate*, 41, in Brazilian edition, Ed. Vozes, no. 1587, p. 622).

In these texts there are thus simply allusions to the Pauline texts. There is no actual theology of reconciliation developed. The term reconciliation was selected to be a pacific term, initiating a dialogue. But there is not so much as an approximation to the Pauline theology of Jews and Gentiles.

Finally, the Council uses the word reconciliation three times to speak of the sacrament of penance, thereby initiating a new practice in sacramental language. In *Lumen Gentium* it states the following: 'Those who approach the sacrament of Penance obtain pardon from the mercy of God for the offense committed against Him and are at the same time reconciled to the Church' (*Lumen Gentium*, 11. In Brazilian edition, Ed. Vozes, no. 30, p. 51). The priests, for the sinners and sick amongst the faithful, exercise the ministry of alleviation and reconciliation' (*Lumen Gentium*, 28. In Brazilian edition, Ed. Vozes, no. 68, p. 74). In the Decree on the priesthood, the Council declared that priests 'through the sacrament of Penance reconcile sinners with God and with the Church'. (*Presbyterorum Ordinis*, 51. In Brazilian edition, Ed. Vozes, no. 1150, p. 447).

Thus in summary we are able to state that the Second Vatican Council cites rather complacently the Pauline texts on reconciliation, re-introduces the word into ecclesiastical language, but does not elaborate any theology of reconciliation.

The Second Vatican Council was extended, in a certain sense, by the Roman Synod of 1983 and by the papal Exhortation, *Reconciliatio et Paenitentia* of John Paul II. This document starts from the very general meaning of reconciliation as it was used by Vatican Council II. Practically, the word reconciliation takes on two differing meanings. On the one hand, it deals with reconciliation with God through the remission of sins. It concentrates attention upon the means of reconciliation which is the sacrament of Penance. The theology of penance is the one defined by the Council of Trent, adding to it the reconciliation with the Church, but without further development. The Exhortation is, in the first place, a new presentation of the traditional doctrine from the Council of Trent. It attempts to provide a remedy for the crisis in the sacrament of Penance.

Besides this sacramental meaning of reconciliation this document uses the word reconciliation in the sense of overcoming conflicts in general. There exist conflicts in the contemporary world, and conflicts within the Church. Reconciliation is able to signify that the Church has a specific mission of overcoming or resolving the conflicts that exist within the Church itself or in the world. It expresses an extension of the concept of reconciliation to politics: internal ecclesial politics and world politics at all levels.

In several instances the Vatican encouraged certain national episcopates to struggle for national reconciliation through the overcoming of social and national conflicts. For example, In Chile, in Nicaragua, in the Republic of El Salvador, in the Philippines, and in other countries. The bishops were given in this way a true political mission. On the other hand though, the Vatican also insists on an ecclesiastical politics of 'reconciliation' in countries where one finds inter-ecclesiastical conflicts, including the episcopacy. In this case, we are dealing with a specific ecclesiastical policy.

The Exhortation does not show how this political task of reconciliation through the suppression of conflicts is linked to the sacrament of Penance and to the appeal for individual conversion. The word reconciliation unites both these areas, but it is being understood in different senses. Since reconciliation with God signifies submission to the will to God. Political reconciliation between parties does not mean the submission of one party to the other, but a form of reconciliation, in which each part offers concessions to the other. Political reconciliation includes renunciation from each side of some of its owns demands.

On the other hand though, the Pope insists on a reconciliation 'in truth': 'The Church promotes a reconciliation in truth, since it well knows that none are possible: neither reconciliation, nor unity outside or contrary to the truth' (*Reconciliatio et Paenitentia*, paragraph 9). This restriction reduces the breadth of reconciliation in the political or social arena as well as in the international arena. The problem really is: What is the truth in the political arena? The apostolic exhortation does not enter into the Pauline theology of reconciliation between Jew and Gentile, nor into the theology of universal reconciliation.


### d.        Reconciliation in Idealist Philosophy and in Marxism

With modernity, the theme of reconciliation extended to new problems and new realities. Modernity emerged it seemed at the end of a lengthy process of the discovery of subjectivity. This experience of subjectivity was for centuries the privilege of a small minority, privileged in all areas of life. Nevertheless, with material development, this experience of subjectivity was extended little by little and then in an accelerated fashion.

The period in which the modern subject was discovered, it appeared that the human subject was a problematical being, in confrontation with the external world. The subject-object opposition emerged, and, with it, the rest of the oppositions were historically linked to this: the opposition between the spiritual and the material, freedom and necessity, reason versus spontaneity, individual and society, human versus the external world, reason versus being, reason versus nature and so forth. This situation created within the human being an internal division, or rather various internal divisions. The human being considered himself/herself as an alienated being, who had lost his/her identity and become torn up, attracted by contrary movements. In the midst of the modern consciousness is the question of freedom: how does one unite freedom with the structure of the given world?

The Modern Revolutions sought to address this problem. The French Revolution, in particular, had enormous repercussions for philosophy. In a way German philosophy became a reflection built upon the concrete experience of the French Revolution, which the Germans witnessed from close hand but from the outside. The central issue again was reconciliation.

Romanticism presented itself over against the Revolution. Schiller chose, contrary to the path of revolution, the aesthetic solution. He saw that the Revolution crushed the individual and sacrificed existing individuals for the happiness of future individuals. He did not see freedom coming from that position. Freedom would come from the aesthetic experience: in art, in the game, in love. Here the individual would realize himself/herself, and exercise the true freedom. Schiller thinks that the artist is capable of transcending the material and social circumstances in which he/she lived. He/she is not a pure reflection of the situation, but able to be a unique individual. Schiller thinks that human beings are not redeemed through the State. He affirms the primacy of the individual over against the State. He thinks that the individual is capable of reaching reconciliation by himself/herself.[38]

## 1. Hegel and Reconciliation

Hegel is understood in relation to Romanticism. He was fascinated by Romanticism, and by Schiller in particular and wished to define himself over against this movement, by denouncing a pure subjectivism, a major danger. For Hegel, the subject and the object are reconciled in the Spirit: The Spirit is God present in His community, God the font and creator of freedom. Morality proceeds from this Spirit. The solution, and reconciliation, according to Hegel, are found in history, and not in the individual. History realizes the advent of the Spirit. The Spirit is actualized through history. In his manner, the conflicts, the contradictions and the contrary conditions are resolved through history. What appears as division, an obstacle to reconciliation, is in reality part of the process of reconciliation. Hegel trusted in history because he thought that history is rational. All the contradictions tend towards reconciliation and are paths to reconciliation. Without conflicts and contradictions there would be no history and no human being. This being alone is able to develop itself and journey to its end through the means of opposites. What Hegel called contradiction has diverse meanings, but

---

38 See Paulus Engelhardt, *Versöhnung und Erlösung* Christlicher Glaube in moderner Gesellschaft, vol. 23 (Munich: Herder, 1982), 137–143.

they all converge: they all represent oppositions which are encountered in the process of history. The human being is made of contradictions because he is the force of the reconciliation of opposites.[39] Consequently, the diverse forms of alienation which are experienced in the present do not constitute obstacles, but on the contrary, are the very paths to reconciliation. Humanity is journeying to its reconciliation. The Spirit is guiding in this process, through provocations, and suffering. Humanity journeys to the unity in which subject and object, reason and nature, will be reconciled.

Hegel trusted the state. He saw in the state the instrument of synthesis and of reconciliation. In the state will be the concrete and historical realization of the Spirit and the overcoming of the antagonisms that have divided human beings until now. The state will realize true freedom, truly different from romantic individualism.

Here the purpose is not to fully present the Hegelian system, but simply to introduce it so as to be taken into consideration by those authors who consider themselves called upon elaborate a theology of reconciliation. For here this concept is central to the consideration at hand.[40]

## 2.    Marx and Reconciliation

Hegel still is of actual relevance: the doctrines of statism, of nationalism, and of national security, which had such importance during the twentieth century right up to the present, are testimonies to his ideas' endurance. Nevertheless, another of his historical roles has been to to have prepared the thought of Karl Marx. Marx began with the problems presented by Hegel and through Hegelianism. He shared the same dialectical conception of history and giving the same emphasis to the concept of reconciliation. For Marx, though, the problem is the reconciliation of the human being. The problem is the diverse forms of human alienation which correspond to exposed antagonisms in history.[41] According to Marx, Hegel reconciled all the contradictions, but only in thought. Besides, he left intact the far more fundamental contradiction between this perfect ideal thought and the miserable reality of the German people. The French Revolution created the state. Thus the state was created to open all the gates to the bourgeoisie who exercised their dominance over a people without alternatives. The state did not supercede individualism, but to the contrary, it consolidated it, for the revolution left individuals isolated and without defenses against the state. Hegel thought that the state had overcome individualism, creating freedom. In Marx's thought the opposite had occurred. Reconciliation ought not to begin from the state, but from the concrete individual.

Hegel sees human beings through his historical dialectical process: within the process of evolution of the Spirit. For Marx only the concrete, particular, individual

---

39 See F. Grégoire, *Etudes hégéliennes. Les points capitaux du système* (Louvain-Paris: : Publications Univentaires de Louvain, 1958), 54–102.

40 F. Grégoire, *Etudes hégéliennes*, 40–61, 279f, 362f; P. Engelhardt, *Versöhnung und Erlösung*, 144–149.

41 See Paulus Engelhardt, *Versöhnung und Erlösung*, 150–153.

human had value. Only this person is the object of legitimate thought. He is talking about the need to go from the level of abstract humanity to the level of concrete humanity, which is the worker, whose condition is defined by his/her position over against other human beings.[42]

For Marx, the concrete root of all forms of alienation lies in the alienation of work.[43] The proletariat is radically alienated because they are separated from nature. The product of labor is not owned by them and it only augments the power of the objective world which dominates them. It augments the force of the system that oppresses them. Their labor does not involve the greater use of their creative faculties, but is simply a factor of production, merchandise which they hire for a salary, dependent upon the capitalist. The worker does not work with rational ends in view, but simply to augment indefinitely the capacity of the system of production. His/her collaborators become his/her competitors and rivals with whom he/she disputes over wages. In turn, the capitalist is also alienated because he/she has become alienated from nature which he/she exploits. He/she lives as a function of production and is not satisfied. The system produces and destroys being through possession. What value is possession if the being has no value?

The root of this fundamental alienation is the system of private property. Communism is the overcoming of private property and consequently the beginning of a true reconciliation between worker and the master of capital, being thus true reconciliation of the human with himself/herself.

In this way, communism will be the true reconciliation between existence and essence, through the liberation of the human creative forces: the true reconciliation of the subject and the object; that the human being ends being separated from the product of his/her labor and works for himself/herself: a true reconciliation between freedom and necessity, that indeed removes the implacable system that maintains all imprisoned; the true reconciliation between individuals and society, indeed that truly removes the rivalry between workers that makes of each one an egoist, and now is able to initiate a true collaboration.

What occurred with historical Marxism is one of the tragedies of history. It is not the first time that the followers of a doctrine made the contrary of what its creator had postulated, and they legitimated it using the texts of the same doctrine. Anyway Marxism belongs to the Western cultural heritage, just like bourgeois nationalism, and capitalism. It exists in real society and will not disappear magically. The problems focused upon by Marx are still present here and in the countries with centralized economies and understood as socialist. The principal problem is that of labour. Without reconciliation in labor, no reconciliation is possible: This is the challenge presented by Marxism.

---

42 See Michel Henry, *Marx I. Une philosophie de la réalité* (Paris: NRF Gallimard, 1976).

43 See Michel Henry, *Marx II. Une philosophie de l'économie* (Paris: NRF Gallimard, 1976).

Amongst the questions raised by Hegel as by Marx and also by Teilhard de Chardin and by modernity itself, is that of the destiny of history. Has human history a purpose, a project, any rationality? This problem has never been fully tackled by the Churches. The Second Vatican Council did not dare to address it. It remains open. Yet it remains at the base of the relationship between the Church and the world. Is reconciliation possible on the earth? Thus where is it legitimate to search for this reconciliation?

Frequently Marxism was considered as a secularized form of messianism, in the sense of leading all history towards a terrestrial end or purpose![44] If there exists a purpose of history, this final purpose tends to absorb all the activities of the generations preceding the end. The individuals of all generations thus exist to serve the final generation.

If there exists an end it can be nothing other than the integral reconciliation of humanity with itself, with nature, with society: a reconciliation that includes all the aspects of human life and resolves all contradictions. If there is no final purpose, reconciliation cannot be an absolute end. Conflict and reconciliation should be evaluated in each circumstance. If a terrestrial messianism is not possible, conflict remains inevitable within history. It is unthinkable to consider without conflict. Reconciliation is good or bad according to the conditions, the means and the consequences: it is judged by truth, as the Pope declares. In every case, the problem of messianism forms part of a theology of reconciliation. It is not possible to say beforehand that every reconciliation is good, nor that every conflict has to be overcome. History will not be judged by its end, but rather by each one of its stages.

### e. Reconciliation as a Political Project and as Theology

*1. Political Reconciliation*

The word reconciliation is also occasionally used in political language. It serves to present or to define certain concrete political projects. Its content is thus by nature political. Thus political projects do not derive directly from reconciliation with God, nor from reconciliation between Jews and Gentiles, nor from the universal reconciliation proclaimed by Saint Paul. Rather they deal with contingent political options which shall be judged from the perspective of political sciences and political ethics.

For example, the word reconciliation is used in the sense of national unity. After a civil war or when a nation's unity and identity is threatened through the existence of separatist parties as a result of race, culture, history, geography, or whatever other reason. Then the defenders of national unity appeal for national reconciliation. For

---

44 Cf. G. Fessard, *Les structures théologiques dans l'Athéisme marxiste*, in *Concilium*, no. 16 (1996), 31–43; H. de Lubac, *La postérité spirituelle de Joachim de Flore*, vol. 2, (Paris: P. Lethielleux, 1981), 356–360.

the defenders of nationality, this means the maintenance of the existence of the nation. For example, in the case of Canada, of Belgium, of Switzerland, of France, of Spain, of Ireland, and so render the nation governable. It deals with this by attempting to accept certain common rules as a basis for a government after a period of profound national crisis. For example, after a long dictatorship it is common to appeal for national reconciliation. The term is utilized in this sense in Chile, in Central America, and in various other nations. The promoters of reconciliation are the defenders of the established nationality. By contrast, the adversaries of reconciliation are the separatists: for these the party of reconciliation is the principal enemy.

In politics, national reconciliation is a characterized political option. It is not possible to deduce from the Gospel that Christians ought to favor reconciliation more than separation. In practice, in the unfolding of history from the time of Constantine, the Catholic Church has been linked to great political entities such as the imperial: it defended the Roman Empire against the separatists as much in Egypt as in Syria, and this attitude led to schisms which have endured to the present (Monophysites and Nestorians). In the Middle Ages the Church defended the the Holy German Empire against the attempts of the independents. Then the Church defended the great monarchies: The Hapsburgs, the French and the Spanish monarchies. It defended the colonial systems of Portugal, of Spain and of France. The Pope only recognized the new nations born from the Spanish empire fifteen years after their independence.[45] The Church always preached reconciliation with the colonial power. The Portuguese Empire itself was defended by the Church up until the last moment, and always in the name of reconciliation. The independent states were only recognized by the Church after the fact. Thus Catholics were exhorted to practice a politics of reconciliation with the colonial power.

Frequently this politics of reconciliation was defended with pseudo-theological and pseudo-evangelical arguments. It used to be said that Christians ought not to enter into conflicts, and should not favor conflictive attitudes, that Christians ought always to seek peace and so forth. This attitude expressed a systematic theological reductionism. The biblical idea of peace was applied to a political programme of supporting the status quo, to a specific political programme.

The parties and nationalist movements often reckon on support amongst the Catholics. Even though the Holy See and part of the national episcopacy have attempted to counter such movements, so many times the Catholic social influence has had an important role in the defense of the established systems, of constituted nations or of colonial empires.[46]

---

45 See J. Leflon, *La crise revolutionnaire* (*Histoire de L'Eglise* by A. Fliche and V. Martin, vol. 20) (Paris: Blout and Gay, 1949), 354–356.

46 See Christine Alix, *Le Saint-Siège et les nationalismes en Europe* (Paris: Sirey, 1962).

## 2. Social Reconciliation

The theme of reconciliation also serves as a foundation for counter-revolutionary ideologies. Over the past two hundred years social conflicts have assumed, each time, greater force throughout the world, under the influence of European culture which is fundamentally – in its historical trajectory – revolutionary.[47] At first the conflict was primarily between the underprivileged classes (bourgeoisie, industrial proletariat, rural labour) and the privileged classes (clergy and nobility). Since then the conflict has become one between the bourgeoisie and the proletariat or working classes.

In the context of social conflicts, the theme of reconciliation forms part of the ideology of the dominant classes, of those classes which occupy privileged positions. The appeal to social reconciliation obscures the desire and the project of maintaining the established situation. In this then, reconciliation consists in the exploiters and the exploited renouncing their claims and accepting the existing situation. The discourse of social peace is the natural discourse of the dominant classes.

Frequently, bourgeois Catholics appeal to the necessity for peace and for social reconciliation in order to struggle against the popular movements. They invoke religious motives: they invoke the evangelical doctrine of peace and of reconciliation.[48] The clergy themselves provide much support for such arguments and thus allow a conservative religious ideology to grow, under cover of the name of evangelical reconciliation. In accord with such an ideology, any social conflict would be contrary to the Gospel. Any supporting action in conflict would be incompatible with Christian confession. This conservative ideology actually practices a theological reductionism: it applies the biblical theme of reconciliation to a specific political project, and attempts to exclude every contrary project in the name of Christianity. It uses Christian themes to base a quite specific political programme that favours the privileges of the establishment.

Reconciliation thus is linked with the famous ideology of 'Order'. This was already the ideology of the state of the Byzantine Empire, and later adopted by Western rulers.[49] It was the ideology of conservative parties through the previous century. It was based in a political Catholicism that is a form of political monotheism.[50] If one examines the documents of the Catholic hierarchy, one lamentably can verify that rarely the conservative social ideologies are distinguished.[51] In the twentieth century

---

47  See Fr. Heer, *Europa, Mutter der Revolutionen* (Stuttgart: W. Kohlhammer, 1964).

48  See P. Pierrard, *L'Eglise et les ouvriers en France (1840–1940)* (Paris: Hachette, 1984), 276–280.

49  See Hélène Ahrweiler, *L'idéologie politique de l'empire byzantin* (Paris: PUF, 1975), 129–147.

50  See P. Droulers, *Catholicisme et mouvement ouvrier au XIXe siècle*, in Francois Bédarida, Jean Maition and J. Baubórot (eds) *Christianisme et monde ouvrier. Etudes.* (Paris: Ed. Ouvrières, 1975), 37–65.

51  See M. D. Chenu, *La 'doctrine sociale' de l'Eglise comme idéologie* (Paris: Cerf, 1979).

the old conservative parties were separated from history through the evolution of events, but they found other expression in the Fascist movements, nationalism, or in national security doctrines, all also based on the fundamental concept of order. Now, the conservative order is indeed quite different from biblical peace and from the Pauline doctrine of reconciliation.

In social order as in national order, each project of political reconciliation ought to be analyzed politically. Analyzed, it has to be interpreted and judged through Christian discernment. At first glance, a political program of social reconciliation ought not to be more Christian than a program of social conflict. It needs to appreciate the value of social conflict or reconciliation in each case. For the biblical doctrine of reconciliation does not include in itself any political or social program of reconciliation. The word reconciliation can become equivocal, for it can designate different realities without any relationship between them.

On the political level reconciliation can bear many meanings. Thus for example, in Chile during 1985 and 1986 the word reconciliation served to indicate the conflict with the established regime. The word reconciliation was chosen by the opposition parties of the 'democratic' opposition to the government of Pinochet. The supporters of reconciliation were the promoters of the conflict with Pinochet. Precisely for this reason, Pinochet declared himself a ferocious opponent of reconciliation. Can one justify this program of 'reconciliation' through the Gospel? Without reductionism, it is not possible. Likewise a theology of reconciliation will have to practice the discernment of the current political situation. It cannot just evangelically legitimate a political program, but rather must discern the best possible, with all the risks which history can dispense. For one can never know in advance what a political programme is going to provide.

### f. Reconciliation in the Latin American Context

Our principal preoccupation with a theology of reconciliation in Latin America will be to avoid any kind of theological reductionism or ideologization of any political programme, which has happened so many times under military regimes. We will also have to avoid confusion between two meanings of reconciliation. This is not to say that theological reconciliation, inspired by Pauline theology, is not able to have implications on the political and social levels. These implications nevertheless ought to be verified and should not be used as word-play.

Our point of departure will be the dialectic of the Jews and the pagans according to Saint Paul. This is not separable from reconciliation between God and humanity, since the purpose and the profound significance of reconciliation given by God is made clear precisely in the dialectic between Jews and pagans. The fulfillment of the law is the sign and the manifestation of the reconciliation intended and realized by God. In the dialectic of the Jews and the pagans is manifested the graciousness of the gift of God and of his pardon, fundament of the new covenant, of reconciliation.

With G. Fessard, we reckon that the dialectic of the Jews and the pagans does not just refer to a single historical period (the debates between Jesus and the authorities of Israel), but reveals a constant in the history of salvation. Judaism remains present (in the Pauline sense) within the Church and paganism (in the Pauline sense) and still exists, even between baptized persons who are formally integrated into the Church. There still exists a 'Judaeo-Christianity' and a 'pagan-Christianity'. The option of God for the pagans still has significance and efficacy today. If so, where does this take place?

The reply to this question depends upon the reply to a prior question: where is the equivalent of the law today? Where is there a law imposed upon a pagan people, a new people, as an indispensable condition to entrance into the Church? This law exists. The canonical law of the Latin American Church imposed upon a people who were not Latin, neither in their history nor in their culture. This law was imposed as an indispensable condition and unique means of adherence to the Church and so Christians made narrow the gate and made the acceptance of the Gospel most difficult.

In Latin America we have two examples: the Native American Indians and the Blacks. Up until the present, the Native American Indians have not been able to enter the Church with their history and their culture. On them was imposed the Christianity of the dominant conquerors. The acceptance of Christianity by the Indians involved still was not effected with profundity, even to the present, because there did not exist an authentic Indian Church, except in some isolated fragments, object of much suspicion.

In the same way, there does not exist an Africanized Christianity. The slaves and their descendants received a Western Christianity, the one of the masters and slavers. They found refuge in their African cults which had to be hidden behind Christian facades. To this day, the descendants of the black slaves are, in the vast majority, animists by conviction, and Christian by convention, both as a mode of adaptation to the dominant culture. In the Latin American Church Blacks do not occupy any high position at all. All their attempts at liturgical accommodation were vetoed, and all of animism condemned, in the name of Christian dogma.

Now, the exclusion of the Native Americans and the Blacks in the Church reinforced or even to a certain point, created their universal social exclusion. The regional Latin American Bishops Conference in Puebla, Mexico, insisted upon the responsibility of the Catholic Church in the formation of Latin American culture, which excludes both Native Americans and Blacks. For this exclusion the Church bears great responsibility We are able to state that the rejection of the 'pagans' by the 'Judaeo-Christians' has had a similar and parallel repercussion on the social an political plane. Only reconciliation on the ecclesiastical plane will be able to carry reconciliation through the social and political planes.

Only a social and political analysis will be able to show whether reconciliation constitutes (or does not) a valid political program for Native Americans and Blacks. Letting the experts and people mainly involved have the responsibility to judge and decide, we may think that there are some reasons in favor of a political and social reconciliation. It would be difficult to conceive a project for independent Native American Indian nations in Latin America, and even less so for black peoples. The races are geographically and historically condemned to live together.

What then are the conditions for reconciliation in Latin America with the Native Americans and Blacks? In the first place, such a reconciliation presupposes the recognition of the great guilt of oppression, of 500 years of systematic oppression lasting to this day. Thus even in the present, Native Americans and Blacks are still in a state of exclusion from society and from culture, both of which originated in the Church. In the second place, reconciliation demands restitution: the construction of a civilization in which all are able to develop their potentialities. But there is not only oppression of the Native Americans and the Blacks, there is also a rejected poor and Mestizo population which continues to be marginalized in the present. The Latin American nations were constructed, and still operate, on behalf of a small minority who control all privileged rights. The visible sign of this rejection of the people's rights was – and still is – the invasion of the land by the powerful elite and their economic interests. The invasion of land of course began with the original Conquest. It continues though to the present through expulsions of tenant farmers, leaseholders, and small farmers. The land is for the smallest minority. Thus likewise in the city, the culture and in the means of social advancement. Reconciliation in Latin America presumes a total inversion of the whole civilizational and cultural process. The ruling elites deny this situation. They proclaim that their country is a model of harmonious community life. In the same manner the great landed estate owners had proclaimed that they formed a great family with their leaseholders and cowboys, with their gunmen and their dependents.

Before any specific political project of reconciliation, it is necessary to reconcile views on that is meant by the proper construction of society: is it to be constructed to serve everyone, or just to serve the minority who have dominated pitilessly for 500 years? Such a political project and the political fundamentals, will be the object of discernment, and not of theology. Yet to the extent that the Church bears an immense responsibility in the formation of Latin American culture, and a responsibility which she has publicly acknowledged, the problematic of Latin American society is also a problem for theology. What then in the Church would permit the development of such a society? How is it possible for a Christian Church to be at the base of such an unjust and oppressive society? What are the basic principles which enable us to comprehend that the Church has produced such a phenomenon? This is a theological problem. Pauline theology is able to offer us some principles, most notably that of the dialectic between the Jews and the pagans.

Everyone knows the traditional Protestant thesis: the horrors of Latin American society are best explained through the paganism of the Roman Catholic Church, and the superiority of the United States of America is explainable by the superiority of the Protestant Churches. To this thesis we will now respond, but in what manner?

Besides internal reconciliation, Latin America also poses the problem of universal, human, reconciliation. The conquest of Latin America coincided with the beginning humanity's unifying epoch. Nevertheless this happened through conquest and domination, and not through dialogue, interchange, and collaboration.

What possible relation can there be between the project of universal reconciliation in Christ-the theological reality-and the project of world peace amongst the nations , the power blocks, and the economic worlds? There is no deduction from one reality to the other. Once again an analysis of the whole world system is necessary, one that discerns the relations between the diverse possible world political projects. It is not possible beforehand to say that Christians should collaborate with any project for world 'peace', if this project simply consolidates the actual relations of domination. The political reason illumined by the Gospel will have to choose between conciliation and conflict, in accord with the historical moment.

In a few years, the Church and the nations will celebrate the five hundredth anniversary of the discovery and conquest of the Americas by Columbus's ships, in the service of the king of Spain. The meeting of the Episcopal Conference of Latin America (CELAM) which will occur in Santo Domingo to commemorate this anniversary will perhaps approach the theme of reconciliation of a society which was founded through invasion, in the exploitation of the inhabitants, and in their extermination, and through the enslavement of Africans violently carried from Africa. This will be an opportune time to reflect upon the Christian significance and human content of a reconciliation with Christian meaning. The Church was involved in conquest – on the side of the conquerors most times, but also, on the side of the conquered, even though always as a vanquished minority, defeated, and never predominant at the institutional level. In this reconciliation the Church will have to bear an enormous part of the culpability, to make a profound act of repentance and ask pardon for all the support which it gave to structural injustices and circumstances. After this it will have to pledge itself to dismantle everything which up to the present day has contributed to its commitment to the apparatus of domination. It will have to examine itself profoundly, and in the light of Pauline theology, discern what there was in itself to lead to such a compounding of sin. One cannot here invoke individual malice. Those who represented the Church during the conquest of America were not worse than the others who were in Europe. We are not dealing with personal sins. We are dealing with something which was and possibly still is in the structure of established Christianity and leads inevitably to what happened. Other Christians would have acted in the same manner in the same situation because the problem lies not in the individual but indeed is structural. Something in the structure of the Church was linked with the apparatus of oppression, and it was not the individuals.

May God illumine us so that we may discover and carry out what the twentieth century Church needs in order to enter into the divine project of reconciliation.

Chapter 7

# Social Sin: Social Reconciliation?

Margaret R. Pfeil

Peru is a political community that will win peace and reconciliation when it wins a minimum of equality of opportunities among its members, when solidarity has triumphed over poverty and has beaten discrimination and indifference, when justice and law impede arbitrariness [and] corruption and repair the harms produced, and when its citizens exercise democracy with the fullest freedom and assume their responsibilities. Then and only then will it be possible to speak with truth of Peru as a country that has reconciled with itself.[1]

The Peruvian Truth and Reconciliation Commission (CVR) released its final report on 28 August 2003. The ninth and final volume offers a careful theoretical consideration of the meaning of reconciliation in general and then specifically in relation to the damage wrought by twenty years of extremely violent conflict in Peru. Noting the fact that the majority of Peruvians are Christian, it acknowledges that tradition's rich history of reconciling practices, but its recommendations articulate socio-political concerns independent from a faith-based conception of reconciliation. In the religiously pluralistic Peruvian context, the CVR maintains, no single tradition can provide a framework for social reconciliation. Furthermore, given their mixed record in defending human life during the conflict, the Christian churches are not well-positioned to facilitate such a process.[2]

Still, mutual advantages emerge from holding the truth commission model in conversation with Christian theology and practices of sacramental reconciliation. An exploration of Christian reconciliation yields valuable conceptual guideposts for assessing the contributions of a truth commission to the work of social restoration. The truth commission model, in turn, proves useful in addressing two questions that current sacramental forms of reconciliation elicit. How might a particular community name 'social sin'? And, once identified, what form of reconciliation might best heal the brokenness revealed? A general treatment of these two issues provides a theological horizon against which to consider the CVR process as a concrete practice of social reconciliation in response to social sin.

---

1    Comisión de la Verdad y Reconciliación, *Informe Final* (Lima: CVR, 2003), IX, 1, 101. In this essay, all citations for the CVR report will include the volume, chapter, and page number, and all translations are my own.

2    CVR, IX, 1, 75.

**Naming Social Sin**

Following the Second Vatican Council, Catholic theological inquiry into the social dimensions of sin coalesced around the Latin American bishops' efforts to attend to the signs of the times of their own people, in particular the brutal reality of systematic oppression and repression experienced by the poor majority. Latin American prelates like Salvadoran Archbishop Oscar Romero increasingly turned to the language of social sin[3] in order to denounce structural manifestations of moral evil:

> It is not a matter of sheer routine that I insist once again on the existence in our country of structures of sin. They are sin because they produce the fruits of sin: the deaths of Salvadorans – the swift death brought by repression or the long, drawn out, but no less real, death from structural oppression. That is why we have denounced what in our country has become the idolatry of wealth, of the absolute right, within the capitalist system, of private property, of political power in national security regimes, in the name of which personal security is itself institutionalized ... No matter how tragic it may appear, the church through its entrance into the real socio-political world has learned how to recognize, and how to deepen its understanding of, the essence of sin. The fundamental essence of sin, in our world, is revealed in the death of Salvadorans.[4]

Romero's account of the Salvadoran experience proves instructive in constructing an account of social sin. First, it represents one instantiation of a general theological trend: the concept of social sin has developed in response to the need for a more comprehensive account of human sinfulness. Traditionally, Catholic moral theology has described sin with reference to freely chosen acts of particular moral agents that involve a rejection of God's love. But, this understanding of personal sin cannot account for wrongly ordered *patterns* of human behaviour that eventually become institutionalized. Individuals may sometimes be held responsible for sinful acts that contribute to an unethical social structure, but in some cases, they may succumb to a kind of moral blindness, participating in a given societal institution or system without realizing that their actions, both of commission and omission, contribute to structures of sin.

---

3    A word about terminology is in order. In this essay, 'the language of social sin' encompasses references to sin that seek to articulate its *structural* manifestations in a given situation. While this language does not exclude consideration of personal sin, it does seek to establish an account of the social dimensions of sin as not merely the effect of personal sin. Such terms include 'social sin', 'structural sin', 'sinful situations', 'structures of sin', and 'institutionalized violence'.

4    Archbishop Oscar Romero, 'The Political Dimension of the Faith from the Perspective of the Option for the Poor', in *Voice of the Voiceless*, trans. Michael J. Walsh (Maryknoll: Orbis Books, 1985), 183–184. See also Jon Sobrino, 'Latin America. Place of Sin and Place of Forgiveness', trans. Dinah Livingstone, in *The Principle of Mercy* (Maryknoll, NY: Orbis Books, 1994), 59. This article also appeared in Casiano Floristan and Christian Duquoc (eds), *Forgiveness Concilium*, 184 (Edinburgh: T. & T. Clark, 1986), 45–56.

Secondly, Romero's description illustrates an important implication of the use of the language of social sin: It signals an epistemological choice to view the damage wrought by sin from the standpoint of those on the margins of societal power. From the vantage point of the primary victims of systemic oppression and repression, the socio-economically poor, the *structural* manifestations of sin come into sharper focus.[5] Having adopted that perspective, Romero found that his central moral and pastoral task shifted from identifying discrete sinful acts to comprehending the ethical significance of institutionalized violence that led inexorably to the deaths of human beings. The language of social sin allowed him to name and denounce not only particular offenses against life but also the social structures that resulted from and prepared the ground for the sins revealed in the crucified bodies of his people.

Prompted by a similar need to name sin fully, John Paul II embraced the language of social sin with growing insistence since the beginning of his papacy.[6] One pivotal point in his developing account of social sin occurred on 3 April 1987 when a bitter clash of Chilean civilians and military personnel erupted as the pope celebrated an outdoor mass for one million people in a Santiago park. Enveloped in tear gas, the crowd nevertheless continued to worship. Greatly moved by such faithful witness, John Paul II invoked the language of social sin to address structures of institutionalized violence at length in the encyclical letter, *Sollicitudo rei socialis*, promulgated later that year:

> 'Sin' and 'structures of sin'are categories which are seldom applied to the situation of the contemporary world. However, one cannot easily gain a profound understanding of the reality that confronts us unless we give a name to the root of the evils which afflict us.[7]

The language of social sin gives articulation to the moral evil at the heart of structural repression and oppression. Its invocation reflects a profound desire to name moral truth precisely in situations where the most vulnerable members of society have been stripped of their names and identities, and have even been 'disappeared', enveloped by a vortex of violence far beyond the intentions and capabilities of any one person or group.

---

5  On the perspectival dimension of the option for the poor, see Gregory Baum, 'Option for the Powerless', *The Ecumenist* 26 (November-December 1987), 5–11. Sandra Harding's account of standpoint epistemology serves to illuminate this aspect of the option for the poor. See "Rethinking Standpoint Epistemology: What Is 'Strong Objectivity?'," Linda Alcoff and Elizabeth Potter (eds.) *Feminist Epistemologies* (New York: Routledge, 1993), 49–82.

6  I offered a detailed exposition of the development of the language of social sin and its significance for Catholic social doctrine in Margaret R. Pfeil, 'Doctrinal Implications of Magisterial Use of the Language of Social Sin', *Louvain Studies* 27 (2002), 132–52.

7  David J. O'Brien and Thomas A. Shannon (eds), 'Sollicitudo rei socialis', in *Catholic Social Thought* (Maryknoll: Orbis Books, 1992), paragraph 36. For an insightful account of the papal Mass in Parque O'Higgins and its impact on the pope's approach to this document, see Roberto Suro, 'The Writing of an Encyclical', Kenneth A. Myers (ed.), *Aspiring to Freedom. Commentaries on John Paul II's Encyclical 'The Social Concerns of the Church* (Grand Rapids: William B. Eerdmans Publishing Company, 1988), 159–69.

**Social Sin: Social Reconciliation?**

If the theological correlative of sin is grace, then the effort to identify social manifestations of sin points to the need to heal the wounds revealed. Theologically and pastorally, however, the pace of development in naming social sin has outstripped correlative evolutions in ritual practices of reconciliation. In the Catholic tradition, a privatized view of sin, unfolding since the advent of the Penitentials in the Fifth Century, has engendered forms of sacramental reconciliation that give primacy to individual confession with priestly absolution.[8] While potentially transformative for persons open to the grace of the sacrament, this private approach to reconciliation is not sufficiently capacious to address the harm caused at the structural level of society by social sin.

This gap between theological development and pastoral reality prompts reflection on alternative practices of reconciliation, and the truth commission model represents one promising option. It embodies the ritual power of naming structures of sin in order that they might be transformed and shares the fundamental purpose of sacramental reconciliation, the restoration of right relationship. José Zalaquett, a member of the Chilean truth commission, affirms this consonance: 'Righting a wrong and resolving not to do it again is, at its core, the same philosophy that underpins Judaeo-Christian beliefs about atonement, penance, forgiveness, and reconciliation'.[9] Although reluctant to characterize reconciliation in religious terms, the Peruvian truth commission also invoked the ecclesial tradition as a touchstone:

> If we recognize our responsibility for the harm caused to society and commit ourselves to put in practice the process of reconciliation, we will be demonstrating true repentance. It would be in this sense desirable for institutions or persons directly involved in acts of violence to publicly acknowledge their guilt before society, that is, to ask for forgiveness. Although this can only be asked properly of the victims ... the request for forgiveness, accompanied by a sincere acknowledgement of responsibility, be it personal or institutional, can help to create the new conditions of solidarity that national reconciliation requires.[10]

The Peruvian commission recognized that the ecclesial tradition of sacramental reconciliation offers a language and wisdom born of centuries of experience in reconciling practices. At the same time, by noting the need for accountability at the institutional level, the CVR identified the growing edge of ecclesial approaches to reconciliation. To be a credible and relevant resource in a process of social

---

8    John Paul II has insisted that individual confession with priestly absolution is the 'only ordinary form' of sacramental reconciliation. See 'Apostolic Exhortation on Reconciliation and Penance' (*Reconciliatio et paenitentia*), *Origins* 14 (20 December 1984), paragraph 32. The pope adopted this language from the *Rite of Penance* in *The Rites of the Catholic Church* (New York: Pueblo Publishing Co., 1983), paragraph 31.

9    José Zalaquett, 'Balancing Ethical Imperatives and Political Constraints: The Dilemma of New Democracies Confronting Past Human Rights Violations', *Hastings Law Journal* 43 (1992), 1432.

10   CVR, I, 'Introducción', 38.

reconciliation, ecclesial rituals of reconciliation need to speak to the social as well as the personal brokenness caused by sin, and they must also reflect awareness of the church's own institutional complicity in structures of sin.

Holding the theology and practice of sacramental reconciliation in conversation with the work of the Peruvian truth commission serves as a test case for the larger project of generating social practices of reconciliation that respond to social sin. Building on the Christian ecclesial tradition, recent theological and pastoral efforts to develop the social dimension of sacramental reconciliation have taken shape around four categories that prove useful in exploring the CVR's work as a societal response to social sin: the process nature of conversion and reconciliation; the formation and examination of conscience; the relationship between personal conversion and structural transformation; and, the ecclesiological implications of social reconciliation.

## Conversion and Reconciliation as a Process

The accumulated wisdom and experience of the Christian tradition indicate that conversion and reconciliation unfold through a gradual process. In his influential work on conversion, Mark Searle observed that 'the primary purpose of ritual is to enable the individual to undergo the journey of conversion, rendering the experience intelligible and less terrifying, and enabling him to complete the journey, through encounter with the sacred, to newness of life'.[11] The rituals of Christian liturgy mediate a process through the three stages of separation, liminal transition, and reintegration. 'What is being left behind? What is this person or this community being called to? How is this transition to be made and what does it involve?'[12]

Contemporary retrievals of the early church's Order of Penitents create space for the emergence of a communal response to these questions.[13] A penitent may confess to a priest but delay absolution until completion of specific penitential practices. The process may unfold over the course of weeks or months as the person journeys along the purifying path of conversion. During this time, the penitent attends liturgy but abstains from receiving the Eucharist. His or her presence allows the local ecclesial community to extend their prayers in solidarity as sinners in need of forgiveness. When the penitent and confessor find it appropriate, the penitent receives absolution and subsequently returns to full participation in the Eucharistic celebration.

---

11 Mark Searle, 'The Journey of Conversion', *Worship* 54 (1980), 47.

12 CVR, 46. Searle built on the work of Arnold van Gennep, *The Rites of Passage* (Chicago: University of Chicago Press, 1960).

13 Joseph Bernardin, 'Proposal for a New Rite of Penance', in *Synod of Bishops, Rome, 1983. Penance and Reconciliation in the Mission of the Church* (Washington, DC: United States Catholic Conference, 1984), 43. Subsequently, several liturgical theologians, notably James Lopresti and Joseph Favazza, have explored this proposal further, and it has been promoted in pastoral settings in the United States through the efforts of the North American Forum for the Catechumenate.

Following a model proposed by James Lopresti, some parishes in the United States have undertaken this process over the course of Lent, with ritual absolution offered in a communal penance service on the Wednesday of Holy Week.

This approach to sacramental reconciliation serves to emphasize the penitential and reconciling journey as an essential aspect of communal life, and therefore it lends itself to addressing social sin, Lopresti argues:

> The penitential process … is holistic. It is not merely a struggle with personal sin. It includes a more demanding and pervasive rescue from the power of evil in its systemic manifestations (i.e., social sin). A community that fully understands the import of Lenten purification and illumination searches out the signs of God's Spirit intervening in human societies and institutions. The community discovers God seeking to rescue whole peoples, to heal division within communities, and to expose the demons that have taken up residence in oppressive structures. The faith community gratefully acknowledges the power of the Gospel to transform culture, prays for a deepening of that transformation, and pledges to cooperate in it as well.[14]

The deepening of cultural and social transformation takes root when holistic ecclesial practices of reconciliation find resonance with the work of other institutions within civil society to repair the damage wrought by structures of sin. The process nature of conversion and reconciliation implies that all entities in a given societal context have a role to play in healing social divisions revealed in a conflict situation. Each institution will have its own particular responses to the questions posed by Searle. Given its particular narrative, what does it need to leave behind? What is it being called to do and to be within an ethically restored society? How will it undertake the transformation required?

Among societal institutions, the truth commission occupies a unique position in the reconciling process because it owes its very existence to a society's efforts to name the truth of a particular conflict. In Peru, the truth commission has contributed significantly to the fulfillment of this goal. The CVR is widely regarded as one of the best among more than twenty-five truth commissions that have been convened worldwide, partly because its original mandate afforded the commission great latitude to envision its work as part of a longer process of reconciliation. Prepared by an inter-institutional working group that encompassed governmental ministries as well as non-governmental organizations, including the Catholic and Protestant churches, the mandate charged the commission with investigating:

---

14 James Lopresti, *Penance: A Reform Proposal for the Rite* (Washington, DC: The Pastoral Press, 1987), 17. See also Joseph Favazza, *The Order of Penitents*, foreword by James Lopresti (Collegeville, MN: The Liturgical Press, 1988). Toinette Eugene similarly situates reconciliation within the context of social and structural expressions of sin in 'Reconciliation in the Pastoral Context of Today's Church and World. Does Reconciliation Have a Future?' Robert J. Kennedy (ed.), *Reconciling Embrace*, (Chicago: Liturgy Training Publications, 1998), 1–16. In the same volume, see also H. Kathleen Hughes, 'Walking on the Edge of Two Great Abysses. Theological Perspectives on Reconciliation', 102, 106–107.

a) assassinations and kidnappings;
b) forced disappearances;
c) torture and other grievous bodily harm;
d) violations of the collective rights of the Andean and native communities of the country;
e) other crimes and grave violations of the rights of persons.[15]

The scope of the CVR's work covered a period from 1980 to 2000 defined by very distinct socio-political landscapes, from the internal armed conflict sparked by the subversive activities of the Shining Path (PCP-SL) guerrilla movement through a subsequent period of state-sponsored repression against legitimate opposition groups during Alberto Fujimori's presidency. The sweeping nature of its mandate complicated the commission's task, but it also created space for nuanced consideration of the systemic nature of the violence that enveloped Peru during those twenty years. Perhaps it may also spare Peru the arduous task of launching subsequent investigations into categories of violations not included in the original mandate, as happened in Chile.[16]

Reflecting a profound understanding of reconciliation as a process, the CVR's final report identifies three dimensions. On a political level, the commission calls the state, including the military and police forces, to re-establish ties with the rest of civil society characterized by justice and accountability. In the social realm, fundamental bonds of relationship must be restored between institutions and civic fora with society as a whole, and in particular with the indigenous peoples and other marginalized groups. Finally, reconciliation needs to unfold on the interpersonal level among members of communities rent by violent conflict.[17]

Nothing can substitute for the role of personal encounter in the process of healing and reconciliation. Without sustained attention on the individual level, victims of violent conflict may have great difficulty in reintegrating into post-conflict society in a fully participative manner.[18] The CVR sought to provide the most dispossessed and marginalized Peruvians an opportunity to tell their horrific stories to people who were willing to accompany them in their suffering and their tears.[19]

Despite these intentions, the commission's work remains unfinished. Stories of torture, murder, and loss have yet be told, and wounds have yet to be healed. The

---

15 CVR, I, 'Introducción', 23, as from Presidencia del Consejo de Ministros, Decreto Supremo 065–2001 (2 June 2001).

16 The Rettig Report did not address acts of torture and illegal detention that did not culminate in death. In November 2003, Chile's National Commission of Political Prisoners and Torture, led by Bishop Sergio Valech, began deliberations regarding these cases in order to offer the victims some measure of compensation.

17 CVR, I, 'Introducción', 38. See also IX.1, 'Fundamentos de la Reconciliación', 14.

18 Yovana Pérez, Verónica Molina, and Victoria Pareja, 'El Tratamiento Individual con Personas Afectadas por la Violencia Política', *Ideele* 157 (September 2003), 84–85.

19 Albano Quinn, 'Un momento de gracia para revisar nuestra Evangelizacion', *Ideele* 159 (November 2003), 32–33.

day after releasing the report, Salomon Lerner Febres, president of the commission, traveled to Ayacucho. 'It was here that the greatest loss of human life was suffered ... And it is for that reason that today Ayacucho should be the place where that spiritual health we call peace should begin and extend throughout the nation'. Among the hundreds of mostly indigenous people gathered, about fifty heckled Lerner from the plaza's margins, claiming that the commission had neglected to hear their stories.[20] This reception served as a painful reminder that the CVR's work represents the annunciation rather than the culmination of a process of reconciliation.

Did the commission announce a new process of reconciliation, or rather was it calling the nation to remember its own story of social reconciliation, one frequently interrupted by extreme violence but still bearing truth claims for the future of its people? The very existence of the truth commission and the dissemination of its report do represent a fresh, deliberate commitment to social reconciliation in Peru, and yet the process nature of conversion and reconciliation suggests historical antecedents. The CVR grew out of an ongoing narrative of reconciling efforts, including the courageous work of rural ecclesial communities to extend the church's sacramentality to the task of social healing even during the height of the Shining Path's reign of terror.

Like an opportunistic disease, the PCP-SL thrived in the absence of vibrant structures of social relationship bridging local communities and national stratifications of social class and status. The institutional church and its pastoral agents in Peru posed a threat to the Shining Path whenever and wherever they attempted to foster communal ties of solidarity rooted in the option for the poor. Over time, Jeffrey Klaiber argues, these local ecclesial efforts bore rich fruit:

> When the civilians – peasants, workers, and urban dwellers – started forging ties among themselves, the Shining Path began to experience its first setbacks. Thus the Shining Path was not defeated by the armed forces or the police, who too often repressed the people and sometimes drove them to support the other side, but by the people themselves, who organized and blocked the advance of terrorism ... By conscientizing the people in Lima and in the mountains the progressive church had already done much to create a sense of solidarity that helped the people organize and defend themselves.[21]

The work of these pastoral agents, in turn, took root in the longer narrative of Christian sacramental practice. In the early church, community members accompanied those recently baptized by reflecting with them on the meaning and mystery of their entry into the Christian community. This process of mystagogy, or 'the interpretation of mystery', finds contemporary application in connection with the sacraments of initiation celebrated at the Easter Vigil. But, the mystagogical method can fruitfully

---

20 Ned Hugo, 'Peru's Truth Commission Visits Birthplace of Bloody Guerrilla Insurgency', *Associated Press* (29 August 2003).

21 Jeffrey Klaiber, *Church, Dictatorships, and Democracy in Latin America* (Maryknoll: Orbis Books, 1998), 143. He developed a similar point in 'Peru: The Church and the Shining Path', *America* 166:6 (22 February 1992).

be extended to other sacraments, including reconciliation.[22] Rooted in dialogue, it bears affinity with the process nature of conversion and reconciliation and provides space for communal participation in the celebration of the sacrament.

## Formation and Examination of Conscience

A mystagogical approach to sacramental reconciliation would be particularly helpful in the formation and examination of socially attuned consciences. By cultivating an atmosphere conducive to communal discernment of sinful aspects of social reality, church members may help one another to come to some awareness of their own individual and collective participation in it. Examination of conscience remains fundamentally the responsibility of the individual, but it comes to fruition through communal support. As they struggle to understand their solidarity in sin, penitents can also encourage one another to remain open to the grace of the conversion process. Dialogue nurtures growth of critical consciousness, or 'conscientization'. The dialogical moment, as Paulo Freire noticed, serves as an encounter between human beings by which they seek to name the world, and in naming it, they transform it.[23]

A dialogical and communal approach to the formation and examination of conscience proves vital in naming and resisting structures of sin precisely because they entail an unconscious and therefore involuntary dimension, or what Gregory Baum calls a sort of 'blindness produced in persons by the dominant culture, blindness that prevents them from recognizing the evil dimension of their social reality'.[24] To the extent that one participates in an ethically disordered structure but does so without knowledge of the moral evil at stake, personal sin cannot be imputed to that person. And yet, such involvement may exacerbate unethical systemic patterns of behaviour.

Because they provide a dialogical space for the formation and examination of social conscience, truth commissions represent a potentially powerful means of unmasking structures of sin. In the case of Peru, the truth commission emphasized community involvement. Eight public audiences were organized in various regions of the country to listen to testimonies, and the proceedings were televised nationwide. The CVR sought to identify particular victims and perpetrators of atrocities as well as to ascertain the patterns of institutionalized violence that created the conditions of the possibility of disappearances, torture, and massacres of socially marginalized ethnic groups.

---

22 Kathleen Hughes makes a compelling case for creative use of mystagogy in the celebration of the sacraments in *Saying Amen. A Mystagogy of Sacrament* (Chicago: Liturgy Training Publications, 1999).

23 Paulo Freire, *Pedagogy of the Oppressed*, trans. Myra Bergman Ramos (New York: Herder and Herder, 1970), 76–77.

24 Gregory Baum, 'Structures of Sin', in Gregory Baum and and Robert Ellsberg (eds), *The Logic of Solidarity* (Maryknoll: Orbis Books, 1989), 113.

The final report emerging from these proceedings begins by articulating the data for communal examination of conscience, explicating the known facts of the Peruvian conflict, and revealing the multivalent structures of sin involved. In the preface, Lerner describes a double scandal, one involving assassination, disappearance and torture on a massive scale, and the other rooted in indolence, incompetence, and indifference among those who possessed the power to halt these atrocities but failed to do so. One of the main lessons of the truth commission process, he finds, is that Peruvians share a collective guilt of omission insofar as they corporately allowed systemic violence to ravage the country without significant resistance. But, he insists, there are also 'concrete responsibilities' and Peru must not countenance impunity.[25]

To flesh out the truth of accountability, the CVR report details the particular dynamics of Peru's experience of institutionalized violence. Unlike the 'classic Latin American schema', the Peruvian conflict was not triggered by state-sponsored repression of subversive groups but rather by the Shining Path's popular uprising against the government beginning in May 1980. The PCP-SL ultimately was responsible for 54 per cent of the deaths and disappearances reported to the commission, making it the primary perpetrator of atrocities in the war. The CVR attributes 37 per cent of the atrocities to government-sponsored forces, including paramilitary groups.[26] In all, an estimated 69,280 people died in the twenty-year internal conflict.[27]

As part of its examination of social conscience, the CVR provides insight into the relationship between individual responsibility and structural sin. Lerner, for example, holds the armed forces accountable for systematic violations of human rights and crimes against humanity in certain times and places. But, he also points to the responsibility of particular moral agents for atrocities committed by state forces, such as extrajudicial executions, torture, disappearances, and sexual violence against women: 'So much death and so much suffering cannot accumulate simply by the blind functioning of an institution or an organization. It requires, as a complement, the complicity or at least the consent of those who have the authority and therefore the means to avoid disgrace'. Those who held political power during these years must answer for their failure to use it ethically. In Lerner's judgment, they too readily ceded to the military their authority and the power entrusted to them by the people.[28]

Responding to the CVR's analysis, some among the Peruvian military have focused narrowly on individual acts of injustice while downplaying suggestions of

---

25  Salomón Lerner Febres, CVR, I, 'Prefacio', 13–14.

26  CVR, I, 1, 54–55.

27       CVR, VIII, 'Conclusiones Generales', 315. Unlike the Chilean commission's approach of offering a conservative estimate of the number of victims, the CVR employed a projection method used previously in Guatemala and Kosovo. Some commentators regard this as the weakest aspect of the report. At the time of its release, 35,000 victims remained unidentified and 2,000 mass graves awaited excavation.

28  Salomón Lerner Febres , CVR, I, 'Prefacio', 15.

systemic problems within the military structure itself. Col. Carlos Romero (Ret.), once commander of a counter-subversive batallion and later chief of operations for the Second Infantry Division in Ayacucho, argues, 'Did the forces of public order commit excesses and violations of human rights? Clearly they did so. But, not in collective form or as institutional policy. They were individual acts and deeds that ought to be prosecuted and viewed in their actual context'.[29]

Col. Romero's assessment finds *prima facie* support in Lerner's emphasis on individual responsibility. At the same time, the scope and depth of the CVR's data indicate that the systemic violence gripping Peru during these years was not reducible to ethical lapses on the part of individual members of the military or their political overseers. Lerner points to a more insidious problem, a kind of false consciousness in Peruvian society in which structures leading to death on a massive scale were not identified, making it harder for individuals to take conscientious action. 'In the moral vacuum in which dictatorships flourish, good reasons fall by the wayside and concepts become inverted, depriving the citizenry of all ethical orientation'.[30] Under such circumstances, it becomes difficult to assign individual responsibility, and yet citizens did participate in upholding judicial, political, and military structures that obscured the truth and perverted the pursuit of justice on behalf of those most directly affected by the institutionalized violence that gripped the nation. Before legal provision was made in 1992 allowing judges to remain anonymous when presiding over terrorism cases, civilian justices had freed 8,500 accused terrorists.[31] President Alberto Fujimori instituted the category of 'judges without faces' to bolster the institutional power of the state in confronting terrorism, but the image of faceless arbiters of justice serves as a powerful symbol of the anonymous quality of structural sin. The PCP-SL leader had succeeded in fomenting a culture of fear in which those in positions of authority forfeited their own identities in the struggle to name the social sinfulness enmeshing Peruvian society.

The CVR also reports that after a marked decline in terrorist activities following the 1992 capture of Abimael Guzmán, the Fujimori regime nevertheless pressed forward with its repressive policies, intentionally stoking the nation's fear of terrorism and institutionalizing corruption in order to remain in power.[32] A legitimate threat to Peruvian society, the PCP-SL had provoked an extremely violent response from an embattled national government. After the immediate danger had passed, the country fell to the mercy of particular moral agents blinded by ambition and greed. The CVR notes that the government initially declared a kind of truce with drug traffickers in order to focus their efforts on PCP-SL as the principal threat, but with the rise of Vladimiro Montesinos as presidential advisor and overseer of the National Intelligence Service, that truce gradually became an alliance.[33] Montesinos

---

29 'Quien esté libre de culpa, que tire la primera piedra', *Ideele* 158 (October 2003), 35.
30 Salomón Lerner Febres , CVR, I, 'Prefacio', 16.
31 Jeffrey Klaiber, *Church, Dictatorships, and Democracy in Latin America*, 142.
32 CVR, I, 1, 75–76 and VIII, 'Conclusiones Generales', 327.
33 CVR, VIII, 'Conclusiones Generales', 327.

and Fujimori can certainly be held accountable legally and morally for turning a national security crisis into an opportunity for personal and political gain through a lethal network of corruption. But, situating their crimes within a larger context, the structural aspects of social sin emerge.

The path trod by Fujimori and Montesinos had already been well worn by others in Peruvian history, just as centuries of structural violence in Peru had paved the way for the likes of the Shining Path organization with its nihilistic ideology.[34] The deep wounds wrought by long years of economic, cultural and social discrimination against indigenous peoples scarred the national consciousness, inuring it sufficiently to permit brutal dehumanization to occur with impunity. In Lerner's estimation, 'these two decades of destruction and death would not have been possible without profound contempt for the country's most dispossessed population, on the part of both the PCP-Shining Path and agents of the state'.[35] The systematic violence perpetrated against mostly poor, rural, uneducated indigenous victims did not attract notice in the rest of the country, a phenomenon that the CVR regards as symptomatic of the underlying racism that has perdured in Peruvian society for nearly two centuries since national independence.[36]

The CVR documents a strong correlation between race-based socio-economic exclusion and the probability of becoming a victim of armed violence. More than 40 per cent of the dead and disappeared lived in Ayacucho, the impoverished Andean region where the conflict began. Seventy-nine per cent of all victims lived in rural areas. Eighty-five per cent of the victims recorded by the CVR lived in six of the poorest departments in the country; their composite income accounts for only nine per cent of the total for all Peruvian families. Sixty-eight per cent of the victims received less than a high school education. Three of every four victims were campesinos whose first language was Quechua or another indigenous tongue, though native speakers comprised only 16 per cent of the national population according to the 1993 census.[37]

In response to early Shining Path attacks, the government placed the most contested areas under special political-military command in 1982. But, repressive treatment of the indigenous population proved a tragic mistake, ratcheting up the level of violence among a population largely sympathetic to the government's efforts to maintain public order.[38] Few among the military forces spoke Quechua, exacerbating an already volatile situation. In a social climate shaped by centuries of racial discrimination, Peru's indigenous peoples were regarded as dangerous aliens in their own lands, their lives expendable in the name of national security.

---

34  Edgardo Rivera Martínez, 'Un lugar muy alto en nuestra historia', *Ideele* 158 (October 2003), 32.

35  Salomón Lerner Febres , CVR, I, 'Prefacio', 13–14.

36  CVR, VIII, 'Conclusiones Generales', 317, 333.

37  Salomón Lerner Febres, CVR, I, 'Prefacio', 13, and VIII, 'Conclusiones Generales', 316, footnote 5.

38  Jeffrey Klaiber, *Church, Dictatorships and Democracy in Latin America*, 147. See CVR I, 1, 65.

Unlike most other Latin American countries experiencing internal armed conflict, Peru lacked strong victims' advocacy organizations, mainly because the majority of the victims were economically poor, indigenous persons living in rural areas with little awareness of or access to legal remedies.[39] The CVR concludes that when the government created the political-military command structure, it abdicated its democratic responsibilities and contributed to a climate of impunity in the face of state-sponsored systematic human rights violations.[40]

The militarization of civil society by the state met with approval among Peru's urban dwellers, the principal beneficiaries of state services from whom the human and social costs of the armed conflict remained at some remove.[41] Insufficient police training and resources at the local level accelerated recourse to military options. When Fujimori engineered a self-coup on 5 April 1992, the majority of Peruvians supported him, rationalizing systematic repression as the necessary price of defending Peru against terrorism.[42] For its part, Congress offered no viable alternatives to military force and likewise failed in its responsibilities after the coup, actively promoting impunity and approving the General Amnesty Law in 1995.[43]

Though Peru has suffered other periods of extreme violence, the CVR regards this twenty-year conflict as the most extensive, intense, and prolonged in the nation's history.[44] The commission's report marks the first time in which Peru has undertaken a process of introspective reflection on the causes of the cycle of violence with a view toward disarming it. The CVR sought to transform structures of sin by embarking upon a national examination of conscience that will continue to unfold as Peruvian civil society contemplates the implications of the commission's findings.

## Personal Conversion and Structural Transformation

At their 1979 meeting at Puebla, the Latin American bishops indicated that 'structural transformation is the outward expression of inner conversion'.[45] These two forms of movement away from sin stand in dialectical relationship.[46] True to the nature of

---

39  CVR, VIII, 'Conclusiones Generales', 347.

40  CVR, VIII, 330, 333.

41  CVR, VIII, 331, 350.

42  CVR, VIII, 336.

43  CVR, VIII, 340.

44  CVR, VIII, 315.

45  Conferencia Episcopal de Latino America, 'Evangelization in Latin America's Present and Future. Final Document of the Third General Conference of the Latin American Episcopate', (Puebla de los Angeles, Mexico, 27 January – 13 February 1979), John Eagleson and Philip Scharper (eds), *Puebla and Beyond*, trans. John Drury (Maryknoll: Orbis Books, 1979), paragraph 1221.

46  Paul Lakeland has noticed this dialectical interrelationship between personal conversion and structural transformation in his commentary on *Sollicitudo rei socialis,* 'Development and Catholic Social Teaching: Pope John Paul's New Encyclical', *The Month* 249 (June 1988), 706–710. See also Rosemary Radford Ruether, 'Feminist Theology and Spirituality', in Judith

reconciliation as a process, transformation of sinful structures of behaviour unfolds both as the fruit of and impetus toward personal conversion.

Truth commissions lend themselves to this dynamic interplay between personal conversion and structural transformation. Typically, they are crafted to ascertain the structural dynamics of a societal conflict and corresponding institutional and individual responsibilities. In the Peruvian case, Lerner indicated the need for purification through reconciliation with and in the truth, effecting justice in the double sense of seeking reparation and just punishment without vengeance as well as of transforming the structures of the state and civil society so that such atrocities might never happen again.[47]

Recognizing a similar need for deep social reparation, Ignacio Martin-Baró, one of the six Jesuits murdered by state security forces in El Salvador in 1989, stressed the radically structural dimensions of the trauma wrought by counterinsurgency conflicts or state repression:

> All this damage is of such magnitude that it becomes almost ingenuous or cynical to act as if it can be forgotten overnight, because fundamentally the problem is not one of isolated individuals whether few or many; it is a problem whose nature is strictly social. The damage that has been produced is not simply in the destruction of personal lives. Harm has been done to the social structures themselves – to the norms that order the common life, to the institutions that govern the life of citizens, to the values and principles by which people are educated and through which the repression has tried to justify itself.[48]

Martin-Baró's assessment was affirmed by a Chilean mental health team treating the individual and social consequences of human rights violations during the Pinochet regime. Their work highlights the psychological dimension of the relationship between personal conversion and structural transformation:

> Political repression creates problems for its direct victims in private and subjective ways, but it also affects a whole society socially and politically. Working for a long period under the dictatorship made us especially aware of the dialectical relationship between therapy

---

L. Weidman (ed.), *Christian Feminism,* (New York: Harper & Row Publishers, 1984), 25–26, and Mark O'Keefe, O.S.B., *What Are They Saying About Social Sin?* (New York: Paulist Press, 1990), 92–95.

47  Salomón Lerner Febres, 'Prefacio', in CVR, I, 17.

48  Ignacio Martin-Baró, 'Reparations: Attention Must Be Paid', in Neil J. Kritz (ed.), *Transitional Justice*, vol. I, (Washington, DC: United States Institute for Peace, 1995), 569–70. This article originally appeared in *Commonweal* (23 March 1990), 184–86. Kritz notes that Martin-Baró wrote it shortly before he was killed, as a prologue for a book on mental health and human rights. Bishop Francisco Claver made similar observations regarding the Philippine experience in '*Sollicitudo Rei Socialis*: A View from the Philippines', in Gregory Baum and Robert Ellsberg (eds), *The Logic of Solidarity* (Maryknoll: Orbis, 1989), 207.

and macrosocial processes. The continuing rule of the dictatorship meant that, within the context of psychotherapy, victims could only aim for a private sort of 'reparation'.[49]

Psychotherapy for victims of such extreme situations requires social expression. '... [T]o be effective it must be elaborated beyond the subjective sphere, charging the social order with responsibility for repairing the damage'.[50] Reparation, they note, has a double significance, referring to both a sort of 'intrapsychic process of repair' as well as legally structured forms of compensation. Thus, social reparation involves inner healing as well as socially mediated forms of redress establishing the truth with a view toward justice for the victim. 'At both the individual and collective levels, the capacity for being *moved* ethically and emotionally must be recovered'.[51] Conversion from sin at the personal level both presupposes and lays the groundwork for some degree of structural transformation.

By cultivating social conscience, the CVR intended to foster reparation in both senses, 'reversing the climate of indifference with acts of solidarity that contribute to the overcoming of discriminatory views and habits ...'.[52] Ideally, the CVR concludes, reparation engenders civic trust and will contribute to a national reconciliation marked by full citizenship for all Peruvians. The commission's threefold understanding of reconciliation points toward the general good of 'building a country that recognizes itself positively as multiethnic, pluricultural, and multilingual. Such recognition is the basis for overcoming the practices of discrimination that underlie the multiple conflicts of our republican history'.[53]

Analogous to the disjunction between current practices of sacramental reconciliation and the phenomenon of social sin, the CVR notes that while national and international legal mechanisms address individual violations of human rights, they are not equipped to respond to widespread, systematic atrocities. Therefore, the Peruvian reparations plan must be flexible enough to meet such needs. Toward that end, the CVR put forth an 'Integral Program of Reparations' (PIR) that seeks to combine individual and collective forms of reparation, as well as symbolic and material compensation. The stated objective of the PIR is 'to repair and compensate for the violation of human rights as well as losses or social, moral, and material harms suffered by victims as a result of the internal armed conflict'.[54]

The PIR distinguishes between personal and social damage in need of restoration. In cases in which a whole social organization or an entire community has been victimized, they would be eligible to receive compensation as a group.

---

49 David Becker, Elizabeth Lira, María Isabel Castillo, Elena Gómez, and Juana Kovalskys, 'Therapy with Victims of Political Repression in Chile: The Challenge of Social Reparation', *Journal of Social Issues* 46:3 (1990), 134.

50 CVR, 141.

51 CVR, 147. Emphasis in the original. The authors cite Melanie Klein, *Love, Hate and Reparation*, 1987, originally published in 1937.

52 CVR, VIII, 'Conclusiones Generales', 351. See also IX, 2, 141.

53 CVR, 352.

54 CVR, IX, 2, 147.

This provision is particularly important given the disproportionate losses suffered by some of the poorest communities in Peru. Repairing the harm done there means rebuilding basic infrastructure and reweaving the fabric of common life through the creation of adequate social, cultural, educational, political and legal structures together with equitable access to them. 'In the long run, to rebuild is to help persons to find renewed purpose in life. This vision of the future distinguishes the program of collective reparations from any public works program of development or campaign against poverty'.[55]

Consistent with its communally-oriented process, the CVR recommends a dialogical approach to bridging ethnic and cultural differences among Peruvians with an emphasis on full and fair participation by all. The commission charges the state with the task of initiating the conversation and recommends that the President begin by formally apologizing on behalf of the state to all victims of the twenty-year conflict, that he publicly embrace the final report, and that his allocution be disseminated nationwide in the various languages of Peru, including Quechua, Aymara, and Asháninka.[56]

Even with judicious beginnings, any program of reparations implemented under the guise of a truth commission will quickly exhaust the limits of adequate response, gauged by the measure of strict justice. But, the object of such efforts springs from a more restorative vision of justice. Viewed from that perspective, the question guiding reparations policy shifts from 'What is due each party in the conflict?' to 'What needs to be mended?' The vindication of justice, then, will take on a communal and dialogical character because that which begs for healing involves the whole society.

This means that no single institution or approach to reconciliation can meet the multivalent need for societal restoration. The truth commission process cannot repair all the damage done, and neither can the church do so by making the Sacrament of Reconciliation available. Taken together, though, these two avenues of reconciliation may contribute to the longer and broader process of personal and social healing. Sacramental practices of reconciliation in ecclesial life may serve to cultivate attitudes and dispositions among church members that better prepare them for participation in societal practices of reconciliation like the truth commission. Engaging in forgiveness calls to mind one's own status as a forgiven sinner still in need of mercy. In turn, this awareness may conscientize communities working for liberation so that they might name their own internal structures of oppression, their own participation in social sin.[57] Reflecting on the Salvadoran experience, Jon Sobrino writes,

> These Christian communities that feel sin in themselves and are capable of forgiving are the ones most involved in the eradication of society's sin, the ones most prepared for the great forgiveness – forgiveness of those who have murdered countless people belonging

55  CVR, IX, 2, 194.

56  CVR, IX, 2, 162.

57  Latin America: Place of Sun, Place of Forgiveness', trans. Dinah Livingstone, in Jon Sobrino, *The Principle of Mercy* (Maryknoll, NY: Orbis Books, 1994), 66.

to them. The communities which seek hardest for internal reconciliation are the ones most prepared to seek social reconciliation ...[58]

Ultimately, processes of social reconciliation emerge through the leadership of reconciled individuals and reveal the vital social role of the church's ministry of reconciliation. Local ecclesial communities foster reconciliation by creating safe, dialogically oriented space for the personal and communal healing needed to sustain societal practices of reconciliation.

## Ecclesiological Implications of Social Reconciliation

In order to bear credible witness to its fundamental mission of reconciliation, the church itself must be reconciled, as the 1971 Synod of Bishops so poignantly declared:

> While the Church is bound to give witness to justice, she recognizes that everyone who ventures to speak to people about justice must first be just in their eyes. Hence we must undertake an examination of the modes of acting and of the possessions and lifestyle found within the Church herself.[59]

In the service of social reconciliation, the church must examine and repent for its own complicity in structures of sin. Since the process of conversion and reconciliation is a journey, the church as a historically conditioned institution will always stand in need of reconciliation, as Vatican II acknowledged: The church 'at once holy and always in need of purification, follows constantly the path of penance and renewal'.[60] In the Peruvian case, Bishop Albano Quinn has observed, the CVR's report signals the grace of conversion for the nation, as well as an opportunity for the church to review its commitment to the gospel in light of its own teaching.[61]

The CVR offers important data for ecclesial discernment, documenting the excellent work of church leaders and pastoral agents in confronting systemic violence and promoting peace. But, it also calls attention to some egregious pastoral and ethical lapses, including Cardinal Juan Luis Cipriani's intransigence regarding human rights issues, his uncritical support of a series of repressive political regimes, and his advocacy of the death penalty for captured Shining Path leader Abimael Guzmán, all positions that put him at odds with the majority of the Peruvian bishops'

58 Latin America: Place of Sun, Place of Forgiveness', trans. Dinah Livingstone, in Jon Sobrino, *The Principle of Mercy* (Maryknoll, NY: Orbis Books, 1994), 67.

59 'Justice in the World', in David J. O'Brien and Thomas A Shannon (eds), *Catholic Social Thought*, 295.

60 'Dogmatic Constitution on the Church', (*Lumen gentium*) (21 November 1964) in Austin Flannery (ed.), *Vatican Council II*, vol.1 (rev. ed), (Collegeville, IN: The Liturgical Press, 1992), paragraph 8.

61 Albano Quinn, O.Carm., 'Un momento de gracia para revisar nuestra Evangelización', *Ideele* 159 (November 2003), 31–33.

conference.[62] In the commission's judgment, Cipriani, together with his predecessor, Federico Richter Prada, actually impeded the work of human rights organizations while serving as archbishop of Ayacucho, the region where the highest per centage of atrocities occurred.[63]

A member of Opus Dei and now archbishop of Lima, Cipriani has rejected the truth commission's report. At a Mass attended by President Alejandro Toledo, he declared, 'I do not accept it because it is not true'.[64] The CVR has provided vital data for communal examination of conscience in Peru, but it remains unclear what role the church can play in the process unless it first holds accountable its own members, and particularly leaders like Cipriani.

Without rigorous accountability and ongoing conscientization, Peru might be vulnerable to the insidious possibility of false reconciliation or a sort of cheap grace. As Gregory Baum warns, the language of reconciliation can be used as an ideological tool to evade the demands of truth, namely structural reform and resistance against evil.[65] Mario Vargas Llosa laments that many citizens have received the CVR report with ambivalence at best. The document portrays a 'horrifically sad' but true image of Peru, compelling even well-intentioned and decent people to recoil in shame.[66]

But, the commission's threefold understanding of reconciliation extends the hope that shame might be transformed into the graced capacity to offer and receive forgiveness as part of restorative justice. The CVR sought to establish grounds for holding the state accountable to civil society and for societal institutions to repair inter-communal ruptures in relationship. At every level of social interaction, the CVR spoke to the need for interpersonal healing as well. 'Reconciliation', the CVR report concludes, 'is fundamentally a re-encounter of society with itself'.[67]

The Peruvian truth commission has succeeded in creating open, public space for societal institutions and local communities to discern their particular commitments to this threefold social remembering. Occupying a singularly powerful role in a predominantly Catholic Christian society, the Peruvian church bears a special responsibility in this regard. Local ecclesial communities can provide the kind of dialogically oriented communal forum needed to continue the personal and corporate formation and examination of conscience so carefully initiated by the CVR. Modern

---

62  CVR, III, 3.3, 414–421, 426–429. For more historical background on courageous pastoral efforts in Ayacucho and Cipriani's opposition to them, see Jeffrey Klaiber, *Church, Dictatorships and Democracy in Latin America*, 152–53.

63  CVR, III, 399.

64  Juan Forero, 'Peru Truth Commission Stirs Up a Hornet's Nest', *International Herald Tribune* (9 September 2003), 5.

65  Gregory Baum, 'A Theological Afterword', in Gregory Baum and Harold Wells (eds), *The Reconciliation of Peoples* (Maryknoll: Orbis Books, 1997), 188. See also'The Kairos Document' (South Africa, 1985), in Robert McAfee Brown (ed.), *Kairos* (Grand Rapids: William B. Eerdmans Publishing Co., 1990), 38–40.

66  Mario Vargas Llosa, 'Nada en común', *Ideele* 158 (October 2003), 39, quoting from Vargas Llosa's article published in *El Pais* (21 September 2003).

67  CVR, I, 3.3, 83.

adaptations of the Order of Penitents and the expanded use of mystagogy offer hope that the Peruvian church might develop its own creative ritual responses to social sin, perhaps in conversation with the traditional healing practices of its indigenous peoples.

Standing in relationship to other institutional actors within civil society and to its own members, the church will need to undertake a public examination of conscience and acknowledge its complicity as an institution in contributing to structures of sin that gave shape to these two decades of extremely violent conflict in Peru. In particular, as the largest religious body in the country, the church must consider its role in perpetuating institutionalized racism. By taking seriously its own examination of conscience, it will be better able to freely and credibly witness to the truth of its own message and ministry of reconciliation. The humble witness of the poor majority of indigenous victims of systemic violence might serve to guide the Peruvian church on the path of conversion by way of the cross.

In the encounter of sacramental reconciliation with the truth commission model, a fuller understanding of the contours of social reconciliation in Peru emerges, one capable of addressing a wounded society's need for systemic healing more adequately than either approach could accomplish alone. The CVR's work has proven critical to the process of naming social sin, situating the data of twenty years of violent conflict within the broader narrative context of Peruvian culture and history. Institutional actors and local communities now have public space within which to imagine the future of their particular stories as part of the larger national narrative of social reconciliation. What do they need to leave behind? What are they being called to do and to be within an ethically restored society? And, how will they undertake the transformation required?

# PART III
# Nations and Churches in the Future

## Chapter 8

# Living in the Wake of the Truth and Reconciliation Commission: A Retroactive Reflection

Charles Villa-Vicencio

To understand and evaluate the Truth and Reconciliation Commission (TRC), it is crucial to understand its origin and identity. It emerged as result of a negotiated settlement between black and white, within which neither side won or lost. The conflict began with a fragile white Portuguese presence in the Cape in the latter part of the fifteenth century. It endured Dutch and English colonialism from the seventeenth century to the beginning of the twentieth. It persisted through generations of institutionalized racism and culminated in a thirty-year race war.

In the words of Shakespeare's Macbeth: 'as two spent swimmers, that do cling together', it drew to a climax in an historic settlement, forged essentially between black Africans and white Boers. The settlement was designed to stop an escalating war that threatened to destroy the very identity, infrastructure and promise of a nation yet to be born. Both sides to the conflict somehow believed that new life could still emerge out of the phoenix strife that characterized the apartheid years. The TRC was expected to facilitate the process. Its brief was to help cultivate a milieu within which the gross violations of the past would not be repeated in the future. Judge Richard Goldstone, Justice of the Constitutional Court and former Prosecutor of the International Criminal Tribunal for the former Yugoslavia and later for Rwanda, put it this way:

> The decision to opt for a Truth and Reconciliation Commission was an important compromise. If the African National Congress (ANC) had insisted on Nuremberg-style trials for the leaders of the former apartheid government, there would have been no peaceful transition to democracy, and if the former government had insisted on a blanket amnesty then, similarly, the negotiations would have broken down. A bloody revolution sooner rather than later would have been inevitable. The Truth and Reconciliation Commission is a bridge from the old to the new.[1]

The events that culminated in the Report being handed to the president on 29 October 1998 are well known: 22,500 victims of gross violations of human rights volunteered to tell the Commission their stories. Over 7,000 people applied for amnesty. The TRC,

---

1  Richard Goldstone, The Hauser Lecture, New York University, 22 January 1997.

with the exception of some amnesty hearings that are still outstanding, is now over. It must be over. It is time to move on. The nation was experiencing what the media called 'TRC fatigue'. Having received saturation coverage in the media, no South African (black or white) can ever again say 'it did not happen' or 'I never knew'. And yet the past dies only with difficulty. Some struggle to put it behind them, others continue to seek to turn away from it too quickly – not wanting to stop to reflect too deeply, to look too carefully, or to take responsibility for what happened.

## Has the Experiment Worked?

Some ask more brashly, has the Commission saved or reconciled the nation? The answer is 'of course not'. It would be presumptuous to think that a Commission of the nature and duration of the TRC could reconcile a nation torn apart by 350 years of colonialism and 50 years of apartheid rule. The mandate of the Commission was captured in the title of its founding act, *The Promotion of National Unity and Reconciliation Act (No 34 of 1995)*. Its mandate was the *promotion* of national unity and reconciliation. The Commission has contributed to this process, in the sense of promoting, consolidating, and advancing a process of reconciliation that had started with the negotiation process and needs to continue to happen if it is to succeed.[2]

I offer three somewhat crude models or typologies of response to the TRC in South Africa:

## • Some rejected the mandate of the Commission

There is an understandable reluctance among some victims to put the past behind them. Chris Ribeiro, the son of the murdered Florence and Fabian Ribeiro, objected to anyone 'pushing reconciliation down my throat'. Marius Schoon, who lost his wife and a daughter in a South African Army raid into Botswana, in turn, complains about 'the imposition of a Christian morality of forgiveness'.

Polish dissident Adam Michnik tells that when he was in prison he resolved never to seek revenge or to refuse to forgive. Yet he kept repeating to himself a fragment of Zbigniew Herbert's poem: 'And do not forgive, as it is not within your power to forgive on behalf of those betrayed at dawn'. He argued that we can forgive harm done *to us*. But, it is not in our power to forgive harm done *to others*. 'We can try to convince people to forgive, but if they want justice, they are entitled to demand it'.[3]

It is the responsibility of the democratically-elected government to govern, mindful that some within the nation are not prepared to put the past behind them.

---

2   See Jakes Gerwel, 'National Reconciliation: Holy Grail or Secular Pact?', in C. Villa-Vicencio and W. Verwoerd (eds), *Looking Back Reaching Forward: Reflections on the Truth and Reconciliation Commission of South Africa* (Cape Town: University of Cape Town Press. London: Zed Books, 2000), 277–287.

3   Adam Michnick in 'Justice or Revenge', *Journal of Democracy* 4:1 (January 1993), 3–27.

The point is well made by Jose Zalaquett, who served on the Chilean National Truth and Reconciliation Commission. 'Leaders', he suggests, 'should never forget that the lack of political pressure to put these issues on the agenda does not mean they are not boiling underground, waiting to erupt'.[4] The demand by many Chileans, almost ten years after the establishment of the Chilean Commission, that General Augusto Pinochet stand trial, following his arrest in the United Kingdom, underlines Zalaquett's point. Some are not prepared to settle for less than retribution. Some even demand revenge.

- **Some enthusiastically embraced the mandate of the Commission**

Having spend twenty-seven years in prison, former President Nelson Mandela was ready to forgive and be reconciled with those who jailed him. Not everyone could emulate his stance. Yet people like Cynthia Nomveyu Ngewu, whose son, Christopher Piet, was one of the Gugulethu Seven shot by the police in an ambush in March 1986, was asked for her response to the position of those who supported the imprisonment of perpetrators, she replied:

> In my opinion, I do not agree with this view. We do not want to see people suffer in the same way that we did suffer, and we did not want our families to have suffered. We do not want to return the suffering that was imposed upon us. So, I do not agree with that view at all. We would like to see peace in this country ... I think that all South Africans should be committed to the idea of re-accepting these people back into the community. We do not want to return the evil that perpetrators committed to the nation. We want to demonstrate humanness towards them, so that they in turn may restore their own humanity.[5]

The testimony of Ginn Fourie, mother of Lyndi Fourie, who was killed in the Heidelberg Tavern massacre, carried out by three young APLA (Azanian People's Liberation Army) operatives in December 1993, captures the importance of discovering the humanity, compassion and courtesy of her daughter's assassins. At the close of the amnesty hearing for the young men responsible for the deed, Mrs Fourie met with them as they were about to be returned to their prison cells. She had on a previous occasion offered them her forgiveness. They had suggested that perhaps there was a need for joint counselling, involving perpetrator and victim or survivor. I quote her account of the meeting:

> The warders insisted that the meeting adjourn, a hug for each indicated the depth of community we had entered into in this short while. The amnesty applicants then shackled themselves, which at that moment symbolized to me the enormous responsibility which accompanies freedom of choice and the sad outcome of making poor choices. Tears came to my eyes. Humphrey Gqomfa (one of the killers) turned to the interpreter and said: 'Please take Mrs Fourie home'. Once more I was amazed by the sensitivity and leadership

---

4    Alex Boraine et al., *Dealing with the Past* (Cape Town: IDASA, 1994), 15.

5    TRC, *Truth and Reconciliation Commission of South Africa Report* (Cape Town, 1998), Vol. 5, chapter 9, para. 33.

potential of this man, the same man who was also a perpetrator of gross violations of human rights against my own daughter.[6]

The magnanimity of spirit shown by Ginn Fourie and the killers of her daughter should never be taken for granted. It cannot be demanded of anyone. It is, at the same time, the kind of response that constitutes the wellspring on which healing is premised for victim and perpetrator alike. There are other stories. They include the story of Neville Clarence who lost his sight in the Church Street bomb detonated outside of the Airforce Headquarters in Pretoria on 20 May 1983. Although blinded by the bomb, Clarence seemed to look Aboobaker Ismael, the commanding officer of the operation of Mkhonto we Sizwe (MK), the armed wing of the African National Congress, in the eye: 'I forgive you for what you have done. I came … to share my feelings with you. I wanted you to know that I harbour no thoughts of revenge'.[7] Brian Mitchell, responsible for the Trust Fields Massacre in December 1988 asked for forgiveness of those who survived the attack and committed himself to working in the community he had destroyed. Jubulisiwe Ngubane, who had lost her mother and her children in the attack observed: 'It is not easy to forgive, but because he stepped forward and asked for forgiveness, I have no choice. I must forgive him …'[8]

Some did forgive. It cannot be demanded. It cannot be presumed. It cannot even be expected. Where it happens it is grace.

- **The majority of South Africans are essentially ambivalent about the mandate of the Commission**

The ambivalence has many different sources. There are those (primarily whites) whose ambivalence comes to expression primarily in indifference. They want to forget the past. Some want to ignore its persisting presence. Few are ready to engage it, reflect on it and ask what it may teach them about the present and the future.

There is another kind of ambivalence about the past which manifests itself in an inability not to remember, while being determined to get on with life. One sees this among private individuals who have borne the brunt of the past and now struggle to engage the future. One also sees this among those in government who are eager to close past wounds and to have the nation move on. Their fear is that too much memory will fuel continuing resentments. It will reopen past divisions and undermine possibilities of peaceful coexistence.

These differing sources of ambivalence, giving expression to opposite political and ideological poles in a nation living between the past and the future, ironically

---

6    In a paper 'The Psychology of Perpetrators of Political Violence in South Africa: A Personal Experience,' delivered at a Medical Research Unit on Anxiety and Stress Disorders conference, Mental Health Beyond the TRC, 8 October 1998.

7    See account in Piet Meiring, *Chronicle of the Truth Commission* (Vanderbijlpark: Carpe Diem Books, 1999), 339–341.

8    Piet Meiring, *Chronicle of the Truth Commission*, 121–23.

find a measure of common ground in a unclear response to the past. They find this in a desire to look forward: to go to school or have their children do so, to get jobs and be successful, to have their offspring succeed in life, to enjoy the 'good things' of life, to live and let live. It is a philosophy that at times makes for a robust competitiveness and at times for a measure of protectionism. It, at the same time, carries the seed of rugged individualism and a potential indifference to the lesson that the past has to teach. (I was recently in conversation with a very bright and ambitious young black student who told me that 'the struggle' of the 1980s was not his struggle. He explained that his struggle is the future. It involves gaining material prosperity and social influence.)

The then president of the then Federal Republic of Germany, Richard von Weizsacker, made an important speech in 1995 concerning Germany's Nazi past, in which he said that while there was no 'zero hour' for the German people in moving the past to the future, there was a fresh start.[9] South Africa has in some ways risked a similar (but, of course, different) kind of transition.

It is too early to say whether it has worked. If those who in different ways supported, promoted, tolerated and invariably benefited from apartheid are not prepared to build a new South Africa, the forces that brought the nation to the brink of disaster in 1989 could be found to still be there – demanding satisfaction, this time, in a less compromising way. In the event that time and space is such that these matters can be dealt with, those at the two poles of the political memory spectrum may just find one another. It is what the present state leadership is hoping for, and yet, there are factors militating against it. Antjie Krog, celebrated author of *Country of My Skull*, tells of her recent visit to Germany. 'I wanted to be there to find out how do you live with the responsibility and guilt of the past', she says. 'I was astounded. I assumed other places are like South Africa, but what I didn't realise, of course, was that there were hardly any Jews left in Germany. Here [in South Africa] we see each other every day – we confront the past daily ...'.[10] The issues that divide the two ends of South African society stand out in sharp relief in the post apartheid period. The past continues to be present – economically, psychologically, spiritually and at a host of other levels from language and humour to art and music. And yet, it is within this diversity that South Africans need to learn to live together. It is here, in the morally murky ambivalence about the past, that nation-building will be required to happen. There is simply no other option. To expect every South African to undergo a cathartic experience in dealing with the past, is to expect everyone to be caught up in the enthusiasm of an evangelical preacher on a Sunday morning. In reality, most people do not even show up to hear the sermon.

---

9  Donald W. Shriver, *An Ethic for Enemies: Forgiveness in Politics* (New York, Oxford: Oxford University Press, 1995), 73–118, 230.
10  Antje Krog, 'Top of the Times', *Cape Times* (25 February 2000).

## Given these Different Responses to the TRC, Can the Nation Heal Itself?

Bad memories do not easily go away. Timothy Garton Ash, the Oxford based historian reminds us that 'often it is the victims who are cursed by memory, while perpetrators are blessed by forgetting'.[11] In South Africa it is primarily those who suffered least (and prospered most) who are most determined to forget the pain of others. Those who survived the nightmare of suffering, torture and death can do no other than remember. And yet, as suggested, some who have suffered and been deprived are, for different reasons, committed to move on. And yet, many of these people *can* do no other than remember.

Speaking in the National Assembly in May 1998, then Deputy President Thabo Mbeki identified two 'interrelated elements' constitutive of the process of the reconciliation needed between what he calls the 'two nations in one country', one which is 'white and relatively prosperous' and the other which is 'black and poor'.

The first element of Mbeki's analysis of the challenge facing South Africa, is the creation of a material base whereby the 'grossly underdeveloped' black nation may be assisted to elevate themselves from the vastly inferior material living conditions they were forced to accept during apartheid. The need for this to happen, as an essential basis for healing and reconciliation, is self-explanatory.

The second challenge that Mbeki identified, is the promotion of what he called a 'subjective factor', aimed at sustaining the hope and conviction among South Africans that the process of reconciliation and nation-building can succeed. As such, reconciliation is seen to involve an enduring process of reconstruction and economic development, but also the promotion of public processes designed to facilitate co-operation and trust between people who have lived in isolation from one another for so long. The Truth and Reconciliation Commission, despite the compromises, risks, shortcomings and court orders has functioned essentially at this 'subjective' level. Now, in the wake of the work of the TRC, several questions need to be asked yet again. These are questions that were asked when the idea of a Commission was first mooted, as an alternative to both trials and amnesia.

## Why does a Nation Remember?

Is it merely because some cannot forget? Can it serve any good? Does time not eventually heal? Hear the words of President Roman Herzog on the occasion of the meeting of the Deutscher Bundestag in 1996:

> The pictures of the piles of corpses, of murdered children, women and men, of starved bodies are so penetrating that they remain distinctly engraved, not just in the minds of survivors and liberators, but in those who read and view accounts of [the holocaust] today. … Why then do we have the will to keep this memory alive? Would it not be an evident desire to let the wounds heal into scars and to lay the dead to rest? … History fades

---

11 In Timothy Garton Ash, *The File* (London: Flamingo, 1997), 201.

quickly if it is not part of one's own experience. [But] memory is living future. We do not want to conserve the horror. We want to draw lessons that future generations can use as guidance. ... In the light of sober description the worst barbarous act shrinks into an anonymous event. If we wish for the erasure of this memory we ourselves will be the first victims of self-deception.[12]

The implication is that we remember in order not to repeat past atrocities. The problem is that there is not much evidence to suggest that history equips as not to repeat past abuses. Terrence McCaughey, President of the former Irish Anti-Apartheid Movement, tells of his student days at Tübingen University in Germany in the late 1950s.[13] There had been a week-long film series on German politics from the Weimer Republic to the rise and fall of Adolf Hitler. Academic life almost came to a standstill. He tells of his Old Testament lecturer, Professor Karl Elliger, addressing his class on the morning after the final presentation: 'You young people no doubt think we were all stupid not to have seen what was happening', he said. 'We have no excuses. But learn this, evil never comes from the same direction, wearing the same face. I hope you will be wiser and more discerning than our generation when the threat of evil next comes around. You need to be vigilant'. The professor turned to his notes and lectured his students on the Book of Joshua.

We remember in the hope that we will not repeat past atrocities. But primarily we remember because we cannot, while the past remains unresolved, lay its ghost to rest. The words of Rebecca Hanse, a relative of Fezile Hanse who, together with Andile Majol and Patrick Madikane was shot dead by riot police on 17 June 1985 in Bongolethu, a black township on the outskirts of Oudtshoorn, are pertinent: 'We must preserve the bones of our children until they can rest in peace. We cannot forget. We must keep our children alive. They were not ready to die. There is much for them still to do. We are not ready to let them go'.[14] Maybe a time will come when their bones *will* rest in peace. In time, hopefully, the past will no longer be with us in as excruciating a way as it is at present.

Why do we remember? Ultimately the nation is called to remember for the sake of those who suffer. It is a manner of restoring the dignity of victims and survivors by ensuring that their suffering does not pass unnoticed. It is to say to victims and survivors: 'Your suffering is part of our healing as a nation. We remember you'.

---

12 Presse und Infromationsdienst der Bundesregierung, 23 January 1996. Translated and quoted in Undine Kayser, 'Improvising the Present: narrative Construction and Re-construction of the Past in South Africa and Germany'. Honours Thesis, Centre for African Studies, University of Cape Town, 1997/98.

13 Dublin, Ireland, March 1999.

14 In conversation at the grave of the Bongolethu Three, June 1996. See also TRC, *Report*, Volume 3, 437–439.

**But, How Reliable is Memory?**

Memory sometimes plays tricks on us. Bad memories are fraught with trauma and often with incomprehension. It gives expression to the inability of language to articulate what needs to be said. What are the implications of this healing and reconciliation?

Memory is perhaps always incomplete. Its very incompleteness is what cries out to be heard. There is the testimony of silence. There is body language. There is fear, anger and confusion. There is a struggle between telling what happened and explaining it away. Mxolisi (Ace) Mgxashe struggles with the very question of truth. 'Inyani iyababa', he observes. In Xhosa it means 'truth is bitter'. '... It is so bitter [that] sometimes we find ourselves quarreling over whether it should be told at all. Even when there has been some consensus that the truth should be told ... we invariably disagree on the extent to which it must be told'.[15]

Sometimes we involuntarily hide the truth as much from ourselves as others. Antje Krog prefers not to even use the word 'truth'. 'I prefer the word lie', she says. 'The moment the lie raises its head, I smell blood. Because it is there ... where truth is closest'.[16] Truth rarely leaps forth to introduce itself unmolested by lies, confusion, forgetfulness and evasion. It needs to be dug out!

What then is the relationship between truth and fiction? Testifying at a Cape Town hearing of the TRC into the killing of the Guguletu Seven in April 1996, Cynthia Ngewu (to whom reference has already been made), the mother of Christopher Piet, one of those killed, wrestled with what had in fact happened. 'Now nobody knows the real-real story', she noted.[17] The ambiguity of memory is real. It is a reality that is frequently exploited by people who seek to discredit those who have suffered and struggle to finds words to articulate their deepest experience of what happened. Thus Anthea Jeffery attacks the Commission because (according to her) insufficient attention was given to the importance of factual or objective truth, by recognizing the importance of what the Commission called *personal or narrative (dialogue) truth*, as well as *social truth* and *healing or restorative truth*. The Commission deliberately chose to wrestle with these notions of truth in relation to *factual or forensic truth*.[18] The Commission was not a court of law and (for good reason) it did not subject victim and survivor testimony to cross-examination.[19]

---

15  Mxolisi Mgxashe, *Argus* (14 June 1996).

16  Antjie Krog, *Country of My Skull* (Johannesburg: Random House, 1998), 36.

17  Human Rights Violations' Committee Hearing, Cape Town, 22 April 1996.

18  Anthea Jeffery, *The Truth About the Truth Commission* (Johannesburg: South African Institute of Race Relations, 1999).

19  It did, however, through its corroboration assess such testimony on the basis of a balance of probability. Graeme Simpson is correct: '... most of the legal and jursiprudential dilemmas presented by the TRC process are actually rooted in its own almost bi-polar roles as both a "fact-finding" and a "quasi-judicial enterprise on the one hand, and as a psychologically sensitive mechanism for story telling and healing on the other". In 'A Brief Evaluation of South

Albert Camus has defined truth as being 'as mysterious as it is inaccessible', and yet, he insisted, worth 'being fought for eternally'.[20] Its discovery involves a long and slow process. It often involves conflict arising from stories that contradict one another. This is part of the process of national reconciliation. Donald Shriver's words are compelling: 'One does not argue long with people whom one deems of no real importance. Democracy is at its best when people of clashing points of view argue far into the night, because they know that the next day they are going to encounter each other as residents of the [same] neighbourhood'.[21] The difficulties of creating democracy out of a culture of gross violations of human rights are immense. It can be facilitated through what the Chileans call *reconvivencia* – a period of getting used to living with each other again. Above all, it involves being exposed to the worst fears of one's adversaries. It requires getting to know one another, gaining a new insight into *what* happened as well as an empathetic understanding of *how* a particular event is viewed by one's adversaries.

## Is there a Role for Story-telling?

Getting to know one another and building relationships between former enemies involves many things. Important among these is welding together a story that unites rather than one that divides. This involves the difficult process of moving beyond testimony which, I have suggested, is frequently fraught with trauma, incompleteness and sometimes incomprehension.

This is perhaps where poetry, music and myth can contribute more to healing than any attempt to explain in some rigid forensic way 'who did what to whom'. Antjie Krog's celebrated novel on the work of the Commission, *Country of My Skull*,[22] weaves fragments from different testimonies and interviews into a semi-fictional historical account of events. The Commission was obliged to do both *more* and *less* than what she accomplished. It was, above all, obliged to be more comprehensive and thus compelled to reduce or translate the richness of raw memory, or what has been called first-generation testimony, into historical narrative. This material awaits a dozen poets, musicians and story-tellers to be retold in a healing way. Silences in testimony need to be heard if not interpreted. There needs to be reading between the lines, behind the words and within the context of the moment. The testimony is to be heard for what it is – a cry from the heart. It is difficult to conceive how any historical text can capture that. And yet, the healing of the nation requires that it be heard.

---

Africa's TRC: Some Lessons for Societies in Transition', Paper delivered at Commissioning the Past Conference, University of the Witswatersrand, June 1999.

20  Cited in Janet Cherry, 'Historical Truth and the Truth and Reconciliation Commission', in C. Villa-Vicencio and W. Verwoerd (eds), *Looking Back Reaching Forward* (Cape Town: UCT Press, 1999), 143.

21  Donald W. Shriver, *An Ethic for Enemies: Forgiveness in Politics*, 230.

22  Antjie Krog, *Country of My Skull* (Johannesburg, Random House 1998), 36.

**Getting on With Life**

Is it ever possible, for those who truly suffered, to put the past behind us? The words of holocaust victim Primo Levi can only haunt the soul of any person of compassion:

> This is the awful privilege of our generation and of my people, no one better than us has ever been able to grasp the incurable nature of the offence, that spreads like a contagion. It is foolish to think that human justice can eradicate it. It is an inexhaustible fount of evil; it breaks the body and the spirit of the submerged, it perpetuates itself as hatred among survivors, and swarms around in a thousand ways, against the very will of all, as thirst for revenge, as a moral capitulation, as denial, as weariness, as renunciation.[23]

Clearly some show a resilience to rise above the anguish of past suffering better than others. Testimony that witnesses both to a willingness or desire to 'get on with life' as well a reluctance or inability to do so is there to be heard and analyzed. I offer rather the comment of a young woman named Kalu that highlights the internalised emotions inherent to the transition from the old to the new:[24]

> What really makes me angry about the TRC and Tutu is that they are putting pressure on me to forgive. ... I don't know if I will ever be able to forgive. I carry this ball of anger within me and I don't know where to begin dealing with it. The oppression was bad, but what is much worse, what makes me even angrier, is that they are trying to dictate my forgiveness.

Her words capture the pathos involved in the long and fragile journey towards reconciliation. No one has the right to prevail on Kalu to forgive. The question is whether victims and survivors can be assisted *to get on with the rest of their lives* in the sense of not allowing anger or self-pity to be the all-consuming dimension of their existence. Reflecting on the response of Kalu, my colleague, Wilhelm Verwoerd, refers to the response of Ashley Forbes to his torture at the hands of the notorious torturer, Jeffrey Benzien. Although critical of the decision to grant Benzien amnesty, arguing that he failed to make full disclosure, he observed: 'I forgive him and feel sorry for him. And now that the TRC has showed what happened, I can get on with the rest of my life'.

Not every victim deals with his or her past in this way. It is important, however, for *their own sake*, that victims and survivors are assisted (to the extent that it possible) to indeed *get on with life*. This does *not* mean forgetting the ghastly deeds of the past. This is usually not possible and probably not helpful. There is indeed a

---

23  Primo Levi, 'The Truce' in Albert A Friedlander (ed.), *Out of the Whirlwind: A Reader of Holocaust Literature* (New York: Schocken Books, 1976), 426.

24  See Wilhelm Verwoerd, 'Forgiving the Torturer but not the Torture', in *Sunday Independent* (14 December 1998). See also my 'Getting on With Life: A Move Towards Reconciliation', in C. Villa-Vicencio and W. Verwoerd (eds), *Looking Back Reaching Forward* (Cape Town: UCT Press, 1999), 199–209.

place for righteous anger, which can be a source of self-worth and dignity. To get on with life does *not* necessarily mean becoming friends with the person responsible for one's suffering. Very few accomplish this. It *does* mean dealing with the 'ball of anger' that prevents one from getting on with life.

And yet, the graph of the journey forward is rarely a progressively even one. Such progress that is made in *getting on with life* tends to take place in concentric circles. Progress can be made. Time and circumstances of different kinds do assist the healing process. But there is also *deep memory* that reminds us that the past is never quite past. Bernard Langer, reflecting on the suicide of Primo Levi, forty years after his release from Auschwitz, speaks of the 'painful and uneasy stress between trauma and recovery'.[25] Levi's prolific writing at no time fails to portray the presence of melancholy. Langer argues that:

> Levi, as a suicide, demolishes the idea that he had mastered his past, come to term with the atrocity of Auschwitz, and rejoined the human community healed and whole. Life went on for him, of course, though it is probably a mistake to think of his writings as a form of therapy, a catharsis that freed him from what he called the memory of the offense. It is clear from everything he wrote that survival did not mean a restored connection with what had gone before. The legacy of permanent disruption may be difficult to accept, but it lingers in his suicide like an abiding parasite.[26]

Levi's testimony is that of one who seeks to wash his conscience and memory clean. Refusing to reduce the immensity of his particular ordeal to 'a capacity for evil buried in human nature somewhere', he is angry at society's apparent indifference to the question as to what makes killers resort to the depths of humanity that they do. And yet he insisted, 'to a greater or lesser degree all were responsible'. The 'greater majority of Germans', he writes, '... accepted [the persecution of the Jews] in the beginning out of mental laziness, myopic calculations, stupidity and national pride...'.[27]

Wrestling with memories of suffering and questions concerning the nature of evil, he killed himself. The concentric circles of others in the quest to get on with life are less decisive. Joe Seremane is angry with the Commission for failing to probe deeply enough into death of his brother Timothy Tebogo Seremane in the ANC Quatro Camp in 1981. 'You owe us a lot', he told the Commission. 'Not monetary compensation, but our bones buried in shallow graves in Angola and heaven knows where else'. He quotes words from Langston Hughes' M*instrel Man*:[28]

---

25  Lawrence Langer, *Preempting the Holocaust* (New Haven and London: Yale University Press, 1998), xv.

26  Lawrence Langer, *Preempting the Holocaust*, xv.

27  Lawrence Langer, *Preempting the Holocaust*, xv.

28  Lawrence Langer, *Preempting the Holocaust*, xv, 23–62.

Because my mouth
Is wide with laughter
And my throat deep with song,
Do you not think
I suffer, after I have held
My pain so long?

Whatever the truth of the various allegations (by Seremane and the counter-charges by the ANC) the pathos of his words should not be missed. The question is what can society do to help those who suffer to move on? In Ndebele's words, the question is how to promote 'visible measures for improving the lives of the victims of the past, who even while they are still in a state of severe disadvantage ought not to experience themselves any more as victims?'

## Are there Lessons to be Learned from the South African Experiment in Healing?

Situations and contexts differ. It is insensitive to dare seek to impose one's own attempt at a solution onto others. But this much we can learn: Where people suffer, healing is needed. And yet healing is never complete. It involves moving on in concentric circles. This means that compassion, support and understanding is required. This constitutes the acid test of the Commission and indeed of the entire South African transitionary process. It involves the question whether our reflection on the past will succeed in making us a more compassionate, supportive and understanding people? And the jury is still out on this one.

Bluntly put. Unless the South African experiment in healing reaches not only victims and survivors of the apartheid years but also heals the hardened hearts of both direct perpetrators of gross violations of human rights as well as the benefactors of apartheid, the healing process that is taking place is likely to be incomplete. This would be a huge tragedy for a nation that has done so incredibly well in seeking to heal itself in so many other ways.

In closing, I cite W. S. Merwin's prose poem, entitled *Unchopping a Tree*. It provides a powerful metaphor, reminding us of the limitations of any human attempt to heal.[29] Merwin describes the incredibly difficult process of how one could go about unchopping a tree – placing each fallen branch, withered twig and dried leaf in its appropriate place, as well as relocating birds' nests. Herewith the final lines of the poem:

---

29  In W. S. Merwin, *The Miner's Pale Children* (New York: Atheneum, 1970), 85–88.

The first breeze that touches its dead leaves …
You are afraid the motion of the clouds will be
enough to push it over. What more can you do?
What more can you do?

But there is nothing more you can do
Others are waiting
Everything is going to have to be put back.

Have the leaves been placed in the correct place? How many twigs are missing? Will the birds recognize their nests? Will the tree take root and grow? Perhaps endurance, not restitution, never full recovery, not even full healing, is all that survivors can strive for. Some dare to hope for more. Some remember. Others are fearful to do so. What is important is the dream of a great tree that can be. It involves a dream. It also involves hard work.

Has the TRC worked? When the British historian E. P. Thompson was asked a few years back whether he thought the French Revolution was a success, he noted that it is still too early to tell. The jury is still out on the South African transition. What is certain is that we cannot afford to wait two hundred years for a verdict.

Chapter 9

# Truth and Reconciliation: From Chile to South Africa

Michael Battle

## Introduction and Summary

Archbishop Desmond Tutu has become South Africa's primary public confessor who articulates why forgiveness is better than retributive justice. The thesis of this paper is that Tutu's role in South Africa's Truth and Reconciliation Commission (abbreviated to TRC) is unique and cannot be displayed in other Truth Commissions such as in Chile. I base my claim on the following argument. The greatest religious challenge in a new South Africa is the maintenance of what has become an amalgam of spiritual and political leadership, especially as displayed in the life and thought of Archbishop Desmond Tutu. Tutu's context of South African apartheid presented the dilemma in which he, as ecclesial head of a historically white Church, negotiated how to act effectively in a society so defined by race that both Afrikaner and African could each claim God's election as the chosen race. Subsequently, as head of the TRC in South Africa, Tutu's urgency toward restorative justice, I argue, is not simply to restore black people to a place of flourishing – such an interpretation of Tutu forfeits his profound contribution toward reconciliation of races. Because of Tutu's Trinitarian spirituality in which diverse personhood flourishes in unity, Tutu is obligated to articulate a theology of community in which all South Africans have an opportunity to grow toward unity. All of this makes sense, however, in South Africa and not in other Truth Commissions such as in Chile.

With this paper, and hopefully a larger work, I attest to Tutu's crucial, albeit controversial, role in the Truth and Reconciliation Commission (TRC). Therefore my argument throughout this paper is that Tutu acts both as theological and political agent of utopian community in his context of warring factions. With this focus, I now address my thesis that it is vital to see Tutu's theological contributions, more particularly his articulation of forgiveness and repentance, in order to understand the impetus for his political involvement in the TRC.

**The Birth of the South African Truth and Reconciliation Commission**

How will South Africans deal with the legacies of the apartheid era? This has been the question lingering over the South African nation for over a century. Upon the final victory of democratic election in 1994, the African National Congress (ANC) tried to answer the previous question with what they called a 'Truth Commission', but their adversary, the National Party (NP), advocated for a 'Reconciliation Commission'. The ANC, Nelson Mandela's Party, was concerned about the victims of the apartheid period, while the NP, F. W. de Klerk's Party, looked for amnesty for the perpetrators. The result was the 'National Unity and Reconciliation Act' of 26 July 1995, which established the 'Truth and Reconciliation Commission' (TRC). At the end of the day, the TRC provided a compromising approach for apparently opposite interests. These disparate interests are stated clearly in Chapter 2 of the Act, which describes the 'Objectives of the Commission' as follows:

§ 3 (1) the objectives of the Commission shall be to promote national unity and reconciliation in a spirit of understanding which transcends the conflicts and divisions of the past by

(a) establishing as complete a picture of the causes, nature and extent of the gross violations of human rights which were committed during the period from March 1, 1960 to the cut-off date,[1] including the antecedents, circumstances, factors and context of such violations, as well as the perspectives of the victims and the motives and perspectives of the persons responsible for the commission of the violations, by conducting investigations and holding hearings;

(b) facilitating the granting of amnesty to persons who make full disclosure of all the relevant facts relating to acts associated with a political objective and comply with the requirements of this Act;

(c) establishing and making known the fate or whereabouts of victims and by restoring the human and civil dignity of such victims by granting them an opportunity to relate their own accounts of the violations of which they are the victims, and by recommending reparation measures in respect of them;

(d) compiling a report providing as comprehensive an account as possible of the activities and findings of the Commission contemplated in paragraphs (a), (b) and (c), and which contains recommendations of measures to prevent the future violations of human rights.[2]

Given the above context of victim and perpetrator discovering compromise, the origin of the TRC is inextricably linked to the evolution of South Africa's negotiated settlement. The greatest concern shared by both black and white South African leaders was that the South African transition would happen, not by force of arms, but through dialogue and an eventual negotiated settlement. Here, it must be understood

---

1    Set for December 1993. Meanwhile the TRC has suggested a prolongation of this period up to 10 May 1994, which is the day President Mandela took office. This extension would provide the inclusion of acts of violence committed prior to the first general elections held on 27 April 1994.

2    Republic of South Africa, *Government Gazette*, vol. 361, no. 16579, Cape Town, 26 July 1995.

that this transition is fundamentally different to that which, for example, Nazi Germany underwent after World War Two, or the revolution which saw Mengistu Haile Mariam deposed from power in Ethiopia. Another example is Argentina's National Commission on the Disappeared (Comisión National sobre la Desaparición de Personas CONADEP). This Commission in Argentina documented almost 9,000 cases of enforced disappearances during the military dictatorship, although the true number is generally thought to have been far higher. Ruth Stanley is helpful here in her comparison between Chile and Argentina.[3]

In many countries in which truth commissions occurred, their conflicts produced a clear victor. For example, after World War Two, the Allies were able to take occupation of Germany and impose their version of justice on the Nazi regime at Nuremberg. In a like manner, the Ethiopian People's Revolutionary Democratic Front (EPRDF) overthrew the Mengistu regime after a period of civil war. One of the EPRDF's first acts after taking power, was the establishment of a Special Prosecutor's Office to try members and supporters of the old regime responsible for widespread violations of human rights. In both cases, Germany and Ethiopia, the approach to those who had committed gross violations of human rights could therefore be imposed in terms dictated by the victorious party. Predictably, both parties chose prosecution as the primary mode of dealing with the past, not only because they believed this to be right but, crucially, because they were able to do so.[4]

These situations of Germany and Ethiopia, in which clear victories emerged, can be contrasted with the transition from military rule to democracy in Chile. It is in the more ambiguous transitions that one may see similarities between Chile and South Africa's Truth and Reconciliation Commissions. When General Pinochet, the former head of the Chilean junta, agreed to restore power to an elected civilian government, he still commanded sufficient power to ensure that he remained in office as head of the armed forces. As a result of the continued influence and strength of the military, the new government was effectively unable to bring charges against those who had been responsible for assassinations, torture and 'disappearances' under Pinochet's rule. Although the new government in Chile did establish a Truth Commission in order officially to investigate, record and acknowledge human rights' abuse under military rule, those who were responsible for these abuses remained unidentified and unpunished. If Germany and Ethiopia represent one element in the justice policy choices, which confront societies during a transition from authoritarian to

---

3    Ruth Stanley, 'Modes of Transition v. Electoral Dynamics: Democratic Control of the Military in Argentina and Chile', *Journal of Third World Studies*: 18:2 (Fall 2001), 71–91. Stanley examines two approaches used to explain how far democratically-elected governments are able to impose civilian control over the military following the transition from authoritarian rule by comparing the cases of Argentina and Chile. They have been selected as representing two opposite poles on the modes-of-transition spectrum, with Argentina standing for transition by collapse and Chile for a transition negotiated by the outgoing military regime from a position of strength.

4    Desmond Tutu, *No Future without Forgiveness* (New York: Doubleday, 2000), especially chapter two: 'Nuremberg or National Amnesia? A Third Way', 13–20.

democratic rule – that of prosecution – then Chile represents another at the other end of the spectrum – blanket amnesties for those who committed gross violations of human rights.[5]

The similarity between the South African TRC and the Chilean National Commission on Truth and Reconciliation (NCTR) is that both were given mandates to go beyond truth finding to promote reconciliation. This similarity framed their common task to use truth as the means toward reconciliation or 'truth for reconciliation'. Both South Africa and Chile's TRC's focused on determining truth in order to understand and hope for the future of their countries. Audrey Chapman states: 'While [Chile's NCTR] focus was on investigating and determining truth, it understood this truth toward the purpose "to work toward the reconciliation of all Chileans".' To this end, continues Chapman's analysis, a variety of groups of victims, human rights' agencies, professional associations and political parties entered the conversation to best reach reconciliation through truth-telling.[6]

Among all the Truth Commissions that have existed, the South African occupies the closest proximity to Chile's, but as I show below, it still remains different from Chile's. South Africa's negotiated settlement it produced a markedly different balance of power to that which prevailed at the time of the post-war German, Ethiopian or Chilean transitions. The struggle between the liberation movements and the former government had reached an impasse in which neither side could claim a victory. Furthermore, the South African conflict created a deeply divided society which produced, at the time of transition, a great deal of hostility, mistrust, and instability. A lasting and peaceful settlement could not have been achieved if one side was to embark on a series of prosecutions against the other. It was therefore important to develop a way of coming to terms with the past, which neither concealed the occurrence of human rights' abuse nor threatened to destroy South Africa's new democracy. The Truth and Reconciliation Commission is precisely such an initiative. By fully investigating human rights' abuses and making the granting of amnesty conditional on full disclosure, it aims to discover the truth about the past. More similar to Chile than Germany and Ethiopia, South Africa sought to consolidate democracy and promote national unity as those who established the TRC chose truth above prosecution. Many critics would say that the TRC chose conciliation above justice. In fairness to the TRC, their work is still unfinished as they now recommend a reparation policy designed to assist those who suffered as a result of abuse. The TRC is a product of South Africa's transition. More importantly it is also about the future, a future which projects and promotes the human rights of all South Africans.[7]

---

5  Desmond Tutu, *No Future without Forgiveness*, 20–33.

6  Audrey Chapman, 'Truth Commissions as Instruments of Forgiveness and Reconciliation', in Raymond Helmick and Rodney Peterson (eds), *Religion, Public Policy, and Conflict Transformation* (Philadelphia: Templeton Foundation Press), 249f.

7  Truth Talk, *The Official Newsletter of the Truth and Reconciliation Commission* 2:1 (March 1997).

## The Birth of the Chilean Truth and Reconciliation Commission

In Chile, the National Commission on Truth and Reconciliation (*Comisión Nacional de Verdad y Reconciliación*) came into being in April 1990 to investigate cases of forced disappearance, execution, and torture resulting in death during the period from 11 September 1973 to 11 March 1990 (the date when Patricio Aylwin assumed the presidency).[8] Chile's NCTR, or Rettig Commission as it became known (after its chairman), reported a total of over two thousand deaths as a result of human rights' abuses under the military regime, the majority having occurred in the initial years of the dictatorship. In presenting the findings of the report, Patricio Aylwin (similar to the manner of President Nelson Mandela in South Africa) asserted that nothing justified human rights' abuses. Stanley states, 'Even if Chile had been in a state of internal war, as the military claimed, this would not excuse the violations of human rights, since even in war there were rules governing the treatment of prisoners'.[9] As those in South Africa's TRC practiced, so too did President Patricio Aylwin as he asked for forgiveness from victims who had suffered and called on the military to recognize the pain it had caused for so many. The future demanded the collaboration of all to lessen such pain and never to repeat such history, but rather to remember it. Stanley states:[10]

> The reaction of the military differed somewhat among the three branches of the armed forces. The Army strongly criticized the report for its alleged one-sidedness, claiming further that the report and the international attention it received could compromise basic aspects of the internal security and the external defense of the Republic – a statement that could be interpreted as a thinly-veiled threat that the military would be prepared, if further provoked by the human rights debate, to intervene once more in political life. The Chilean Navy also responded critically, although less confrontationally, while the Airforce Commander, General Fernando Matthei, defended the coup d'etat of September 1973 but also expressed regret for the loss of life and support for the democratic President in his search for reconciliation. These differing reactions to the Rettig Commission's report reflect the varying degrees of involvement of the three branches of the armed forces in the human rights' abuses committed under the dictatorship.

Whereas many Truth Commissions result in prosecutions of human rights' violators, this did not occur in Chile and South Africa. The Chilean military dictatorship passed an Amnesty Law covering all acts committed between 1973 and 1978, the period of greatest repression.[11] Prosecutions were possible in countries like Germany, Ethiopia,

---

8   I am indebted to Ruth Stanley's work for the following history. See 'Modes of Transition v. Electoral Dynamics', referred to earlier.

9   I am indebted to Ruth Stanley's work for the following history.

10  Ruth Stanley, 'Modes of Transition v. Electoral Dynamics', 4–5.

11  According to the report of the Rettig Commission, 1,886 of the total of 2,298 deaths established as having occurred during the dictatorship occurred between 1973 and 1978. The figure of 2,298 includes 2,130 victims of human rights' violations and 168 victims of political violence – in other words, victims whose death is not attributable to the state or its agents.

and Argentina because their governments repealed self-amnesty as one of the first acts after the return to stability; by contrast, South Africa and Chile's Amnesty Law remains in force. The precise application of the Amnesty Law has remained contentious in both Chile and South Africa as many argue that, though the respective TRC's guaranteed amnesty to violators of human rights, it did not preclude judicial proceedings against them. This contention carries over into the courts, claiming that the Amnesty Law prevents any judicial investigation of the crimes it covers.

In Chile, the Rettig Commission strongly criticized this approach, pointing out that according to Article 413 of the Code of Criminal Procedure, a case may only be definitively closed after a full investigation into the alleged crime and the attempt to identify the criminal. The Commission also pointed out that the approach favoured by the courts was more restrictive than had been envisaged by the authors of the Amnesty Law. However, the Supreme Court, in a case brought before it after President Aylwin assumed office, upheld the view that the Amnesty Law did prevent judicial investigation of human rights' abuses perpetrated between 1973 and 1978.[12] Where one begins to see the differences between South Africa and Chile's Commissions is in the Chilean exceptions to their limitation on prosecution, although they are few in number. However, the few in number are extremely contentious cases. Such an example has been the conviction of both retired General Manuel Contreras and Brigadier Pedro Espinoza in May 1995 for their part in the assassination of Allende's former Foreign Minister Orlando Letelier, together with the US citizen Ronnie Moffitt, in Washington D.C. in 1976. [13]

The most famous example of Chile's practice of amnesty is General Augustino Pinochet. As some prosecutions were allowed in spite of the NCTR, the armed forces challenged the Supreme Court's decision. Pinochet condemned the prosecutions as unjust. According to press reports, Pinochet took advantage of the stand-off between the civilian authorities and the armed forces to press for a definitive resolution of the human rights' issue and increased salaries for members of the armed forces. Relating specifically to the case at hand, Pinochet was reported to have demanded a pardon for both Contreras and Espinoza after they had served half of the sentence handed down by the Supreme Court, as well as military custody of the two prisoners. The Frei

---

See *Informe de la Comisión Nacional de Verdad y Reconciliación* (Santiago: Corporacion Nacional de Verdad y Reconciliación, 1996), 2 vols, vol. I Pt. 2, Statistical Annexe, Tables I and 7, pages 945, 947.

12   See Lois Hecht Oppenheim, *Politics in Chile. Democracy, Authoritarianism, and the Search for Development* (Boulder and Oxford: Westview, 1993), 217.

13   Although Contreras and Espinoza did not enter their specially designed prison units until 21 October 1995, almost five months after sentence had been passed, having spent the intervening period of time in a Navy hospital on grounds of supposed ill-health. Stanley adds this complexity: 'that the Letelier case had been expressly excluded from the Amnesty Law; hence, the prosecution and conviction of Contreras and Espinoza did not, of itself, represent a threat to the order bequeathed by the Pinochet regime'. See Ruth Stanley, 'Modes of Transition v. Electoral Dynamics', 5.

government compromised on the latter demand, agreeing to mixed civilian-military custody of the prisoners under the command of the prison service (*Gendarnerfa*).

Perhaps, it is too early tell whether the following will happen in South Africa, but Chile's practices of amnesty are slowly being challenged. More recently, human rights' violations have again been the subject of judicial proceedings. Prosecutions relating to abuses committed before 1978 have been accepted by some courts, the Amnesty Law notwithstanding.

The rationale behind this is that cases of disappeared persons whose whereabouts has never been established are to be treated as continuing cases of kidnapping (*delito de ejecución permanente*) in which the crime has persisted beyond 1978 and is therefore not covered by the Amnesty Law. In line with this interpretation of the law, former high-ranking military officers are currently being investigated for human rights' abuses committed during the dictatorship. The Supreme Court has upheld this interpretation of the limits to the Amnesty Law. In response to these judicial investigations, whose onset coincided with the extradition proceedings against Senator Pinochet (and which may eventually implicate Pinochet himself), the commander in chief of the Army, Ricardo Izurieta, has stated publicly that any investigation of human rights' abuses committed by the Pinochet regime must also look at the responsibility of the other side. Effectively, Izurieta's discourse resuscitates the argument that the army was involved in an internal war and seeks to justify the human rights' abuses perpetrated by the dictatorship by apportioning the blame to its opponents.[14]

Developments in Chile do not parallel those in South Africa in the sense that the issue of human rights' violations during the period of apartheid has not remained in the courts, not as a result of policies adopted by political actors, but because of leadership like that of Desmond Tutu and Nelson Mandela. Whereas in Chile the activities of human rights' activists on behalf of the disappeared have used the judicial system to seek an end to impunity. This contention separates Chile and South Africa's Commissions further as the judicial proceedings in Chile itself and the detention of Senator Pinochet in London have weakened the common memory of what was supposed to occur with the NCTR. For example, now any events deemed 'enforced disappearances' are not covered by the Amnesty Law which means that army officers, including some still on active duty, may be convicted of criminal offenses committed during the period of military dictatorship. In response, military representatives and right-wing politicians question the weakened common memory

---

14 Ricardo Izurieta stated in a speech on 7 June 1999: 'If there really exists the will to move towards a true reconciliation and thus to reach the desired (goal of) national unity, we must have the courage to accept that the judgment being demanded of the military government in general and its armed forces in particular necessarily calls for a judgment on those who caused the political crisis that gave rise to the intervention of (the armed forces), whereby one would also evaluate the position subsequently adopted by them (i.e. those who caused the political crisis), first in creating an atmosphere of rising violence and then in exacerbating hatreds and revanchism'. Izurieta's speech was quoted in its entirety in *El Mercurio*, 8 June 1999.

of what the NCTR was about. Such politicians question the decision of the Supreme Court, claiming that it limits the application of the Amnesty Law and effectively amounts to the derogation of legal norms without the consent of the legislature.

In July 1999 army chief Izurieta convened a meeting of superior officers to discuss this development and the proceedings against Pinochet. According to unofficial sources, the army generals present reflected on the armed forces' role as the guarantor of the constitution and discussed whether the criminal proceedings now before the courts violated this constitutional role. Given this extra-military function accorded to the armed forces by the constitution, such deliberations implicitly challenge the democratic order. [15]

The government of the *Concertación* called for a round table on human rights' abuses, the so-called *mesa de diálogo*,[16] incorporating members of the armed forces, human rights' activists, representatives of the church, historians and journalists.[17] This initiative has been rejected by many human rights' organizations and lawyers who see it as an attempt to distract attention from the judicial investigations of human rights' abuses at the precise moment when these investigations twenty-six years after the military coup, finally are beginning to bear fruit. The human rights' organization CODEPU has roundly criticized the government's initiative, viewing it as a maneuver aimed at achieving a *punto* final with respect to past human rights' abuses. CODEPU firmly rejected the attempt to find the political solution to this issue that the army has frequently called for and by which is meant a renewed pact guaranteeing impunity. Significant groups and individuals have therefore refused to participate in the *mesa de diálogo*. The government's approach appears to favor the kind of elite negotiation that has characterized Chile's transition from the start, rather than an open debate. Thus, Defense Minister Edmundo Perez Yoma originally proposed that the deliberations of the *mesa de diálogo* should remain secret. A compromise was achieved whereby the statements of the participants were to be made available to the public, but the debate among them would remain confidential; participants also committed themselves to refrain from airing their views on the proceedings to the media.

There is no doubt that Chile's NCTR is similar to South Africa's TRC, but it is important to see how they differ. Perhaps, South Africa's vow to learn from history is an indicator of how important it is to see what is happening in Chile as amnesty is apparently disappearing. Even though the decision to call for collaboration among many public sectors in Chile was in response to military pressure to put an end to the debate on human rights' violations, Chile is in the midst of revising its understanding of amnesty as it reopens the case of Senator Pinochet and the cases now before the courts in Chile. It remains to be seen what Chile will achieve, but it is already apparent that the Chilean expectations differ from their original NCTR. While many

---

15  See Ruth Stanley, 'Modes of Transition v. Electoral Dynamics', 7.

16  See Mario Aguilar's chapter in this volume.

17  See article in *El Mercurio* (1 September 1999). Significantly, it was the Defense Minister, Edmundo Pdrez Yoma, who launched this initiative.

hope for information on the fate of those who disappeared during the Pinochet dictatorship, the army claims that it has no such information and is concerned with a broader agenda:

> ...the *mesa de diálogo* is a mechanism that can serve to solve the problem, as they see it, that the conditions dictated by the military when it withdrew from government have not met with full compliance. It is apparent that the military regards the terms of the amnesty transition as inviolable and any attempt to modify those terms as a threat to the established constitutional order of which the military is the guarantor. This intransigent position is all the more striking in that, in fact, the Amnesty Law has not been abrogated and thus human rights' violations including torture and assassination committed between September 1973 and March 1978 continue to enjoy impunity.[18]

To summarize, Chile and South Africa's efforts at Truth and Reconciliation Commissions are noble efforts at reaching compromise in order not to slide into perpetual civil war. A notable aspect of the Chilean situation is that the current governing coalition is responding to the military's unease without lessening the demand for a political solution to the issue of human rights' abuses. Perhaps, now as we turn to Archbishop Tutu and South Africa, one will see that the unfolding dynamic in Chile appears to be conditioned less by electoral politics than by the corporate interests of the military. In South Africa, electoral politics and spiritual leadership has distinguished South Africa's TRC. However, South Africa must learn from Chile's older Truth process because South Africa can ignore recent events in Chile only at its peril.

## Tutu and the Truth and Reconciliation Commission

In *Truth Talk*, the official newsletter of the Truth and Reconciliation Commission,[19] Tutu salutes the remarkable magnanimity and generosity of spirit of South Africans who have exposed their pain to the world. Tutu believes that the vast majority of South Africans should, by right, be consumed by bitterness, anger, resentment, and the desire for revenge. By displaying a willingness to forgive, however, South Africans, through the TRC, are paying a very high price for the freedom South Africa is now enjoying. For Tutu, that price is multi-faceted. First, the high price for freedom in South Africa relates to the suffering they experienced as a result of gross apartheid violations. Secondly, to speak about these violations was no guarantee that the South African nation would embrace healing. Thirdly, there was the concern that the perpetrators of apartheid may obtain amnesty without even apologizing for what

---

18 See Ruth Stanley, 'Modes of Transition v. Electoral Dynamics', 6. Since the military cannot in the circumstances argue that the letter of the Amnesty Law has been violated, they assert that its spirit is not being applied; *La Tercera* en Internet: Mesa de Diálogo, '?Qua busca la Mesa de Diálogo?'(n.d.).

19 *Truth Talk*, The Official Newsletter of the Truth and Reconciliation Commission 1:1 (November 1996).

they did. And fourthly, the victims who testified in the TRC hearings relinquished their rights to institute civil proceedings for compensation.

At the heart of Tutu's logic for defending the high cost of the TRC was that whatever reparation the victims of apartheid may get, at the end of the day, such reparation would in no way match the high cost of suffering during the apartheid era. For this high price, all that may be shown is the knowledge that South Africans hope more for a future than they resent the past. Tutu proceeds to explain the TRC above and beyond logic. Underlying much of Tutu's rationale for the TRC is his atonement theory by which he understands the process of creating a future – a process in which communities practice forgiveness. Tutu states:

> We regret that there are still both victims and perpetrators who are not coming forward. We had hoped that they would not forfeit the possibility of healing the hurt. But there is something I would like to say to those perpetrators: You are free to hope you will get away with it, you are free to take the risk that you will not in fact be prosecuted if you don't ask for amnesty. Being inhabitants of a moral universe, you should understand there is no lie, which can prevail forever. The truth will eventually win out and you will regret it if you did not take advantage of the amnesty provisions. When you come forward to confess you are guilty, you will lighten the burden for us all. After all, it is better to live in a country which is stable and peaceful, where people are reconciled, than in one which is torn apart by strife because people are angry and wanting revenge. Reconciliation is not easy. Stability and forgiveness are not easy to obtain.[20]

Tutu's atonement theory for a future South Africa assumes that there is no such thing as a reprobate.[21] As a pastor Tutu is trained to be sensitive to even a flickering ember of remorse in the hope it could be nurtured into a flame of reconciliation; as Tutu believes, '… we all have the capacity to become saints'.[22] Understanding Tutu in my previous book, it is not surprising that South Africa needed Tutu as a head of the truth commission, which was headed actually by two churchmen.[23] The TRC has been described as a mixture of the ecclesiastical and the judicial. Implicit to the theology of the TRC is that civic judges can not discover 'the truth', instead, like Pontius Pilate, they merely satisfy themselves as to the discharge of an onus. Tutu's theological impetus of community, however, understands true confession occurring between sinners and the only sinless one, the triune God – the only one qualified to judge whether the truth has been told and forgiveness merited.

---

20  Desmond Tutu 'Address', in *Truth Talk*, The Official Newsletter of the Truth and Reconciliation Commission 1:1 (November 1996).

21  To illustrate Tutu's passion for universal atonement, Professor Liz Bounds told me that several divinity students in Tutu's class at the Candler School of Theology at Emory University had great difficulty accepting Tutu's position on universal salvation.

22  David Beresford, 'Fisher of Men, Seeker of Truth', *Mail & Guardian* (a South African weekly newspaper), Johannesburg (19 December, 1997).

23  The other chair of the TRC being the Reverend Dr Alex Boraine, of the Methodist Church of Southern Africa.

Critics of Tutu's theological impetus behind the TRC state that the idea of a person being 'required' to confess 'the truth' to a human commission in the name of the law, dressed up in the robes of the church, takes one back to the Inquisition. 'If we were the Inquisition we would have had electric prods', Tutu chuckles. 'We have to try and persuade people that ultimately their own healing is going to depend on their owning up. And the [National Unity and Reconciliation Act] makes it quite clear that the truth is sought, not for the purpose of prosecution, it is sought for the purpose of healing the land'.[24]

## Amnesty or Amnesia?

Before I proceed to discuss Tutu's presupposition of personhood as informing his views of forgiveness, a further word must be said about the controversy of the TRC and the unrecognized affliction of many South Africans.[25] Such affliction may be seen on 11 October 1996, when the news went out that the former Defense Minister Magnus Malan and the nineteen co-accused persons left their Durban court acquitted from the indictment of murdering thirteen persons, among them many women and children. The 'Malan-Trial' took place before the Supreme Court of KwaZulu Natal and referred to a massacre committed in 1987 in Kwamakutha, a township close to Durban. Many black South Africans bitterly interpreted this decision as a sign that even after the end of apartheid everything is meant to remain the same.[26]

Despite Tutu's controversial approach of advocating forgiveness for criminals, many South Africans believe that the TRC under Tutu's leadership is the way to deal with affliction so that the nation may not be held hostage to the past. During the TRC hearing, victims and survivors from all sides of the political spectrum told of their suffering during the apartheid era.[27] This led people in some communities to dub the TRC 'the Kleenex Commission' because of the tissues used by witnesses to wipe away their tears. Behind this derogatory description of the TRC is the crucial significance of how past crimes, particularly military crimes were never prosecuted. For both South Africa and Chile, to establish the record of the past regime through truth commissions entailed the danger of delegitimizing the current or successor

---

24 David Beresford, 'Fisher of Men, Seeker of Truth', *Mail & Guardian*, Johannesburg (19 December 1997).

25 Here Simone Weil's distinction between pain (suffering that can be alleviated) and affliction (suffering that leaves a permanent scar) is insightful. See Simone Weil, *Waiting on God* (New York: G.P. Putnam's & Sons, 1951), 69.

26 This is only one example of the depths of affliction faced in South African society. I was deeply struck by this affliction when I attended a TRC hearing in which a young man, unable to walk, wept bitterly on the witness stand – TRC Hearing, Worcester, South Africa, 21 June 1999.

27 See TRC, *Truth and Reconciliation Commission of South Africa Report*, Five Volumes (Cape Town: Juta & Co, 1998).

regime. Prosecutions for human rights' abuses are even more contentious, since, if successful, they not only delegitimize but criminalize the former military rulers.

The Amnesty Committee – which makes the decisions on whether to grant amnesty to perpetrators – because they were dealing with prisoners whose crimes were already known, conducted hearings in which people had grave difficulty providing complete disclosures. New information was slow in coming in revealing what happened under apartheid. The hope of the Amnesty Committee in particular was that in the summoning of people such as police generals, investigative inquiries would reveal new information that would subvert any future machinations. Herein, was one of Tutu's most potent political arguments in favor of the TRC. If members of the corrupt police could convince the Amnesty Committee that they had made full disclosure of their acts and that these were politically motivated then they are entitled to amnesty. Such disclosure was not simply to grant amnesty for the guilty; even more important, such disclosure would ensure that the subversive 'Third Force' agitating for a return to apartheid, would completely abort.

These perpetrators of affliction did not even have to say that they felt sorry for what they had done, as long as they gave complete disclosure which would implicate those who created the infrastructure of apartheid. The Christian mystic, Simone Weil, is helpful in understanding the irony of feeling sorry for such a perpetrator, even when such a person could not feel sorry for self. Weil states:

> Affliction hardens and discourages us because, like a red-hot iron, it stamps the soul to its very depths with the scorn, the disgust and event the self-hatred and sense of guilt and defilement which crime logically should produce but actually does not. Evil dwells in the heart of the criminal without actually being felt there. It is felt in the heart of the man who is afflicted and innocent ... Everybody despises the afflicted to some extent.[28]

Weil is helpful in explaining the dangers and strains of forgiveness and repentance in that she discusses the 'blindness' of mechanistic structures in society as analogies between affliction and mere pain and makes interesting distinctions. If, for example, oppressive people in power thereby creating oppressive structures were not blind there would not be an affliction. Affliction is anonymous before all things, it deprives its victims of their personality and makes them into things. As Weil concludes, affliction 'is indifferent; and it is the coldness of this indifference, a metallic coldness, which freezes all those it touches right to the depths of their souls. They will never find warmth again. They will never believe any more that they are anyone'.[29]

Tutu concedes Weil's insight that, at times, he feels 'overwhelmed by the extent of evil' emerging from the commission hearings. One story which particularly haunts him is the police murder of Siphiwe Mtimkulu in the Eastern Cape. Mtimkulu was drugged, shot behind the ear, and burned. 'Which is bad enough', states Tutu, 'But while they are burning his body they are having a braai [a barbecue] on the side. I

---

28  Simone Weil, *Waiting on God* (New York: G.P. Putnam's & Sons, 1951), 69.

29  Simone Weil, *Waiting on God* (New York: G.P. Putnam's & Sons, 1951), 69.

can't actually get over it!'[30] Like Weil's insight into affliction, Tutu sees the need for catharsis in making a full and public disclosure of past crimes. To admit guilt even in the secrecy of the bedroom is not easy. It is 'facile' to say that confession is only between a penitent and God. Tutu states, 'If I quarrel with my wife and I say to her, "It's between me and God", that marriage is not going to last very much longer'. The relationship is both vertical and horizontal. Tutu believes, 'The Bible is quite clear about it when it says: Love God and love thy neighbour. The two are linked together'.[31]

How much more difficult must it be to reveal the most heinous crimes right before the eyes of the nation! And how difficult it must be to name superiors and colleagues and thereby to 'betray' the 'comrades' and the entire organization. It does take considerable determination to break rank and to resist the circle of subtle threats and compensations; for such people will appear to the system as traitors and deserters. Despite Tutu's political argument for the TRC, it seems that a considerable portion of the implicated police and security forces are still trying to protect the 'system' and themselves with the hope that they will somehow manage to avoid the TRC and the courts.

It is reasonable, of course, to admonish citizens to live with compromises. But on the other hand it must be understood that the anger of the disadvantaged and victimized human beings must increase before true forgiveness occurs. If victims of apartheid experience that their oppressors escape their evil acts while they themselves continue to wait for decent houses, jobs and professional training, there will be no true community. The acceptance of amnesties will largely depend on the measure in which the needs of the victims are being met. There must be a clear willingness on the part of white South African society to make amends in unequivocal terms. This is called repentance. If such repentance is not forthcoming the work of the TRC might well appear as a strategy to placate people's feelings rather than to bring them peace with justice. In other words, repentance naturally follows forgiveness. If there is no natural sign of repentance, then forgiveness easily follows cheap grace. This means that, as a Christian and as a person who is a member of the church, processes of dehumanization cannot be tolerated. In this light Tutu reasons, 'Is it not revealing how when we meet people for the first time we soon ask, "by the way, what do you do?" meaning what gives you value?'[32]

## Cheap Grace or Invaluable Personhood

For Tutu, the TRC does not misunderstand justice as cheap grace. Instead, deeply laden within Tutu's theology is an understanding of personhood that sheds light on

---

30  David Beresford, 'Fisher of Men, Seeker of Truth', *Mail & Guardian* (19 December 1997).

31  David Beresford, 'Fisher of Men, Seeker of Truth', *Mail & Guardian* (19 December 1997).

32  Tutu, 'Grace Upon Grace', in *Journal for Preachers* XV:1 (Advent 1991), 20.

the image of God as triune. One may never understand Tutu's political contributions until one understands his theology. From Tutu's perspective of *Ubuntu*, godless systems of justice encourage a high degree of competitiveness and selfishness. Such systems demonstrate the greatest discrepancy in a triune God's creation of interdependence.[33] Tutu shows this discrepancy as he recounts the creation narrative in which Adam needs Eve as a sign of our interdependency.[34]

> Apartheid says people are created for separation, people are created for apartheid, people are created for alienation and division, disharmony and disunity and we say, the scripture says, people are made for togetherness, people are made for fellowship.
>
> You know that lovely story in the Bible. Adam is placed in the Garden of Eden and everything is honky-dory in the garden. Everything is very nice, they are all very friendly with each other. Did I say, everybody was happy? No, actually Adam was not entirely happy and God is solicitous for Adam and He looks on and says, 'No, it is not good for man to be alone'. So God says, 'Adam, how about choosing a partner?' So God makes the animals pass one by one in front of Adam. And God says to Adam, 'What about this one?' Adam says, 'Not on your life'. 'What about this one?' 'No'. God says, 'Ah, I got it'. So God puts Adam to sleep and out of his rib he produces this delectable creature Eve and when Adam awakes, he says 'wow', 'this is just what the doctor ordered'. But that is to say, you and I are made for interdependency.[35]

Tutu's interpretation of the creation narrative illustrates the profound truth that instead of being made for disproportionate differences, God's creation continually informs persons that identity and relationship go hand in hand. The obsession with individualism and self-achievement is countered for Tutu in Jesus' claims of discipling individuals to move outside of competitive cosmologies. Tutu states:

> Now the radical point about Jesus' question [re: the Good Samaritan] is: Who proved a neighbour to the man in need? You, gathered here, are in fact not meant to discover who your neighbour is (whom you are supposed to love as yourself as the second great commandment). No, you are meant to be asking, 'To whom am I going to be a neighbour – Who is in need and whose need I must meet as a neighbour with this privilege and this responsibility'. You and I are the ones who are to be judged for failing to be neighbour to those in need.[36]

It is with this evidence of proving to be a neighbor that African community is intelligible. According to much of current African scholarship, African epistemology begins with community and moves to individuality, whereas Western epistemology moves from individuality to community. For example, western definitions of 'community' connote a 'mere collection of self-interested persons, each with private

---

33  Tutu, Sermon, printed after 7 October 1989.

34  Tutu provides the following humorous account of Adam's search for a wife in 'Birmingham Cathedral Address', and 'Why We Must Oppose Apartheid'.

35  Tutu, 'Birmingham Cathedral Address', 3.

36  Tutu, Address, 'Love Reveals My Neighbour, My Responsibility' (16 December 1981).

sets of preferences, but all of whom get together nonetheless because they realize that in association they can accomplish things which they are not able to accomplish otherwise. This definition of community is really an aggregation, a sum of individuals. Not only does this go against ontological claims of community but methodologically, this definition of community becomes a tautology. Ifeanyi A. Menkiti states that 'John Mbiti's aphorism: "I am because we are" does not include an additive "we" but a thoroughly fused collective we'.[37] However, Tutu's *ubuntu* anticipates its own problematic, namely, the needs of the many outweighing the few.

Tutu stresses the Christian definition of relationship, as opposed to other social forms of communalism to define *Ubuntu*. Influenced deeply by the spirituality of the Anglican Church, Tutu is able to overcome any tendency to go to the extreme of discounting personality for the sake of community. For Tutu, being properly related in a theological *Ubuntu* does not denigrate individuality. So he declares that:

> No real human being can be absolutely self-sufficient. Such a person would be sub-human. We belong therefore in a network of delicate relationships of interdependence. It is marvelous to know that one who has been nurtured in a living, affirming, accepting family tends to be loving, affirming and accepting of others in his or her turn. We do need other people and they help to form us in a profound way.
>
> You know just how you blossom in the presence of someone who believes in you and who helps you have faith in yourself, who urges you to great thoughts and yet accepts you as who you are and not for what you have or can achieve, who does not abandon you because you have failed. And you know just how you tend to wilt in the presence of someone who is forever complaining and finding fault with you. You didn't know you could be so clumsy being all thumbs until you got to this lady's house and trust you to break her favourite antique or to drop ashes on her beautiful Persian carpet.
>
> Jesus has had tremendous faith in people and got them having faith in themselves with a proper kind of self assurance, exorcising them from the horrible paralysing sense of inadequacy that plagues so many of us. After the resurrection He met Peter and did not berate Him for denying Him because he helped him cancel it out through a three-fold positive assertion: 'Yes, I love you'. To this man who had denied Him, Jesus gave not less but increased responsibility – Feed my sheep. Become – (you vacillating old so and so) – my chief apostle and pastor.[38]

It is worthwhile to explore a bit more what I mean by an African extreme of community. There are three senses of human groupings: first, collectivities, second, constituted human groups, and the third is random collections of individuals. African social and philosophical understandings of human society usually adopt the first usage of human grouping – collectivities; whereas the Western understanding is more like the second category of human groups constituted of individuals. The difference between the two is both an 'organic' and 'non-organic' dimension to the

---

37 Ifeanyi A. Menkiti, 'Person and Community in African Traditional Thought', in R. A. Wright (ed.), *African Philosophy* (New York: University Press of America, 1971), 166.

38 Tutu's Handwritten Sermons, 'Genesis Chapter 3', St. Mary's, Blechingly, Surrey, (6 October 1985).

relationship between the component of individuals. In an African understanding, human society is something constituted organically; whereas, in Western, egalitarian societies there is more of a non-organic organization of individuals into a unit more akin to an association than to an African community. These distinctions also play out on the level of personhood.

Many Western views of personhood include primarily the perception of the lone individual whose essential characteristics are that of self-determination; whereas, the African view of a person depicts the meaning or intelligibility of a person only in the context of that persons' surrounding environment. In the African concept of *Ubuntu*, human community is vital for the individual's acquisition of personhood, however, in Western thought, especially in existentialism, the individual alone defines self-existence. Jean-Paul Sartre's individual illustrates this Western attribute. The Western individual is 'nothing [and] will not be anything until later, and then he will be what he makes himself'.[39] This Sartrean view of person is as a 'free unconditioned' being, a being not constrained by social or historical circumstances. Such Western individualism flies in the face of African beliefs. Not only does the location of meaning solely within the individual separate African and Western discourse, there is also the problem of materialism.

**Catharsis and Conclusion**

Some observers have described the work of the TRC as a cathartic process. They argue that this self-cleansing must of necessity lead to a turmoil of emotions. Anger, sadness, grief and shock must be allowed to surface. Why is it that many black South Africans cannot accept the slogans so widely shared among whites such as 'Let bygones be bygones!'? When white business people, for example, say that they accept the new constitution of South Africa, how does one know that such people are not engaged in selective acts of amnesia? The emotions that rise in many black South Africans conflict deeply with a disposition that is typical for Western European culture which regards the past as over and finished. Although Europeans tend to honour their dead they do not often live with the awareness that the spirits of the dead are still with them and that it is of vital importance to reconcile the unredeemed spirits of the past.

This, however, is a conviction deeply rooted in black African spirituality. For them there can be no peaceful presence as long as the spirits of the dead are not laid to rest. Therefore many relatives of murdered or disappeared persons ask the TRC to help them get back from the police whatever remains of their loved ones exist in order to bury them in a decent and dignified manner. The burial is the ritual by which a lost member of the family can finally be brought home. This is the way in which the harmony between the generations is restored and maintained. The bringing home

---

39 Jean-Paul Sartre, 'Existentialism Is a Humanism', in Nino Languilli (ed.), *The Existentialist Tradition: Selected Writings*, trans. Philip Mairet (New York: Doubleday-Anchor Books, 1971), 399.

of the one who is lost, even the one who is guilty, to the place of the ancestors is a vital aspect of the peace of the living.

This is a spirituality that should not be denounced as belief in 'spirits' but as a worldview which knows something of the fundamental connectedness of all life. It is a spirituality which sees each individual human being as a member of the community, a community which includes the past and the coming generations. In this context coming to terms with the past is more than settling legal claims, it is an act of re-membering, of bringing together that belongs together. African re-membering has a lot to do with healing, redemption and liberation.

Tutu is in the heritage of African peoples whose concepts and rituals provide the notion of reconciliation with profound meaning. Often reference is made to *Ubuntu*, a term which connotes the basic connectedness of all human beings beyond all lines of race and class. It is concepts like these which help African peoples to transcend the violent mechanisms of denial retaliation that are so typical for Western cultures. It is a misunderstanding of Tutu to think his forgiveness rests in itself. Forgiveness assumes God's sovereignty of enticing all to repentance. White people in South Africa are faced with the question: Will they be prepared to see the TRC as an opportunity to get a deeper grasp on the spiritual power of their black fellow citizens? Will they learn from them to work for processes of re-membering, of bringing peace to the past for the sake of the present and future? Will they grasp the great readiness of the victims to forgive them as a chance to leave the prisons of shame and the dungeons of denial so that all the people at the Cape of Good Hope can finally be of good hope?

To face these profound emotions is the beginning of healing. As one observes Tutu and the TRC one encounters something profoundly uplifting. As women and men recall their memories they are again faced with all their pain and anguish. And yet, as these persons face their suffering, and as they name it in public, they leave the witness stand with their heads held high. They have been recognized in their pain, and this is the beginning of a renewed dignity. There is deep satisfaction, of course. Were they not destined to be annihilated? Now they are poised as heroes. When they were tortured in the prisons were they not told: 'Yell as loud as you wish, nobody will ever hear you!'? Now the nation hears. And the accounts of their suffering is received into the memories of the nation. They were made voiceless, now there voice can be heard across radio and television. Now the names of the torturers that were beyond reproach only a few years ago can openly be mentioned. This correction of history is restoring for all who had been humiliated. The Magnificat of Mary comes to mind: 'He has put down the mighty from their thrones, and exalted those of low degree' (Luke 1:52).

But this profound satisfaction is not a subliminal form of revenge but expresses itself in genuine readiness to forgive. Many victims repeat the phrase expressed by a witness during the first days of the TRC hearings: 'I am ready to forgive, but I need to know whom and for what'. There is no need to repeat that the TRC process is unprecedented and merits close international attention by persons involved in peace research, legal questions, religious studies, theology, social psychology, and other disciplines. In light of projections of millennial violence associated with racism, it would be important to study possibilities for transferring this process to other conflict areas.[40] It is significant, for instance, that some members of the TRC have already been invited to visit Rwanda in order to relate their approach to a country that is still reeling from the aftermath of the genocide between Hutus and Tutsis.

The future of the African continent is uncertain as African leadership changes hands. The vanguard of African leaders like Tutu are slowly bowing out of leadership, as for example the recent death of Julius Nyerere.[41] As leadership changes, it will be interesting to see how an African leader maintains spiritual leadership that is also political leadership. At the end of the day, it must be seen that the success of African community depends largely on the leadership with which some of the most pressing problems of Africa and the world can be met. For example, in South Africa, the townships are time bombs that need immediate attention. This would also seem to be the case in many inner – cities around the world. Unemployment is rampant, so are the flagrant disparities between the small 'elites' and the poor masses. There is an urgent need to establish spirituality and political reform.

---

40 David Welna reports that Northwestern University is warning a white supremacist group not to distribute its racist pamphlets on the University's campus. The warning, also informed by FBI reports of a rise of white supremacist groups spawned by the year 2000, is aimed at the World Church of the Creator, based in East Peoria, and the church's leader, Matthew Hale. National Public Radio, Morning Edition, 21 October 1999.

41 Thousands of people attended a Roman Catholic funeral Mass 19 October, 1999 for former President Julius Nyerere, revered as Tanzania's founding father, in Dar Es Salaam, Tanzania. Cardinal Polycarp Opengo, who led scores of bishops and priests in the service, praised Nyerere for his honesty and integrity on a continent where so many leaders succumb to corruption. Nyerere is remembered at home as the man who led the drive for Tanzania's independence from Britain in 1961 and later forged a nation from the union of then Tanganyika and the Indian Ocean islands of Zanzibar. He is credited with peacefully uniting the 120 ethnic groups in Tanzania under a national flag and bringing education to even the poorest Tanzanians during his 23 years as president. Since his death in a London hospital on Oct. 14, messages of praise have poured in from world leaders paying tribute to Nyerere, who championed struggles for independence across the continent. He led the drive to oust dictator Milton Obote from Uganda, and spearheaded international efforts to dismantle South Africa's apartheid. *The New York Times* (19 October 1999).

Chapter 10

# Reconciliation as a Contested Future: Decolonization as Project or Beyond the Paradigm of War

Nelson Maldonado-Torres

The future of social reconciliation in countries such as South Africa, Argentina, Chile, Guatemala, El Salvador, and many others, to a great extent depends on addressing the challenges posed by colonial legacies and neo-colonial realities. This is one of the ideas that ties together the different chapters in this anthology. The authors point to a 'truth' which is not only that of specific events or unspeakable acts. The 'truth' in question relates to our very modern experience. It intimates that modernity is complicit with a paradigm of war.[1]

Reconciliation faces peculiar challenges if war is found to be not so much an extraordinary affair, but a constitutive feature of modernity. I will argue here that the ethics, if not the very practice of war, is maintained alive in modernity through enduring colonial relations of power. Colonialism, or, better put, coloniality, may be understood as a naturalization of the ethics of war. Slavery, death, and even torture form part of the structure of power and horizon of meaning sustained by coloniality. If violence and war persist in modernity through colonial forms of power, then it must be said that reconciliation demands processes of decolonization that introduce a new ethics beyond coloniality and war. I submit that the future of reconciliation resides in the possibility of profound processes of decolonization.

Similar reflections to the ones that I have indicated took place in the context of understanding the nature and significance of the Second World War, and, more specifically, the Jewish Holocaust. Truth and Reconciliation Commissions respond to different conditions from those that led to the Nuremberg trials, but they all have understood themselves as attempting to deal with questions about justice, prosecutions, amnesties, and reparations after Nuremberg.[2] That is, they all learnt from the mechanisms for seeking justice after the Second World War. Also relevant are the reflections of intellectuals such as Zygmunt Bauman, Emmanuel Lévinas, Theodor Adorno, and Max Horkheimer who saw in the Jewish Holocaust not so much

---

1   I have developed this view in Nelson Maldonado-Torres, *Against War: Views from the Underside of Modernity* (Durham: Duke University Press, forthcoming).

2   The link between certain post-Second World War events and Truth and Reconciliation Commissions are clearly stated by Iain Maclean in the first chapter of this volume.

a departure from the ideals of Western civilization as the very accomplishment of certain tendencies in modernity.[3] My reflections here take a similar route, but where they focused quite exclusively on modernity as an intra-European phenomenon, I take the perspective here that modernity is a product of the action and counter-action of Europe and the colonial periphery.[4] This perspective can hardly be avoided when one includes reference to Truth and Reconciliation Commissions in South Africa and Latin America as part of the enquiry. Indeed, as I will show below, modernity's complicity with a paradigm of war cannot be fully understood without reference to colonialism and to the precise definition (through colonial relations) of Europe, Africa, and the Americas.

The exploration of modernity as a paradigm of war and the implications of this reflection for the search for truth and reconciliation leads me here to an exploration of the modern episteme and its links with colonialism, anti-black racism, and anti-indigenous views. The emergence of the modern postreligious episteme involves a move away from social ideas based on religious differences to social and geo-political relations defined in ontological and, later on, allegedly biological or racial differences. Reconciliation will thus be said to require both decolonization and deracialization, as well as a systematic questioning of the ways in which human bodies are conceived when they are made objects of domination, exploitation, and/or rape. In short, reconciliation requires the overcoming of modernity as a paradigm of war. And such overcoming requires the birth and sustenance of a particular kind of attitude: a decolonial attitude. The first step in these investigations lies in dispelling the idea that the search for truth and reconciliation itself is part and parcel of such a paradigm. And with that I shall begin.

**Truth and Reconciliation in the Modern/Colonial World**

The impetus of searching for truth in Truth and Reconciliation Commissions occurs in a context where, at least in certain influential academic and social circles, the search for truth has long been discredited. Nietzsche suggested long ago that the unconditional search for truth is an expression of the will to death.[5] He argued that the search for truth is tied to ascetic views of subjectivity. Nietzsche traces the search

---

3   Zygmunt Bauman, *Modernity and the Holocaust* (Ithaca, NY: Cornell University Press, 1989); Max Horkheimer and Theodor W. Adorno, *Dialectic of Enlightenment*, trans. John Cumming (New York: Continuum, 2002); Emmanuel Lévinas, 'Reflections on the Philosophy of Hitlerism', in *Critical Inquiry* (1990), 17 (Autumn 199), 63–71.

4   In this I follow to some extent 'post-colonial' figures such as Enrique Dussel and Edward Said. See Enrique Dussel, *The Underside of Modernity: Apel, Ricoeur, Rorty, Taylor, and the Philosophy of Liberation*, trans. and edited by Eduardo Mendieta (Atlantic Highlands, NJ: Humanities Press, 1996); Edward Said, *Orientalism* (New York: Pantheon Books, 1978).

5   I base my account here on Friedrich Nietzsche, *Beyond Good and Evil: Prelude to a Philosophy of the Future*, trans. Walter Kaufmann (New York: Vintage Books, 1966); Friedrich Nietzsche, *On the Genealogy of Morals and Ecce Homo*, trans. Walter Kaufmann

for truth or sincerity and asceticism to Christian morals. The French philosopher Michel Foucault expanded these intriguing reflections later on in the twentieth century. For him, asceticism and martyrdom hide behind a demand for constant self-examination that surpasses the horizons of Christianity and defines modern hermeneutics of the self. The search for truth becomes equivalent to self sacrifice. There is, according to Foucault, 'No truth about the self without a sacrifice of the self'. Consciousness becomes the police of the libido: the task is to turn 'our eyes continuously downwards or inwards in order to decipher, among the movements of the soul, which ones come from the libido'.[6] The search for truth becomes the motivation of a fight against ourselves.

As much as one should learn from great masters of suspicion like Nietzsche and Foucault, the search for truth in Truth and Reconciliation Commissions obeys different imperatives than those denounced by them: instead of fomenting a will to death (of the self) expressed in terms of ascetic inclinations or martyrdom it seeks to locate the roots of and to oppose a murderous will to death (of the Other). To make this idea more lucid consider the predicament of one of Fyodor Dostoyevsky's most enigmatic characters, Dimitri Raskolnikov. His desire for confession and penance in *Crime and Punishment* cannot be reduced to the notion of self-sacrifice that Nietzsche and Foucault found so pervasive in modernity.[7] In it we are dealing not with the policing of the self, but with the coming to terms with a lie: that the old lady he killed deserved in one way or another to die. Like Raskolnikov, Truth and Reconciliation Commissions aim to locate and neutralize the force of a murderous lie. They make clear that murderous lies cannot be tolerated. In this context their calls for truth are a cry for life and not a call for the dissolution of the self. Quite the opposite, truth is searched for here so that a new and responsible self/nation can emerge from the ashes of death, murder, and deceit.

With all their limits and problems Truth and Reconciliation Commissions are expressions of the need and desire to speak 'truth to power'. The goal of searching for truth is, in this context, healing nations that have long been besieged by the evils of systematic murder and state sponsored terrorism. But the truth hardly ends in the knowledge of the amount of people murdered, the names of the disappeared, or the methods of killing. There are underlying truths that begin to surface once one tries to understand the meaning and ultimate reference of the demands for truth and reconciliation. If the search for truth in Truth and Reconciliation Comissions is not a subtle expression or continuation of the suicidal moral of modernity, but an attempt to overcome the effects of violence and war by opposing murderous silence and bringing into light murderous lies, then how does it exactly stand in relation to the paradigm of modernity? I submit that when looked at from the point of view of

---

and R. J. Hollingdale (New York: Vintage Books, 1989); Friedrich Nietzsche, *The Will to Power*, trans. Walter Kaufmann and R. J. Hollingdale (New York: Random House, 1968).

6    Michel Foucault, *Religion and Culture* (New York: Routledge, 1999), 180.

7    See Fyodor Dostoyevsky, *Crime and Punishment*, trans. Jessie Coulson (Oxford: Oxford University Press, 1998).

efforts to search for truth and reconciliation, modernity appears not so much as a suicidal episteme, but rather as a warring paradigm, or as a way of thinking and being that promotes war. I also submit that the modern paradigm of war is intrinsically connected with colonialism as well as with the legacies of racism, particularly anti-indigenous and anti-black.

The links between modernity, war, colonialism, and racism come to the fore very clearly in the discussion of efforts to find the truth and to promote reconciliation in several chapters in this volume. In his contribution to this volume, the former Research Director of the South African Truth and Reconciliation Commission, Charles Villa-Vicencio, asserts that a proper understanding of the nature of the Truth and Reconciliation Commission (TRC) in South Africa requires some sense about its origin and identity, which should be traced, precisely, to colonial times. 'The conflict', Villa-Vicencio points out, 'began with a fragile white Portuguese presence in the Cape in the latter part of the fifteenth century to the beginning of the twentieth. It persisted through generations of institutionalized racism and culminated in a thirty-year race war'.[8] To the question about the success of the TRC Villa-Vicencio responds: 'It would be presumptuous to think that a Commission of the nature and duration of the TRC could reconcile a nation torn apart by 350 years of colonialism and fifty years of apartheid rule.... Its mandate was the promotion of national unity and reconciliation'.[9]

In his chapter on the 'Maya "Greening Road" and Globalization', Brett Greider asserts that

> For the indigenous Maya of Guatemala, the encounter with 'Globalization' began in 1524 with the arrival of the Spanish conquistador Pedro de Alvarado. It was a clash of cosmovisiones (sacred world views) that persists today in conflicting social and political movements of contemporary Guatemala ... The Maya kingdoms were subjugated and colonized, and continue today suffering the oppression of nearly five hundred years of colonization.[10]

'The new war on indigenous people in Guatemala', Greider adds, 'is an economic war waged by perpetuating poverty, the result of the colonial paradigm of modernity'.[11] Military rule in Guatemala continued a pattern of subordination which existed under colonial rule. That same pattern continues now under the auspices of global capital. 'International banking has slowly replaced the traditional national production with a

---

8    Charles Villa-Vicencio, 'Living in the Wake of the Truth and Reconciliation Commission: A Retroactive Report' (see this volume), 193.

9    Charles Villa-Vicencio, 'Living in the Wake of the Truth and Reconciliation Commission' (see this volume), 194.

10   Brett Greider, 'The Maya "Greening Road" and Globalization: The Pan-Mayan Movement as Transmodern Paradigm' (see this volume), 103.

11   Brett Greider, "The Maya 'Greening Road' and Globalization" (see this volume), 105.

globalized elite: the former military elite changing masks for transnational power'.[12] The special weight of war and poverty in indigenous populations is, to be sure, not unique to Guatemala, Central America, or Mexico. Margaret Pfeil reports, for instance, that the conflict in Peru between the government and Shining Path rebel forces ensued in the killing of hundreds, if not thousands, of mostly indigenous people.[13] Consider that three of every four victims were campesinos whose first language was Quechua. The underlying premise of the conflict, presupposed by both Shining Path forces and the government, was that 'Peru's indigenous peoples were regarded as dangerous aliens in their own lands'.[14]

Efforts to search for truth and to promote reconciliation in South Africa and different parts of the Americas cannot but attempt to come to terms in one way or another with modernity and its colonial underside. Anti-black and anti-indigenous racism also comes into view very strongly. This element of racism and its link with colonialism comes more sharply into focus in João Comblin's chapter on 'The Theme of Reconciliation and Theology in Latin America'.[15] Comblin makes very strong points about the particular responsibility of the Church toward Native American Indians and Blacks:

> Up until the present, the Native American Indians have not been able to enter the Church with their history and their culture ... In the same way, there does not exist an African Christianity. The slaves and their descendants received a Western Christianity, the one of the masters and slavers ... In the Latin American Church blacks do not occupy any high position at all. All their attempts at liturgical accomodation were vetoed, and all of animism condemned, in the name of Christian dogma.

More pointedly, Comblin asserts:

> Now, the exclusion of the Native Americans and the blacks in the Church reinforced or even to a certain point, created their universal *social exclusion* [italics mine]. The regional Latin American Bishops Conference in Puebla, Mexico, insisted upon the responsibility of the Catholic Church in the formation of Latin American culture, which excludes both Native Americans and blacks. For this exclusion the Church bears great responsibility. *We are able to state that the rejection of the 'pagans' by the 'Judeo-Christians' has had a similar and parallel repercussion on the social and political plane.* [italics mine]. Only reconciliation on the ecclesiastical plane will be able to carry reconciliation through the social and political planes. Only a social and political analysis will be able to show if reconciliation constitutes a valid political program for Native Americans and blacks.

---

12 Brett Greider, 'The Maya "Greening Road" and Globalization' (see this volume), 102.

13 Margaret R. Pfeil, 'Social Sin: Social Reconciliation?' (see this volume), 178, 182.

14 Margaret Pfeil, 'Social Sin: Social Reconciliation?', (see this volume), 182.

15 João Comblin, 'The Theme of Reconciliation and Theology in Latin America' (see this volume), expecially page 168.

Comblin states that reconciliation in Latin America requires coming to terms with the ways in which both Church and state have sustained a racial regime of exclusion, poverty, and death that targets indigenous peoples and Black populations. Recognizing the gravity of this somber picture Comblin concludes, 'Reconciliation in Latin America presumes a total inversion of the whole civilization and cultural processes'.[16]

Comblin accentuates the role of the Catholic Church not only in promoting, but also, and more fundamentally, in helping to create a structure of social and political power which targets, specially though not uniquely, indigenous peoples and Blacks. Greider adds economics to the social and political dimensions of modern/colonial power. To the social, the political, and the economic structure one must also add the level of the symbolic, which helps define the meaning given to indigeneity and blackness in Latin America. But, are these reflections limited to one region of the world, in this case, Latin America? Comblin suggests that with the exclusion of indigenous and Blacks the Church 'created their universal social exclusion'. Anti-black racism in South Africa and other parts of colonial Africa, as documented in part by Villa-Vicencio and Michael Battle in this volume, along with the continued existence of anti-indigenous structures in the Americas, Australia, New Zealand, and other territories around the world, points to the widespread assumption of the inferiority of Black and indigenous peoples. Comblin suggests a link between the form of power that defined social and political relations in Latin America, Africa, and other regions in the globe. He also compares the significance of the Church's role in those 'universal social exclusions' to the 'rejection of the 'pagans' by the 'Judeo-Christians'. Such rejection, defined much of the way in which power operated in the Middle Ages. Implicit in Comblin's comments there is thus the idea of a parallel between the way in which the division between the pagan and the Christian functioned in the Middle Ages and the way in which anti-black and anti-indigenous racism works in modernity. He also hints that the behavior of the Church in Latin America may be connected with the production of the modern model of power. Is there any justification for these claims? Is the rejection of Blacks and indigenous peoples in modernity equivalent to the way in which the divide between pagan and Christian worked in the Middle Ages? And, how to understand the link between the role of the Church in Latin America and the modern global model of power? If Comblin is right that reconciliation 'presumes a total inversion of the whole civilization and cultural processes', it is important to know more about the 'truth' of modern civilization and its culture.

### '1492: A New World View': A Continuing Dialogue

Reflections on efforts to find truth and to promote reconciliation in Latin America and South Africa point to a triadic model that makes reference to the white European,

---

16 J. Comblin, 'The Theme of Reconciliation and Theology in Latin America' (see this volume), 168.

indigenous populations, and black African and Afro-diasporic people. The Afro-Caribbean theorist, Sylvia Wynter, has reflected on the nature of this model. My account here is based on her reflections, in addition to further research that I have done inspired by her work and by that of the Peruvian sociologist Anibal Quijano.[17] The first idea that must be taken into consideration when thinking about the triadic model that Wynter examines is that 'white', 'black', and 'indigenous' are not categories that existed prior to the contact among the peoples to which the terms refer. That is, what occurs in the encounter between Europeans on the one hand, and black Africans and indigenous peoples in the Americas on the other is not merely an encounter among previously existing peoples, but more fundamentally the creation of new subjectivities. Just as there was no 'pagan' without a Christian to define it in the Middle Ages, there was no 'black' without a 'white' to create it in modernity. There is an important difference, though, between these two binary categories of differentiation: while the Christian may have existed without the existence or prior to the creation of the category 'pagan', the 'white' did not exist prior to the designation of another as 'black'. It is by naming the 'black' that Europeans became 'white'. But whiteness and blackness themselves did not come into being as categories that denoted race until after the encounter of the Europeans and native peoples in the Americas. The categories of 'natives' and 'indigenous', of course, did not exist prior to the conquest and colonization of what acquired the name 'America'.

What is 'America?' According to Anibal Quijano and Immanuel Wallerstein, America is the first space/time model of power with global vocation and the first identity of modernity.[18] According to Quijano, this space/time model of power is the result of the convergence of two historical processes that converged and established its two axes:

> One was the codification of the differences between conquerors and conquered in the idea of 'race', a supposedly different biological structure that placed some in a natural situation of inferiority to the others. The conquistadors assumed this idea as the constitutive, founding element of the relations of domination that the conquest imposed. On this basis, the population of America, and later the world, was classified within the new model of power. The other process was the constitution of a new structure of control of labor and its

---

17 See especially Anibal Quijano, 'Coloniality of Power, Eurocentrism, and Latin America', *Nepantla: Views from South* 1:3 (2000), 533–580; Anibal Quijano, 'Raza, "etnia, y 'nación": cuestiones abiertas', in Roland Forgues (ed.), *José Carlos Mariátegui y Europa: la otra cara del descubrimiento* (Lima, Peru: Amauta, 1992); Sylvia Wynter, '1492: A New World View', in Vera Lawrence Hyatt and Rex Nettleford (eds), *Race, Discourse, and the Origin of the Americas: A New World View* (Washington, DC: Smithsonian Institution Press, 1995). See also Sylvia Wynter, 'Unsettling the Coloniality of Being/Power/Truth/Freedom: Towards the Human, After Man, Its Overrepresentation – An Argument', *The New Centennial Review* 3:3 (2003), 257–327. My research on this topic will appear in Nelson Maldonado-Torres, 'Imperio, raza y religión', in Eduardo Mendieta (ed.), *Enciclopedia iberoamericana de las religiones: religion e imperio* (Madrid: Trotta, forthcoming).

18 Anibal Quijano and Immanuel Wallerstein, 'Americanity as a Concept, or the Americas in the Modern World-System', *International Social Science Journal* 134 (1992), 549–557.

resources and products. This new structure was an articulation of all historically known previous structures of control of labor, slavery, serfdom, small independent commodity production and reciprocity, together around and upon the basis of capital and the world market.[19]

The two axes in question are then, on the one hand, a new mental category (race), and on the other, a new structure for the control of labour (capital).

'The idea of race, in its modern meaning', Quijano states, 'does not have a known history before the colonization of America'.[20] As other scholars who specialize on the examination of the category 'race', Quijano believes that ethnocentrism and prejudice, even discourses based on caste differences, all of which existed well before the sixteenth century of the common era, do not have the same connotation of the modern category 'race'.[21] Quijano speculates that 'race' may have originated in reference to the phenotypic differences between conquerors and conquered, but he does not identify race with color. For him the association with color came much later, and it was probably initially established in Anglo-America where Blacks were not only the most important exploited group but also the most important colonized race. Indians were not an intrinsic part of the colonized society, which rested on their exclusion, persecution, and marginalization. I will complicate this account with reference to Wynter's work below. Suffice it to say now that for Quijano the important idea is that, however it was originated, race was constructed to refer to the supposed differential biological structures between conquerors and conquered, and more precisely, I would like to add, to the differences between legitimate subjects of the Spanish and Portuguese Christian empires and legitimately enslavable populations in the colonies. Thus the differences between conquerors and conquered were themselves understood through a new (colonial) prism that defined relations between masters and slaves.

Capital, the other axis of the modern global model of power, existed before the sixteenth century, but it functioned as one form of labour control among others and it was not oriented toward a world-market. The 'discovery' of America was crucial for the formation of a capitalist oriented world-market as well as it served as the place where every other known form of labour control was first gradually subordinated to capital. The subordination of different forms of labour to capitalism and the racial ideology of domination were not so much parallel, as entangled structures of power. This happened as the new historical identities came to be identified with different geo-historical places and different social and labour roles. Race domination worked thus in favour of the subordination of different labor forms to capital, which came to be associated with European and, later on, 'white' labour. Indigenous peoples

---

19  Anibal Quijano, 'Coloniality of Power, Eurocentrism, and Latin America', 533–34.

20  Anibal Quijano, 'Coloniality of Power, Eurocentrism, and Latin America', 534.

21  Such scholars include Ivan Hannaford, *Race: The History of an Idea in the West* (Washington, DC: The Woodrow Wilson Center Press; Baltimore: The Johns Hopkins University Press, 1996); Frank M. Snowden, Jr., *Before Color Prejudice: The Ancient View of Blacks* (Cambridge, MA: Harvard University Press, 1983).

served a role as 'serfs' and Blacks came to be seen and treated as the primary source for slavery. This way of defining labor roles equally fortified the idea of race, which came to define the common sense of modern subjects. 'In this way', Quijano remarks, 'both race and the division of labor remained structurally linked and mutually reinforcing, in spite of the fact that neither of them were necessarily dependent on the other in order to exist or change'.[22] In short, Quijano's main argument is that since the sixteenth century globalization has been driven by a form of power that brings together capitalism and race. And, since it was the colonial enterprise which gave a precise meaning to the modern category of race and since it also provided the context that brought capital, race, and the world market together, he refers to this mutually reinforcing modern structure of power as the 'coloniality of power'. It was this matrix of power ('patrón de poder') that also shaped the social and labour roles of genders and that motivated an epistemic framework that legitimated the concentration of capital in Western Europe, that is, Eurocentrism.[23]

'Coloniality of power' does not merely refer to the form of power exercised by modern colonial administrations – and by modern I mean from the late fifteen century on. It is rather a form of power that brings together race and capital. Modern colonialism was the fire in which race and capital came to be so combined. But, once constituted, the 'coloniality of power' came to define relations of power, both nationally and geo-politically, well beyond the end of colonial administrations. Indeed, the 'coloniality of power' denotes the darker side of modernity itself and its rationalistic emancipatory project. That is why it makes sense for Greider to combine modernity and coloniality in his reference to the 'colonial paradigm of modernity'. Indeed, what Villa-Vicencio, Greider, and Comblin characterize as the legacy of colonialism in the regions to which they refer is best understood as the effect of the coloniality of power. They are not referring so much to the effects of something that once existed, as to the concrete operation of an actually existing system of power. That is the reason why any attempt at reconciliation needs to come into terms with coloniality. The coloniality of power explains the continued salience of racial problems, systematic poverty, and dependency. And when Comblin states that 'Reconciliation in Latin America presumes a total inversion of the whole civilization and cultural processes', he is referring to a concept and ideal of 'civilization' that presupposes the coloniality of power. According to Comblin, the Church played a vital role in the design of the modern view of civilization, particularly as it relates to the exclusion of indigenous and Blacks. But how is it that the Church came to play such a crucial role in creating the coloniality of power? In order to get some clarity about this it is necessary to understand the mechanisms at work in the displacement of the dichotomy between pagan and Christian and the creation of a triadic model which created and brought together 'indigenous', 'Blacks', and Europeans – who only later came to be known as 'whites'. In short, if the colonial enterprises of the late fifteenth and early sixteenth century were the fire under which the coloniality

---

22 Anibal Quijano, 'Coloniality of Power, Eurocentrism, and Latin America', 536.
23 Anibal Quijano, 'Coloniality of Power, Eurocentrism, and Latin America', 533–80.

of power was formed or constituted, 'indigeneity' and 'blackness' became both the tools and the primal ingredients for such a task. And both 'indigeneity' and 'blackness' depended for their precise meaning on a fundamental break with the symbolic apparatus of medieval Christianity.

In order to understand the role of Christianity in the emergence of a new, specifically modern model of power, it is necessary to trace the beginnings of the triadic model prior to 1492. As Sylvia Wynter points out, the basis of the triadic model was established about fifty years prior to the 'discovery' of the Americas. It began with Portuguese excursions in the coast of West Africa. Following historian Daniel Boorstin, Wynter argues that:

> Columbus's 1492 voyage cannot be detached from the overall sequence of historical events that began with the Portuguese state's dispatching, during the first half of the fifteenth century, of several expeditions, whose goal was to attempt to find a sea route around the hitherto nonnavigable Cape Bojador on the bulge of West Africa—a cape that had been projected, in the accounts of the earth's geography given by medieval Christian geographers, as being the nec plus ultra line and boundary marker between the habitable temperate zone of Europe and the inhabitable torrid zones.[24]

In order to understand the implications of the Portuguese's voyages in Africa in mid-fifteenth-century Europe, and later on the significance of 1492, it is necessary to comment on the Christian medieval system of symbolic representations. The Christian medieval system of symbolic representations was strongly defined by three kinds of hierarchies: one social, one geographical, and another cosmological. Social hierarchy was defined by a divide between believers in the true religion and believers in false religions and heretics (including also pagans, idolaters and infidels). Then, believers in the true religion, that is Christians, were themselves divided among noble and non-noble, with some of them occupying positions in the clergy. The geographical hierarchy consisted on a division between habitable lands and inhabitable torrid zones. According to the Christian medieval imaginary it was the grace of God which made possible life on earth, and such grace extended to the then known habitable lands. The cosmological hierarchy consisted in the idea that the earth was in the center of the universe. In the Christian imaginary it was the Christian God who revealed true religion, who located the earth in the center of all creation, and who also, by his grace, allowed life to emerge and flourish as well as the heaven to appear in the known world. The centrality of God and the cosmology that such centrality sustained were being gradually undermined by the Renaissance celebration of the human being along with astronomical observations which defied the geocentric view of the universe. The voyages of the Portuguese in Africa began to undermine Christian geography, and with it, also challenged its system of social classifications.

The challenge of finding human populations in the inhabitable lands was first dealt by extending or applying the existing social system of classification. So, the newly

---

24  Sylvia Wynter, '1492: A New World View', 9.

'discovered' peoples of Africa were referred to as 'idolaters' and 'Moors'. Idolatry, which was a feature of paganism, had already been used to identify and justify the exploration of the Neolithic Berber peoples of the Canary Islands.[25] The category of 'Moor' was seemingly justified first because Muslims had already extended over parts of Africa and second, because many Muslim Africans, were, just like the newly 'found' people, black. The association between the Moor and the black African is made evident by the very etymology of the word Moor which can be traced back to the Latin word *maurus* and to the Greek word *mauros* which were used to refer to people of dark skin in the northwest of Africa.[26] Once the Muslims dominated those areas, Christians began to refer to them as Moors. Moor, thus, gradually became an ethnic and geopolitical category based on religion and skin color. When the Portuguese arrived at Cape Bojador in Africa and at other supposedly inhabitable areas, it did not matter much if the people whom they encountered practiced Islam or not for them to identify them as Moors. To begin with, as John Tolan points out in his study of Christian representations of Muslims in the Middle Ages, Christians were rather ignorant about Islam in that era.[27] Thus, they could not always indicate what qualified as Moor and what did not. Being black in Africa was enough indication to raise the possibility, if not to legitimize the characterization of a group of people as Moor. And once characterized as such their enslavement was legitimized by the then valid terms of the Christian feudal episteme, according to which it was possible to enslave vanquished combatants and declared enemies of the Christian faith.

In order to understand the way in which black Africans in Cape Bojador and other areas of exploration in the previously assumed non-habitable lands were conceived, one must also consider the plasticity of terms within a system of symbolic representations. Such plasticity was evinced, for instance, when later on in the Americas Hernando Cortés notes what he perceives to be beautiful *mezquitas* (mosques) in Tenochtitlán when he sees the city for the first time.[28] The imperatives for the preservation of any given episteme have priority over the accuracy of description. Referring to the newly found people in Africa, and later on in the Americas, in terms which were already part of the social system of classification in medieval Christian Europe was a way to contain the potentially devastating effects of the empirical disproof of the geographical order for the medieval Christian episteme. What we find here is a severe case of epistemological bad faith, which, in many ways, is required by all epistemes to survive. Here we have a case of masking the

---

25 See Felipe Fernández-Armesto, *Before Columbus: Exploration and Colonization from the Mediterranean to the Atlantic, 1229–1492* (London: Macmillan, 1987); Sylvia Wynter, '1492: A New World View', 11.

26 See Jack D. Forbes, *Africans and Native Americans: The Language of Race and the Evolution of Red-Black Peoples*, 2nd ed (Urbana and Chicago: University of Illinois Press, 1993), 26.

27 See John V. Tolan, *Saracens: Islam in the Medieval European Imagination* (New York: Columbia University Press, 2002).

28 See Jonathan Z. Smith, 'Religion, Religions, Religious', in M. C. Taylor (ed.), *Critical Terms for Religious Studies* (Chicago: The University of Chicago Press, 1998), 270.

new and strange with the familiar to the point of a perverse misrecognition. For such misrecognition is the one which led the Portuguese, under the presupposition that Muslims were at war with Christians and that therefore they could be legitimately enslaved, to massively ship them as slaves out of Africa.

The challenge of identifying the unknown peoples of Africa was met by applying the socio-religious system of classification in medieval Christianity. This application allowed the Portuguese to expand the horizon of slavery to include people regarded as Muslims. Christian slave-trade in Africa was thus first justified in relation to existing laws of war, which applied to adherents of Islam, or 'moors'. Slavery in this context was not racial. It rather depended on a socio-religious system of classification and on classical notions of just war. In order for racial slavery to emerge there needed to be a shift in the socio-religious system of classification to a similar extent as there was one in relation to the cosmological and geographical dimensions of the medieval system of symbolic representations. This shift occurred only after 1492 in the context of the 'discovery' and conquest of the Americas.

As Pierre Chaunu, William Phillips, Carla Phillips, and Paolo Taviani, among others, have made clear, the trips of the Portuguese to Africa had a strong impact on Christopher Columbus, who had himself joined Portuguese explorations of Africa after 1482.[29] Columbus was fascinated with the explorations of previously assumed non-habitated lands. He was familiar with the ways in which these peoples were conceived, and what the Portuguese did with them. Thus, it was more or less natural for him to suggest, upon his encounter with indigenous peoples of the Americas, that they could legitimately be enslaved. After noting that they are all naked, Columbus remarks that 'And I thought and still believe that others come from the mainland to take them as captives. They should be good servants ... since I see that they promptly do what one asks of them. And I believe that they will rapidly become Christians, since it seemed to me that they had no religion'.[30] It was clear for Columbus that the people whom he found were not 'Moors', so he could not rely on the same system of classification in order to justify slavery. Instead of applying the terms that he knew, Columbus rather identifies the indigenous peoples that he first encounters as *tabula rasa*. He indicates that they had no clothes. Also, different from the Moors or other religious subjects in his known world, the indigenous peoples gave him the impression that they could be easily Christianized since 'it seemed to me that they had no religion' ('me parecio que ninguna secta tenían'). The indigenous people appeared to Columbus as neither pagan nor Moor, not even idolaters ('porque ellos no tienen secta ninguna ni son idólatras').[31]

---

29  Pierre Chaunu, *La expansión europea: siglos XII al XV*, trans. Ana María Mayench (Barcelona: Labor, 1972); William D. Phillips and Carla Rahn Phillips, *The Worlds of Christopher Columbus* (Cambridge: Cambridge University Press, 1992); Paolo Emilio Taviani, *Columbus: The Great Adventure. His Life, His Times, and His Voyages*, trans. Luciano F. Farina and Marc A. Beckwith (New York: Orion Books, 1991).

30  Cristóbal Colón, *Los cuatro viajes. Testamento*. (Madrid: Alianza Editorial, 1986), 63. My translation.

31  Cristóbal Colón, *Los cuatro viajes. Testamento*, 110.

A clear understanding of the significance of the idea that indigenous peoples had no religion requires further elaboration.[32] As I pointed out before, medieval Christianity relied on a social differentiation between noble and non-noble as well as on one among Christians, heretics, infidels, and pagans. The second conception of social classification is based on the divide between believing the true religion or practicing false religions. All religious subjects, with either true or false religions, were understood as part of the human oecumene. They all shared a ground in the divine. The question was whether such religious beliefs and practices related human beings adequately with the creator. Since at least the fourth century after the Common Era, Christians conceived Christianity as the only religion through which it was possible to have such a relation with the divine. Christianity was the one true religion, while other religions were false. But having 'no religion' indicated an ontological and not so much an epistemological problem with the subjects in question. Having 'no religion' introduces the suspicion that certain subjects are ontologically different from others. That is, subjects with 'no religion' would be fundamentally disconnected from the divine, which raises questions about whether ultimately they had 'souls' or not. The famous debates in Valladolid about whether indigenous peoples had 'souls' and the notion that rather than mere 'pagan' or 'idolaters' they were to be considered as 'natural slaves', were clearly first intimated by Columbus's idea that indigenous peoples had 'no religion' and that they would make 'good servants'.[33] The persistence of that idea in the sixteenth and seventeenth centuries testifies to a larger shift in the understanding of humanity and social relations, which characterizes a fundamental part of our own very modern experience – just as the divide between Christians, infidels, heretics, and pagans defined life earlier in the Christian medieval world.

The characterization of indigenous peoples as subjects with no religion gave them the dubious advantage that they could now easily be Christianized, while at the same time relegated to a sub-human status – a status beyond the medieval Christian classificatory scheme. Thus, this idea of Columbus came to serve a twofold role: it justified heavy and constant Christianization, while at the same time it legitimized slavery on a new basis. Now slavery was not going to be seen as the outcome of war with infidels, pagans, or idolaters, but as the natural condition of subjects whose very humanity was put in question. We find here the beginnings of a shift from forms of slavery justified by existing laws of war to a new mode of geo-political relations where geography and ideas about the constitution of subjectivity merge in order to justify oppressive relations beyond the limits of the feudal Christian episteme. The disproof of the core geographical ideas of the feudal episteme did not lead to a radical abandonment of a geographical divide. Rather, the feudal geographical

---

32 I have elaborated further the ideas below in Nelson Maldonado-Torres, 'Imperio, raza y religión', 2005.

33 See the classic study of these debates by Lewis Hanke, *All Mankind Is One: A Study of the Disputation Between Bartolomé de Las Casas and Juan Ginés de Sepúlveda in 1550* (DeKalb: Northern Illinois University Press, 1974). It should be noted that the Pope did side with de Las Casas on the humanity of the Indians.

hierarchy gave way to a new geo-political hierarchy according to which the subjects in the previously believed unhabitated lands lack, at an ontological level (and not merely epistemological), a fundamental relation with God. Since these subjects live in lands where, according to the geographical ideas of the Christian episteme, God did not extend his grace and there were neither heavens nor life, the existence of human subjects in those territories indicated that they may not have any 'soul'. That is, the disproof of core geographical ideas of the Christian episteme motivated, not a complete abandonment, but rather a translation or reconfiguration into a new post-feudal episteme. In short, as Wynter has indicated, the collapse of the divide between habitated and non-habitated lands begins to give way to a fundamental differentiation between people who are entirely human and people who lack (at the ontological level) degrees of humanity. It is perhaps here that we find the birth of the master/slave relation in modernity. It may also be here where feudal geography gives way to the racial geo-politics that will be so central to Eurocentrism and other continental visions of knowledge.

In his first voyage to the Americas, Columbus commits a double transgression of the medieval Christian episteme: he challenges dominant ideas about the geography of the known world while he simultaneously (re)introduces a new term in the medieval system of religio-social classification.[34] Columbus's characterization of the indigenous people as having no religion fulfilled a twofold role: on the one hand it made clear that, contrary to peoples who held false religions, they could be easily Christianized, and, on the other, that they could just as easily or as naturally be conceived as subjects who could be enslaved. The shift initiated by Columbus and continued through the first decades of the conquest of the Americas will be of utmost significance. As Wynter indicates, just like geographical ideas about the division of the earth in terms of habitable and non-habitable zones defined the 'conventional wisdom' of the feudal-Christian episteme, the idea of certain groups of people being constitutively inferior from others or less human than others gradually came to be part of the 'conventional wisdom' of post-feudal modern subjects. It continued to persist even after Christians concluded that indigenous peoples did in fact have a soul. This persistence was made possible by the introduction of a third population group in the Americas, black slaves.

The decimation of indigenous populations in the Americas not too long after the 'discovery' led to the introduction of enslaved labour force from Africa. But black Africans did not only provide slave labour. They came to occupy a crucial role in the new system of material relations and symbolic representations that began to emerge in the Americas. 'In this role', explains Wynter, 'they would not only serve to free the indigenous peoples from the outright slavery to which many had been reduced in the immediate decades after 1492 ... one that had been initiated by Columbus himself ... As the liminal category whose mode of *excluded difference*, based on the

---

34 As I point out elsewhere there is at least a precedent of discourse centered on the idea of some people having 'no religion'. See Nelson Maldonado-Torres, 'Imperio, raza y religión', 2005.

hereditary slave status of its members as the only *legitimately enslavable* population group, they would also generate the principle of similarity or of conspecificity that would come to bond, if on the terms of sharply unequal relations, the incoming Spanish settlers with the indigenous peoples. From the mid-sixteenth century on, this principle would come to bond the latter as members of a category whose status was that of *hereditarily free* subjects of the Spanish state'.[35] From this ideal Wynter concludes that

> This third population group, therefore, would come to embody the new symbolic construct of *Race* or of innately determined difference that would enable the Spanish state to legitimate its sovereignty over the *lands of the Americas* in the **postreligious** legal terms of Western Europe's now-expanding state system. It would do so by instituting by means of the physical referent of the group's enslaved lives and labor the empirical basis, of, in Cerio's terms, the 'moral and philosophical foundations' on which the Spaniards 'accepted' the indigenous peoples 'into their societies, however rudely.[36]

The introduction of the black African in the Americas represents the third term that forms the triadic social-existential model in the Americas. In face of the decimation of indigenous peoples and increasing attempts to incorporate them within the socio-religious model based on epistemic differences among subjects with different religions, black Africans not only provided labour but also served to confirm and deepen the standards of sub-humanity opened up by the new postreligious episteme. That is, black Africans become the ultimate anchor of the new episteme. They alone represented the legitimately enslavable subjects in the Spanish territories. Such slavery was hereditary and phenotypically determined by color. Blackness thus became the non-religious, purely phenotypical and thus biological, determinant that indicated inferiority and enslaved nature. In this context, black Africans ceased to be Moors or mere 'idolaters' and became *negros* and *negras* (black male and black females). *It was as if in the Middle Passage black Africans were born again into a new system of symbolic representations where the colour of the skin, rather than religion (true or false, existent or not), became in itself the mark of sub-humanity.* This transformation was possible, however, only after the existing laws of slavery had been contested and an alternate system based on ontologically constitutive difference between subjects was introduced in relation to 'indigenous' peoples. Once the premises of the feudal Christian system of symbolic representations were contested and new ideas to legitimate slavery were introduced, the conditions were created for a radical change in the perception toward Africans. The Middle Passage provided the condition for a transformation of their identity from Moors to pure Blacks, that is, from a system based on religious differences to a postreligious modern system which would legitimize slavery and systematic forms of oppression with reference to racial and geo-political considerations. The transformation of the Moor into Black also

---

35 Sylvia Wynter, '1492: A New World View', 11.
36 Sylvia Wynter, '1492: A New World View', 11.

meant a deepening of the racist logic and a shift from ontological difference between subjects to purely biological ones.

The emergence of a postreligious system of human differentiation, social classification, and geo-political relations did not mean that other systems ceased to exist. What it meant was that the other existing epistemes were gradually subordinated and highly influenced by the emerging one. Just like capitalism does not do away with other forms of labor control, modern racism does not necessarily eliminate other forms of considering human differences either. But that does not mean that they remain untouched either, or that they can escape, by sheer force of will, the terms imposed by the reigning episteme. The question is to describe in every case how racism intersects with other forms of conceiving human difference, either by affecting them directly or by allowing them to exist. One crucial issue is to determine how anti-blackness and anti-indigeneity continue to exist notwithstanding the formal recognition of the humanity of ex-slave Afro-descent and indigenous peoples. It is also important to consider why about eighty percent of the planet's poor people live in racialized geo-political areas, and why poor people in richer countries tend to be also people of colour. How is reconciliation possible in such a world?

## Reconciliation: A Contested Future

The explorations in this volume of Truth and Reconciliation Commissions in South Africa and Latin America suggest that reconciliation is not possible without incessant processes of decolonization. They all make clear that undergirding the lack of 'conciliation' in South African and Latin American societies there is colonialism, or more precisely, coloniality. Colonialism changed the historical course of societies, created new identities, and new challenges for all those involved in its path. The coloniality of power has likewise affected the lived possibilities of subjects around the world. Truth and Reconciliation Commissions often take as their more direct goal the healing and restoration of nations. But what we have learnt is that oftentimes these nations themselves are premised on colonial premises that reproduce anti-black and anti-indigenous racism, along other forms of evils, many of which can be traced to modernity as a warring paradigm. Thus, true reconciliation can hardly be achieved by nationalization alone. Decolonization, not nationalization, imposes itself as the ultimate horizon for reconciliation.

The challenges for reconciliation not only lie in the need to think about peace and conciliation beyond the horizons of assumed ideas about the nation and the nation-state. This difficulty itself is indicative of a more profound problem: that of seeking the 'truth'. As Wynter explains, the problem that the search for 'truth' confronts at any given moment is that the dominant episteme establishes the parameters of what is going to be considered as 'true'. The common sense of people and their ability to judge tend to work in favor of the dominant episteme. They serve the episteme's preservation, and the preservation, to be sure, of those who obtain power by virtue of it. But the episteme also tends to define the goals of all subjects and their self-definition, without which they would lack a sense of who they are. Here the root of a particularly modern form of bad faith.[37] Before truth can be found and reconciliation achieved there need to be changes at both the personal and institutional levels that defy and put in question the existing dominant episteme, as well as nurture the idea that a different form of understanding world, self, and others is possible.

I submit that nothing short of a fundamental change of attitude in the subject of knowledge could begin to undo or to question the perverse expressions of the episteme. I refer to this attitude as a *decolonial attitude*. Although individual expressions of this attitude are most important and relevant, the challenge that humanity confronts demands the promotion of a shift in thought as massive and influential as Columbus and the subsequent conquerors and missionaries did in the late fifteenth and sixteenth centuries. Wynter calls for a new way of conceiving the human community. Alternative decolonial conceptions of the humanity of the human were articulated in the 1960s, and before that, one can argue, in the process of decolonization of different territories after the end of the Second World War. What we find there arguably is the beginnings of a decolonial turn that opposes directly the racial and colonial turn of the sixteenth century and its many reincarnations from the sixteenth to the twentieth centuries in Europe and elsewhere. The chapters in this volume all suggest in one way or another that the work of Truth and Reconciliation Commissions and related mechanisms for promoting reconciliation could be seen as part of this struggle against racist, sexist, and colonial hegemony.

Demands for truth and reconciliation after wars, social conflicts, and military regimes contribute to efforts to promote decolonization by reminding everyone of the continued existence of a paradigm of social relations inspired by the naturalization of the ethics of war, in which certain subjects are marked for death, and human bodies, particularly, but not only, women's bodies, appear as marked for rape ... and death.[38] Demands for truth and reconciliation also promote decolonization by maintaining alive the interests for a renewed conception of humanity, one which would no longer reproduce racist and sexist attitudes. In Margaret Guider's words, Truth and Reconciliation Commissions 'contribute to redemocratization through processes of truth-telling that open the way to confession and remorse, restitution and forgiveness, healing and reconciliation, deterrence and an unwavering commitment to "never

---

37  For an analysis of this form of bad faith see Lewis R. Gordon, *Bad Faith and Antiblack Racism* (Atlantic Highlands, NJ: Humanities Press, 1995).

38  Much has been written about the connections of militarism and sexual violence. In his contribution to this volume, David Tombs explores the limits of Truth and Reconciliation Commissions in dealing with the truth about sexual violence. See David Tombs, 'Unspeakable Violence: The UN Truth Commissions in El Salvador and Guatemala', (this volume), chapter 3. I explore the connections between war, coloniality, and sexual violence in Ramón Grosfoguel, Nelson Maldonado-Torres, and José David Saldívar (eds), 'On the Coloniality of Being', in *Coloniality, Transmodernity, and Border Thinking* (forthcoming), and Nelson Maldonado-Torres, *Against War: Views from the Underside of Modernity*.

again".[39] Such commitment to truth-telling and to 'never again' along with the hope that 'another world is possible' are two of the most fundamental aspects of what I have referred to as the decolonial attitude.[40] Truth and Reconciliation Commissions have served, in various degrees, as sites for the promotion of such an attitude. Other sites for the promotion of that attitude include the Catholic Church, provided that it takes seriously the efforts to undo the system of symbolic representations that it helped to generate and with which it has remained in complicity for more than five centuries, as Comblin suggests. Other churches and organizations, including state institutions such as the university, have much to do in order to promote decolonization as a project and help to break or at least defy the perverse effects of global coloniality – that is, global capital working side by side with global racism.

At the beginning of this chapter I indicated that reconciliation demands processes of decolonization that introduce a new ethics beyond coloniality and war. I regard the 'decolonial attitude' as the basic existential, epistemological, and political posture that sustains and promotes this ethics. The decolonial attitude is itself an expression of an ethical subjectivity that defines and positions itself in a way that promotes decolonization and re-imagines human relationships. In addition to decolonial 'truth-telling' and hope, the decolonial attitude also involves an ethics of decolonial memory and a decolonial economy of giving. They are all parts of the technologies and set of ideas that form part of philosophies of liberation and the methodology of the oppressed.[41]

There can be no reconciliation without an effort to remember what has been actively produced as 'forgotten' or 'invisible' by narratives of the nation-state, modernity, and liberal democracy.[42] The 'forgotten' here not only makes reference to relevant events in history when modernity has shown its evil side, or when the oppressed have rebelled successfully against it. As Barnor Hesse remarks, and as I have suggested here, 'What remains forgotten … is the colonial, foundational relation of slavery to the modern constitution of racialized governmentalities'. Hesse refers with this to the:

---

39  Margaret Eletta Guider, 'Reinventing Life and Hope: Coming to Terms with Truth and Reconciliation – Brazilian Style' (see this volume), 123–27.

40  'Another world is possible' is the distinctive motto of the World Social Forum. See http://www.forumsocialmundial.org.br.

41  For an elaboration of philosophies of liberation and the methodology of the oppressed see Enrique Dussel, *Etica de la liberación en la edad de la globalización y de la exclusión* (Madrid: Editorial Trotta; México, D.F.: Universidad Autónoma Metropolitana – Iztapalapa, and Universidad Nacional Autónoma de México, 1998); Frantz Fanon, T*he Wretched of the Earth*, trans. Constance Farrington (New York: Grove Press, 1991); Chela Sandoval, *Methodology of the Oppressed* (Minneapolis: University of Minnesota Press, 2000).

42  For a systematic formulation of a sociological view that focuses on the investigation of what is produced as invisible see Boaventura de Sousa Santos, 'A Critique of Lazy Reason: Against the Waste of Experience' in Immanuel Wallerstein (ed.), *The Modern World-System in the Longue Durée*, forthcoming.

political formations of 'race' and racism … which inscribed the written and unwritten constitutions of social relations of governance and dominant forms of cultural representation in Western societies. This continues in the post-slavery and postcolonial eras to animate the administration of the state, the conduct of civil subjects, and their regulation of the conduct of 'others'.[43]

Hesse alludes here to what I have elaborated in this chapter under the rubrics of the coloniality of power – at least to one of its axes, the idea of race, and its links with the political. He rightly focuses on the relevance of slavery for the formation of the colonial matrix of power. His own ethics of postcolonial memory are designed to respond to the challenges of remembering the relationship of modern racism to slavery, particularly in his case, to Atlantic slavery. Now, this ethics of decolonial/postcolonial memory, Hesse continues:

is not concerned with the (colonial) past through an obsession with the past, but through an engagement with the (liberal-democratic) present. In the West to remember in a postcolonial idiom is to encounter or confront the (liberal-democratic) contemporaneity in terms of what has constituted its (imperial) history. It is triggered by an awareness of the discontinuities of decolonization and global justice and continuities of racism and global inequality.[44]

The ethics of decolonial memory, which Hesse elaborates under the rubrics of postcolonial memory, involve a *questioning of liberal democracy* and its attempts to erase the traces of the past in the present and thus questions of justice and radical transformation that follow from them. The idea that derives from here is that efforts to promote reconciliation need to approach critically liberal democracy, instead of taking it as its sole inspiration or expressed end. This message is very important for leaders who participate in efforts to promote reconciliation sponsored by states. As Hesse puts it, 'The *oughtness* of Atlantic slavery's memory and the justness of its excavation reside in refusing to efface through forgetfulness the historical complicity and contemporary failures of Western liberal democracies'.[45] What this 'ought' demands is 'a critical excavation and inventory of the marginalized, discounted, *unrealized objects of decolonization* and the political consequences of their social legacies'.[46] Beyond the liberal project of the Enlightenment, Hesse hints here at a distinct project of decolonization, which remained unfinished in the twentieth century.[47] Truth and Reconciliation Commissions obtain their most radical meaning when understood in the context of this unfinished project.

---

43 Barnor Hesse, 'Forgotten like a Bad Dream: Atlantic Slavery and the Ethics of Postcolonial Memory', in David Theo Goldberg and Ato Quayson (eds), *Relocating Postcolonialism* (Oxford: Blackwell, 2002), 164–65.

44 Barnor Hesse, 'Forgotten like a Bad Dream', 165.

45 Barnor Hesse, 'Forgotten like a Bad Dream', 165.

46 Barnor Hesse, 'Forgotten like a Bad Dream', 165. Italics mine.

47 Walter Mignolo, Enrique Dussel, and Ramón Grosfoguel and others have also articulated ideas around this project. See Enrique Dussel, *El encubrimiento del Indio: 1492.*

'Truth-telling', hope, and the ethics of memory need to be complemented with a decolonial economy of the gift. While formal attempts at reconciliation often provide the occasion for cathartic processes and for the telling and listening of stories, nevertheless, as Pal Ahluwalia indicates, it is important to move beyond them. A decolonial/postcolonial economy of giving 'seeks to break down the cycle of revenge'. In South Africa and Latin America, as well as the places that Ahluwalia studies (Australia, Palestine, and Rwanda), this cycle is begun by colonialism. And so Ahluwalia states: 'It is colonialism that breaks down conciliation and necessitates reconciliation. And it is here that postcolonialism is instructive, recognizing that it is possible to imagine both a reconciled present and future. It is in this act of reimagining that the gift occupies a key role'.[48] The gift invites thought in an economy based on responsibility and generosity. It also calls for renewed ideas on leadership and intellectual life, as well as on innovative ideas about citizenship.[49] A decolonial/ postcolonial economy of giving aids in the breaking down of 'categories and identities that have been ascribed or constructed in order to maintain power structures'.[50] In this sense, an economy of giving appears to be crucial to dismantle not only identities constructed by colonialism, but more fundamentally, central aspects that keep alive

---

*Hacia el origen del mito de la modernidad*, 2nd edn. (Mexico, D.F.: Editorial Cambio XXI, 1992); Ramón Grosfoguel, 'Subaltern Epistemologies, Decolonial Imaginaries and the Redefinition of Global Capitalism', *Review 28* (forthcoming 2005); Ramón Grosfoguel and Nelson Maldonado-Torres, 'Latinas and the 'Euro-American' Menace: The Decolonization of the US Empire in the 21st Century' in Ramón Grosfoguel, Nelson Maldonado-Torres, and José David Saldívar (eds), *Latinas in the World-System* (Chicago: Paradigm Press, forthcoming); Nelson Maldonado-Torres, *Against War*; Nelson Maldonado-Torres, 'Intervenciones filosóficas al proyecto inacabado de la descolonizacion', in Juan Manuel Contreras Colín and Mario Rojas (eds), *Filosofía y liberación, Homenaje a Enrique Dussel* (México, D.F.: Universidad de la Ciudad de México, forthcoming); Walter Mignolo, *Local Histories/Global Designs: Coloniality, Subaltern Knowledges, and Border Thinking* (Princeton, NJ: Princeton University Press, 2000). For a feminist account of decolonization as project see Chela Sandoval, *Methodology of the Oppressed*. (Minneapolis: University of Minnesota Press, 2000).

48 Pal Ahluwalia, 'Towards (Re)Conciliation: The Postcolonial Economy of Giving', in Theo Goldberg and Ato Quayson (eds), *Relocating Postcolonialism* (Oxford: Blackwell, 2002), 197–98. Frantz Fanon has noted with acuity the way in which colonialism interrupts the history of the colonized and disrupts the metaphysical coordinates of their culture and conception of the world. I have argued elsewhere that his response to such devastating effects involves a radical decolonial ethics of the gift. See Frantz Fanon, *Toward the African Revolution: Political Essays*, trans. Haakon Chevalier (New York: Grove Press, 1988); Nelson Maldonado-Torres, 'The Cry of the Self as a Call from the Other: The Paradoxical Loving Subjectivity of Frantz Fanon', *Listening: Journal of Religion and Culture* 36:1 (2001), 246– 60.

49 See Ahluwalia, 'Towards (Re)Conciliation', 198–201.

50 Ahluwalia, 'Towards (Re)Conciliation', 201.

the coloniality of power.[51] Any attempt to promote reconciliation today must come into terms with the perverse expressions of coloniality in the modern world.

---

51 For an elaboration of an ethics of the gift in response to coloniality and the modern paradigm of war see Maldonado-Torres, *Against War*. See also Nelson Maldonado-Torres, 'The Cry of the Self as a Call from the Other: The Paradoxical Loving Subjectivity of Frantz Fanon', *Listening: Journal of Religion and Culture* 36:1 (2001) 46–60. Available on-line at: http://www.listeningjournal.org/articles.htm.

# Bibliography

**Primary Literature (Commission reports, church documents)**

*Commission Reports:*

Commission reports are listed below for

Argentina:
Commisión Nacional sobre la Desaparición de Personas (CONADEP). *Argentina Nunca Más.* Buenos Aires: Editorial Universitaria, 1984, and in English, Commisión Nacional sobre la Desaparición de Personas. (CONADEP). *Nunca Más: The Report of the Argentine National Commission on the Disappeared.* Translated by Writers and Scholars International, Ltd. New York: Farrar, Straus, 1986.

**Brazil:** (non-official)
Arquidiocese de São Paulo. *Brasil nunca mais. Un relato para a história.* Prefacio de Paulo Evaristo Arns. 18th Ed. Petropolis: Vozes, 1985, and in English Archdiocese of São Paulo, *Torture in Brazil: A Shocking Report on the Pervasive Use of Torture by Brazlian Military Governments, 1964–1979.* Translated by Jaime Wright, edited by Joan Dassin. Austin: University of Texas, 1998.

Chile:
Comisión Nacional de Verdad y Reconciliación. *Informe de la Comisión Nacional de Verdad y Reconciliación, Informe Rettig.* Texto Oficial Completo. 3 Volumes. Santiago, Chile: La Nación, 1991. In English, National Commission on Truth and Reconciliation, *Report of the Chilean National Commission on Truth and Reconciliation,* translated by Phillip Berryman. Notre Dame, Ind.: Notre Dame Press, 1993.

El Salvador:
United Nations Commission on the Truth for El Salvador. *From Madness to Hope: The 12-Year War in El Salvador: Report of the Commission on the Truth for El Salvador.* New York: UN Security Council, 1993.

Guatemala:
Comisión para el Esclarecimiento Histórico (CEH). *Guatemala: Memoria Del Silencio, Informe de la Comisión para el Esclarecimiento Histórico.* 12 Volumes. Guatemala: Comisión para el Esclarecimiento Histórico, 1999. In English, Commission for Historical Clarification. *Guatemala: Memory of Silence. Prologue.* Guatemala: United Nations, 1999. See also the Roman Catholic Church independent report by *Recuperación de la Memoria Histórica.* (REMHI)

and Menschenrechtsbüro des Erzbistums Guatemala ODHAG (eds) *Guatemala: Never Again!, The Official Report of the Human Rights Office, Archdiocese of Guatemala.* Translated by G. Tovar Siebentritt. Maryknoll, NY: Orbis Books, London, Catholic Institute for International Relations and Latin America Bureau, 1999.

Haiti:
Commission national de verité (CNVJ). *Si M Pa Rele.* Port-au-Prince: Minstère Nationale de la Justice de la République d'Haiti, 1996.
Paraguay:
Comité de Iglesias para Ayudas de Emergencia (CIPAE). *Nunca Más: La Dictadura de Stroessner y los Derechos Humanos.* Asunción: Comité de Iglesias para Ayudas de Emergencia, 1990.
Peru:
Comisión de la Verdad y Reconciliación. *Comisión de la Verdad y Reconciliación, Informe Final.* 9 volumes. Lima: Comisión de la Verdad y Reconciliación, 2003.
South Africa:
Truth and Reconciliation Commission. *Truth and Reconciliation Commission of South Africa: Final Report.* 5 volumes. Cape Town: Juta and Co., 1998.
**Uruguay:**
Servicio Paz y Justicia de Uruguay. *Uruguay Nunca Más. Informe Sobre la Violación a los Derechos Humanos (1972–1985).* Montevideo, 1989. In English, The Peace and Justice Service of Uruguay. *Uruguay Nunca Mas: Human Rights Violations, 1972–1985.* Translated by Elizabeth Hampsten. Philadelphia: Temple University Press, 1992.
Church Documents:
Abbott, Walter M. *The Documents of Vatican II.* New York: America Press, 1966.
Archdiocese of São Paulo. *Torture in Brazil: A Shocking Report on the Pervasive Use of Torture by Brazlian Military Governments, 1964–1979.* Translated by Jaime Wright, edited by Joan Dassin. Austin: University of Texas Press, 1998.
Archdiocese of São Paulo. *Brasil: Nunca Mais.* Petrópolis: Vozes, 1985.
Comissão Pastoral dos Direitos Humanos e dos Marginalizados da Arquidiocese de São Paulo. 'Violência contra os Humildes,' SEDOC 10 (1978), 961–983.
Comité de Iglesias para Ayudas de Emergencia (CIPAE). *Nunca Más: La Dictadura de Stroessner y los Derechos Humanos.* Asunción: Comité de Iglesias para Ayudas de Emergencia, 1990.
Conferencia Episcopal Argentina (CEA). 'Camino de la Reconciliación.' *Clarin* (17 March 1983) and (6 May 1983).
Conferencia Episcopal Argentina (CEA). *'Dios, el hombre y las consciencia.' Clarin* (21 & 28 June, 1983), 14–15. (editorials by José Ignacio López, 28 June 1983).
Conferencia Episcopal Argentina (CEA). *Documentos del Episcopado Argentino, 1965–1981. Colección Completa del Magisterio Postconciliar de la Conferencia Episcopal Argentina.* Con un Indice Analytico preparado por César H. Belaunde.

2<sup>nd</sup> Edition. Buenos Aires: Editorial Claraetinia, 1982.

Conferencia Episcopal Argentina (CEA). *Documentos Basicos*, Buenos Aires: CEA, 1980.

Conferencia Episcopal Argentina (CEA). *Iglesia y Communidad Nacional.* Buenos Aires: CEA, 1981.

Conferencia Episcopal Argentina. *La Iglesia y los derechos humanos.* Buenos Aires: CEA, 1984.

Conferencia Episcopal de Chile. 'Reconciliacion en Chile.' (Santiago: CEC, 24 April 1974).

Conferencia Episcopal de Guatemala. *Al servicio de la vida, la justiticia y la paz: Documentos de la Conferencia Episcopal de Guatemala, 1956–1997.* Guatemala de la Asunción: La Conferencia, 1997.

Conferencia Episcopal de Guatemala. *El Clamor por la Tierra: carta pastoral colectiva del episcopado Guatemalteco.* Guatemala de la Asunción: Impr. Gutenburg, 1988.

Conferencia Episcopal de Chile. *El renacer de Chile y outros documentos.* Santiago, Chile: Centro Nacional de Comunicación Social del Episcopado de Chile, 1984.

Conferencia Episcopal de Latino America. 'Evangelization in Latin America's Present and Future. Final Document of the Third General Conference of the Latin American Episcopate,' (Puebla de los Angeles, Mexico. 27 January – 13 February 1979), in John Eagleson and Philip Scharper (eds), *Puebla and Beyond.* Trans. John Drury. Maryknoll, NY: Orbis Books, 1979.

Denzinger, Henricus and Adolfus Schönmetzer, S.J. (eds). *Enchiridion symbolorum. Definitionum et Declarationum de rebus fidei et morum.* Edition XXXII, Barcelona: Herder, 1963.

Eagleson, John and Philip Scharper (eds). *Puebla and Beyond: Documentation and Commentary.* Translated by John Drury. Maryknoll, NY: Orbis Books, 1979.

Episcopado de São Paulo, 'Testemunho de Paz', SEDOC Servico de Documentacão, 5 (1972), 107–109.

Flannery, Austin (ed.). *Vatican Council II*, vol. 1, Collegeville, IN: The Liturgical Press, 1992.

Fundación Documentación y Archivo de la Vicaría de la Solidaridad (FDAVS). *Informe de Derechos Humanos del Primer Semestre de 2001.* Santiago, Chile: Arzobispado de Santiago Fundación Documentación y Archivo de la Vicaría de la Solidaridad, 2001.

General Synod of the Dutch Reformed Church. *Human Relations and the South African Scene in the Light of Scripture.* Cape Town: Dutch Reformed Church Publishers, 1976.

John Paul II. 'Apostolic Exhortation on Reconciliation and Penance' (*Reconciliatio et paenitentia*), *Origins* 14, 20 December 1984.

John Paul II. 'On Social Concern' (Sollicitudo rei socialis), in David J. O'Brien and Thomas A. Shannon (eds), *Catholic Social Thought*, Maryknoll, NY: Orbis Books, 1992.

John Paul II. *Post-Synodical Apostolic Exhortation RECONCILIATION AND*

*PENANCE of John Paul II to the Bishops, Clergy and Faithful on Reconciliation and Penance in the Mission of the Church Today.* Rome: Vatican, December 1984.

O'Brien, David J. and Thomas A. Shannon (eds). *Catholic Social Thought: The Documentary Heritage.* Maryknoll, NY: Orbis Books, 1992.

Rouët de Journel, Marie Joseph. *Enchiridion patristicum: loci ss. Partum, dectorum, scriptorium ecclesiasticorum.* 24th edition, Barcelona: Herder, 1969.

South African Council of Churches. *Confessing Guilt in South Africa. The Responsibility of Churches and Individual Christians.* Johannesburg: SACC, 1989.

Synod of Bishops. 'Justice in the World' (1971), in David J. O'Brien and Thomas A. Shannon (eds). *Catholic Social Thought.* (1992), 287–300.

Tutela Legal. *Investigación sobre la massacre de centenares de campesinos en los caseríos El Mozote, Ranchería y Jocote Amarillo del cantón Guacamaya, en los cantones La Joya y Cerro Pando, de la jurisdicción de Meanguera y en el caserío Los Toriles de la jurisdicción de Arambala, todos del departamento de Morazán, por tropas del BIRI Atlacatl durante operativo militar los días 11, 12 y 13 de Diciembre de 1981: Hechos conocidos como Masacre de El Mozote.* San Salvador: Tutela Legal, 1991.

Western Cape Council of Churches. 'Statement on Amnesty', *Journal of Theology for Southern Africa* 81 (December 1992), 94.

World Council of Churches. *From Cottesloe to Cape Town. Challenges for the Church in a Post-Apartheid South Africa. The WCC Visit to South Africa, October, 1991.* Geneva, PCR Information, No. 30, 1991.

Other Reports:

Agrupación de Familiares de Detenidos Desaparecidos (AFDD), Años de Historia de la Agrupación de Familiares de Detenidos Desaparecidos de Chile: Un camino de imágenes que revelan y se revelan contra una historia no contada. Santiago, Chile: Corporación Agrupación de Familiares de Detenidos Desaparecidos, 1997.

Agrupación de Familiares de Detenidos Desaparecidos (AFDD). *Resúmen de Actividades Año 1992.* Santiago Chile: AFDD, 1992, 1993.

Americas Watch. *Chile Since the Coup: Ten Years of Repression.* New York: Americas Watch, 1983.

Americas Watch. 'The Argentine Military Junta's "Final Document:" A Call for Condemnation.' An Americas Watch Report, 1983.

Amnesty International. *Chile: Amnesty International Briefing.* London: Amnesty International, 1998.

Amnesty International. *Chile: Evidence of Torture, An Amnesty International Report.* London: Amnesty International, 1983.

Amnesty International. *Brazil: Corumbiara and Eldorado de Carajás: Rural Violence, Police Brutality an Impunity.* http://web.amnesty.org/library/print/ENGAMR190011998

Amnesty International. *Brazil:.Eldorado de Carajás – Hopes Betrayed.* http://www.amnesty.org.yk/deliver?document=12904

Amnesty International News. 'Brazil: Carandiru Trial – A Clear Message To Those in Charge.' http://www.amnesty.org.uk/news/press/12903.shtml

Boutros Boutros-Ghali. UN Secretary, Letter to the UN Security Council, UN Document S/25500, 29 March 1993.

Congreso Argentino de la Cooperación. *Documento Final*. Buenes Aires: Consejo Intercooperativo Argentino, 1983.

Corporación Nacional de Reparación y Reconciliación (CNRR). *Informe Sobre Calificación de Víctimas de Violaciones de Derechos Humanos y de la Violencia Política*. Santiago, Chile: Corporación Nacional de Reparación y Reconciliación, 1996.

European Economic Community and FONPAZ/COPREDE. *Los Acuerdos de Paz*. Guatemala City, 1997.

Human Rights Watch. *El Salvador: Extradition Sought for Alleged Death Squad Participant*. New York: Human Rights Watch, August 1991.

Human Rights Watch. *Global Report on Women's Human Rights*. New York: Human Rights Watch, 1995.

Human Rights Watch and National Coalition for Haitian Refugees. *Rape in Haiti: A Weapon of Terror*. New York: Human Rights Watch, July 1994.

Jahanger, Asma. Report of the Special Rapporteur, 'Civil and Political Rights, including the Questions of Disappearances and Summary Executions – Mission to Brazil,' Sixtieth Session of the U.N. Commission on Human Rights. http://www.unhchr.ch/huridocda/huridoca.nsf, January 28, 2004.

Nizich, Ivana. *War Crimes in Bosnia-Hercegovina, Vol. I–II*. New York: Human Rights Watch, 1992–1993.

*Relator sobre a Tortura da Comissão* DH - ONU 05/03/2003 http://www.midiaindependente.org/eo/blue/2003/03/249039.shtml.

Truth Talk, The Official Newsletter of the Truth and Reconciliation Commission, Vol. 1, No. 1, November 1996.

Truth Talk, The Official Newsletter of the Truth and Reconciliation Commission, Vol. 2, No. 1, March 1997.

U.S. Department of State Human Rights Report for 2000, 59th Session of the U.N. Commission on Human Rights, "Brazil." http://www.humanrights-usa.net/reports/brazil.html.

van Boven, Theo. Report of the Special Rapporteur, 'Civil and Political Rights, including the Questions of Torture and Detention,' Sixtieth Session of the U.N. Commission on Human Rights. http://www.unhchr.ch/huridocda/huridoca.nsf, 20 December 2003.

**Dissertations and Speeches**

Du Toit, Stephanus Francois. 'Ideas of Truth and Revelation in the Light of the Challenge of Postmodernism', Ph.D. Dissertation, Cambridge University, 1995.

Fourie, Ginn. 'The Psychology of Perpetrators of Political Violence in South Africa: A Personal Experience.' Paper delivered at a Medical Research Unit on Anxiety and Stress Disorders conference, Mental Health Beyond the TRC, 8 October

1998.

Goldstone, Richard. The Hauser Lecture, New York University, January 22, 1997.

Ignatief, Michael. 'Truth, Justice, and Reconciliation', Lecture to the Canadian Bar Association, Toronto, 30 August 1996.

Kayser, Undine. 'Improvising the Present: Narrative Construction and Reconstruction of the Past in South Africa and Germany.' Honours Thesis, Centre for African Studies, University of Cape Town, 1997–98.

Koll, Karla Ann. 'Struggling for Solidarity. Changing Mission relations between the Presbyterian Church (USA) and Church Organizations in Latin America during the 1980s', Ph.D. Dissertation, Princeton Theological Seminary, chapter 3, 2003.

Simpson, Graeme. A Brief Evaluation of South Africa's TRC: Some Lessons for Societies in Transition.' Paper delivered at Commissioning the Past Conference, University of the Witswatersrand, June 1999.

Tombs, David. 'Crucifixion, Rape and the Body-Politics of Power in the Roman Empire,' unpublished paper presented at the Society of Biblical Literature International Meeting, Rome, July 9, 2001.

Tutu, Desmond. Address, 'Love Reveals My Neighbour, My Responsibility,' December 16, 1981.

Tutu's Handwritten Sermons, 'Genesis Chapter 3,' St. Mary's, Blechingly, Surrey, October 6, 1985.

Secondary Literature

Abraham, Garth. *The Catholic Church and Apartheid. The Response of the Catholic Church in South Africa to the First Decade of National Party Rule 1948–1957.* Johannesburg: Ravan Press, 1989.

AFDD – Agrupación de Familiares de Detenidos Desaparecidos. *20 Años de Historia de la Agrupación de Familiares de Detenidos Desaparecidos de Chile: Un camino de imágenes que revelan y se revelan contra una historia no contada.* Santiago, Chile: Corporación Agrupación de Familiares de Detenidos Desaparecidos, 1997.

Aguilar, Mario I. 'The Disappeared: Ritual and Memory in Chile,' *The Month: Review of Christian Thought and World Affairs* 32/12 (1999), 472–475.

Aguilar, Mario I. 'El Muro de los Nombres de Villa Grimaldi (Chile): Exploraciones sobre la Memoria, el Silencio y la Voz de la Historia,' *European Review of Latin American and Caribbean Studies* 69 (October 2000), 81–88.

Aguilar, Mario I. '"Evangelio y Paz': A Dialogue between Church and State in 1970s Chile,'" *The Month: Review of Christian Thought and World Affairs* 34/3 (2001), 103.

Aguilar, Mario I. 'The Vicaría de la Solidaridad and the Pinochet Regime (1976–1980): Religion and Politics in 20th Century Chile.' *Iberoamericana: Nordic Journal of Latin American and Caribbean Studies.* xxxi/1 (2001), 101–115.

Aguilar, Mario I. *Current Issues on Theology and Religion in Latin America and Africa.* Lampeter: Edwin Mellen Press, 2002.

Ahluwalia, Pal. 'Towards (Re)Conciliation: The Postcolonial Economy of Giving.' In David Theo Goldberg and Ato Quayson (eds), *Relocating Postcolonialism.* (Oxford: Blackwell,

2002), 184–204.

Ahrweiler, Hélène. *L'idéologie politique de l'empire byzantin*. Paris: PUF, 1975.

Ahumada, Eugenio, Javier Luis Egaña, Augusto Góngora, Carmen Quesney, Gustavo Seball and Gustavo Villalobos. *Chile, La Memoria Prohibida: Las Violaciones a los Derechos Humanos 1973–1983*. Santiago, Chile: Pehuén Editores, 1989.

Alberts, L. and F. Chikane (eds). *The Road to Rustenburg: The Church Looking Forward to a New South Africa*. Cape Town: Struik, 1991.

Alcoff, Linda and Elizabeth Potter (eds), *Feminist Epistemologies*. New York: Routledge, 1993.

Aldunate, J. 'The Christian Ministry of Reconciliation.' In G. Baum and H. Wells (eds), *The Reconciliation of Peoples: Challenge to the Churches*. Maryknoll, NY: Orbis Books, 1997.

Allen, Beverly. *Rape Warfare: The Hidden Genocide in Bosnia-Herzegovonia*. Minneapolis: University of Minnesota Press, 1996.

Alliens, Madeleine. *Le Désert et la Nuit*. Paris: Cerf, 1981.

Alix, Christine. *Le Saint-Siège et les nationalismes en Europe*. Paris: Sirey, 1962.

Alves, Rubem A. *A Theology of Human Hope*. Washington, D.C.: Corpus Books, 1969.

Andrade, Jorge. *Milagre na Cela*. Rio de Janeiro: Paz e Terra, 1997.

Argueta, Manlio. *One Day of Life*. Trans. W. Brow. London: Chatto and Windus, 1984.

Armony, Ariel C. *Argentina, the United States and the Anti-Communist Crusade in Central America 1977–1984*. Athens, OH: Ohio University Press, 1997.

Arns, Dom Paulo Evaristo. *Da Esperança à Utopia: Testemunho de Uma Vida*. Rio de Janeiro: Editora Sextante, 2001.

Arnson, Cynthia (ed.). *Comparative Peace Processes in Latin America*. Washington DC: Woodrow Wilson Center Press, and Stanford, CA: Stanford University Press, 1999.

Aron, A. *et al.* 'The Gender Specific Terror of El Salvador and Guatemala: Post-traumatic Stress Disorder in Central American Refugee Women,' *Women's Studies International Forum*. 14 (1991), 37–47.

Aronson, Cynthia J. *Crossroads: Congress, the President and Central America*. 2nd Edition. University Park, PA: Penn State Press, 1993.

Ash, Timothy Garton. *The File*. London: Flamingo, 1997.

Askin, Kelly. *War Crimes Against Women: Prosecution in International War Crimes Tribunals*. The Hague: Martinus Nijhoff, 1997.

Asmal, Kader, L. Asmal, and L. Roberts (eds). *Reconciliation through Truth: A Reckoning of Apartheid's Criminal Governance*. Cape Town: David Philip, 1996.

Araya, Eduardo. *Relaciones Iglesia-Estado en Chile 1973–1981*. Santiago: Instituto Chileno de Estudios Humanísticos, 1982.

Azpuru, Dinorah. 'Peace and Democratization in Guatemala: Two Parallel Processes.' In Cynthia Arnson (ed.), *Comparative Peace Processes in Latin America*. Stanford

University Press, 1999.

Bale, Joanna, Melissa Kite and Richard Beeston. 'Pinochet Flies Out a Free Man.' *The Times* (3 March 2000), 1.

Barahona de Brito, Alexandra, Carmen Gonzalez-Enriquez and Paloma Aguilar (eds). *The Politics of Memory and Democratization: Transitional Justice in Democratizing Societies.* Oxford Studies in Democratization. Oxford: Oxford University Press, 2001.

Barth, Karl. *Kirchliche Dogmatik.* III/2, Zurich: Evangelischer Verlag, 1948.

Bartmann, B. *Teologia dogmática.* 3 volumes, Sao Paulo: Ed. Paulinas, 1962.

Batstone, David, Eduardo Mendieta, Lois Ann Lorentzen and Dwight Hopkins (eds). *Liberation Theologies, Postmodernity, and the Americas.* New York: Routledge, 1997.

Battle, Michael. *Reconciliation. The Ubuntu Theology of Desmond Tutu.* Cleveland, Ohio: Pilgrim Press, 1997.

Baum, Gregory. 'A Theological Afterword,' in Gregory Baum and Harold Wells (eds), *The Reconciliation of Peoples.* (Maryknoll, NY: Orbis Books, 1997), 184–192.

Baum, Gregory. 'Option for the Powerless,' *The Ecumenist.* 26 (November-December 1987), 5–11.

Baum, Gregory and Robert Ellsberg (eds). *The Logic of Solidarity.* Maryknoll, NY: Orbis Books, 1989.

Bauman, Zygmuut. *Globalization: The Human Consequences.* New York: Columbia University Press, 1998.

Bauman, Zygmunt. *Modernity and the Holocaust.* Ithaca, NY: Cornell University Press, 1989.

Bax, Douglas. *A Different Gospel: A Critique of the Theology Behind Apartheid.* Johannesburg: Presbyterian Church of Southern Africa, 1979.

Becker, David, Elizabeth Lira, Maria Isabel Castillo, Elena Gómez and Juana Kovalskys. 'Therapy with the Victims of Political Repression in Chile: The Challenge of Social Reparation,' *Journal of Social Issues.* 46/3 (1990), 133–149.

Beresford, David. 'Fisher of Men, Seeker of Truth,' *Mail & Guardian, A South African Weekly Newspaper.* Johannesburg (19 December 1997).

Bernardin, Joseph. 'Proposal for a New Rite of Penance,' in *Synod of Bishops, Rome, 1983. Penance and Reconciliation in the Mission of the Church.* Washington, DC: United States Catholic Conference (1984), 41–44.

Betto, Frei. *Batismo de Sangue: A Luta Clandestina Contra a Ditadura Militar – Dossiês Carlos Marighella e Frei Tito.* 11ª ed., São Paulo: Editora Casa Amarela, 2000.

Betto, Frei, et al. *Frei Tito: Resistência & Utopia.* São Paulo: CEPIS, 1994.

Binford, Leigh. *The El Mozote Massacre: Anthropology and Human Rights.* Tuscon: University of Arizona Press, 1996.

Boesak, Willa. *God's Wrathful Children. Political Oppression & Christian Ethics.* Grand Rapids, MI: William B. Eerdmans Publishing, 1995.

Boraine, Alex, J. Levy, R. Scheffer (eds). *Dealing with the Past: Truth and*

*Reconciliation in South Africa*. Cape Town: IDASA, 1994.

Brain, Joy, Philippe Denis (eds). *The Catholic Church in Contemporary Southern Africa*. Pietermaritzburg: Cluster Publications, 1999.

Brody, Reed. 'The United Nations and Human Rights in El Salvador's Negotiated Revolution,' *Harvard Human Rights Journal* 8 (Spring 1995), 229–258.

Brownmiller, Susan. *Against Our Will: Men, Women and Rape*. London: Secker and Warburg, 1975.

Bruner, Jerome S. *Making Stories: Law, Literature and Life*. Cambridge: Harvard University Press, 2003.

Buergenthal, Thomas. 'The United Nations Truth Commission for El Salvador,' *Vanderbilt Journal of Transnational Law* 27/3 (1994), 497–544.

Bunster-Burotto, Ximena. 'Surviving Beyond Fear: Women and Torture in Latin America,' in Miranda Davies (ed.). *Women and Violence*. (1994), 156–76.

Burdick, John. *Looking for God in Brazil*. Berkeley, CA: University of California Press, 1996.

Burdick, Michael A. *For God and Fatherland: Religion and Politics in Argentina*. New York: The State University of New York Press, 1995.

Burnett, Virginia Garrard. 'Identity, Community and Religion Change Among the Maya of Chiapas and Guatemala,' *Journal of Hispanic/Latino Theology* 6/1 (August 1998), 61–79.

Byrne, Hugh. *El Salvador's Civil War: A Study of Revolution*. Boulder, CO and London: Lynne Rienner, 1996.

Cambe, M. 'Puissances,' in Louis Pirot (ed.). *Supplément au Dictionnaire de la Bible*. Paris: Letouzey et Ané, 1926.

Cañas, Antonio and Héctor Dada. 'Political Institutionalization in El Salvador,' in Cynthia Arnson (ed.), *Comparative Peace Processes in Latin America*. (Washington, DC: Woodrow Wilson Center Press and Stanford, CA: Stanford University Press, 1999), 69–95.

Carmack, Robert M. (ed). *Harvest of Violence: The Maya Indians and the Guatemalan Crisis*. Norman, OK: University of Oklahoma Press, 1998.

Carothers, Thomas. *In the Name of Democracy: U.S. Policy Toward Latin America in the Reagan Years*. Berkeley: University of California Press, 1991.

Casaldáliga, Dom Pedro. *Missa da Terra Sem Males*. São Paulo: Edições Paulinas Discos, 1980.

Cavanaugh, William T. *Torture and Eucharist: Theology, Politics and the Body of Christ*. Oxford: Basil Blackwell, 1998.

César, Murilo Días, Licínio Ries Neto and Jaci Bezerra. *Teatro Social: Três Dramas*. Rio de Janeiro: Ministério da Cultura- Instituto Nacional de Artes e Cênicas, 1986.

Chapman, Audrey and Bernard Spong (eds). *Religion & Reconciliation in South Africa*. Philadelphia: Templeton Foundation Press, 2003.

Chapman, Audrey. 'Truth Commissions as Instruments of Forgiveness and Reconciliation.' In Raymond Helmick and Rodney Peterson (eds). *Religion, Public Policy, and Conflict Transformation*. (Philadelphia: Templeton Foundation

Press, 2001), 247–268.

Chaunu, Pierre. *La expansión europea: siglos XII al XV*. Translated by Ana María Mayench. Barcelona: Labor, 1972.

Chenu, M. D. *La 'doctrine sociale' de l'Eglise comme idéologie*. Paris: Cerf, 1979.

Cherry, Janet. 'Historical Truth: Something to fight for,' in C. Villa-Vicencio and W. Verwoerd (eds). *Looking Back Reaching Forward*. (Cape Town: UCT Press, 1999), 134–143.

Claver, Francisco. '*Sollicitudo Rei Socialis*: A View from the Philippines,' in Gregory Baum and Robert Ellsberg (eds). *The Logic of Solidarity: Commentaries on Pope John Paul II's 'Encyclical on Social Concern.'* Maryknoll, NY: Orbis Books, 1990.

Cloete, G. D. and D. J. Smit (eds). *A Moment of Truth. The Confession of the Dutch Reform Mission Church 1982*. Grand Rapids: Wm. B. Eerdmans Publishing, 1984.

Cochrane, James, John W. De Gruchy and Stephen Martin (eds). *Facing the Truth: South African Faith Communities and the Truth & Reconciliation Commission*. Cape Town: David Philip Publishers, 1999.

Coenen, Lothar, E. Bayreuther and H. Bietenhard (eds). *Theologisches Begriffslexikon zum Neuen Testament*. Wuppertal: Brockhaus, 1971.

Cojti Cuxil, Demetrio. *Configuracion delpensamiento politico del pueblo Maya*. Quetzaltenango: Associacion de escritores Mayenses de Guatemala 1995.

Cojti Cuxil, Demetrio. 'Global Fragments: a Second Latinamericanism,' in Frederick Jameson and Masau Miyoshi (eds). *Cultures of Globalization*, Chapel Hill: Duke University Press, 1998.

Cojti Cuxil, Demetrio. 'The Politics of Maya Revindication,' in Edward Fischer and R. McKenna Brown (eds), *Maya Cultural Activism in Guatemala*. Austin: University of Texas Press, 1996.

Colón, Cristóbal. *Los cuatro viajes. Testamento*. Madrid: Alianza Editorial, 1986.

Comblin, José. *Reconciliación y Liberación*. Santiago, Chile: CESOC, Ediciones Chile y América, 1987.

Comblin, José. *The Church and the National Security State*. Maryknoll, NY: Orbis Books, 1979.

Cox. Elizabeth Shrader. 'Gender Violence and Women's Health in Central America,' in Miranda E. Davies (ed.), *Women and Violence: Realities and Responses Worldwide*. New York: Palgrave Macmillan, 1994.

Crichton, J. D. *The Ministry of Reconciliation. A Commentary on the Order of Penance, 1974*. Ordo Paenetentia translated by Geoffrey Webb. London: Geoffrey Chapman, 1974.

Crouzet, Edward. *Sangre sobre la Esmeralda: Sacerdote Miguel Woodward, Vida y Martirio*. Santiago, Chile: Ediciones Chile-América – CESOC, 2001.

Daniélou, C. F. J. *Origène*. Paris: La Table Ronde, 1948.

Danner, Mark. *The Massacre at El Mozote*. New York: Vintage, 1993.

Davies, Miranda E. (ed.). *Women and Violence: Realities and Responses Worldwide*.

New York: Palgrave MacMillan, 1994.

Daye, Russell. *Political Forgiveness: Lessons from South Africa.* Maryknoll, NY: Orbis Books, 2004.

de Alvarado, Pedro. *Cartas de relacion.* Madrid: M. Rivadeneyra, 1863.

de Gruchy, John W. *Reconciliation: Restoring Justice.* Cape Town: David Philip, 2002.

de Gruchy, John and Charles Villa-Vicencio (eds). *Apartheid is a Heresy.* (Grand Rapids, MI: Wm B. Eerdmans Publishing, 1983).

de Klerk, F. W. 'South Africa Panel Didn't Serve Truth.' *New York Times,* (28 November 1998), A14.

de Oliveira Costa, Homero. 'Incursões na História das Anistias Políticas no Brasil,' http://www.dhnet.org.br/direitos/anthistbr/Redemocratizacao1988/homeroanistia.html.

de Lubac, Henri. *La pensée religieuse du Père Teilhard de Chardin.* Paris: Aubier, 1962.

de Lubac, Henri. *La postérité spirituelle de Joachim de Fiore.* 2 vols. Paris: P. Lethielleux, 1979, 1981.

de Souza, Percival. *Autópsia do Medo – Vida e Morte do Delegado Sérgio Pasranhos Fleury.* São Paulo: Editora Globo, 2000.

Delumeau, *J. Le péché et la peur. La culpabilisation en Occident, XIII–XVII siècles.* Paris: Fayard, 1983.

Didion, Joan. *Salvador.* London: Chatto & Windus, 1983.

Digeser, P.E. *Political Forgiveness.* Ithaca: Cornell University Press, 2001.

Doggett, Martha. *Death Foretold: The Jesuit Murders in El Salvador.* Washington, DC: Georgetown University Press & Lawyer's Committee for Human Rights and Americas Watch, 1983.

Dorsman, Robert, Hans Hartman, and Lieneke Noteboom-Kronoemeijer (eds). *Truth and Reconciliation in South Africa and the Netherlands.* Utrecht: Studie-en Informatiecentrum Menschenrechten, 1999.

Dostoyevsky, Fyodor. *Crime and Punishment.* Translated by Jessie Coulson. Oxford: Oxford University Press, 1998.

Dri, Rubem. *Teologia y Dominación.* Buenos Aires: Roblanco, 1987.

Dri, Rubem. *Processo a la Iglesia argentina: las relaciones de la jerarquia eclesiástica y los gobiernos de Alfonsín y Menem.* Buenos Aires: Editorial Biblos, 1997.

Droulers, P., Francois Bédarida, Jean Maition and J. Baubérrat (eds). *Catholicisme et mouvement ouvrier au XIXe siècle,* in *Christianisme et monde ouvrier.* Paris: Ed. Ouvrières, 1975.

Dugard, John. 'Dealing with Crimes of a Past Regime. Is Amnesty Still an Option?' *Leiden Journal of International Law* 12/4 (2000), 1001–1015.

Dupont, J. *La reconciliation dans la Théologie de Saint Paul.* Lovain, Bruges-Paris: Publications Universitaires de Louvain, 1953.

Dussel, Enrique. 'Beyond Eurocentrism,' in Frederick Jameson and Masao Miyoshi (eds), *The Cultures of Globalization.* Durham and London: Duke University

258 *Reconciliation, Nations and Churches in Latin America*

Press, 1998.

Dussel, Enrique. *El encubrimiento del Indio: 1492. Hacia el origen del mito de la modernidad.* 2da ed. Mexico, D.F.: Editorial Cambio XXI, 1992.

Dussel, Enrique. *Etica de la liberación en la edad de la globalización y de la exclusión.* Madrid: Editorial Trotta; México, D.F.: Universidad Autónoma Metropolitana–Iztapalapa, and Universidad Nacional Autónoma de México, 1998.

Dussel, Enrique. *The Invention of the Americas: Eclipse of 'the Other' and the Myth of Modernity.* New York: Continuum, 1995.

Dussel, Enrique. *The Underside of Modernity: Apel, Ricoeur, Rorty, Taylor, and the Philosophy of Liberation.* Trans. and ed. Eduardo Mendieta. Atlantic Highlands, NJ: Humanities Press, 1996.

Eblak, Luis. 'Madre Maurina, uma vítima da ditadura' *Jornal do Commercio* 7 junho 1998.

Engelhardt, Paulus. *Versöhnung und Erlösung.* Christlicher Glaube in moderner Gesellschaft, Vol. 23, Munich: Herder, 1982.

Escalante, Jorge. *La Misión Era Matar: El Juicio a la Caravana Pinochet-Arellano.* Santiago: LOM Ediciones, 2000.

Escribano, Judith. 'The Cook, the Dog, the Priest and His Lover: Who Killed Bishop Gerardi and Why?' In M. A. Hayes and D. Tombs (eds). *Truth and Memory: The Church and Human Rights in El Salvador and Guatemala.* Leominster: Gracewing, 2001.

Eugene, Toinette. 'Reconciliation in the Pastoral Context of Today's Church and World. Does Reconciliation Have a Future?' Robert J. Kennedy (ed.). *Reconciling Embrace.* (Chicago: Liturgy Training Publications, 1998), 1–16.

Falla, Ricardo. *Massacres in the Jungle.* Boulder, CO and Oxford: Westview Press, 1995.

Falla, Ricardo. *The Story of a Great Love.* Washington, DC: Epica, 1998.

Fanon, Frantz. T*he Wretched of the Earth.* Trans. Constance Farrington. New York: Grove Press, 1991.

Fanon, Frantz. *Toward the African Revolution: Political Essays.* Trans. Haakon Chevalier. New York: Grove Press, 1988.

Favazza, Joseph. *The Order of Penitents.* foreword by James Lopresti. Collegeville, MN: The Liturgical Press, 1998.

Fernández-Armesto, Felipe. *Before Columbus: Exploration and Colonization from the Mediterranean to the Atlantic, 1229–1492.* London: Macmillan, 1987.

Ferreira, José Inácio. *Anistia: Caminho e Solução.* Vitória: JANC, 1979.

Fessard, Gaston. *De L'Actualitè historique.* Paris: Desclée de Brouwer, 1960.

Fischer, Edward and R. McKenna Brown. *Maya Cultural Activism in Guatemala.* Austin: University of Texas Press, 1996.

Fleet, Michael and Brian H. Smith. *The Catholic Church and Democracy in Chile and Peru.* Notre Dame: University of Notre Dame Press, 1997.

Forbes, Jack D. A*fricans and Native Americans: The Language of Race and the Evolution of Red-Black Peoples.* 2nd ed. Urbana and Chicago: University of

Illinois Press, 1993.

Forero, Juan. 'Peru Truth Commission Stirs Up a Hornet's Nest,' *International Herald Tribune* (9 September 2003), 5.

Forgues, Roland (ed.). *José Carlos Mariátegui y Europa: la otra cara del descubrimiento*. Lima, Peru: Amauta, 1992.

Foucault, Michel. *Religion and Culture*. New York: Routledge, 1999.

Fox, Thomas C. 'Arns is a Symbol of Human Rights in Latin America,' *National Catholic Reporter* (21 September 2001), 24.

Franklin, Jonathan. 'Chilean Army Admits 120 Thrown into the Sea,' *Guardian* (9 January 2001), 14.

Freire, Paulo. *Pedagogy of the Oppressed*. Translated Myra Bergman Ramos. New York: Herder and Herder, 1970.

Freyre, Gilberto. *Order and Progress: Brazil from Monarchy to Republic*. Edited and translated from the Portuguese by Rod W. Horton. Westport, Conn.: Greenwood Press, 1980.

Friedlander, Albert A. (ed.). *Out of the Whirlwind: A Reader of Holocaust Literature*. New York: Schocken Books, 1976.

Gamini, Gabriella. 'Pinochet is Fit Enough to Leave Hospital,' *The Times* (4 March 2000), 4.

Garabal, Tito. El *Viaje comienza ahora: Juan Pablo II en Uruguay, Chile y la Argentina*. Buenos Aires: Ediciones Paulinas, 1987.

Garzón, Baltasar. *La Acusación del Juez Baltasar Garzón contra el General (R) Augusto Pinochet. Auto de Procesamiento contra Augusto Pinochet Ugarte (10.12.98), Procedimiento, Sumario 19/97 Terrorismo y Genocidio, 'Operativo Cóndor', Juzgado Central de Intrucción Número Cinco, Audiencia Nacional, Madrid*. Santiago, Chile: Ediciones ChileAmérica – CESOC, 1999.

Gerwel, Jakes. 'National Reconciliation: Holy Grail or Secular Pact?' in C. Villa-Vicencio and W. Verwoerd (eds), *Looking Back Reaching Forward: Reflections on the Truth and Reconciliation Commission of South Africa*. (Cape Town: University of Cape Town Press, 2000), 277–286.

Gibson, James L. 'Overcoming Apartheid: Can Truth Reconcile a Divided Nation?' Cape Town: Institute for Justice and Reconciliation, 2002.

Goldberg, Theo and Ato Quayson (eds). *Relocating Postcolonialism*. Oxford: Blackwell, 2002.

Golden, R. and M. McConnell. *Sanctuary: The New Underground Railway*. Maryknoll, NY: Orbis Books, 1986.

Goldman, Francisco. 'Murder Comes for the Bishop,' *The New Yorker*, (15 March 1999) 60–77.

Goldstone, Richard. 'Justice as a Tool for Peace-making: Truth Commissions and International Criminal Tribunals.' *New York University Journal of International Law & Politics* 28/3 (1996), 485–504.

Gordon, Lewis R. *Bad Faith and Antiblack Racism*. Atlantic Highlands, NJ:

Humanities Press, 1995.

Gorender, Jacob. *Combate nas Trevas.* 5ª ed., São Paulo: Editora Atica., 1998.

Graziano, Frank. *Divine Violence: Spectacle, Psychosexuality, and Radical Christianity in the Argentine 'Dirty War.'* Boulder, CO and Oxford: Westview Press, 1992.

Grégoire, F. *Etudes hégélienn, Les points capitaux du système.* Louvain-Paris: Publications Univentaires de Louvain, 1958.

Grelot, P. *Sens Chrétien de L'Ancien Testament.* Tournai-Paris: Desclée, 1962.

Grosfoguel, Ramón, and Nelson Maldonado-Torres. 'Latinas and the "Euro-American" Menace: The Decolonization of the US Empire in the 21st Century,' in Ramón Grosfoguel, Nelson Maldonado-Torres and José David Saldívar (eds) *Latinas in the World-System.* (Chicago: Paradigm Press, 2005). Forthcoming.

Grosfoguel, Ramón. 'Subaltern Epistemologies, Decolonial Imaginaries and the Redefinition of Global Capitalism,' *Review*, 28 (forthcoming 2005).

Guedes, Ana. 'História da Luta: 25 Anos da Anistia Política no Brasil,' http:/www. vermelho.org.br/diario/2004/0828/0828_anaguedes-anistia.asp.

Guider, Margaret Eletta. *Daughters of Rahab.* Minneapolis: Fortress Press, 1995.

Gunton, Colin (ed.). *The Theology of Reconciliation: Essays in Biblical and Systematic Theology.* London, New York: T & T Clark, 2003.

Gutiérrez, Gustavo. *A Theology of Liberation. History, Politics and Salvation*, Translated and edited by Sister Caridad Inda and John Eagleson. Maryknoll, NY: Orbis Books, 1973.

Gutiérrez, Gustavo. *En busca de los pobres de Jesuscristo: El pensamiento de Bartolome de Las Casa.* Lima: Ediciones Siquerre, 1992.

Gutiérrez, Gustavo. *Las Casas: In Search of the Poor of Jesus Christ.* Marynoll, NY: Orbis Books, 1993.

Guzmán, Nancy. *Romo: Confesiones de un Torturador.* Santiago, Chile: Editorial Planeta, 2000.

Hanke, Lewis. *All Mankind Is One: A Study of the Disputation Between Bartolomé de Las Casas and Juan Ginés de Sepúlveda in 1550.* DeKalb: Northern Illinois University Press, 1974.

Hannaford, Ivan. *Race: The History of an Idea in the West.* Washington, D.C.: The Woodrow Wilson Center Press and Baltimore: The Johns Hopkins University Press, 1996.

Harding, Sandra. '"Rethinking Standpoint Epistemology: What Is 'Strong Objectivity"?' in Linda Alcoff and Elizabeth Potter (eds). *Feminist Epistemologies.* New York: Routledge, 1993.

Harper, Charles (ed.). *Impunity: an Ethical Perspective. Six Latin American Case Studies.* Geneva: World Council of Churches, 1996.

Hay, Mark. *Ukubuyisana: Reconciliation in South Africa.* Pietermaritzburg, Cluster Publications, 1998.

Hayes, M. A. and D. Tombs (eds). *Truth and Memory: The Church and Human Rights in El Salvador and Guatemala.* Leominster: Gracewing, 2001.

Hayner, Priscilla B. 'Commissioning the Truth: Further Research Questions,' *Third*

*World Quarterly* 17/1 (1996), 19–29.

Hayner, Priscilla B. 'Fifteen Truth Commissions–1974 to 1994: A Comparative Study.' *Human Rights Quarterly.* 16/4 (November 1994), 597–655.

Hayner, Priscilla B. *Unspeakable Truths: Confronting State Terror and Atrocity.* New York and London: Routledge, 2001.

Hebblethwaite, Margaret. 'Brazil's Moral Giant,' *The Tablet*, 26 January 2001.

Heer, Fr. *Europa, Mutter der Revolutionen.* Stuttgart: W. Kohlhammer, 1964.

Helmick, Raymond G., S.J. and Rodney L. Peterson (eds). *Forgiveness and Reconciliation: Religion, Public Policy and Conflict Transformation.* Philadelphia: Templeton Foundation, 2001.

Henry, Michel. *Marx I. Une philosophie de la réalité.* Paris: NRF Gallimard, 1976.

Henry, Michel. *Marx II. Une philosophie de l'économie.* Paris: NRF Gallimard, 1976.

Herkenhoff, João Baptista. 'A Cidadania no Brasil Contemporâneo: O Povo como Construtor da Própria História,' http://www.dhnet.org.br/direitos/militantes/herkenhoff/livro2/brasil2/html.

Herman, Judith L. *Trauma and Recovery: From Domestic Abuse to Political Terror.* London: Pandora, 2001.

Hesse, Barnor. 'Forgotten like a Bad Dream: Atlantic Slavery and the Ethics of Postcolonial Memory,' in David Theo Goldberg and Ato Quayson (eds). *Relocating Postcolonialism* (Oxford: Blackwell, 2002), 143–173.

Horkheimer, Max, and Theodor W. Adorno. *Dialectic of Enlightenment.* Translated by John Cumming. New York: Continuum, 2002.

Hugedé, Norbert. *Commentaire de l' Epître aux Colossiens.* Geneva: Ed. Labor et fides, 1968.

Huggins, Martha, et al. *Violence Workers: Police Torturers and Murderers Reconstruct Brazilian Atrocities.* Berkeley: University of California Press, 2002.

Hughes, Kathleen. *Saying Amen. A Mystagogy of Sacrament.* Chicago: Liturgy Training Publications, 1999.

Hughes, Kathleen. 'Walking on the Edge of Two Great Abysses. Theological Perspectives on Reconciliation,' in Robert J. Kennedy (ed.). *Reconciling Embrace.* (Chicago: Liturgy Training Publications, 1998), 1–16; 102; 106–107.

Hugo, Ned. 'Peru's Truth Commission Visits Birthplace of Bloody Guerrilla Insurgency,' *Associated Press*, 29 August 2003.

Jameson, Fredrick and Masao Miyoshi (eds). *The Cultures of Globalization.* Duke University Press, 1998.

Jameson, Fredric. *The Seeds of Time.* New York: Columbia University Press, 1994.

Jandt, Fred E. *Intercultural Communication: An Introduction.* Thousand Oaks, CA: Sage Publications, 1998.

Jeffery, Anthea. *The Truth About the Truth Commission.* Johannesburg: South African Institute of Race Relations, 1999.

Joest, W. 'Versöhnung,' *Religion in Geschichte und Gegenwart.* Vol. VI (Tübingen: J. C. B. Mohr, 1962), column 1378.

Jonas, Susanne. *The Battle for Guatemala: Rebels, Death Squads, and U.S. Power.*

Boulder, CO. and London: Westview Press, 1996.

Jones, L. Gregory. *Embodying Forgiveness. A Theological Analysis.* Grand Rapids, MI: Wm. B. Eerdmans Publishing, 1995.

Jordá Sureda, Miguel. *Martirologio de la Iglesia Chilena: Juan Alsina y Sacerdotes Victimas del Terrorismo de Estado.* Santiago, Chile: LOM Ediciones, 2001.

Kennedy, Robert J. (ed.). *Reconciling Embrace.* Chicago: Liturgy Training Publications, 1988.

Keshgegian, Flora A. *Redeeming Memories: A Theology of Healing and Transformation.* Nashville: Abingdon Press, 2000.

Kettler, F. H. 'Versöhnung', *Religion in Geschichte und Gegenwart.* Vol. VI (Tübingen: J.C.B. Mohr, 1962), columns 1373–1378.

Klaiber, Jeffrey. *Church, Dictatorships, and Democracy in Latin America.* Maryknoll, NY: Orbis Books, 1998.

Kritz, Neil J. (ed.). *Transitional Justice: How Emerging Democracies Reckon with Former Regimes.* 3 vols. Washington, DC: U.S. Institute of Peace Press, 1995.

Krog, Antjie. *Country of My Skull.* Johannesburg: Random House, 1998.

Krog, Antjie. 'Top of the Times', *Cape Times.* (25 February 2000).

Lakeland, Paul. 'Development and Catholic Social Teaching: Pope John Paul's New Encyclical,' *The Month* 249 (June 1998), 706–710.

Langer, Lawrence. *Preempting the Holocaust.* New Haven and London: Yale University Press, 1998.

Languilli, Nino. (ed.). *The Existentialist Tradition: Selected Writings.* Trans. by Philip Mairet. New York: Doubleday-Anchor Books, 1971.

Leflon, Jean. *La crise revolutionnair:1789–1846.* Vol. 20 of *Histoire de L'Eglise* by A. Fliche and V. Martin. Paris: Blout and Gay, 1949.

Leon-Portilla, Miguel. *El reverso de la Conquista. Relaciones aztecas, mayas e incas.* Mexico City: Joaquin Mortiz, 1964.

Leone, Matilde. *Sombras da Repressão: O Outono de Maurina Borges.* Petrópolis: Vozes, 1998.

Levi, Primo. 'The Truce,' in Albert A Friedlander (ed.). *Out of the Whirlwind: A Reader of Holocaust Literature.* New York: Schocken Books, 1976.

Lévinas, Emmanuel. 'Reflections on the Philosophy of Hitlerism,' *Critical Inquiry,* 17 (1990), 63–71.

Link, H. G. 'Reconciliación,' in *Diccionario teológico del Nuevo Testamento.* Vol. IV. Salamanca: Sigueme, 1984.

Lira, Elizabeth. *Las Suaves Cenizas Del Olvido Vía Chilena De Reconciliación Política 1814–1932.* Santiago, LOM-DIBAM, 1999.

Lopresti, James. *Penance: A Reform Proposal for the Rite.* American Essays in Liturgy, 6, Washington, DC: The Pastoral Press, 1997.

Loucky, James and Marilyn M. Moors (eds). *The Maya Diaspora: Guatemalan Roots, New American Lives.* Philadelphia: Temple University Press, 2000.

Louw, Alberts and F. Chikane. *The Road to Rustenburg. The Church Looking Forward to a New South Africa.* Cape Town: Struik, 1991.

Maclean, Iain S. *Opting for Democracy? Liberation Theology and the Struggle for*

*Democracy in Brazil*. Pieterlen, Suisse: Peter Lang, 1999.

Maclean, Iain S. 'Truth and Reconciliation: Irreconcilable Differences?' *Religion & Theology* 6/3 (1999), 269–302.

Malamud-Goti, Jaime. *Game Without End: State Terror and the Politics of Justice*. Norman, OK and London: University of Oklahoma Press, 1996.

Maldonado-Torres, Nelson. *Against War: Views from the Underside of Modernity*. (Durham: Duke University Press), Forthcoming.

Maldonado-Torres, Nelson. 'Imperio, raza y religión,' in Eduardo Mendieta (ed.) *Enciclopedia iberoamericana de las religiones: religion e imperio* (Madrid: Trotta), Forthcoming.

Maldonado-Torres, Nelson. 'Intervenciones filosóficas al proyecto inacabado de la descolonizacion', in Juan Manuel Contreras Colín and Mario Rojas (eds). *Filosofía y liberación. Homenaje a Enrique Dussel*. México, D.F.: Universidad de la Ciudad de México). Forthcoming.

Maldonado-Torres, Nelson. 'On the Coloniality of Being,' in Ramón Grosfoguel, Nelson Maldonado-Torres and José David Saldívar (eds), *Coloniality, Transmodernity, and Border Thinking*. Forthcoming.

Maldonado-Torres, Nelson. 'The Cry of the Self as a Call from the Other: The Paradoxical Loving Subjectivity of Frantz Fanon,.' *Listening: Journal of Religion and Culture* 1 (2001), 46–60.

Maluleke, Tinyiko Sam. 'Truth, National Unity and Reconciliation in South Africa. Aspects of the Emerging Theological Agenda.' *Missionalia* 25/1 (April 1997), 59–86.

Marighella, Carlos. *The Terrorist Classic: Manual of Urban Guerrillas*. Translated by Gene Hanrahan. Chapel Hill: Documentary Publications, 1985.

Mariz, Beatriz. *Refugees of a Hidden War: Counterinsurgency in Guatemala*. Albany, NY: State University of New York Press, 1988.

Martin-Baró, Ignacio. 'Nada en comuún.' *Ideele* 158 (October 2003), 36–39.

Martin-Baró, Ignacio. 'Reparations: Attention Must Be Paid,' in Neil J. Kritz (ed.). *Transitional Justice*, Vol. I (Washington, D.C., United States Institute for Peace, 1995), 569–571.

Marzal, Manuel M, Eugenio Maurer, Xaverio Albo, Bertomeau Melia. *The Indian Face of God in Latin America*. (Faith and Cultures Series), Maryknoll NY: Orbis Books, 1996.

Maybury-Lewis, David. *Millennium: Tribal Wisdom and the Modern World*. New York: Viking, 1979.

McClintock, M. *The American Connection: State Terror and Popular Resistance in Guatemala*. London: Zed Books, 1985.

Meiring, Piet. *Chronicle of the Truth Commission*. Vanderbijlpark: Carpe Diem Books, 1999.

Melander, Veronica. *The Hour of God: People in Guatemala Confronting Political Evangelicalism and Counterinsurgency, 1976–1990*. Uppsala: Uppsala University, 1999.

Mendieta, Eduardo (ed.). *The Underside of Modernity*. New Jersey: Humanities

Press, 1996.

Menkiti, Ifeanyi A. 'Person and Community in African Traditional Thought,' in R. A. Wright (ed.). *African Philosophy*. New York: University Press of America, 1971.

Merwin, W.S. *The Miner's Pale Children*. New York: Atheneum, 1970.

Mignone, Emilio Fermin. *Witness to the Truth: The Complicity of Church and Dictatorship in Argentina, 1976–1983*. Translated by Phillip Berryman. Maryknoll, N.Y: Orbis Books, 1988.

Michnick, Adam and Vaclav Havel. 'Justice or Revenge,' *Journal of Democracy* 4/1 (January 1993), 3–27.

Mignolo, Walter. *Local Histories/Global Designs: Coloniality, Subaltern Knowledges, and Border Thinking*. Princeton, NJ: Princeton University Press, 2000.

Montgomery, Tommie Sue. *Revolution in El Salvador: From Civil Strife to Civil Peace*. Boulder, CO and Oxford: Westview Press, 1995.

Moreiras, Alberto. 'Global Fragments. A Second Latinamericanism,' in Frederick Jameson and Masao Miyoshi (eds). *The Cultures of Globalization.* Duke University Press, 1998.

Munoz, Braulio. *Sons of the Wind: The Search of Identity in Spanish American Indian Literature.* New Brunswick, NJ: Rutgers University Press, 1982.

Myers, Kenneth A. (ed.). *Aspiring to Freedom. Commentaries on John Paul II's Encyclical 'The Social Concerns of the Church.'* Grand Rapids, MI: William B. Eerdmans, 1988.

Nelson, Diane M. 'Maya Hackers and the Cyberspatialized Nation-State: Modernity, Ethnostalgia, and a Lizard Queen in Guatemala,' *Cultural Anthropology* 11/9 (1998), 287–308.

Nietzsche, Friedrich. *Beyond Good and Evil: Prelude to a Philosophy of the Future*. Translated by Walter Kaufmann. New York: Vintage Books, 1966.

Nietzsche, Friedrich. *On the Genealogy of Morals and Ecce Homo*. Translated by Walter Kaufmann and R.J. Hollingdale. New York: Vintage Books, 1989.

Nietzsche, Friedrich. *The Will to Power*. Translated by Walter Kaufmann and R. J. Hollingdale. New York: Random House, 1968.

Nino, Carlos Santiago. *Radical Evil on Trial*. New Haven: Yale University Press, 1996.

O'Keefe, Mark, O.S.B. *What Are They Saying About Social Sin?* New York: Paulist Press, 1990.

Oppenheim, Lois Hecht. *Politics in Chile, Democracy, Authoritarianism, and the Search for Development*. Boulder, CO and Oxford: Westview Press, 1993.

Otzoy, Antonio. 'The Struggle for Maya Unity.' *NACLA Report on the Americas*, Vol. XXIX/5 (March–April 1996), 33–35.

Owen, K. 'Can South Africans Really Face the Past? The Truth Hurts.' *The New Republic* (23 November 1998), 21.

Pasqualucci, J. M. 'The Whole Truth and Nothing But the Truth: Truth Commissions, Impunity and the Inter-American Human Rights System.' *Boston University*

*International Law Journal* 12/2 (1994), 321–370.

Perera, Victor. *Unfinished Conquest: The Guatemalan Tragedy*. Berkeley: University of California Press, 1993.

Pérez, Yovana, Verónica Molina, and Victoria Pareja. 'El Tratamiento Individual con Personas Affectadas por la Violencia Política,' *Ideele* 157 (September 2003), 84–87.

Peterson, E. 'Die Kirche aus Juden und Heiden,' *Theologische Traktate*, Vol. V, Munich: Kosel, 1951.

Pfeil, Margaret R. 'Doctrinal Implications of Magisterial Use of the Language of Social Sin,' *Louvain Studies* 27 (2002), 132–52.

Philipose, Liz. 'The Laws of War and Women's Human Rights,' *Hypatia* 11/4 (Fall 1996), 46–62.

Phillips, William D., and Carla Rahn Phillips. *The Worlds of Christopher Columbus*. Cambridge: Cambridge University Press, 1992.

Pierrard, P. *L'Eglise et les ouvriers en France (1840–1940)*. Paris: Hachette, 1984.

Pion-Berlin, David. 'The National Security Doctrine, Military Threat Perception and the "Dirty War" in Argentina.' *Comparative Political Studies* 21/3 (October 1998), 382–407.

Popkin, Margaret and Naomi Roht-Arriaza. 'Truth as Justice: Investigatory Commissions in Latin America,' *Law and Social Inquiry: The Journal of the American Bar Foundation*, 20 (1995), 79–116.

Popkin, Margaret. *Peace Without Justice: Obstacles to Building the Rule of Law in El Salvador*. University Park, PA: Pennsylvania State University Press, 2000.

Quijano, Anibal. 'Coloniality of Power, Eurocentrism, and Latin America.' *Nepantla: Views from South*. 1/3 (2000), 533–80.

Quijano, Anibal. '"Raza," etnia, y "nación": cuestiones abiertas,' in Roland Forgues (ed.), *José Carlos Mariátegui y Europa: la otra cara del descubrimiento*. (Lima, Peru: Amauta, 1992).

Quijano, Anibal, and Immanuel Wallerstein. 'Americanity as a Concept, or the Americas in the Modern World-System,' *International Social Science Journal* 134 (1992), 549–57.

Quinn, Albano. 'Un momento de gracia para revisar nuestra Evangelización,' *Ideele* 159 (November 2003), 31–33.

Quizar, Robin Ormes. *My Turn to Weep: Salvadoran Refugee Women in Costa Rica*. Westport, CT and London: Bergin & Garvey, 1998.

Rama, Angel. *Transculturación narrativa en America Latina*. Mexico: Siglo Veintiuno Editores, 1982.

Rey, Terry. 'Junta, Rape, and Religion in Haiti, 1993–94,' *Journal of Feminist Studies in Religion* 15/2 (Fall 1999), 73–100.

Rivera Martínez, Edgardo. 'Un lugar muy alto en nuestra historia,' *Ideele* 158 (October 2003), 32.

Romero, Carlos. 'Quien esté libre de culpa, que tire la primera piedra,' *Ideele* 158 (October 2003), 33–35.

Romero, Oscar. 'The Political Dimension of the Faith from the Perspective of the Option for the Poor,' in *Voice of the Voiceless*, translated Michael J. Walsh (Maryknoll: Orbis Books, 1985), 177–187.

Rotberg, Robert I. and Dennis Thompson (eds). *Truth V. Justice: The Morality of Truth Commissions*. Princeton: Princeton University Press, 2000.

Ruetler, Rosemary Redford. 'Feminist Theology and Spirituality,' in Judith L. Werdner (ed.), *Christian Terrorism* (New York: Harper and Row, 1984).

Said, Edward. *Orientalism*. New York: Pantheon Books, 1978.

Salinas, Luis A. *The London Clinic*. Santiago, Chile: LOM Ediciones, 1999.

Sandoval, Chela. *Methodology of the Oppressed*. Minneapolis: University of Minnesota Press, 2000.

Sartre, Jean-Paul. 'Existentialism Is a Humanism,' in Nino Languilli (ed.), *The Existentialism Tradition: Selected Writings*. Translated by Philip Mairet, New York: Doubleday-Anchor Books, 1971.

Schele, Linda and David Freidel. *A Forest of Kings: The Untold Story of the Ancient Maya*. New York: William Morrow, 1990.

Schnackenburg, R. *Die Brief an die Epheser*. Evangelisch-Katholisch Kommentar zum Neuen Testament, Zurich-Neukirchen: Benzinger-Neukirchener Verlag, 1982.

Schweizer, Eduard. *Der Brief and der Kolosser*. Evangelisch-Katholisch Kommentar zum Neuen Testament. Zurich-Neukirchen: Benzinger-Neukirchener Verlag, 1980.

Searle, Mark. 'The Journey of Conversion,' *Worship* 54 (1980), 35–55.

Serbin, Kenneth P. *Secret Dialogues: Church-State Relations, Torture, and Social Justice in Authoritarian Brazil*. Pittsburgh: University of Pittsburgh Press, 2000.

Shriver, D. W. *An Ethic for Enemies: Forgiveness in Politics*. New York and Oxford: Oxford University Press, 1995.

Shutte, Augustine. *Ubuntu: An Ethic for a New South Africa*. Pietermaritzburg: Cluster Publications, 2001.

Sieder, Rachel. *Central America: Fragile Transition*. Basingstoke: Macmillan Press, 1996.

Sieder, Rachel (ed). *Guatemala after the Peace Accords*. London: Institute of Latin American Studies, 1998.

Sieder, Rachel. 'War, Peace and Memory Politics in Central America,' in Alexandra Barahona De Brito, Carmen González-Enríquez and Paloma Aguilar (eds). *The Politics of Memory: Transitional Justice in Democratizing Societies*. Oxford: Oxford University Press, 2001.

Sigmund, Paul. *Religious Freedom and Evangelization in Latin America. The Challenge of Religious Pluralism*. Maryknoll, NY: Orbis Books, 1999.

Skidmore, Thomas. *Brasil: de Castelo a Tancredo*. Rio de Janeiro: Paz e Terra, 1998.

Smith, C. *Resisting Reagan: The U.S. Central America Peace Movement*. Chicago: Chicago University Press, 1996.

Smith, Jonathan Z. 'Religion, Religions, Religious,' in Mark C. Taylor (ed.), *Critical Terms for Religious Studies*. (Chicago: The University of Chicago Press, 1998),

269–84.

Smuts, Jan Christian. *Holism*. London: MacMillan, 1926.

Snowden, Frank M., Jr. *Before Color Prejudice: The Ancient View of Blacks*. Cambridge, MA: Harvard University Press, 1983.

Sobrino, Jon. 'Latin America: Place of Sin and Place of Forgiveness,' in Jon Sobrino, *The Principle of Mercy*. Maryknoll, NY: Orbis Books, 1994.

Souza, Raoul. 'The Church: A Witness to the Truth on the Way to Freedom,' in Charles Harper (ed.) *Impunity: an Ethical Perspective. Six Latin American Case Studies*. Geneva: World Council of Churches (1996), 60–72.

Spence, Jack et al. *Chapultepec: Five Years Later: El Salvador's Political Reality and Uncertain Future*. Boston: Hemispheres Initiative, 1997.

Stanley, Ruth. 'Modes of Transition v. Electoral Dynamics: Democratic Control of the Military in Argentina and Chile' Journal of Third World Studies; Americus, 18/2 (Fall 2001), 71–92.

Stanley, William. *The Protection Racket State: Elite Politics, Military Extortion, and Civil War in El Salvador*. Philadelphia: Temple University Press, 1996.

Steigenga, Tim. 'Guatemala,' in Paul Sigmund, *Religious Freedom and Evangelization in Latin America. The Challenge of Religious Pluralism* (Maryknoll, NY: Orbis Books, 1999), 150–174.

Stiglmayer, Alexandra (ed.). *Mass Rape: The War Against Women in Bosnia-Herzegovonia*. Translated by Marion Faber. Lincoln: University of Nebraska Press, 1993.

Stoll, David. *Between Two Armies in the Ixil Towns of Guatemala*. New York: Columbia University Press, 1993.

Stoll, David. *Is Latin America Turning Protestant? The Politics of Evangelical Growth*. Berkeley: University of California Press, 1999.

Suro, Roberto. 'The Writing of an Encyclical,' in K. A. Myers (ed.), *Aspiring to Freedom. Commentaries on John Paul II's Encyclical 'The Social Concerns of the Church*. Grand Rapids: William B. Eerdmans Publishing Company, 1988.

Swarns, Rachel L. 'Unthinkable Attack Jolts a Crime-Weary Country,' *New York Times* (16 November 2001), A3.

Swift, Anthony. 'The Street Kids Who Took on a Government,' *Guardian*, London (18 November 1995), 31.

Taviani, Paolo Emilio. *Columbus: The Great Adventure. His Life, His Times, and His Voyages*. Translated by Luciano F. Farina and Marc A. Beckwith. New York: Orion Books, 1991.

Taylor, M. C. (ed.). *Critical Terms for Religious Studies*, Chicago: The University of Chicago Press, 1998.

Taylor, Mark Lewis. 'Transnational Corporations and Institutionalized Violence,' in David Batstone (ed.). *New Visions for the Americas: Religious Engagement and Social Transformation*. Minneapolis: Fortress Press, 1993.

Tedlock, Barbara. *Time and the Highland Maya*. Albuquerque: University of New Mexico Press, 1982; Revised 1992.

Tedlock, Dennis. *Breath on the Mirror: Mythic Voices and Visions of the Living*

*Maya.* New York: HarperCollins 1993.

Tedlock, Dennis. Translator. The *Popol Vuh, The Definitive Edition of the Mayan Book of Life and the Glories of Kings.* New York: Vintage, 1985.

Tolan, John V. *Saracens: Islam in the Medieval European Imagination.* New York: Columbia University Press, 2002.

Tombs, David. 'Crucifixion, State Terror and Sexual Abuse,' *Union Seminary Quarterly Review* 53 (Autumn 1999), 89–108.

Tombs, David. 'Honour, Shame and Conquest: Male Identity, Sexual Violence and the Body-Politic.' *Journal of Hispanic/Latino Theology.* 9/4 (May, 2002), 21–40.

Tutu, Desmond. 'Grace Upon Grace,' *Journal for Preachers*, Vol. XV/1 (Advent 1991), 20.

Tutu, Desmond. *Healing a Nation' Index on Censorship: Wounded Nations Broken Lives- Truth Commissions and War Tribunals.* 25/5, Issue 172 (September/October 1996), 38–42.

Tutu, Desmond. *No Future without Forgiveness.* New York: Doubleday, 2000.

Tutu, Desmond. 'The Process of Reconciliation and the Demands of Obedience,' *Transformation* (1985), 3–8.

Valente, Marcela. '"Repentant" Captain Adolfo E. Scilingo arrested,' in *Press Service* (October 1997).

Van Gennep, Arnold. *The Rites of Passage.* Chicago: University of Chicago Press, 1960.

Verdugo, Patricia. *Chile, Pinochet, and the Caravan of Death.* Boulder, CO: Lynne Rienner, 2001.

Verwoerd, Wilhelm. 'Forgiving the Torturer but not the Torture,' *Sunday Independent* (14 December 1998).

Vidal, Hernán. *Chile: Poética de la Tortura Política.* Santiago, Chile: Mosquito Editores, 2000.

Villa-Vicencio, Charles. *A Theology of Reconstruction: Nation-Building and Human Rights.* Cambridge: Cambridge University Press, 1992.

Villa-Vicencio, Charles and Willem Verwoerd (eds). *Looking Back, Looking Forward. Reflections on the Truth and Reconciliation Commission of South Africa.* Cape Town: University of Cape Town Press, 2000.

Villa-Vicencio, Charles and Erik Doxtader (eds). *The Provocations of Amnesty. Memory, Justice and Impunity.* Cape Town: Institute for Justice and Reconciliation, 2003.

Volf, Miroslav. *Exclusion & Embrace. A Theological Exploration of Identity, Otherness, and Reconciliation.* Nashville, TN: Abingdon Press, 1996.

Von Rad, G. *Theologie des Alten Testaments.* Munich: Kaiser Verlag, 1958.

Warren, Kay. *Indigenous Movements and Their Critics: Pan-Maya Activism in Guatemala.* Princeton, NJ: Princeton University Press, 1998.

Weidman, Judith L. *Christian Feminism.* New York: Harper & Row, 1984.

Weil, Simone. *Waiting on God.* New York: G.P. Putnam's Sons, 1951.

Weschler, Lawrence. *A Miracle, A Universe: Settling Accounts with Torturers.* New York: Penguin, 1991.

West, Gerald. 'Don't Stand on my Story: The Truth and Reconciliation Commission,

Intellectuals, Genre and Identity,' *Journal of Theology for Southern Africa* 98 (July 1997), 3–12.

Whitfield, Teresa. *Paying the Price: Ignacio Ellacuría and the Murdered Jesuits of El Salvador*. Philadelphia: Temple University Press, 1994.

Whitfield, Teresa. 'The Role of the United Nations in El Salvador and Guatemala: A Preliminary Comparison,' in Cynthia J. Arnson (ed.). *Comparative Peace Processes in Latin America*. Stanford: Stanford University Press, 1999, 447–463.

Wilson, Richard. *Maya Resurgence in Guatemala: Queqchí Experiences.* Norman, OK: University of Oklahoma Press, 1995.

Wynter, Sylvia. '1492: A New World View,' in Vera Lawrence Hyatt and Rex Nettleford (eds). *Race, Discourse, and the Origin of the Americas: A New World View*. (Washington, DC: Smithsonian Institution Press, 1995), 5–57.

Wynter, Sylvia. 'Unsettling the Coloniality of Being/Power/Truth/Freedom: Towards the Human, After Man, Its Overrepresentation – An Argument,' *The New Centennial Review* 3/3 (2003), 257–337.

Zahrnt, Heinz. *Die Sache mit Gott*. Munich: Piper, 1996.

Zalaquett, José. 'Balancing Ethical Imperatives and Political Constraints: The Dilemma of New Democracies Confronting Past Human Rights Violations,' *Hastings Law Journal* 43/6 (1992), 1425–1438.

Zalaquett, José. The Ethics of Responsibility: Human Rights, Truth and Reconciliation in Chile. Washington: Washington Office on Latin America, 1991.

Zerbine, Therezinha Godoy. *Anistia: Semente da Liberdade*. São Paulo: Escolas Profissionais Salesianas, 1979.

Zur, Judith. 'The Psychological Impact of State Terror,' *Anthropology Today* 10/3 (June 1994), 12–17.

# Index